THE ARABIC MANUSCRIPT TRADITION

HANDBOOK OF ORIENTAL STUDIES
HANDBUCH DER ORIENTALISTIK

SECTION ONE

THE NEAR AND MIDDLE EAST

EDITED BY

H. ALTENMÜLLER · B. HROUDA · B.A. LEVINE · R.S. O'FAHEY
K.R. VEENHOF · C.H.M. VERSTEEGH

VOLUME FIFTY-EIGHT

THE ARABIC MANUSCRIPT TRADITION

THE ARABIC MANUSCRIPT TRADITION

A Glossary of Technical Terms and Bibliography

BY

ADAM GACEK

BRILL
LEIDEN · BOSTON · KÖLN
2001

This book is printed on acid-free paper.

Library of Congress Cataloging-in-Publication Data

Gacek, Adam.
The Arabic manuscript tradition : a glossary of technical terms and bibliography / by Adam Gacek.
p. cm. — (Handbuch der Orientalistik. = Handbook of Orientalistik. Section one, the Near and Middle East, ISSN 0169-9423 ; v. 58)
Includes bibliographical references and index.
ISBN 9004120610 (alk. paper)
1. Manuscripts, Arabic—History—Bibliography. 2.Codicology–Dictionaries. 3. Paleography, Arabic—Bibliography. I. Title. II. Handbuch der Orientalistik. Erste Abteilung, Nahe und der Mittlere Osten ; 58. Bd.

Z6605.A6 G33 2001
[Z106.5]
011'.31—dc21 2001018082
CIP

Die Deutsche Bibliothek – CIP-Einheitsaufnahme

Gacek, Adam:
The Arabic manuscript tradition : a glossary of technical terms and bibliography / by Adam Gacek.. – Leiden ; Boston ; Köln : Brill, 2001
(Handbuch der Orientalistik : Abt. 1, Der Nahe und Mittlere Osten ; Bd. 58)
ISBN 90-04-12061-0

ISSN 0169-9423
ISBN 90 04 12061 0

PRINTED IN THE NETHERLANDS

To

Joanna,

Julian and Helenka

CONTENTS

ACKNOWLEDGEMENTS

I am very grateful to Prof. David Pingree for recommending this work for publication and my colleague Prof. François Déroche for his comments and suggestions. My gratitude also goes to Steve Millier and Khaleel Mohammed for having kindly proof-read this text. Last but not least, I am thankful to McGill University for granting me a sabbatic leave, without which this work would most probably not have seen the light of day.

PREFACE

One of the principal characteristics of Arab Islamic civilization is undoubtedly the cult of books. This central position of the book in Arabic culture has its roots in Islam itself, more specifically in the Qurʾān, the Arabic book par excellence. From the early 1st / mid 7th century until the end of the 13/19th century, Islamic civilization produced several tens of thousands of works in Arabic on a variety of subjects, both religious and scientific in nature, and most probably several millions of manuscript copies. This very rich heritage has survived in the hundreds of thousands of manuscripts found in almost all major university libraries and in numerous public and private collections throughout the world.

Along with this manuscript output, Arab authors, scholars, calligraphers and craftsmen produced a rich literature dealing with the actual making and decoration of books. This literature is gradually being discovered and edited. Apart from numerous compositions on calligraphy and penmanship, most notably from the Mamluk period (see 'Bibliography', VII. 2), we have now at our disposal three manuals dealing with a wealth of information on writing implements, the preparation of inks, papermaking and bookbinding. They are: *ʿUmdat al-kuttāb* (UK) by al-Muʿizz ibn Bādīs (d.454/1062), *al-Mukhtaraʿ fī funūn min al-ṣunaʿ* (MB) attributed to al-Malik al-Muẓaffar Yūsuf al-Ghassānī (d.694/1294), and *al-Nujūm al-shāriqāt* (NW) by Muḥammad ibn Abī al-Khayr al-Ḥasanī al-Dimashqī (fl.10/16th cent.).

To these should be added the *Taysīr* (TS) of al-Ishbīlī (d.628/1231), the *Tadbīr al-safīr* (HT) of Ibn Abī Ḥamīdah (fl.9/15th) and the *Ṣināʿat tasfīr al-kutub* (ST) of al-Sufyānī (fl.1029/1619), all of which deal with bookbinding techniques and materials. Furthermore, the *Tuḥaf al-khawāṣṣ* (TK) of Abū Bakr Muḥammad al-Qalalūsī (d.707/1307), which deals with the preparation of inks, also contains a chapter on *misṭarah* (ruling, lineation). Finally, mention should be made of Badr al-Dīn al-Ghazzī (d.984/1577), who in his work on education, *al-Durr al-naḍīd* (TP), included the most comprehensive chapter to be found in Arabic literature on scribal etiquette, as well as on the collation and correction of books.

The present work consists of two major parts: a glossary of

technical terms and a bibliography arranged by subject.* Although there are a few good general monographs on Arabic manuscripts, there is as yet no comprehensive introduction in English to various Arabic codicological phenomena, and Arabic palaeography is only in its initial stages of development. For this reason the bibliography is envisaged as an indispensable aid for the student of Arabic manuscripts. It brings together, for the first time, some of the most important research in this field published to date.

The technical terms contained in the glossary have been collected and selected from a variety of sources: classical, medieval and post-medieval texts, contemporary studies and catalogues, as well as extant specimens. The glossary is a by-product, as it were, of my research on Arabic manuscripts and therefore should not be taken as comprehensive. Nevertheless, even in its present form, it does reveal a very rich picture of Muslim book culture in the manuscript age, which spans almost 14 centuries. It includes terms encountered in the literature produced by or for government officials and secretaries (*kuttāb*), traditionists (*muḥaddithūn*), calligraphers (*khaṭṭāṭūn*), lexicographers (*lughawīyūn*) and other scholars (*ʿulamāʾ*), as well as craftsmen (*ṣunnāʿ*), book lovers and cataloguers. The exploration of this rich written tradition is necessary for a better understanding of the various scripts, writing surfaces and implements used, as well as the way Arabic manuscript books were transcribed, corrected, bound and decorated.

Although there may be some doubt as to the exact form or meaning of a given term, due to the obscure context or the fact that the word is used in only a single surviving manuscript, nevertheless it was deemed important to include at this stage all terms encountered, unless their exact meanings could not be verified. Some terms, especially those relating to book formats, are recorded the way they appear in various sources, without the specific corresponding equivalents in English. This is due to the fact that we do not as yet know their exact meanings. To translate, e.g. *qaṭʿ al-rubʿ* and *qaṭʿ al-thumn* as 'quarto' and 'octavo', respectively, could be very misleading.

A glossary of terms used in the production of manuscripts would

* This work was originally to appear under the title "Glossary of the Arabic manuscript book" and to contain an edited chapter on bookbinding taken from "al-Mukhtaraʿ fī funūn min al-ṣuna'" by al-Malik al-Muẓaffar. Since an edition of this work has recently been published, this chapter has been omitted.

not be complete without including the names of at least some of the most important scripts in use during the manuscript age. Here, however, great caution is in order. The art of calligraphy is a living art and scripts (and often their labels) were subject to changes and modifications depending on the 'school' (tradition), period and/or region in which they were employed. Thus, for example, the *naskh* or *riqāʿ* scripts in the Mamluk period were very different from the *naskh* or *riqāʿ* of a later period. We do not, as yet, have a clear picture of these variations in formal scripts and there is besides quite a lot of confusion in the modern literature on calligraphy as to the labels themselves. Therefore, the definitions as given in the glossary are very general and sometimes linked only to the use of a given script in a given period or region. These descriptions should not be taken as definitive.

Most of the terms included here concern the Arabic manuscript book. Some, however, having been drawn from sources relating to public administration (diplomatic), may have been used exclusively in those circles. The technical vocabulary relating to the mixing of inks and the use of pigments has, on the other hand, been largely omitted here. This terminology constitutes a well-defined field of study and has been exposed and dealt with in a number of publications but principally in Martin Levey's "Medieval Arabic bookmaking" (MP).

In view of the fact that the terms contained in the glossary were collected from sources which originated in various parts and historical periods of the Arab world, the list contains a considerable number of synonyms. Thus, for example, for the characteristic envelope flap we find *udhn* (Andalusia, North Africa), *marjiʿ* (Morocco), *lisān* (central Arab lands), *miqlab* (Levant, Iraq), *raddah* (Levant), and *sāqiṭah* (Yemen). The same applies to such terms as endband (headband), case (box), medallion, serif, catchword, inkwell and the like.

It is interesting to note also the association of a number of terms with the human body and its various parts. This is particularly apparent in the physical description of the codex. Here we find, for example, *udhn* ('ear'; flap), *lisān* ('tongue'; envelope flap), *raʾs* ('head'; upper margin, fore-edge, flap), *wajh* ('face'; recto, upper cover), *ʿaqb, ʿaqib* ('heel'; lower margin, catchword), *ṣadr* ('chest'; incipit, recto, fore-edge), *khadd* ('cheek'; outer or inner margin), *shidq* and *fakk* ('jawbone'; book cover), and *raqqāṣ* ('dancer'; catchword). Undoubtedly some of the words in the glossary are newly coined terms but the majority can be traced to a medieval usage.

Due to the limitations of the computer program used, an Arabic font was used only where absolutely necessary. The glossary is thus arranged alphabetically according to the root of the word which is given in Arabic script. Arabic script has also been used for abbreviations of some technical terms found in the glossary. Most words are traced to a source, either contemporary or earlier. This is done either in order to document the usage of a given word or to provide a reference for topical study or both. On the whole, the terms without references are either commonly encountered in the existing literature or are easily found in standard dictionaries. Apart from English technical terminology the glossary contains also a number of Greek, Greek/Latin and Latin terms still encountered in the English technical literature. As far as transliteration is concerned, the Library of Congress romanization tables have been used.

PART ONE

GLOSSARY

ا

al-alif al-muḥarrafah see taḥrīf.
al-alif al-murawwasah – the letter alif provided with a serif, tarwīs (q.v.).
al-alif al-musha“arah see musha“ar.
al-alif al-muṭlaqah see muṭlaq.

ا بجد

abjad, abjadīyah, al-ḥurūf al-abjadīyah 1. the first of the eight mnemotechnical terms (voces memoriales) into which the twenty-eight consonants of the Arabic alphabet were divided; the letters of the alphabet arranged according to this mnemonic system (EI, I, 97; GA, 176-178) 2. also **ḥisāb abjad, ḥisāb al-jummal (al-jumal)** – alpha-numerical notation used, among other things, for the creation of chronograms and chronosticons (EI, I, 97-98; SA, III, 18-19; RN, 60; GA, 182).

ا بر

ibrah (pl. ibar) – needle (UK, 154; TS, 11: ʿinda ḥabkih lil-maṣāḥif al-mulawwanah; AG, 107; MB, 103, 104; IA, 59; ST, index, 8).
ibarī, abbār – needle maker (QS, II, 215; DB, I, 8).
miʾbar 1. needle case (DM) 2. syn. of **minfadh** (q.v.) (DD, I, 392).
muʾabbar – sewn (KC, 33: bi-ghishāʾ muʾabbar).

ا برجمة

ibrijmah – paste (used for work with parchment) (TS, 12, 13; AG, 107; SD, I, 2: **ibrishmah**).

ا بردي

abardī see bardī.

ا برو

abrū (Turk. ebrû, from Pers. abrī – ‘cloud’) – marbled paper (MN, 9, 161: ūbrū, waraq al-ūbrū !).

ا بريسم

ibrīsam, **ibrīsim**, **ibrīshim** – silk, comp. burshmān.

ا خر

ākhir (pl. awākhir) – closing matter of the text (composition); explicit (TP, 62, n.14).
ilá ākhirih – et cetera, abbrev. الخ (DB, I, 53).
awākhir al-shahr – the last 10 days of the month (DM).
taʾkhīr, muʾakhkhar see taqdīm.

ا د ب

adab (pl. ādāb) – etiquette (EI, I, 175-176).
adab maʿa al-kutub 1. scribal etiquette 2. primitive critical apparatus (apparatus criticus) in manuscripts (TP, 52).

ا د م

adam(ah), **adīm** (pl. udum) 1. leather (UK, passim; AE, 106-108) 2. tanned red leather (DB, I, 63; IW, 71-72; MF, 201: fa-lam yazal Rasūl Allāh (ṣ) yumlī wa-ʿAlī yaktub ḥattá malaʾa baṭn al-adīm wa-ẓahrahu wa-akāriʿah; MU, XIV, 84: mujallad bi-adam mubaṭṭan bi-dībāj), comp. jild.
addām – tanner (DM).

ا د و

adāh (pl. adawāt) – syn. ālah (EI, I, 345), tool, implement, instrument, e.g. **adawāt (ālāt) al-tajlīd** = bookbinding tools (UK, 153-156, MB, 103-105) or **adawāt (ālāt) al-khaṭṭ (al-kitābah)** = writing implements, accessories (SA, II, 440-468; AE, 117-127).

ا ذ ن

udhn, udhun (pl. ādhān) – flap, envelope flap (TS, 25: idh al-ḥukm fī al-udhn an takūn maṭbūʿah ʿalá al-sifr ḥattá lā taḥtāj ilá ʿurwá wa-lā zirr tazurr bi-hi, ammā al-udhn fa-al-aṣl fīhi an yakūn aqall min niṣf al-sifr bi-miqdār raʾs al-zirr; AG, 109; BA, III, 372).

ارخ

urkhah – date (LL, I, 46).
taʾrīkh (pl. tawārīkh), **tawrīkh** (KK, 55; IK, 102-103; SK, 137: wa-yuqāl al-tawrīkh li-annahu yuqāl warrakhtu al-kitāb wa-arrakhtuh) – date, dating; chronology (SA,VI, 243-251; TP, 53-54; EI, X, 257-302; ER, IV, 668-677); chronogram, chronosticon (also **qiṭʿat al-taʾrīkh**, AM, nos.10, 26, 141; ER, V, 550-551).
al-taʾrīkh al-ʿArabī (**al-taʾrīkh al-Islāmī, al-sanah al-hijrīyah, al-sanah al-qamarīyah, al-sanah al-hilālīyah**) – Muslim calendar beginning July 16th 622 A.D. (SA, VI, 240, 243; EI, X, 258-261).
al-taʾrīkh al-Fārisī (**al-sanah al-Yazdijirdīyah**) – Persian calendar beginning June 16th 632 A.D. (SA, VI, 242, 254, 256; EI, X, 262).
al-taʾrīkh al-Hindī – Vikrama era (Vikrama samvat) beginning in 58 B.C.
al-taʾrīkh al-Ilāhī – Mughal calendar with the starting point March 21st 1584 A.D. (EI, X, 263).
al-taʾrīkh al-mudhayyal, also known as **al-taʿmiyah bi-al-ziyādah** – cryptographic dating, chronosticon, in which more than the second hemistich (miṣrāʿ) of a verse (bayt) is counted in calculating the date (TI, 47-48; TP, 54; EI, IV, 468).
al-taʾrīkh al-mustathná, also known as **al-taʿmiyah bi-al-naqṣ** – chronosticon, in which the value of one letter or word from the first hemistich is subtracted from the cumulative value of the second hemistich in calculating the date (TI, 47-48; TP, 54; AM, nos.109, 213).
al-taʾrīkh al-mutawwaj – chronosticon, in which only the numerical values of the first letters of each verse are counted in calculating the date (KB, 10-12).
al-taʾrīkh al-Qibṭī or **al-Qubṭī** (**taʾrīkh al-shuhadāʾ, sanat Diqliṭyānūs al-Malik**) – Coptic calendar beginning August 29th 284 A.D. (SA, VI, 242, 253, 255; EI, X, 261).
al-taʾrīkh al-Rūmī (**al-taʾrīkh al-Suryānī, taʾrīkh Dhī al-Qarnayn, taʾrīkh ghalabat al-Iskandar, al-sanah al-Yūnānīyah**) – Seleucid era (era of Alexander) beginning Oct.1st 312 B.C. (SA, VI, 242, 253-254; EI, X, 261).
taʾrīkh al-ṣufr – Spanish era beginning Jan. 1st 38 B.C. (EI, X, 261).
al-taʾrīkh bi-ajzāʾ al-yawm aw al-laylah – dating by the hours of day or night, e.g. **shurūq** – the first hour of day, **shafaq** – the first

hour of night, **ghurūb** – the last hour of day, **ṣabāḥ** – the last hour of night (SA, VI, 250).
al-ta'rīkh bi-al-ʿashr min al-shahr – dating by the ten-day segments (decades) of the month, e.g. fī al-ʿashr al-ūlá (al-uwal) (1-10), al-ʿashr al-wusṭá (al-wusaṭ) (11-20), al-ʿashr al-ukhrá (al-ākhirah, al-ukhar, al-awākhir) (21-30) (SA, VI, 248-249).
al-ta'rīkh bi-al-bāqī – dating by the nights of the month using the verb 'baqiya' to indicate how many nights are remaining until the end of the month, e.g. li-arbaʿ ʿashrata laylah (in) baqiyat min shahr kadhā (SA,VI, 244-248).
al-ta'rīkh bi-al-julūs – dating by a ruler's accession to the throne (CM, nos. 106, 235).
al-ta'rīkh bi-al-kusūr (ta'rīkh Ibn Kamāl Pāshā, al-ta'rīkh al-kinā'ī) – dating by fractions attributed to Ibn Kamāl Pāshā (TP, 54; CI, II, 178).
al-ta'rīkh bi-layālī al-shahr – dating by the nights of the month (SA, VI, 244-249).
al-ta'rīkh bi-al-māḍī – dating by the nights of the month using the verb 'maḍá' or 'khalá' to indicate how many nights have elapsed from the beginning of the month, e.g. lil-laylatayn khalatā (maḍatā) min shahr kadhā (SA,VI, 244-248).
al-ta'rīkh bi-al-mawāsim – dating by feasts and festivals, e.g. fī yawm ʿīd al-fiṭr (1st Shawwāl), fī yawm ʿarafah (9th Dhū al-Ḥijjah), fī yawm ʿīd al-naḥr or ʿīd al-aḍḥá (10th Dhū al-Ḥijjah), fī yawm al-qarr (11th Dhū al-Ḥijjah), fī yawm al-nafr al-awwal (12th Dhū al-Ḥijjah), fī yawm al-nafr al-thānī (13th Dhū al-Ḥijjah) (SA, VI, 249; CM, 66/2: fī laylat al-Miʿrāj = 27th Rajab).
al-ta'rīkh al-Jalālī (ta'rīkh-i Jalālī, ta'rīkh-i malakī, ta'rīkh-i sulṭānī) – Jalālī calendar beginning March 15th 1079 A.D. (EI, X, 262; ER, IV, 670).
ta'rīkh kawn al-ʿālam (ta'rīkh al-khilqah) – era of creation (era of Adam) beginning Sept.1st 5509 B.C.

ا رض

arḍīyah – background (LC, 22; FZ, 218: arḍīyat al-matn; JL, 88: arḍīyah mulawwanah).

ا سكرجة

uskurrujah – inkwell (KD, II, 713: wa-uskurrujah al-dawāh Fārisīyah muʿarrabah wa-lā yuqāl sukurrujah wa-taṣghīruhā usay kirah).

ا شر

ushārah, **taʾshīr** see nushārah.

ا شفى

ishfá (pl. ashāfin) – awl, punch (TS, 11, 15; AG, 107; ST, 10: **ishfah**; MB, 103; IA, 59; IB, 43: **shafā**; IK, 90; KM, I, sifr 4, 115).

ا صل

aṣl (pl. uṣūl) 1. author's original, holograph (MU, VIII, 39) 2. copy, transcript (from which another copy is made); exemplar, also referred to as **al-nuskhah al-aṣl** (LC, 26; MH, 92: yajib ʿalá man kataba nuskhah min aṣl baʿḍ al-shuyūkh an yuʿāriḍ nuskhatahu bi-al-aṣl; MU, VIII, 39: wa-al-aṣl yashtamil ʿalá sittat ajzāʾ bi-khaṭṭih kulluh; SD, II, 27) 3. original (main) text, as opposed to a commentary (sharḥ) or gloss (ḥāshiyah); usually abbreviated as ص or صل (VA, no.1845, 1858, 2024; MI, 136), but also ل (MZ, II, 412); text commented upon (LC, 23) 4. main (principal) script such as thuluth or muḥaqqaq (from which other scripts are derived) (NC, 126; SM, 269: aṣlān; AS, 145: al-uṣūl al-khamsah, al-uṣūl al-sabʿah) 5. major work (TM, 174: al-uṣūl al-qadīmah) 6. spine (of a quire or book) (ST, index, 8; ST, 8, 9, 11: ʿalá uṣūl al-karārīs aʿnī qafā al-kitāb) 7. root of a verb or noun (EI, X, 928).
al-aqlām al-uṣūl see qalam.

ا طر

iṭār (pl. iṭārāt, uṭur) 1. rules, rule-border, i.e. textual surround (LC, 24; FT, 402) 2. border (of a book cover) (LC, 24; KR, 80) 3. frame (within a border) (TF, 141: ḥawāshīhā mutaʿadditat al-uṭur) 4. rectangular panel (LC, 24; UI, 29) 5. tabula ansata (UI, 27) 6. headpiece (LC, 24).
maʾṭūr, muʾaṭṭar – ruled (LC, 25; DB, I, 145).

ا فريقي

(al-khaṭṭ) al-Ifrīqī – properly 'a general term for the style of the Arabic script current in Ifriqiyyah (modern Tunisia and eastern Algeria) in the early Middle Ages, (...) used by the historian Ibn Khaldun, writing circa 1375' (DW, 32); according to other sources al-Ifrīqī is identified with al-Sūdānī, a script which originated from the Maghrebi family of scripts and came to be associated with sub-Saharan Africa (AO, 46).

ا فشان

afshān (Pers.) – decoration of paper with flecks of gold and silver (MN, 6; ER, I, 581-582).

ا لف

taʾlīf(ah) (pl. taʾālīf, tawālīf, taʾlīfāt), **muʾallaf** (pl. muʾallafāt) – composition, compilation, work (of prose or poetry) (SD, I, 33; EI, X, 360), comp. taṣnīf.
muʾallif – author, writer, comp. muṣannif.

ا م

umm, ummah (IN, I, 246) (pl. ummahāt) 1. also **al-nuskhah al-umm** – holograph (LC, 26); copy, transcript (from which another copy is made), exemplar; archetype (LC, 26; SD, I, 35; TM, 180: qif ʿalá al-iltizām li-muqābalat al-kitāb ʿalá al-shaykh aw muʿāraḍatih ʿalá al-umm) 2. original (main) text, as opposed to a commentary, sharḥ (IN, I, 246) 3. model codex of the Qurʾān, usually of a large format and without vocalization, used in mosques (KN, 130) 4. fundamental (essential) work (composition) (LC, 29).
umm al-kitāb 1. heavenly prototype (aṣl) of the Qurʾān (EI, X, 854) 2. the first sūrah of the Qurʾān (DM).
Umm al-qurá, **Umm al-buldān**, **Umm al-bilād** – Mecca.
imām – exemplar; archetype, textus receptus (NT, II, 137 : wa-huwa al-imām alladhī lam yakhtalif fī mukhtalaf).
al-muṣḥaf al-imām – ʿUthmanic canon, codex (**al-muṣḥaf al-ʿUthmānī**) (MD, 99; KF, II, 294).
al-Musnad al-imām – the *Musnad* of Ibn Ḥanbal (SL, II, 37, 39).

ا مل

taʾammulāt (sg. taʾammul – 'consideration') – notabilia, comp. tadabbur.
fa-taʾammal(hu) – nota bene, abbrev. فتـ (CI, II, xiv; LL, I, 99).
fīhi taʾammul – a phrase (syn. **fīhi naẓar**) implying doubt and insinuating 'politely that the words to which it relates are false or wrong' (LL, II, 2812).

ا من

taʾmīn – saying (writing) **āmīn (amīn)**; one of the standard closing formulae in manuscripts, usually abbreviated as لم (alif joined to mīm) or ا م (LD, 89, 140, 149; AD, 6; EI, I, 436), comp. tatmīm, tafqīṭ.

ا نبوبة

unbūb(ah) (pl. anābīb) – unpared, unnibbed reed (FN, 31; KU, 153: wa-lā yusammá al-unbūb qalaman ḥattá yuqṭaʿ; BA, III, 370; LM, 31).

ا نس

insī see sinn.

ا نف

anfah – nib (of the calamus) (BA, III, 370).
taʾnīf – nibbing (of the calamus) (KD, II, 701: annaftuhu taʾnīfan idhā ḥaddadtu ṭarafahu al-mabrī wa-qaṭaṭṭuhu qaṭṭan).

ا نق

(qalam) al-muʾannaq see **al-ashʿār**.

ا ول

ālah – implement, instrument, syn. adāh (q.v.).
awwal (pl. awāʾil) – introductory matter of the text (composition); incipit; initia, (TP, 52, n.14; JA, I, 264: rasm al-tasmiyah fī awwal kitāb al-shiʿr; AA, 40: wa-al-taṣdīr fī awwal al-kitāb wa-al-duʿāʾ fī ākhirih).

awāʾil al-shahr – the first 10 days of the month (DM).
taʾwīl (pl. taʾāwīl) – interpretation, explanation (e.g. taʾwīl al-Qurʾān).

****

ب

بتر

mabtūr 1. acephalous, imperfect, incomplete (of text) (KC, passim) 2. truncated letter (especially of a descender) (KH, 34).

بحر

baḥr (pl. buḥūr) – panel on a book cover; cartouche (TS, 33; AG, 110; JL, 103: iṭār fīhi manāṭiq wa-buḥūr mustaṭīlah dhāt fuṣūṣ fī nihāyatihā; SD, I, 53).
tabḥīr – creating panels on book covers (NH, 355).

بخر

tabkhīr – fumigation (TS, 40: wa-yubakhkhir bi-aʿḍāʾ al-hud'hud wa-rīshih fa-innahu yaqtul al-araḍah).

بدل

badal, **bidl** (DB, I, 452) (pl. abdāl) 1. variant reading (varia lectio), usually abbreviated as ل (CI, II, xiii) or خ ل or خ د for nuskhah and badal respectively (KG, 473: see the quotation under ẓāhir; MI, 119, 120, 166: ay fī nuskhah ukhrá badalan ʿan al-nuskhah al-madhkūrah fī al-matn, comp. خ ل for nuskhah-aṣl, MZ, II, 412) 2. also **tabdīl** – substitution, alteration (CL, fasc.3, 296); conjectural substitution, conjecture.

بدوح

budūḥ – artificial talismanic word (seal) formed from the simple threefold magic square, wifq (US, 49; EI, suppl. fasc.3-4, 153-154; SD, I, 59-60; DT, 100-103).

برد

bardī, abardī (waraq al-bardī), bardīyah – papyrus, papyrus sheet or roll (DB, I, 521-522; EI, VIII, 407; WS, 64-66), comp. qirṭās.
mibrad – file, rasp (HT, lin.84; QS, II, 417; IA, 60; DD, I, 390: for trimming).

برز

ibrāz – bringing out (a book), publishing (KM, IV, sifr 13, 6: abraztu al-kitāb nashartuhu wa-huwa mabrūz).
ibrāz bi-al-ḥumrah see ḥumrah.

برشم

barshamah – decorating a text with multi-coloured dots (DB, I, 545).
burshmān (or **barshmān**, pl. barāshim, DC, I, 189) – endband (headband) (ST, index, 8; ST, 17-18; IB, 81, n.148); **barshīm**, **barīshim**, pl. barshimān (LA, pt.5, 386: barshimān jamʿ barshīm aw barīshim ay ibrīshim aw ibrīsim wa-huwa al-ḥarīr wa-al-barshīm Fārisīyah wa-al-burshmān jamʿuhā).

برك

al-mubārak(ah) – epithet of the months of Ṣafar, Shaʿbān, Ramaḍān, Shawwāl, and Rabīʿ al-Thānī (q.v.), as well as such words as kitāb, jāmiʿ, nuskhah, etc.

بركار

birkār (pl. barākīr) – compass; (pair of) dividers (SA, III, 41: used for measuring letters; MU, XVI, 60; DM), see also bīkār and tabkīr.

بركان

burkān (pl. barākīn), **ḥajar al-burkān** – pumice (TS, 12, 18).

برنامج

barnāmaj (pl. barāmij) 1. table of contents (LC, 23) 2. work containing a record of attested study similar to **fihris** and **fahrasah** (q.v.).

برى

bary, **birāyah** – paring, trimming (of a reed) (IR, 232; SA, III, 455-464; SK, 105; UD, 9: arkān al-bary arbaʿah: fatḥ wa-naḥt wa-shaqq wa-qaṭṭ).
burāyah – a shaving (from a reed) (KU, 154: IK, 85; KK, 49).
barrāyah, **mibrāh** (pl. mabārin) – pen knife (AA, 88; IK, 90; DB, I, 591).

بزق

mibzaq – lancet-like knife, **mibzaq al-faṣādah** (ST, index, 8; MP, 64; DA: **mibzagh**; SD, I, 81).

بسط

basṭ – spreading out, flattening (of a letter), as opposed to rounding it, taqwīr (SA, III, 11, 50; AS, 144).
mabsūṭ 1. horizontal stroke, line (KU, 120) 2. (**qalam**) **mabsūṭ** – reed pen, having its nib cut (evenly) straight (not obliquely), syn. jazm (IK, 87) 3. rectilinear (of a script, **al-qalam al-mabsūṭ**) (SA, III, 11: wa-huwa mā lā inkhisāf wa-lā inḥiṭāṭ fīhi ka-al-muḥaqqaq; KH, 34; AS, 144) 4. original (comprehensive), unabridged work, comp. mukhtaṣar.
al-aqlām al-mabsūṭah (al-yābisah) – rectilinear scripts such as muḥaqqaq, maṣāḥif, rayḥān and naskh (AS, 144).
(al-khaṭṭ) al-mabsūṭ – clear, well-spaced Maghrebi script used predominantly for the copying of the Qurʾān and prayer books (LT, 365; TW, 13, 47, 322).

بسمل

basmalah (pl. basāmil) – the propitiatory formula 'Bism Allāh (al-Raḥmān al-Raḥīm)', written usually on its own, a number of lines down from the head of the page, and opening a composition (TP, 52; JM, 12: qāla al-nabī ṣallá Allāh ʿalayhi wa-sallam kull amr dhī bāl lā yubdaʾu fīhi bi-Bism Allāh fa-huwa abtar ay maqṭūʿ al-barakah; EI, I, 1084-1085).

بشر

bashr 1. paring, dressing (of leather) (UK, 161; MP, 58; TS, 23-24; AG, 109; ST, index, 9; IA, 63; LF, 78: 'racler, ratisser des peaux'; HT, lin.111) 2. erasure with a pen knife or scraper (TP, 58; LF, 78; 'effacer des mots avec un grattoir') 3. cancellation by means of drawing lines above a word or words to be erased (LF, 79-81: 'en passant quelques traits de plume par dessus').
mabshūr – pared; erased.

بشرط

bashraṭ 1. silk thread used for endbanding (headbanding) 2. silk endband (headband) (HT, lin.97, 155).

بطاقة

biṭāqah (pl. baṭāʾiq) 1. piece, slip (of paper) 2. catalogue, register (AD, 12).
(qalam) al-baṭāʾiq – the smallest of the curvilinear scripts, also known as **al-ghubār** (q.v.) (AS, 145).

بطن

baṭn (pl. buṭūn), **bāṭin** (pl. bawāṭin) – inner side; flesh side (of parchment); inner cover.
baṭn al-ghilāf (al-sifr, al-kitāb) – inner cover; doublure (LC, 23; AG, 112).
biṭānah (pl. baṭāʾin) 1. lining (FT, 408) 2. doublure (TS, 22-23; MB, 117; IA, 60; HT, lin.73-79) 3. endpaper; paste-down endpaper; endleaf (ST, passim; IB, 47, 49; UK, 157: waraq al-baṭāʾin wa-hiya waraqatān fa-waraqah takūn fī al-jild wa-ukhrá takūn bāqiyatan ʿalá al-karārīs li-taṣūn al-kitāb min al-adhá wa-al-wasakh) 4. pasteboard (UK, 159; HD, 102; MA, IV, 89, 90: wa-lā baʾs an yubaṭṭin al-jild bi-al-awrāq allatī fīhā al-ḥisāb) 5. basan, sheep skin (AG, 110; SD, I, 92).

tabṭīn 1. lining of the insides of book covers with paper, leather or silk (ST, index, 9; MU, XIV, 84: mujallad bi-adam mubaṭṭan bi-dībāj) 2. removal of shaḥmah (q.v.) from the reed (IK, 87); paring (of the calamus) (KD, II, 701: baṭṭantu al-qalam tabṭīnan idhā raqqaqtu baryah; MB, 61; BA, III, 370), comp. bary.

بعد

baʿdu – after; used for a transposed word, abbrev. ب (LE, 134).
baʿdīyah – the epistolary and textual formula 'ammā (or wa-) baʿdu', also known as **faṣl al-khiṭāb**, separating doxological statements from the preface proper (TP, 53, n.20).

بعض

tabʿīḍ – word division, separation (MM, 135: wa-karihū tabʿīḍ al-kalimah al-murakkabah).

بكر

bīkār (pl. bayākīr, bawākīr; comp. birkār) – compass, (pair of) dividers (UK, 153, 156; MP, 58; IB, 44; MB, 101, 103; IA, 59, 60; TU, 105), comp. birkār.
tabkīr, also **bīkārīyah** – working with a compass by drawing circles, measuring distances, etc. (MB, 103, 104, 105: fa-al-bīkārīyah istikhrāj al-shumūs wa-al-dawāʾir al-manqūshah allatī taqaʿu fī wasaṭ al-kitāb); geometrical figure, design.
al-dawāʾir al-bīkārīyayh see dāʾirah.
misṭarat al-tabkīr see misṭarah.
mibkar(ah) – case (for a compass) (NH, 380; DD, I, 391).

بلط

balāṭah – marble slab (UK, 153; IB, 42; MB, 103; IA, 59), comp. rukhām.

بلغ

balāgh (pl. balāghāt), **tablīgh** (pl. tablīghāt), also known as **ʿalāmat al-balāgh (al-tablīgh)** – collation statement or mark indicating the

place where collation was interrupted (MF, 81: balaghtu qirā'atan min al-balāgh bi-khaṭṭī ilá hunā; MF, 85: fa-samiʿa mā fī hāmish al-nuskhah ʿinda al-tablīgh; CD, IV, pl.119; TP, 56; JA, I, 268; CT, 45: **bulūgh**), comp. muʿāraḍah, muqābalah.
muballigh see mustamlin.

بلو / بلى

balī, **bālin** – worn, damaged (TS, 28: al-asfār al-bawālī).

بنق

tabnīq – elegant writing, copying (TE, 15), comp. tanmīq.

بهاري

(al-khaṭṭ) al-bihārī or **al-Bihārī** (also known as **bāhar** (thus), **khaṭṭ-i bāhar**, EI, IV, 1127) – script used in India mostly but not exclusively for the copying of the Qur'ān from the late 8/14th century to the end of the 10/16th century (CA, 36).

بوب

bāb (pl. abwāb) – chapter, abbrev. ب (MI, 103).
tabwīb – arrangement (division) of the text into chapters (MF, 609; TP, 53, n.20).
mubawwib – compiler (DF, IV, 376), comp. murattib.

بيت

bayt (pl. buyūt) 1. wooden box (for housing a multi-volume copy of the Qur'ān) (SJ, nos.2 and 5: fī bayt ʿūd laṭīf mubaṭṭan bi-al-ḥarīr, fī bayt ʿūd rabʿah mughashshá bi-al-jild 2. compartment (in such a box) 3. compartment (in a book cover design) (TS, 31, 32; AG, 110) 4. frame (as part of the border, ṭurrah) (TS, 33).
bayt al-ghurāb – hexagonal element in a Mamluk book cover design (JL, 95, 97; KR, 82).
Bayt al-Maqdis, al-Bayt al-Muqaddas – Jerusalem.
tabyīt – creation of compartments and frames (on book covers) (TS, 31-33; AG, 110).

بيض

bayāḍ (pl. bayāḍāt) 1. blank space, gap; space, spacing (e.g. TM, 169: bayāḍ al-fawātiḥ wa-al-khawātim; AK, 351: fa-inna al-bayāḍ min jumlat ʿalāʾim al-faṣl; SA, III, 146: wa-kuttāb al-rasāʾil yajʿalūn lil-fawāṣil bayāḍan yakūn bayna al-kalāmayn; SA,VI, 195: miqdār al-bayāḍ qabla al-basmalah; SA, III, 50: an yakūn al-bayāḍ bayna al-aḥruf ka-mithlih bayna al-suṭūr) 2. lacuna, abbrev. ض (TN, 51; LC, 23; MI, 138) 3. also **mubayyaḍah**, **tabyīḍah** – fair copy (as opposed to a draft, musawwadah (q.v.) (MU, VI, 157: wa-baqiya baqīyat al-kitāb musawwadatan ghayr munaqqaḥah wa-lā mubayyaḍah fa-bayyaḍahu Abū Isḥāq; MU, XV, 23: al-sawād wa-al-bayāḍ; FK, I, 978; KF, II, 333) 4. counter ('eye') of a letter (KH, 36) 5. white colour, ink or paint.
bayāḍ ṣaḥīḥ – expression used for a blank space or page created by mistake or left deliberately blank in order to indicate a lacuna in the exemplar (hic nullus est defectus).
tabyīḍ 1. creating adequate space (bayāḍ) between letters and lines; spacing (TE, 15) 2. execution (of the fair copy) (TE, 15; KF, II, 333, 346) 3. copying, transcription (TE, 15).
mubayyiḍ – author; fair copyist.

بين

bayān (pl. bayānāt) – marginal correction or explanatory note (usually for a smudged or clumsily written word, i.e. cacographical error), abbrev. ب or ن (TP, 58; CI, I , xiv; MI, 182; MM, 136).

****

ت

تابوت

tābūt (pl. tawābīt) 1. wooden box, chest (for housing a multi-volume copy of the Qurʾān) (SJ, no.47: fī tābūt ʿūd murakkan bi-al-nuḥās; TS, 39: tawābīt al-rabaʿāt; TS, 33: al-tawābīt al-jāfiyah al-ajrām; ME, 568-569) 2. pentagonal figure or panel (TS, 29: thumma tarsum fī al-udhn tābūtan ʿalá wasaṭ al-khātim aw al-dāʾirah; also TS, 30-31; AG, 110).

تاسومة

tāsūmah – octagonal element in a Mamluk book cover design (JL, 95, 97; KR, 82).

تبر

tibr – gold, gold dust (AQ, 246: kataba wa-dhahhaba wa-zayyana arkānah bi-al-tibr wa-al-lawn wa-al-taḥrīr; LL, I, 293).

تخت

takht (pl. tukhūt) 1. wooden board (UK, 149; KT, 135: used for book covers) 2. wooden pressing board (TS, 22, 24; AG, 107) 3. also **takht al-ziyār** (**al-ziyyār**) bookbinder's press (ST, index, 9; IB, 42; HT, lin. 82, 120).
takhtīt – pressing (ST, index, 9).

ترب

turāb – dust, earth, sand.
tatrīb – sprinkling a freshly written text with sand (IK, 94; KM, IV, sifr 13, 6; KU, 156; TD, I, 127-136), comp.tarmīl.
mitrabah – sandbox; compartment for sand in the dawāh (q.v.) (SA, II, 478-480).

ترجم

tarjamah (pl. tarājim) 1. designation of the sender in the ʿunwān (ML, 32: makān al-tarjamah qabla al-basmalah) 2. title (of a book) (LC, 28; AH, 165); detailed title of a book, indicating its contents (DB, II, 122) 3. key word (LC, 28) 4. chapter heading (IN, 252: wa-al-murād bi-al-tarājim al-abwāb wa-al-fuṣūl wa-naḥwuhā) 5. decorative panel around a chapter heading (LC, 27) 6. paragraph (LC, 27) 7. headpiece or tailpiece (LC, 27) 8. decorative figure of any shape or size used in the text (e.g. disc) or margins (e.g. medallion)

(MS, 20: tarājim mudhahhabah mulawwanah mutanawwiʿat al-ashkāl, also MS, 28, 29, 30) 9. biographical note, biography (EI, X, 224) 10. table of contents (tarjamat al-abwāb, LC, 28) 11. interpretation; translation (EI, X, 224) 12. explanation, exegesis (DB, II, 1021) 13. also **mutarjam** (e.g. 'Qaṣīdat Ibn al-Durayhim fī al-mutarjam') – cypher, cryptography (AA, 186; IT, 29-31; DB, II, 1021).
mutarjim 1. translator; biographer 2. illuminator (TW, 260, 270).

ترس

tirs, turs (pl. turūs) – principal (often central) element in a Mamluk book cover design in the shape of a pointed star (JL, 95, 97; KR, 82).

ترنج

turunj(ah) 1. oval, citrus-shaped stamp (mandorla) for center-medallions (IB, 69; LC, 28) 2. center-medallion in the shape of a mandorla (ST, index, 9; IB, 44) 3. illuminated oval medallion, rosette (HD, 103; IP, 145; PA, 116), comp. shamsah.
rubʿ al-turunjah – quarter-medallion, corner-piece (ST, 15).

تفتر

taftar see daftar.

تم

tatmīm – completion, execution; writing **tamma** (lit. 'it is finished') at the end of the colophon, abbrev. م or م م م (any number) (CI, I, xiii; CM, 46), comp. taʾmīn, tafqīṭ.
tamām – end, finish; used in manuscripts of Persian/Indian provenance in the expression **tamām shud** ('it is finished'), often abbreviated as ١٢ , ٢٢ or ١۴ at the end of marginal quotations or glosses (CI, II, xiii), comp. ḥadd.
tatimmah – supplementation; supplement ; continuation and end (of a composition) (DM).
tamīmah (pl. tamāʾim) – amulet, talisman (EI, X, 177-178).

****

ث

ثبت

thabt, ithbāt – writing, copying (MH, 100, 101; FK, II, no.1202-3: hādhā ākhir mā athbatnāhu fī hādhā al-kitāb), used very often in the formula of attestation 'ṣaḥḥa wa-thabata'.
thabat (pl. athbāt) 1. certificate or document attesting a didactic transmission of a text; document, written testimony (SD, I, 157) 2. record of attested study (HB, 234; GA, 288: syn. muʿjam, mashyakhah, in the East, and barnāmaj or fahrasah, in the West) 3. table of contents.
thabāt – signature (SD, I, 157).
ithbāt 1. vocalization (AD, 18) 2. also **tathbīt** – attestation, authentication (formula), usually expressed by: ṣaḥḥa (or ṣaḥīḥ) (dhālika) wa-thabata (or kataba) or hādhā ṣaḥīḥ wa-katabahu (TP, 53, n.25; CT, 45; GA, 289).
muthabbit, muthbit – writer, recorder (syn. kātib), particularly in the expression muthbit al-samāʿ, i.e. kātib al-samāʿ, writer of the audition note (MH, 101; CT, 45).

ثبج

thabaj(ah) – obscurity or indistinctiveness of handwriting (LL, I, 330).

ثقب

mithqab (pl. mathāqib) – drill for making holes in boards when endbanding (headbanding) (TS, 11; AG, 107).

ثقل

thaqīl (lit. 'heavy') – larger variety (version) of a script (SA, III, 58: al-thuluth al-thaqīl, thaqīl al-thuluth; AS, 147).

ثلث

(qalam) al-thuluth (al-thulth) – the principal curvilinear script used in codices mostly for book titles and chapter headings (SA, III, 50: ṭarīqat al-thuluth fa-tajrī al-ḥāl fīhi ʿalá al-mīl ilá al-taqwīr; AS, 147; JM, 32-38: **al-thuluth al-muʿtād**; JM, 46-53: **jalīl al-thuluth**; TU, 106: li-anna alif al-thuluth fī ṣadrihā taḥdīb mā wa-fī ʿajzihā ka-dhālika; LM, 47: wa-al-thuluth lil-taʿlīm; LM, 53: wa-in kunta taktub thuluthan aw tawāqīʿ aw riqāʿan fa-amil ākhirahu (ay ḥarf al-alif) muraṭṭiban ilá naḥw al-yasrah qalīlan; EI, IV, 1123- in Persia, 1125- in Turkey).
al-thuluth al-Maghribī see Mashriqī.
(qaṭʿ) al-thulth see qaṭʿ.
tathlīth – providing a letter with three diacritical points, abbrev. ث (TN, 51), hence **muthallathah** – having three diacritical dots; epithet added to thāʾ to prevent its being mistaken for bāʾ or tāʾ or yāʾ (LL, I, 349).
al-ḥibr al-muthallath see ḥibr.

ثمن

(qālib) al-thumn, al-thumānī see qālib.
muthamman – octagonal, octagon (EI,VII, 795-796), comp. khātim muthamman.

ثنى

tathniyah – providing a letter with two diacritical points (DM), hence **muthannāh** – having two diacritical dots (points).
muthannāh fawqīyah – marked with two points above; epithet added to tāʾ to prevent it from being read as bāʾ, or thāʾ or yāʾ (LL, I, 361).
muthannāh taḥtīyah – marked with two points below; epithet added to yāʾ to prevent its being mistaken for bāʾ or tāʾ or thāʾ (LL, I, 361).
al-taʾrīkh al-mustathná see taʾrīkh.
istithnāʾ – the formula of submission to the will of God 'in shāʾa Allāh' (SA, VI, 232-234) , abbrev. انش , انشه or شا (CI, II, xiv; FM, 167; MZ, Taf. 12, no.13; SA,VI, 232-234; MI, 102), see also mashʾa-lah.

****

ج

جامة

jāmah 1. decorative medallion or panel; either illuminated or stamped (KI, 258: al-manāṭiq wa-al-buḥūr; LC, 25) 2. center-piece (on a book cover) (FI, 87, 88; JL, 83: **jāmah wusṭá**; KR, 87: ashkāl lawzīyah) 3. palmette, roundel (ZM, 44, 45).
rubʿ al-jāmah – quarter-medallion, corner-piece (JL, 83, 99).
dhayl al-jāmah – pendant (JL, 99, 100).

جبر

jabr – repairing, mending, restoring manuscripts; repair (SJ, nos.41, 43).

جد

tajdīd – repair, restoration (KR, 87).

جد ل

jadīlah (pl. jadāʾil) – plait, braid; interlace (TF, 141).
majdūl (pl. majādīl) – leather strap, thong (KC, 33; KC, 42).

جد ول

jadwal(ah) (pl. jadāwil) 1. also **tajdawīl** – ruling (of borders), creating rule-borders (WB, 50, 56; TW, 148, 160) 2. rules, rule-border (LC, 24: jadāwil al-ṣafaḥāt, jadāwil al-hawāmish; HD, 105; PA, 63) 3. diagram, chart, table (LC, 24) 4. column (of text) (SD, I, 175) 5. table of contents (CM, no.6/2) 6. magic square, talismanic seal (EI, II, 370; DT, 108).
mujadwal – ruled (LC, 26).
mujadwil – ruler (maker of rule-borders) (TC, 32).

جذ

judhādhah – slip (of paper); inset (DM), comp. juzāzah.

جر

jarrah, jurrah – horizontal stroke, line, as in the median kāf, isolated ḥā᾽ or sīn 'without teeth' (SA, III, 61, 72 ,81), comp. shaqq.
mijarr – wooden part of the clasp (KC, 33: fī sifr bi-mijarr min khashab).

جرد

jard al-matn see matn.
jarīdah – list, register, inventory (SD, I, 184; DG, 27).
tajrīd 1. edition or composition involving collection or selection of material from an original work; collection (gathering) of glosses from the margins of a manuscript (TT, 107; KF, II, 331: wa-lam yujarridhu ʿan al-musawwadah) 2. extract, abridgement (SD, I, 183).
mijrad(ah) – file; scraper (MB, 112; DD, I, 390: instrument for cleaning a dawāh; UA, 393).

جرم

jirm (pl. ajrām) – format (of a book), e.g. jirm kabīr or kabīr al-jirm, jirm wasaṭ, jirm laṭīf or laṭīf al-jirm (SJ, passim).

جرى

majran (pl. majārin) – compartment for reed pens in the dawāh (KU, 154).

جز

jazz – trimming, shaving (MB, passim: **ḥazz**; IA, 62).
juzāzah (pl. juzāzāt) 1. loose sheet of paper used for notes, quotations or drafts, rough copies 2. also **jizzah** – slip of paper used for glosses and tipped into a volume; inset (UI, 19; MU, VII, 132, n.2: wurayqāt tuʿallaq fīhā al-fawā᾽id; KF, I, 103).

جزء

juz' (pl. ajzā') 1. booklet; single-quire codex; volume (in the sense of mujallad) (MK, 79; AI, 117: wa-yuwassiʿu al-ṭālib kummah li-yaḍaʿ fīhi al-kutub wa-al-ajzā') 2. the 30th part of the Qur'ān (= 3 ḥizbs); one of the 30 volumes of the Qur'ān 3. quire (gathering), abbrev. ج or جـ (CI, I, xii) 4. chapter or section of a text (composition) 5. independent, small piece of writing, usually not more than a quire (IJ, 128) 6. small collection of ḥadīth without any structured arrangement (EI, VII, 705).
mujazza' – volume consisting of bound quires, ajzā' (IJ, 128).
juz'ah – handle (of a knife) (KD, II, 711).
mijza'ah – pen knife (IK, 90).
tajzi'ah – set of a number of volumes (Fr. tomaison) (SJ, passim: tajzi'at sabʿah; WR, 83, 86, 92: e.g. khumāsīyat al-tajzi'ah, tajzi'ah ʿushārīyah, tajzi'ah thumānīyah).

جزع

jazʿ – onyx (for burnishing gold) (UK, 143; MB, 99; MP, 38).
al-waraq al-mujazzaʿ see waraq.

جزم

jazm – reed pen, having the nib cut (evenly) straight (not obliquely) (IK, 87: qalam jazm; LL, I, 421).
(khaṭṭ or **qalam) al-jazm** – ancient script of al-Ḥīrah used for the copying of the Qur'ān (khaṭṭ al-maṣāḥif) and having 'a stiff and angular appearance' (RN, 7-9; IK, 89, 90).
majzūm – well-balanced (of writing) (IK, 94: fa-idhā sawwá ḥurūf kitābatih wa-lam yukhālif baʿḍuhā baʿḍan qīla jazama yajzimu jazman wa-khaṭṭ majzūm).
jazm(ah) – diacritical mark (ہ or جـ) indicating an unvowelled final consonant (DS, 196: wa-ḥudhdhāq al-kitāb yajʿalūn al-jazmah jīman laṭīfatan bi-ghayr ʿarāqah ishāratan lil-jazm; for other signs representing jazmah see GL, 13).

جسد

jasad (pl. ajsād) – background (UK, 149: ṣifat kitābah bayḍā' ʿalá jasad aswad).
tajsīd – tinting in red (AD, 23).

جف

mujaffif – dryer (for sand), comp. tarmīl (UA, 393).

جل

(qalam) al-jalīl – according to Ibn al-Nadīm, the 'father of all scripts' (abū al-aqlām) (FN, 11, 12; IK, 89: wa-khaṭṭ ahl al-Shām al-jalīl yaktubūna bi-hi al-maṣāḥif wa-al-sijillāt; SA, III, 12).
al-khaṭṭ al-jalīl (also **jalī**) – name given to a larger variety of the script, e.g. jalīl al-muḥaqqaq (q.v.), jalīl al-thuluth (q.v.), dīwānī jalī (SA, III, 50: wa-al-maʿná fīhi anna al-ṭams lā yalīq bi-al-khaṭṭ al-jalīl; EI, IV, 1123).
tajlīl – the formula of glorification 'jalla jalāluh' or 'jalla sha'nuh' (abbrev. جش), placed after the word Allāh (TP, 54).
(ism) al-jalālah – the name of God (the word Allāh) (LC, 25).
majallah (pl. majāll) 1. writing surface (like ṣaḥīfah) (BA, III, 371: al-majallah ṣaḥīfah kānū yaktubūna fīhā al-ḥikmah); parchment roll (ND, 57, n.67) 2. booklet (SL, I, 48; SL, II, 5) 3. composition, work (e.g. Majallat Luqmān; FK, I, no.892: wa-baʿdu fa-hādhihi majallah mushtamilah ʿalá sharḥ...).

جلد

jild (pl. julūd) 1. leather (EI, II, 540-541; KM, I, sifr 4,100-111; WS, 56-60; AE, 106-109); parchment (AE, 108; EP, 17) 2. volume.
jild (raqq) al-ghazāl – gazelle skin (hide) (EI, VIII, 408); fine (good quality, vellum-like) parchment, not necessarily made of gazelle skin (EP, 19-21).
jild(ah) – book cover; binding (JL, 81: jildat muṣḥaf; LC, 25).
jildah yumná – upper cover (LC, 25).
jalādah, **mijlad**, **tajlīdah** – book cover (LC, 25; SD, I, 206).
tajlīd – covering with leather; bookbinding (SD, I, 206).

mujallad(ah) – volume (MU, VIII, 123 and IX, 47; LC, 26).
mujallid – bookbinder (QS, II, 416-417).

جلس

majlis (pl. majālis) – session, sitting.
majlis al-samāʿ – audition/reading session (EI, VIII, 1020).
majlis al-muqābalah – collation session (CI, II, 60: balagha qibālan ... fī majālis).
julūs – accession to the throne (DM).
al-taʾrīkh bi-al-julūs see taʾrīkh.

جلف

jilfah, **julfah** – nib (of the calamus; the whole part of the reed which is cut away) (SA, II, 459-460; KU, 154: wa-julfat al-qalam min mubtadaʾ sinnayh ilá ḥaythu intahá al-bary).

جلم

jalam (pl. ajlām) – (pair of) scissors (DS, 181: wa-yaḥtāj ilayhi al-kātib fī qaṣṣ al-waraq lil-taswiyah wa-naḥwih; IK, 91-92; IR, 230).

جمادى

Jumādá al-Ūlá, Jumād al-Awwal – the fifth month of the Muslim calendar, abbrev. ج١ / جـ / جا (OS, 89; CI, II, 203: **Jamīd al-Awwal**; CM, no.190: **Jamīdah al-Thānī** !).
Jumādá al-Ākhirah (al-Ākhir), Jumādá al-Thāniyah, Jumād al-Thānī – the sixth month of the Muslim calendar, abbrev. ج٢ / ج (OS, 89).

جمع

jamʿ (pl. jumūʿ) 1. contraction (of letters) (KU, 126; SA, III, 146: al-jamʿ wa-al-mashq) 2. rounding (of the descender to resemble a semi-circle) (KH, 34) 3. composition, compilation.
jāmiʿ 1. compiler, author (DF, IV, 376) 2. (pl. jawāmiʿ) – comprehensive work, major original compilation, e.g. the Qurʾān (UI, colophon: kataba hādhā al-jāmiʿ ʿAlī ibn Hilāl bi-Madīnat al-Salām; SL, I, 21; FN, 352).

majmūʿ(ah) (pl. majāmīʿ, majmūʿāt) 1. compendium; work, book (MU, III, 98: wa-lahu fī kull fann taṣānīf wa-majāmīʿ wa-tawālīf; FK, II, 359: tamma al-majmūʿ al-musammá bi-Fawāt al-wafayāt) 2. composite volume, codex compositus (LC, 25).
majmaʿ (pl. majāmiʿ), **mujammaʿ** (UA, 393) 1. tool box, case with compartments (TS, 12, 37; AG, 106; SD, I, 217; DG, 32) 2. inkwell (SD, I, 217; DD, I, 389: dawāh murabbaʿah dhāt baṭn wasīʿ min nuḥās aw ghayrih); inkwell for coloured ink (TC, 13) 3. case, box (NM, 683) 4. writing case, escritoire (TW, 52, 233; TM, 52; NH, 380).

جمل

jumal, **jummal** see ḥisāb.

جنب

janb (pl. junūb, ajnāb) – book cover (ST, index, 10).

جنح

janāḥ (pl. ajniḥah) – hinge (guard) (MB, 109, 110; IA, 61; ST, index, 10).
(qalam) al-janāḥ – the smallest of the curvilinear scripts, better known as **al-ghubār** (q.v.) (AS, 145).

جوب

jawāb (pl. ajwibah) – responsum, abbrev. ج (CI, II, xiv; MI,111).
jūbah see jūnah.
mijwab – cutter, knife (TS, 11; AG, 107: for cutting gold leaf ; IA, 61: mijwab al-takhrīm).

جوز

ijāzah (pl. ijāzāt) – authorization, licence; certificate of transmission; statement of authorization to transmit one or more than one text; diploma in the form of a note appended to a manuscript or existing independently and often containing autobibliographical data (LC, 24; EI, III, 27, 1020-1021; LB, 126-130; ER, VIII, 273-275; IJ).
ijāzat al-munāwalah see munāwalah

ijāzat al-qirāʾah see qirāʾah.
ijāzat al-riwāyah see riwāyah
ijāzat al-samāʿ see samāʿ.
ijāzah bi-al-kitbah – certificate granted to a calligrapher allowing him/her to sign his/her calligraphy with the expression 'katabahu' (NI, 181).
(khaṭṭ) al-ijāzah – Ottoman variety of riqāʿ script having a long tarwīs which often wraps round the shaft of the alif (EI, IV, 1125).
mujāz, mustajāz 1. licensee (recipient of an ijāzah) 2. (pl. mujāzāt, mustajāzāt) licensed work.
mujīz – licensor (person who has the authority to grant an ijāzah; signer of a license).

جون

jūnah – compartment (place) for an inkwell (in the dawāh); inkwell (HI, 73: wa-ammā al-jūnah allatī fīhā ḥuqq al-midād fa-yanbaghī an yakūn shaklan mudawwar al-raʾs; SA, II, 468; al-jūnah wa-hiya al-ẓarf alladhī fīhi al-līqah wa-al-ḥibr; DS, 179; AT, 133; NH, 381: **jawn**; KU, 154: wa-al-jūbah (!) allatī tujʿal fīhā al-ḥuqq, also known as **waqabah**; see also the quotation under miqlamah).

جوهر

(al-khaṭṭ) al-mujawhar – Maghrebi script used most commonly in official correspondence and as a book hand for the copying of non-Qurʾānic texts (LT, 365: TW, 13, 47, 322).

****

ح

حبر

ḥibr (pl. aḥbār) 1. gallnut or tannin ink; ink (in general) (UK, 91-100 and MB, 71-75: **al-aḥbār al-sūd –** black inks; UK, 101-110 and MB, 75-78: **al-aḥbār al-mulawwanah –** coloured inks; MJ, 212-213: **ḥibr al-kāghad, ḥibr al-raqq**; IR, 236-237: **al-aḥbār al-murakkabah –** compound inks; MP, 13, n.53; MP, 18-21; KM, IV, sifr 13, 6: wa-al-

ḥibr al-midād wa-al-zāj min akhlāṭ al-ḥibr; MR, 93: wa-al-kitābah bi-al-ḥibr awlá min al-midād li-annahu athbat; MA, IV, 84: wa-yataʿayyan ʿalayhi an lā yansakh bi-al-ḥibr alladhī yaḥriq al-waraq; SA, II, 471-477: wa-ammā al-ḥibr fa-aṣluhu al-lawn; AT, 134-135; AE, 127-131; IK, 68: **al-ḥibr al-muthallath** – ink produced by cooking the ingredients until two thirds of the substance evaporates , see LL, I, 349; IK, 68: **al-ḥibr al-maṭbūkh** – 'cooked' ink; LM, 72-73: **al-ḥibr al-dukhānī**), comp. midād 2. also **ḥabr** – flourish, embellishment (DB, III, 2016).
ḥarq ḥibr – ink burns (SJ, 354).
miḥbarah (pl. maḥābir) 1. also **ḥibrīyah** – inkwell (BA, III, 372; SA, II, 443: al-miḥbarah al-mufradah ʿan al-dawāh; SA, II, 468: wa-hiya al-maqṣūd min al-dawāh; TW, 57) 2. compartment for ink in the dawāh (AT, 132-133; SA, II, 443, 468-469), comp. dawāh.
ḥabbār, **ḥibrī** – ink maker (QS, I, 89).
taḥbīr 1. inking, inscribing in ink (SM, 264: al-taḥbīr al-naqsh min al-ḥibrah) 2. elegant, embellished writing (composition) or copying, transcription (TE, 15; SA, II, 472: ḥabbartu al-shayʾ taḥbīran idhā ḥassantuhu; WR, 87; SK, 119).
misṭarat al-taḥbīr see misṭarah.
muḥabbir – author, compiler (SS, 73: qaraʾtu jamīʿ hādhā al-kitāb ʿalá muʾallifih wa-muḥarririh wa-muhadhdhibih wa-muḥabbirih).

حبس

ḥubs (pl. aḥbās), **taḥbīs** (pl. taḥbīsāt) 1. endowment, bequest 2. certificate or statement of endowment; bequest note (LC, 28), comp. waqf.

حبك

ḥabk 1. also **taḥbīk** – endbanding (headbanding), endbanding with silk 2. also **ḥabkah** – endband (headband), decorative endband (UK, 154, 157; TS, 18-20; AG, 109; MB, 104 ff.; IA, 62, n.15: **al-kutub al-maḥbūkah**; MM, 132) 3. sewing, stitching (of a book) (TM, 170: shadd awrāqih; DB, III, 2044) 4. spine (TQ, 23).
al-ḥabk al-Rūmī – Graeco-Coptic (Byzantine) endband (headband) (TS, 19; AG, 109).
al-ḥabk al-dālī – trellis-like endband (headband) (TS, 19; AG, 109; PA, 120: of the letter dāl).

al-ḥabk al-shaṭranjī – chessboard-like endband (headband) (TS, 19; AG, 109).
al-ḥabk al-muḍallaᶜ – chevron-like endband (headband) (TS, 19; AG, 109).
ḥabakah – bookbinding (IB, 19, n. 478).
ḥabbāk – ornamental sewer; bookbinder (IB, 11; AD, 28).
ḥibākat al-kitāb – raised band (on the spine) (SD, I, 246).

حج

Dhū al-Ḥijjah (al-sharīfah, al-ḥarām) – the twelfth month of the Muslim calendar, abbrev. ذ (OS, 89).

حجاب

ḥijāb (pl. ḥujub) – talisman, amulet (DT, 69).

حجر

ḥajar baḥrī lil-ḥakk – polishing stone (IA, 60).
ḥajar al-burkān, ḥajar al-qawṣarī, ḥajar al-qushūr – pumice (TS, 12; AG, 107; ST, index,10; MB, 112: ḥajar al-qayshūr (!); IA, 62).
ḥajar al-jumāhun – burnisher (for gold) (MB, 99; MP, 38; UK, 142: ḥajar al-ḥumāḥim).
ḥajar al-misann – whetstone, hone (TS, 10).
ḥajar al-ṭiḥn – mill stone (OM).
ḥajar al-ᶜuṣṣār – stone slab for pressing (OM).
miḥjar, maḥjar (pl. maḥājir) 1. **maḥājir** – letters such as wāw, mīm, fā' and ᶜayn (TU, 36) 2. counter ('eye' of a letter) (KH, 36).

حجازي

(al-khaṭṭ) al-Ḥijāzī – generic name given to a number of very early scripts (1st and early 2nd centuries A.H.) used in the region of Mecca and Medina (hence orginally referred to as **al-Makkī** and **al-Madanī**) characterized by elongated ascenders and a slant to the right (AV, 27-33; FN, 8: fa-ammā al-Makkī wa-al-Madanī fa-fī alifātih taᶜwīj ilá yamnat al-yad wa-aᶜlā al-aṣābiᶜ wa-fī shaklih inḍijāᶜ yasīr), comp. Kūfī.

حد

ḥadd, taḥdīd – whetting, honing (of a knife) (KD, II, 711).
ḥadd (pl. ḥudūd) – limit, end; used in the form of its numerical value (١٢) at the end of marginal glosses (RA, 20, 45, 248), comp. tamām.
ḥadd al-qalam – place where the cutting of the nib begins (KU, 154: mabdaʾ maqaṭṭih).
ḥadīd(ah) (pl. ḥadāʾid) – iron tool or stamp (for leather work) (ST, 10; MP, 59; TS, 29, 31; AG, 109; MB, 105; IA, 59).
taḥdīd – tooling (of leather) (TF, 138).
mustaḥadd – knife (UA, 393; MJ, 188).

حدر

ḥadr (pl. ḥudūr) – descender (down-stroke, terminal of a letter) (AA, 50), comp. ṣaʿd.

حر

ḥarīr – silk (ST, index, 10; AG, 109; DB, IV, 2408; EI, III, 215-227).
taḥrīr 1. elegant writing, copying, transcription (TE, 15; SK, 119) 2. fair copying (TE, 15) 3. composition (GA, 286); revised version (edition); redaction (CM, 13; TE, 15) 4. writing (of a vocalized text) (TE, 16) 5. secretarial style of **shikastah** script, known in Persian as **khaṭṭ-i taḥrīr, taḥrīrī** (EI, IV, 1124; ER, IV, 701; TE, 16) 6. outlining of figures and/or letters executed in gold, with black ink (TE, 16; IP, 145; AF, 50, 52; AQ, 246) 7. ornamental surround, frame; outline, contour of letters or illuminated pieces (AF, 38, 48; PA, 58, 64, 214) 8. editing (of a manuscript text).
muḥarrir – 1. author, compiler (SS, 73) 2. penman, calligrapher, e.g. al-Aḥwal al-Muḥarrir al-Babartī (AC, 42; TE, 15-16; MU, XVII, 280: wa-kāna fī awwal amrih muʿalliman fa-lammā jāda khaṭṭuh ṣāra muḥarriran; IK, 67: warrāqan kāna aw muḥarriran) 3. editor.
muḥarrar (pl. muḥarrarāt) – piece of calligraphy, calligraph (DP, 53).

حرد

ḥard al-matn see matn.

حرز

ḥirz (pl. aḥrāz, ḥurūz) – talisman, amulet (DT, 69).

حرس

maḥrūsah ('protected by God') – epithet of major cities in the Islamic world, e.g. Miṣr al-maḥrūsah, maḥrūsat Ḥalab and the like (DB, IV, 2430: aw Ḥalab ḥarasahā Allāh).

حرض

miḥraḍah, muḥruḍah – vessel for making potash from ḥurḍ (kali or glasswort) (IR, 230; LL, I, 549).

حرف

ḥarf (pl. ḥiraf) – edge, border; sharp edge (of a knife, cutter).
ḥarf (pl. ḥurūf, aḥruf) 1. letter; word 2. variant reading (varia lectio) in the Qurʾān (DB, IV, 2457), comp. qirāʾah.
ḥarf al-qalam – right-side (of the) half-nib (SA, II, 464: ḥarf al-qalam huwa al-sinn al-ʿulyā wa-hiya al-yumná; DS, 177: huwa al-sinn al-yumná al-murtafiʿah).
ḥurūf al-ghubār see al-arqām al-ghubārīyah.
ḥurūf al-hijāʾ – letters of the alphabet (EI, III, 596-560).
ḥurūf al-jummal see ḥisāb al-jummal.
al-ḥurūf al-muhmalah see al-muhmalāt.
ḥurūf al-muʿjam see muʿjam.
al-ḥurūf al-muʿjamah see al-muʿjamāt.
al-ḥurūf al-muqaṭṭaʿah see muqaṭṭaʿāt.
al-ḥurūf al-murakkabah see tarkīb.
ḥurūf al-zimām see zimām.
tiḥrāf – shaving, trimming (HT, lin.80-86).
taḥrīf 1. oblique nibbing (cutting of the point of the nib) (SA, II, 463; KK, 50: wa-lil-qalam sinnān sinn ayman wa-sinn aysar fa-idhā kāna al-ayman aʿlá min al-aysar qīla qalam muḥarraf wa-qad ḥarraftuhu taḥrīfan; SK, 50; KD, II, 702: muḥarraf al-sinnayn; LM, 39-42) 2. distortion, error, usually involving either transposition of letters within a word, e.g. عمل /علم or شرق / شقر , or mispronunciation, e.g.

طرة / طغرا (MU, X, 57; MQ, 641: al-taḥrīf bi-al-ziyādah aw bi-al-naqṣ); falsification (of a text), comp. al-qalb al-makānī, taṣḥīf.
al-alif al-muḥarrafah – the letter alif with its tail (foot) tapered slightly to the left (SA, III, 59; MJ, 224).
al-qaṭṭ al-muḥarraf see qaṭṭ.

حرق

ḥarq ḥibr see ḥibr.

حرك

ḥarakah (pl. ḥarakāt) – vowel (GL, 8), comp. shakl.
taḥrīk – vocalization, vowelization (DM).
miḥrāk – spatula, stirrer (for an inkwell) (AA, 112-113; KD, II, 704; MB, 65; UA, 393).

حرم

al-Ḥaramān – the two Holy Places, Mecca and Medina.
Muḥarram (al-ḥarām), **al-shahr al-ḥarām** – the first month of the Muslim calendar, abbrev. م (OS, 89).
al-ḥarām – also an epithet of Rajab, Dhū al-Qaʿdah and Dhū al-Ḥijjah (q.v.).

حزب

ḥizb (pl. aḥzāb) – the 60th part of the Qurʾān (DM).

حزم

ḥazm , taḥzīm – sewing (of quires) (TS, 28; ST, index, 11; ST, 8: ḥazm al-karārīs; MB, 107: khazm).
ḥazzām – sewer of paper into bundles (IB, 11).

حسب

ḥisāb – calculation, computation.
ḥisāb al-jummal (or **ḥurūf al-jummal**) – chronogram, chronosticon (TP, 54: EI, III, 468).

ḥisāb al-ghubār see al-arqām al-ghubārīyah.
al-ḥisāb al-Hindī see al-arqām al-Hindīyah.

حسبل

ḥasbalah – the formula 'ḥasbunā Allāh wa-niʿma al-Wakīl' or 'ḥasbī Allāh' (placed usually at the end of a document, composition and/or colophon, abbrev. ح with a reversed tail of the descender (?) or what looks like حر, see SA, VI, 269-270; EI, II, 302).

حشو

ḥāshiyah (pl. ḥawāshin) 1. edge, turn-in (HT, lin.112; MB, 119; IA, 63) 2. border (on a book cover) (MB, 118; IA, 63; FZ, 217-219; MD, 109) 3. margin (of a page) 4. also **taḥshiyah** – marginal gloss, scholium, apostil; marginalia, often abbreviated as ح or حشـ ; collection of glosses; supergloss (ḥāshiyat al-ḥāshiyah) (TP, 59; MM, 139; EI, III, 268-269; DB, IV, 1820).
al-ḥāshiyah al-yumná – outer margin.
al-ḥāshiyah al-yusrá – inner margin, gutter.
(qalam) al-ḥawāshī – the smaller version of al-naskh script (NA, IX, 222; AS, 145; JM, 89-90).
ḥashw(ah) 1. decorative panel or geometrical figure (in illumination or book cover decoration) (TS, 30; AG, 110; FT, 412; FI, pl.54, 60, 63, 65, 71) 2. interpolation, parenthesis.
al-ḥashw al-baladī – Mamluk-type decorative panel (DE, 977).
ḥāshin (pl. ḥawāshin), **muḥashshin** – glossator, abbrev. المح (MI, 26; CI, II, xi; AD, 34).
taḥshiyah – glossing, gloss (AM, nos.74, 296, 322, 332).
muḥashshá – provided with glosses, glossed.

حصرم

ḥaṣramah – paring, trimming (of a reed) (BA, III, 372: wa-ḥaṣrama al-qalam barāhu; LL, I, 584).

حصل

taḥṣīl – copying, transcription (FK, I, no.89, 546).

حط

ḥaṭṭ – rubbing, smoothing leather (ST, 6; TS, 29, 34), comp. tamḥīt.
miḥaṭṭ – wooden tool used for smoothing leather and tooling; burnisher, polisher (KM, I, sifr 4, 110: al-ḥaṭṭ dalk al-adīm bi-al-miḥaṭṭ wa-huwa khashabah yuṣaqqal bi-hā al-adīm wa-yunqash; AG, 107; MB, 118: mikhaṭṭ (!); IA, 60, 63: **al-miḥaṭṭ al-khashab**, often confused with **mikhaṭṭ** (q.v.); IB, 5, n.31).
inḥiṭāṭ – syn. inkhisāf, downward curvature (of a letter, especially of descenders, ʿarāqāt) (see the quotation under mabsūṭ; KH, 34, 35; RN, 22: **makhsūf** – deeply curved).

حظر

ḥaẓīrah (pl. ḥaẓāʾir) 1. surround, frame (SD, I, 302) 2. headpiece (LC, 24).

حفظ

ḥifẓ – learning by heart, memorization (TP, 51).
ḥifāẓ (pl. aḥfiẓah), **miḥfaẓah** – case, box (KC, 55; NT, II, 142: wa-mimmā ṣuniʿa lil-muṣḥaf al-ʿaẓīm al-aṣwinah al-gharībah wa-al-aḥfiẓah al-ʿajībah; ME, 559, 575), comp. ṣiwān.
muḥāfaẓah – conservation, preservation.

حق

ḥuqq(ah) 1. small box (DG, 44) 2. the main part of the inkwell in the dawāh; inkwell (KU, 154: wa-al-ḥuqq mā yujʿal fīhi al-midād min al-ṣufr aw al-ḥadīd), comp. jūnah.
taḥqīq – establishing the correctness and authenticity of a text; text editing; critical edition (of a text) (MH, 89; MR, 103: idhā waqaʿa fī al-kitāb khaṭaʾ wa-ḥaqqaqahu kataba ʿalayhi kadhā).
muḥaqqiq – corrector; editor.
(al-khaṭṭ or **qalam) al-muḥaqqaq** – 1. ancient bookhand used by the scribes (warrāqūn) of Baghdad, hence also known as **al-ʿIrāqī** and **al-warrāqī** (FN, 12, 13) 2. family of scripts characterized by a clear execution of letters (SA, III, 22: fa-ammā al-muḥaqqaq fa-mā ṣaḥḥat ashkāluh wa-ḥurūfuh ʿalá iʿtibārihā mufradatan; AS, 144) 3. the principal rectilinear script (used mostly for the copying of the Qurʾān)

characterized by tapered descenders (SA, III, 50: ṭarīqat al-muḥaqqaq fa-tajrī al-ḥāl fīhi ʿalá al-mīl ilá al-basṭ dūna al-taqwīr; AS, 146; JM, 67-72: **jalīl al-muḥaqqaq**; TU, 106: wa-alif al-muḥaqqaq laysa fīhā taḥdīb; LM, 47: fa-al-muḥaqqaq wa-al-rayḥān lil-maṣāḥif wa-al-adʿiyah; LM, 53: fa-in kunta taktub muḥaqqaqan aw rayḥānan fa-lā taʿawwij ākhirahu (ay ḥarf al-alif) al-battah; EI, IV, 1123- in Persia, 1125- in Turkey), comp. rayḥān.
al-lām alif al-muḥaqqaqah see lām alif.

حك

ḥakk – rubbing out, effacement (TP, 58; MM, 137); erasure, syn. of bashr (LF, 78; IR, 237: wa-al-ḥakk bi-al-rāsakhth (?) wa-al-nushādir wa-al-qily wa-al-kibrīt ʿinda al-māhir).
miḥakk(ah), miḥakk al-rijl 1. pumice (MB, 112; IA, 62) 2. syn. mibrad (q.v.) (DD, I, 392; NH, 381: wa-al-miḥakkah li-iṣlāḥ ruʾūs al-jarāʾid wa-al-dafātir ka-mibrad).

حل

al-dhahab al-maḥlūl see dhahab.

حلب

qalam al-ḥalbah see ghubār.
Ḥalab al-Shahbāʾ – Aleppo.

حلزون

ḥalazūn 1. snail (used for the preparation of paste, ghirāʾ al-ḥalazūn, q.v.) (UK, 141) 2. screw (of the bookbinder's press) (MB, 104; IA, 59) 3. scroll (in design) (UI, 31).

حلق

ḥalqah (pl. ḥalaq, ḥalaqāt) 1. ring (on a book cover, or a lid of the chest, part of a clasp) (BA, III, 372) 2. study circle, scholar's circle (SL, II, 48; AI, 27).
ḥalqah lawlabīyah, miḥlāq (pl. maḥālīq) – tendril (FT, 422; AB, 136, 139).

ḥalqīyah – roundel (FT, 416).

حلى / حلو

ḥilyah, taḥliyah – decoration, embellishment (KT, 150-151).
ḥilyat al-saʿādah al-sharīfah, al-ḥilyah al-sharīfah – calligraphic composition containing the ḥadīth describing the physical appearance of the prophet Muḥammad (MC, 204-209).

حمد

ḥamdalah, taḥmīd(ah) – the doxological formula 'al-ḥamd li-Allāh' (AD, 38; TP, 53, n.20; EI, III, 122-123).

حمر

ḥumrah 1. red colour, red ink (LC, 24) 2. rubrication, rubrics (CM, 152: tammat al-ḥumrah al-mubārakah; TE, 15; MM, 139: kitābah bi-al-ḥumrah, kitābat al-ḥumrah; TB, 95), also referred to as **ibrāz (iẓhār, kitābah) bi-al-ḥumrah** (LC, 24; TP, 55).
taḥmīr – rubrication (TE, 15; LC, 24).
ḥimār al-kutub – book support, book cradle (TC, 29).

حمل

maḥmil 1. exemplar; archetype (KM, IV, sifr 13, 4: al-maḥmil al-kitāb al-awwal; ME, 566: al-muʿtamad) 2. ʿUthmanic canon, codex (MA, IV, 86) 3. also **miḥmal, maḥmal** – copyist's book support (ME, 566; TW, 56-57, 169; WA, 12: ʿūd al-nasākhah; SD, I, 328: 'pupitre').
ḥamīlah (pl. ḥamāʾil) – talisman, amulet (DT, 69).
taḥammul al-ʿilm – transmission of knowledge (GA, 286; TP, 51).

حنش

taḥnīsh (pl. taḥānīsh) 1. straight or curved line (executed on leather, etc.) (MP, 58; ST, index, 11) 2. rope work; interlace (TF, 138, 143) 3. compass, (pair of) dividers (IB, 44).

حنف

ḥanīfah – inkwell (KD, II, 700).

حنو / حنى

munḥanin – downward (inclined) sloping stroke (from right to left or left to right, as in the isolated dāl) (UD, 11; LM, 49: wa-al-munḥanī wa-al-munkabb fī al-jumlah huwa alladhī yadkhul fīhi al-iʿwijāj min yamnah ilá yasrah).

حور

miḥwar (pl. maḥāwir) 1. spine (of a book) (AB, 140) 2. central panel (on a book cover), as opposed to the border (TF, 138, 144).
maḥār(ah) – oyster shell (for burnishing gold decoration or writing) (KA, 104-105), see also tamḥīr.
taḥwīr – lining books with sheepskin leather, ḥawr (LL, II, 665).

حوط

taḥwīṭah – circular talismanic seal (DT, 109, 149-150).

حوق

taḥwīq – parenthesis (IM, 171; MH, 97, 99; TP, 58: as a means of cancellation; TP, 59: as a means of indicating an addition or omission in a different recension).

حوقل

ḥawqalah, **ḥawlaqah** – the formula 'lā ḥawla wa-lā quwwata illā bi-Allāh', often found at the end of a composition or colophon (MG, I, 483).

حول

ḥāʾil, taḥwīl, ḥaylūlah – place separating (separation of) one isnād from another, abbrev. ح (TP, 56).

iḥālah , ʿalāmat al-iḥālah – reference mark (signe de renvoi) (LC, 24; MI, 35).

****

خ

خانة

khānah – compartment, panel (in decoration) (UI, 3, 31).

ختم

khatm 1. seal, sealing; stamp, stamping; tool, tooling 2. stamping (of a book cover) (FZ, 214) 3. colophon (TM, 174: wa-ka-dhālik yafʿal fī khatm al-kitāb aw ākhir kull juzʾ) 4. also **khatmah** – lecture delivered to mark the end of a series of study sessions on a given composition (e.g. Ṣaḥīḥ al-Bukhārī) or subject; work compiled for this occasion (KS).

khatm al-Qurʾān – the final sūrah of the Qurʾān (AD, 43).

khatmah (pl. khatamāt, khitam) – 1. recital of the entire Qurʾān (esp. on festive occasions) 2. complete copy of the Qurʾān (SJ, 370: al-khitam al-mubārakah; MA, IV, 86).

khātim, khātam khātām, khītām (pl. khawātim, khawātīm, khayātīm, KK, 54) 1. seal, signet; seal impression (EI, IV, 1102-1105; OS) 2. talismanic seal (DT, 108) 3. stamp or medallion (on a book cover), e.g. **khātim murabbaʿ** – lozenge-shaped medallion; **khātim musaddas –** six-pointed medallion (star); **khātim muthamman** – eight-pointed medallion (star) (TS, 29, 34; AG, 109, 110, IA, 63).

al-khātim al-Sulaymānī – Solomon's seal (cryptographic talisman representing the greatest name of God, al-Ism al-Aʿẓam) (CM, 169; CI, I, 130; DT, 144).

khātimah (pl. khawātim), **ikhtitām** 1. conclusion, epilogue 2. explicit, closing matter (in manuscripts) (TP, 52, n.14) 3. colophon (UI, 5, 8; FT, 396) 4. tailpiece (HD, 108).

خد

khadd (pl. khudūd) – inner or outer margin (IM, 165: fa-kāna al-takhrīj fī ṭurratayh ṭurar ṣuffifat bi-bīḍ al-khudūd; AA, 67).

خدع

takhḍīʿ – rounding, backing (of the spine) (HN, 385).

خرج

takhrīj, ikhrāj 1. also **istikhrāj** (TW, 210) – edition or composition involving correction, selection and/or rearrangement (tabwīb) of the material from the original work (TW, 126-130: mukharraj min al-mubayyaḍah, takhrīj ḥāshiyah min al-mubayyaḍah, kharraja taʿālīq jaddih), comp. tajrīd 2. tracing a ḥadīth back to its original source; explanation and evaluation of the sources of a ḥadīth (MH, 88) 3. omission; insertion, comp. laḥaq (TP, 58; TM, 187-188;) 4. writing an omission in the margin (MH, 94: kayfīyat takhrīj al-sāqiṭ fī al-ḥawāshī; MR, 94, 95; IM, 163) 5. marking the place of omission (MF, 606) 6. extract from a book; quotation (TM, 169) 7. copying, transcription (TW, 243: akhraja minhu bi-khaṭṭ yadih mujalladāt kathīrah; KF, II, 333: ghayr mukhraj ilá al-bayāḍ) 8. **takhrīj** – 'kharraja kitāban – he wrote a book leaving [blank] the places [of the titles] of the sections and chapters' (LL, I, 718).

takhrījah 1. omission; insertion 2. reference mark (signe de renvoi), also known as **ʿalāmat (khaṭṭ) al-takhrīj** (TP, pl.XXIIA: wa-yajʿalu badala al-takhrījah ishāratan bi-al-hindī; TP, 58, n.73: in the form of a curved line, ʿaṭfah, or a caret; KF, I, 222: wa-lā kalimah fī al-ḥāshiyah wa-lā takhrījah) 3. marginal note, comment (AD, 45; LC, 27).

mukharraj, mukhraj – insertion (MH, 95: kharraja al-mukharraj fī al-ḥāshiyah).

mukhraj – discarded leaf of calligraphy (AC, 39).

istikhrāj 1. excerpting; copying (DM) 2. catchword, vox reclamans (MA, IV, 90: fa-yaḥtāj al-ṣāniʿ an yakūn ʿārifan bi-al-istikhrāj li-yaʿrif bi-dhālik ittiṣāl al-kalām bi-mā baʿdih; NM, 683).

mustakhrij, mukharrij – compiler, selector (DF, II, 384; TW, 126-130).

خرز

kharz – sewing (of leather) (TS, 35; ST, index, 12; MP, 59).
mikhraz, mikhrāz – awl, punch (SA, II, 481; DS, 181).
al-qirāb al-makhrūz see qirāb.
kharzah – glass bead (for burnishing gold or paper) (MB, 99; OM).

خرش

mikhrash – tool resembling a churn-staff (for mixing paper pulp) (OM).

خرط

kharīṭah (pl. kharāʾiṭ) – case, book pouch (for hanging a copy of the Qurʾān on the wall) (TM, 171: kharīṭah dhāt ʿurwah wa-mismār; TB, 93-94).

خرطوش

kharṭūsh(ah) (pl. kharāṭīsh) 1. cartouche (FI, 82; FT, 394) 2. ansa, roundel, palmette (KH, 36), comp. ṭurrah.

خرطوم

khurṭūm (pl. kharāṭīm) – nib (of a calamus) (SA, II, 459), comp. jilfah.

خرق

khirqah (pl. khiraq) 1. cloth (used for doublures and endbanding) (TS, 15, 17, 27; MB, 109) 2. polishing cloth (MB, 114; HT, lin.166); eraser (cloth) (DM) 3. scrap (of paper) (DM).

خرم

kharm 1. sewing (of quires) (UK, 154, 157; MB, 104; IA, 60; SA, II, 481) 2. undoing the sewing (ST, index, 12; MP, 59) 3. gap, blank, lacuna (SJ, 347, 354: wa-fīhi kharm wa-taqṭīʿ wa ḥarq ḥibr; MI, 76: al-kharm al-saqṭ fī al-makhṭūṭāt).

khurūm – loose leaves from a disbound codex, fragments (HB, 233: feuillets décousus, en vrac; TC, 26).
makhrūm, **munkharim** – imperfect, incomplete (TC, 26; KF, II, 526: makhrūm al-awwal, makhrūm al-ākhir).
makhārīm, makhrūmāt – incomplete, imperfect manuscripts (volumes) (KF, II, 527).

خرمش

kharmashah – uneven lineation (KM, IV, sifr 13, 7: wa-al-kharmashah ifsād al-suṭūr wa-al-kitāb wa-naḥwih).

خز

khazz (pl. khuzūz) – silk; cloth made of silk and wool (TS, 27; AG, 107; AD, 46).

خزم

takhzīm – sewing (of quires) (TS, 14-15; AG, 107), comp. kharm and ḥazm.
makhzūmah – document written on 'a sheet of paper folded twice vertically in the middle so as to form four narrow pages, each page is divided into two parts divided by a fold' (DR, 119).

خزن

khizānah, khizānat al-kutub – bookcase; library, comp. maktabah.

خسف

inkhisāf see inḥiṭāṭ.

خصر

mukhtaṣar 1. concise composition, comp. mabsūṭ 2. abridgement, epitome (EI, VII, 536-540; EA, I, 23-24) 3. abbreviation (contraction, suspension, siglum, TP, 55-56. For various abbreviations used in manuscripts see CI, II, xiii-xiv, 159-160; GL, 25-26).
al-sharḥ al-mukhtaṣar see sharḥ.

خط

khaṭṭ (pl. khuṭūṭ) 1. mark, sign; stroke, line (for various technical terms connected with the shapes of letters and strokes see KH, 34-38) 2. writing, handwriting; script, calligraphy, penmanship (ML, 52: iʿlam anna al-khaṭṭ huwa ṣuwar tatashakkal fī al-ʿaql tashakkulan kullīyan wa-al-yad tukharrij tilka al-ṣuwar bi-wāsiṭat al-qalam bi-qadr quwwat al-yad wa-kathrat idmāniha wa-līn aʿṣābihā).
al-khaṭṭ al-Fāsī – numerical system of Graeco-Coptic origin, also known as **al-qalam al-Fāsī** or **al-qalam al-Rūmī**, used in Maghrebi manuscripts for the purpose of dating and in the law of inheritance (AK, 358).
al-khaṭṭ al-muʿjam – pointed letters, script (text) see also ʿajam.
al-khaṭṭ al-mansūb (also **al-kitābah al-mansūbah**, LM, 29) – proportionate writing or scripts, which according to the Arabic tradition, use the principle of 'tanāsub' elaborated by Ibn Muqlah (SA, III, 41; EI, III, 887: ER, IV, 681), comp. al-aqlām al-sittah.
al-khaṭṭ al-mushakkal – vocalized script (text), scriptio plena, as opposed to unvocalized (ghayr mushakkal), scriptio defectiva.
bi-khaṭṭ – in the hand(writing) of, copied by (e.g. CI, I, 83, 103), comp. yad.
khuṭūṭ al-kuttāb – chancery (secretarial) scripts (KU, 114; AS, 144).
khuṭūṭ al-maṣāḥif – Qurʾānic scripts; book hands used principally for the transcription of the Qurʾān (FN, 9; KU, 114; RN, 17; AS, 144).
khuṭūṭ al-warrāqīn – book hands associated with the copying of texts other than the Qurʾān itself (KU, 114; AS, 144).
khaṭṭāṭ – calligrapher, penman, comp. muḥarrir, kātib.
khaṭṭāṭīyah – female calligrapher (SD, I, 380).
khiṭāṭah – writing; paleography (KJ, no.1, 26); calligraphy (WR, 80).
makhṭūṭ (pl. makhṭūṭāt) 1. handwritten 2. also **makhṭūṭah** – manuscript, manuscript codex.
mikhaṭṭ 1. implement (made of wood, bone or iron) in the shape of a gendarme's hat used for tracing lines on leather (ST, index, 12); tracer (ME, 555; LL, I, 760; MB, 110, 118; IA, 60, 61) 2. reed pen, calamus (AA, 98, 103; UA, 393: wa-qalam al-ṭarḥ yusammūn miḥaṭṭ!).
mikhṭāṭ – wooden ruler, straightedge (LL, I, 760).
takhṭīṭ 1. tracing, drawing (MB, 110) 2. ruling (of lines); writing,

calligraphy (KM, IV, sifr 13, 4: al-takhṭīṭ al-tasṭīr; WR, 80; LF, 81, n.1).

خطب

khiṭāb (pl. akhṭibah) 1. letter, note; address, speech 2. honorific (e.g. Fakhr al-Dīn, Shihāb al-Dīn) 3. also **khuṭbah** – exordium, preface (LC, 25; TP, 53, n.20).
faṣl al-khiṭāb see faṣl.

خف

khafīf (lit, 'light') – smaller variety (version) of a script (e.g. al-thuluth al-khafīf, khafīf al-muḥaqqaq) (AS, 145).
mukhaffaf – letter without doubling (shaddah), abbrev. خف (often unpointed) (GL, 14).
al-lām alif al-mukhaffafah see lām alif.

خفض

takhfīḍ – shaving, trimming (TS, 18; AG, 109).

خلد

khālidī – oval or round-shaped tool (UK, 156; MB, 105; IA, 59; IB, 44: ornament).

خلص

khulāṣah – excerpt, extract; abridgement, epitome, comp. mukhtaṣar.
takhalluṣ – pseudonym; pen-name (nom de plume) (EI, X, 123).

خلف

khilāf (pl. khilāfāt), **ikhtilāf** – variant reading, varia lectio (e.g. ikhtilāf al-riwāyah, ikhtilāf al-nuskhah, MH, 95; MU, XI, 46; XII, 273; XVII, 52; TP, 58).

خمس

khams (pl. akhmās), **khāmisah** (pl. khawāmis) – mark in the shape of a circle, disc or floret separating a group of 5 verses (āyah) of the Qurʾān (MS, 15).
al-khamsah al-ghubārīyah – the number 5 written in the ghubār notation (٦) to mark the middle folio of a quire (ST, 9).
takhmīs 1. marking a group of 5 verses of the Qurʾān; the mark itself (MD, 126; thumma raʾaynā baʿda kull khams āyāt anna al-dāʾirah tataḍamman raʾs ḥarf al-khāʾ badalan min al-sharṭ wa-aṣbaḥat tusammá bi-al-takhmīsāt) 2. (pl. takhāmīs) – pentastich amplification of a poem, pentameter (SD, I, 405; AD, 50; EI, X, 123-125).
makhmūs – pentagonal element in a Mamluk book cover design (JL, 95, 97).

خوصة

khūṣah – fillet (in decoration) (FT, 401).

خير

al-khayr – epithet of the month of Ṣafar (q.v.).
ikhtiyār, **mukhtār** 1. selected passage 2. (pl. ikhtiyārāt, mukhtārāt) – anthology (EA, I, 94-95).

خيط

khayṭ (pl. khuyūṭ) – thread (ST, index, 12).
al-khayṭ al-tashbīk – thread for preliminary endbanding (headbanding), i.e. endbanding without silk (TS, 19; AG, 109).
khiyāṭah – sewing (of quires) (ST, index, 12; MB, 107-108).
mikhyaṭ, mikhyāṭ – large, thick needle (ST, index, 12; IB, 43; IR, 230; DS, 181: huwa mā yukhāṭ bi-hi al-waraq ʿinda al-ḥājah ilá dhālik; NH, 381).

****

د

دأدأ

al-da'ādī (pl. of du'du') – the last three nights of the month (SA, VI, 250).

د بج

dībāj (pl. dabābīj) – silk brocade (MU, XIV, 84: mubaṭṭan bi-dībāj).
dībājah 1. preface, exordium, embracing the matter before and after al-baʿdīyah (q.v.) (LC, 23) 2. headpiece; frontispiece (MD, 127; PA, 65, 115).
ṣafḥat al-dībājah see ṣafḥah.
tadbīj 1. adorning something with arabesques; creating headpieces (AD, 52; TW, 259) 2. composition (of a text) (DM).

د بر

tadabbur – consideration, reflection; **fa-tadabbar(hu)** – syn. of fa-ta'ammal(hu) (q.v).

د بغ

dibāgh(ah) – tanning (MB, 114-115; IA, 63; MP, 60).
dabbāgh – tanner (QS, I, 140-143; EI, suppl., fasc.3-4, 172).

د خن

dukhān – soot, smut (one of the ingredients of ink, midād) (UK, 80; IR, 236: ṣifat ikhrāj al-dukhān).
al-ḥibr al-dukhānī see ḥibr.

د رج

darj, dirj (WS, 87) (pl. durūj, adrāj) 1. rolled up or folded sheet of papyrus, parchment or paper (AJ, 138, 141; LL, I, 868: also **daraj**; IK, 68: al-adrāj al-ʿarīḍah) 2. roll, rotulus (IK, 68; SA, I, 138: al-

murād bi-al-darj fī al-ʿurf al-ʿāmm al-waraq al-mustaṭīl al-murakkab min ʿiddat awṣāl; WS, 89; IA, 63, n.18;).
mudraj(ah) (pl. madārij) 1. syn. darj (FN, 61; AJ, 120, 152: ṣuḥuf mudrajah) 2. bifolio (bifolium) (AJ, 142) 3. inset (SD, I, 432).

د رس

tadrīs – explication (of a reading) (GA, 287).

د رفش

dirafsh – awl, punch (IA, 60).

د رمك

darmak – farina; paste (used for work with parchment) (TS, 13; AG, 107).

د ست

dast(ah) (pl. dusūt) 1. quire (Fr. main de papier), usually consisting of 25 sheets (AJ, 145; AB, 92; MA, IV, 81; PT, 39; WS, 92, 94, 96; SD, I, 524) 2. stack of 5 folded sheets of paper (5 bifolia) (OM), comp. rizmah, kaff 3. wide polisher, burnisher (UK, 156; MB, 105; IA, 59; IB, 44).

د ستور

dustūr (pl. dasātīr) 1. holograph in the form of a draft or notes (FN, 113: irtijālan min ghayr kitāb wa-lā dustūr; FN, 416: wa-raʾaytu bi-khaṭṭih shayʾan kathīran fī ʿulūm kathīrah musawwadāt wa-dasātīr lam yukhraj minhā ilá al-nās kitāb tāmm; KF, II, 332, 363) 2. author's original, holograph (LC, 23) 3. also **al-nuskhah al-dustūr** – archetype (AL, I, 29: al-aṣl al-waḥīd alladhī taʿūd ilayhi ākhir al-amr kull al-nusakh al-khaṭṭīyah).

د شت

dasht – loose leaves; unbound book, book consisting of loose leaves (KF, II, 357: mustakhraj min dasht al-Muʾayyad; HB, 233: 'feuillets en vrac').

دعو

duʿāʾ (pl. adʿiyah) 1. supplication, pious invocation, 'prayer of request' (EI, II, 617-618) 2. formula of benediction, such as 'raḥimahu Allāh, raḍiya Allāh ʿanhu, ʿalayhi al-salām', etc. (see e.g. TP, 54; AA, 150-156).

دغم

idghām – assimilation, contraction (of letters, such as rāʾ, sīn, mīm, nūn, hāʾ), hence **mudgham** – contracted, assimilated (KU, 123-124: wa-iʿlam anna aṣl kull khaṭṭ wa-ʿamūdah al-fatḥ dūna al-taʿmiyah fa-al-tabyīn wa-al-tawqīm dūna al-idghām wa-al-taʿwīr; SA, III, 89; KH, 35).

د ف

daffah (pl. difaf, daffāt) 1. wooden board 2. pressing board (in the screw press) (MB, 104) 3. book cover, pasteboard (ST, index, 13; ST, 5: al-alwāḥ min al-kāghaṭ alladhīna yaksūnahum bi-al-jild ʿalá al-kitāb; MB, passim).
al-daffah al-ūlá (ST, index, 13), also **al-daffah al-yumná (al-ʿulyā)** – upper cover.
al-daffah al-thāniyah (ST, index, 13), also **al-daffah al-yusrá (al-suflá)** – lower cover.

د فتر

daftar (Gr. diphtera) (pl. dafātir)**, taftar** (SK, 108, 321; KK, 57) – booklet (consisting of a number of bifolia or diplomas); notebook (e.g. *Daftar kutub*, 14 leaves, 40 x 14 cm., see LS) 2. bound or unbound codex ; volume (IK, 96: al-daftar fa-yuwaqqiʿūnahu ʿalá mā jullida wa-ʿalá mā lam yujallad; FK, I, nos.108, 662, 1096) 3. account book, register (EI, II, 77-81; SL, I, 4, 22-25, 29, 48; IA, 63, n.18) 3. pen wiper (SA, II, 481).

د ق

daqq 1. rubbing, pounding (MP, 60) 2. beating (of the pulp) (OM)
tadqīq – compact, fine writing (TM, 192).

د قماق

duqmāq – small mallet (OM).

د لك

dalk, tadlīk – polishing, burnishing; glazing (ST, index, 13; MB, 118; HT, lin.163; KM, I, sifr 4, 110; NH, 363: glazing of paper with a wooden ball; OH, 139).
midlak – polisher, burnisher (for doublures) (TS, 11; AG, 107).

د لو

dallāyah – pendant (FZ, 217; FJ, 48-50; KR, 85, 87).
al-ḥabk al-dālī see ḥabk.

د مغ

damghah (sometimes **tamghah**) – ownership stamp (LC, 23; SD, I, 461).
waraq damghah see waraq.

د هن

duhn (pl. adhān, duhūn) – fat, grease; oil.
midhan, mudhun – container for oil (IR, 230: LL, I, 927).

د ور

Dār al-Fatḥ – Constantinople.
Dār al-Hijrah – Medina.
Dār al-ʿIbādah – Yazd.
Dār al-Irshād – Ardabīl.
Dār al-Khilāfah – Baghdad, Tehran, Shāhjahānābād.
Dār al-Saʿādah – Constantinople.
Dār al-Salṭanah – Constantinople, Herat, Tabriz, Isfahan.
Dār al-Salām – Baghdad.
Dār al-Surūr – Burhānpūr (for other epithets of towns see ER, I, 905-906).

dārah, dāʾirah (pl. dawāʾir) 1. circular motif (used as a textual divider, paragraph mark, fāṣilah) (MR, 93: yajʿal bayna kull ḥadīthayn dārah, faʿala dhālika jamāʿat min al-mutaqaddimīn wa-istaḥabba al-Khaṭīb an takūn ghuflan; JA, I, 272; TP, 55) 2. circular motif (used as a collation mark) (TP, 56; JA, I, 273: fa-istaḥabba an takūn al-dārāt ghuflan fa-idhā ʿūriḍa bi-kull ḥadīth naqaṭa fī al-dārah allatī talīhi nuqṭah aw khaṭṭ fī wasaṭihā khaṭṭan) 3. circular motif representing the letter hāʾ (for intahá or intihāʾ) and its numerical value, i.e. (5) 4. circular mark indicating the end of a gloss (TP, 59) 5. round motif in textual or book cover decoration, e.g. roundel, medallion, disc (UK, 156; TS, 30; MB, 105; UD, 13: al-dawāʾir al-bīkārīyah – circles drawn with a compass).
tadwīr 1. straight, even (as opposed to oblique, taḥrīf) nibbing (of a calamus) (UD, 9, 10; LM, 39-40) 2. rounding (of the spine) (IA, 61) 3. also **istidārah** – rounding (of letters) (KH, 35), hence **mustadīr** – round, curvilinear (e.g. RN, 22; LM, 49: wa-al-mustadīr huwa alladhī lā yumkin an yufraḍ ʿalayhi thalāth nuqaṭ ʿalá samt wāḥid ka-dawr al-ḥāʾ wa-al-ʿayn).

د و ن

dīwān (pl. dawāwīn) 1. collection (of records or sheets); register; account book; office, chancellery (KM, IV, sifr 13, 8: al-dīwān majmaʿ al-ṣuḥuf; EI, II, 323; SA, I, 90) 2. book (collection) of prose or poetry (FK, I, 129; EI, II, 323); collection of poems written by one author (DM).
tadwīn 1. collecting (collection), writing down (of ḥadīth) (EI, X, 81; TP, 51), comp. taqyīd 2. writing, composition (CM, no.80; TE, 15) 3. copying, transcription (LC, 28; TE, 15; UI, 8: al-nusakh al-mudawwanah bi-khaṭṭ al-tadwīn al-ʿādī).
(al-khaṭṭ or **khaṭṭ) al-dīwānī** – Ottoman chancery hand having a much more pronounced tarwīs (q.v.) than the Persian taʿlīq (q.v.) from which it is derived (EI, IV, 1125-6).

د و ى

dawāh (pl. dawayāt, duwīy, dawāyā, dawan) 1. inkwell (IK, 82-85; KU, 154: wa-fī al-dawāh majrāhā wa-jūbatuhā wa-ḥuqquhā wa-ṭabaquhā; TW, 52-56, 169-170; BA, III, 370) 2. escritoire, writing case (containing among other things compartments for ink and pens,

ruler, wiper and sand) (SA, II, 440-443; ND, 54; UK, 77; MB, 65; AT,132-133; EI, suppl. fasc.3-4, 203-204; ER, VII, 137-139).
dawwā', **dawātī** – maker of inkwells or writing cases (KD, II, 713; DG, 73).

****

ذ

ذ أ ب

dhu'ābah (pl. dhawā'ib) 1. leather thong attached to a ḥalqah (q.v.) in 'boxed books' (BA, III, 372) 2. descender (of a letter) (AA, 53).

ذ بر

dhabr, **midhbar** see mizbar.

ذ كر

tadhkirah 1. memorandum, aide-mémoire (EI, X, 53) 2. commonplace book (often of oblong format, safīnah) (HB, 234; EI, X, 53).

ذ نب

dhanab (pl. adhnāb) – tail (foot) of a letter, ḥarf (SA, III, 24; UD, 21).
tadhnīb – appendix, supplement (AD, 59).

ذ هب

dhahab, **mā' al-dhahab** – gold ink, paint (MU,V, 226; UK, 130-132; MB, 89-91; SA, II, 477; LC, 25; LL, I, 983: 'water-gold, gold powder mixed with size for ornamental writing, etc.').
al-dhahab al-maḥlūl – liquid gold (ST, index, 13).
al-dhahab al-masḥūq – gold powder (QS, I, 151).
(qalam) al-dhahab – script written in gold ink in the form of al-

thuluth or al-tawqīʿ with its letters outlined in a colour other than gold (NA, IX, 222; AS, 145).
tadhhīb 1. gilding; writing with liquid gold, chrysography (LC, 27; TE, 15; KA, 104-105: **al-tadhhīb al-muṭfá** = matt, **al-tadhhīb al-lammāʿ** = brilliant, glossy, glazed) 2. (pl. tadhāhīb) gilt object (SD, I, 490).
tadhhīb maṭrūq – gold tooling (HN, 385).
mudhahhib – gilder; chrysographer (AB, 132; PA, 141).
idhhāb – chrysography (SJ, 27; MU, XV, 120: ṣāḥib al-khaṭṭ al-malīḥ wa-al-idhhāb al-fāʾiq; TE, 15).

ذ يل

dhayl (pl. dhuyūl) 1. tail or foot (of a book or page) 2. supplement, appendix.
dhayl al-jāmah see jāmah.
dhayl al-kitāb – tail (of the book) (LC, 23).
dhayl al-waraqah – foot of the page, lower margin.
dhaylah – 'tail of the text' colophon (TW, 206).
al-taʾrīkh al-mudhayyal see taʾrīkh.

****

ر

ر أ س

raʾs (pl. ruʾūs) 1. head (of a letter, i.e. character, page or book, e.g. **raʾs al-waraqah**, **raʾs al-ṣafḥah**, **raʾs al-kitāb**); upper margin (TS, 14; SA, III, 24; LC, 26) 2. fore-edge of the codex, as opposed to the spine (MB, 108, 109; IA, 61) 3. envelope flap (MB, 107, 113: al-sāqiṭ wa-huwa al-raʾs; IA, 62) 4. beginning of something, e.g. **ruʾūs al-suṭūr**, **ruʾūs al-ḥurūf** (MM, 136; TM, 172).
raʾs al-fiqrah or **raʾs al-kalām** – chapter heading or subheading (LC, 26).
raʾs al-kaʿb – endband (headband) (MB, 109).
raʾs al-lawḥah – headpiece, frontispiece (LC, 26).
(qalam) al-riʾāsī, sometimes **al-riyāsī** or **al-riyāshī** (!) 1. one of the early scripts apparently associated with the vizier Dhū al-Riʾāsatayn

al-Faḍl ibn Sahl (d.202/817-8) (FN, 12, 13) 2. script akin to a large naskh, but having a left-sloping tarwīs as one of its characteristics (AS, 146; HI, 84; JM, 83-84; TU, 42: fa-inna qalam al-riyāshī yamīl ilá al-muḥaqqaq wa-al-naskh wa-laysa fīhi insikhāf wa-lā inḥiṭāṭ wa-huwa murawwas jamīʿuh).
tarwīs 1. execution of the head of a letter (the manner of drawing it) 2. also **tarwīsah** (see AQ and MO below) – barbed letter-head or serif-like downward stroke (either right-sloping or left-sloping) on the head of such letters as alif, bāʾ, jīm, dāl, rāʾ, ṭāʾ, kāf and lām (SA, III, 46: thumma qad dhakara ahl al-ṣināʿah anna tarwīs al-alif ka-subʿih wa-dhahaba Yāqūt ilá al-ziyādah ʿalá dhālik; IR, 241-242; KH, 35; RN, 33; AS, 144; AQ, 100, 126, 226, 236; MO, 30, 100).

ربط

rābiṭ (pl. rawābiṭ) – fore-edge flap (FJ, 37; FZ, 213, 215).
rābiṭah – catchword, vox reclamans (NZ, 65).

ربع

(qaṭʿ or **qālib) al-rubʿ**, **rubāʿī** see qaṭʿ and qālib.
rubʿ al-jāmah see jāmah.
rubʿ al-turunjah see turunjah.
Rabīʿ al-Awwal (al-sharīf) – the third month in the Muslim calendar, abbrev. ع١ / عل / را (OS, 89; CM, 39/2: **Rabīʿ al-Mawlūd**).
Rabīʿ al-Thānī, **Rabīʿ al-Ākhir** (al-mubārak) – the fourth month in the Muslim calendar, abbrev. ر / ر٢ / ع٢ (OS, 89).
rabʿah (pl. rabaʿāt) 1. square chest, box for copies of the Qurʾān, divided into compartments, buyūt (SD, I, 503) 2. copy of one part (juzʾ) of the Qurʾān (TS, 25, 39) 3. multi-volume Qurʾān, **al-rabʿah al-sharīfah** (SJ, nos.21, 48, 51; MS, 15: inna al-murād bi-al-rabʿah ṣundūq murabbaʿ al-shakl min khashab mughashshá bi-al-jild dhū ṣafāʾiḥ wa-ḥalaq yuqsam dākhiluh buyūtan bi-ʿadad ajzāʾ al-muṣḥaf yujʿal fī kull bayt minhu juzʾ min al-muṣḥaf wa-iṭlāquhā ʿalá al-muṣḥaf majāzan; HI, 94; SD, I, 503; CA, 49).
mirbaʿah – small tool resembling a piece of wood used for lifting; stalk (?) (TS, 11; AG, 109).
tarbīʿ – square (an instrument) (HT, lin.128).
al-kaʿb al-murabbaʿ see kaʿb.

رتب

tartīb 1. arrangement (of the text); composition (MU, I, 50, 51: wa-jaʿaltu al-tartīb ʿalá ḥurūf al-muʿjam; AM, no.170) 2. the expression 'rattabtuhu(hā)' used in a preface (khuṭbah) and indicating the chapter arrangement of the composition in question (TP, 53, n.20).
murattib – author, compiler (DF, II, 384; SS, 72), comp. mubawwib.

رتم

ratm – close, compact writing, copying (KM, IV, sifr 13, 5: ratamtu al-kitāb qarrabtu bayna suṭūrih).

رجب

Rajab (al-murajjab, al-ḥarām, al-aṣamm, al-aṣabb, al-fard) – the seventh month of the Muslim calendar, abbrev. ب / ر (OS, 89).

رجز

urjūzah – poem composed in rajaz metre in which one and the same rhyme is obligatory; didactic poem (EI, VIII, 376).

رجع

rajʿ (pl. arjāʿ) – reference mark (signe de renvoi), often in the shape of an upward rising stroke or the abbreviation ـج (MI, 35, 145; AR, 35: ـج ʿalāmat al-rajʿ ilá al-hāmish; IN, I, 252), comp. SD, I, 513: 'barrage, barrière qui ferme une rivière'.
rujūʿ – reference, source (in a text) (IN, I, 252).
rājiʿ (pl. rawājiʿ) – strip of leather for lining the spine (TS, 28; AG, 109), comp. muʿallaqah.
al-yāʾ al-rājiʿah – the letter yāʾ with its tail (foot) pointing to the right (SA, III, 99; MJ, 239: not allowed in al-muḥaqqaq).
tarjīʿ 1. retouching, retouchage (of a letter); writing in bold characters (TE, 17) 2. polychrome illumination (TE, 17; KM, IV, sifr 13, 5: al-tarjīʿ washy al-kitāb) 3. also **istirjāʿ** – formula 'innā li-Allāh wa-innā ilayhi rājiʿūn', used at the end of a conclusion, epilogue (AD, 62).

marjiʿ – envelope flap (ST, index,13; ST, 13: yusammá al-lisān; IB, 81, n.185).
al-marjiʿ al-aṣghar – fore-edge flap (ST, index, 13).
al-marjiʿ al-akbar – envelope flap (ST, index, 13).

رحل

raḥl(ah) – book cradle, book support (MD, 137; RI, 31: MD, 132: al-raḥlah aw kursī al-muṣḥaf min lawḥayn min al-khashab mutadākhilayn bi-ṭarīqat al-taʿshīq min al-wasaṭ ka-annahumā kaffān qad shabakat aṣābiʿuhā; AD, 62: 'pupitre pour le Coran').

رحم

tarḥīm, taraḥḥum – the formula of benediction, requiescat (used after the name of a deceased person) 'raḥimahu Allāh, raḥmat Allāh ʿalayhi, taghammadahu Allāh bi-raḥmatih', abbrev. رحم / رحمه / ره (the rāʾ and hāʾ in manuscripts of Persian and Indian provenance often resemble a long horizontal line with a loop at its end, comp. numrah) (TP, 54; VA, nos. 294, 419, 584, 1223, 1038, 1055, 1062, 1035, 2152, 3099, 3185).

رخم

rukhām(ah) , also **lawḥ al-rukhām** – marble, marble slab (MB, 103; IA, 59; TS, 11; AG, 107; ST, 10, 14; OM).

رد

raddah – envelope flap (TM, 172: al-qiṭʿah al-rāʾidah min al-jild fawqa al-daffah al-yusrá; TP, pl. XXIB).

ردأ

radāʾat al-khaṭṭ – inelegance (poorness) of handwriting, similarly **al-khaṭṭ al-radīʾ** – bad, inelegant hand (FN, 16: wa qīla radāʾat al-khaṭṭ zamānat al-adab wa-qīla al-khaṭṭ al-radīʾ jadb al-adab).

رزم

rizmah (pl. rizam) 1. ream (of paper), consisting of five quires, dast (q.v.) (PT, 39; AB, 92; AJ, 145; WS, 96: wa-al-dast khams wa-ʿishrūn waraqah wa-al-rizmah khamsat dusūt; SD, I, 524), comp. dast 2. also **ruzmah** – booklet (SD, I, 524: 'cahier').

رسل

risālah 1. letter, epistle 2. tract, treatise; monograph (EI, VIII, 532).
irsāl(ah) – final stroke, extension of the tails of such letters as sīn, rāʾ, ḥāʾ, mīm, nūn, yāʾ ʿayn, qāf, ṣād, wāw, hāʾ without an upward curvature (KH, 35: huwa iṭlāq al-ʿarāqah min ghayr taqwīs; SA, III, 36: wa-kull irsālah yajib an takūn bi-sinn al-qalam al-yumná; LM, 72: fa-yajib an yakūn qadruhā mithl subʿ alif khaṭṭihā).
tarassul – art of letter writing, epistolography (DM).

رسم

rasm 1. marking, making a mark (ST, index, 14) 2. writing, execution; copying, e.g. rasm al-muṣḥaf, rasm al-tasmiyah (DP, 45) 3. drawing, designing, sketching (ME, 561; MB, 100, 101; PA, 100; EI,VIII, 451-453) 4. (pl. rusūm) – stroke, line (traced with a pen) (SD, I, 527) 5. unpointed letter or word (NO, 15) 6. letter or word in a dictionary (SD, I, 527) 7. chapter (in a composition) (SD, I, 527), comp. faṣl.
rasm al-ghubār – see raqm.
bi-rasm see mustanad.
misṭarat al-rasm see misṭarah.
rāsim, rassām – draftsman, designer, painter (ME, 560; SD, I, 528).
rawsam (pl. rawāsim) – woodcut, wood block (AB, 137).

رش

rashshāsh – reed pen, calamus (BA, III, 370).

رشم

rashm, tarshīm 1. marking (syn. rasm) (ST, index, 14) 2. tooling (HT, lin.129, 164) 3. decorating centers of book covers with medallions (ST, index, 14).

rashmah 1. mark (TS, 18) 2. ream (of paper) (SD, I, 532), comp. rizmah.
marshim, marsham (pl. marāshim) 1. small bookbinder's tool (HT, lin. 125) 2. hot iron (SD, I, 532).

رصع

raṣīʿah – central medallion (on a book cover) (AB, 135).
tarṣīʿ 1. illumination, decoration (MS, 28: wa-qad raṣṣaʿtu hawāmish al-kitābah bi-tarājim akbar) 2. illumination (in gold and saffron) (IP, 145; TE, 17) 3. decoration (with liquid gold); covering the entire surface with liquid gold (HD, 103, 126); gilding the inside of the surround (outline), taḥrīr (q.v.) (AF, 48).

رصف

raṣf, tarṣīf 1. joining letters together (AP, 79; SA, III, 140; KH, 35) 2. writing, composition (NS, 184: faraghtu min taʾlīfih wa-raṣfih wa-taṣnīfih; QF, 65: faraghtu min tarṣīf hādhā al-Ḥiṣn al-ḥaṣīn).

رضى

tarḍiyah, taraḍḍin – the formula of benediction 'raḍiya Allāh ʿanhu' or 'riḍwān Allāh ʿalayhi', used for the companions of the Prophet, abbrev. رضه / رض / ض / ره (TP, 54; SL, II, 89; AR, 34, 35; MI, 125).

رطب

tarṭīb – rounding (of letters) (UD, 15; KH, 35: al-tarṭīb hiya shaddat al-istidārah), comp. taqwīr.
al-aqlām al-muraṭṭabah (or **al-raṭbah**, ant. of yābis) – curvilinear scripts, such as the thuluth, tawqīʿ and riqāʿ (UD, 14, 15, 16, 19; AS, 144).

رعى

istirʿāʾīyah – note, statement (LC, 24).

رفع

rafʿ – gouge-like tool (HT, lin.133, 137).
mirfaʿ 1. book support, book cradle (IN, I, 230, 231; ND, 44, n.11; KK, 70) 2. support (for an inkwell) (AA, 111-112).

رق

raqq, riqq (pl. ruqūq) 1. thin leather, parchment (SA, II, 484-485; IW, 74-75; AE, 108-111; WS, 60-63; KJ, no.1, 42: al-raqq al-azraq, al-raqq al-aḥmar; EI, VIII, 407-410; EP) 2. parchment leaf (ND, 53, n.67).
raqq ghazāl see jild.
raqq manshūr – 'unfolded parchment' (EI, VIII, 407).
raqqāq, ruqūqī – parchment maker, parchmenter (DG, 85).

رقش

raqsh, tarqīsh 1. elegant, embellished writing, copying (TE, 17; AA, 105; SK, 119; KK, 53; KM, IV, sifr 13, 5: al-tarqīsh al-kitābah wa-al-tasṭīr fī al-ṣuḥuf) 2. vocalization by means of points; diacritical pointing (TE, 17; IK, 93; LL, I, 1135) 3. making something multi-coloured (LL, I, 1135) 4. arabesque decoration (KA, 105; KR, 86: **al-raqsh al-ʿArabī**).
raqshah – pointing, diacritical point (JA, I, 269).
mirqash – reed pen, calamus (IR, 230).

رقص

raqqāṣ – catchword, vox reclamans (NM, 683; AK, 353).

رقع

ruqʿah (pl. riqāʿ) 1. piece (slip) of leather, paper or other writing surface (MU, I, 133: wa-kuntu aʿriḍ ʿalayhi kull yawm riqāʿan fa-yuwaqqiʿu lī fīhā) 2. letter, brief message, note.
(khaṭṭ) al-ruqʿah (Turk. rikʿa) – script developed most probably in the 2nd half of the 12/18th cent. on the basis of dīwānī (q.v.) and used commonly by the Arabs in correspondence and occasionally as a book hand (EI, IV, 1126).

(qalam) al-riqāʿ – smaller version of tawqīʿ (q.v.) script (AS, 146; JM, 78-82; LM, 47: wa-al-riqāʿ lil-tawāqīʿ al-ṣighār wa-al-murāsalāt; EI, IV, 1123- in Persia, 1125- in Turkey).
ruqayʿah – slip of paper (used for glosses and inserted in between the leaves of the codex, often sewn in); inset (MK, 86).
tarqīʿ (pl. tarāqīʿ) – repair, patchwork.
muraqqaʿ – album of paintings, drawings and/or calligraphy (consisting of a number of pieces joined together and forming a book-accordeon) (AC, passim; MN, 139; EI, VII, 602-603).

رقم

raqm 1. writing (KM, IV, sifr 13, 5: al-raqm al-khaṭṭ fī al-kitāb) 2. also **tarqīm** – elegant writing, copying (TE, 17) 3. (pl. ruqūm) – piece of calligraphy, calligraph (AC, 41; DP, 54; NI, 180: al-ijāzah al-mubārakah li-kātib hādhā al-raqm; AW, 266) 4. diacritical pointing (of letters) (IK, 93: raqqamtuhu tarqīman) 5. (pl. arqām), also **tarqīm** – numbering; number, numeral 6. (pl. ruqūm) – abbreviation, siglum (CL, fasc. 2, 141, 160).
al-arqām al-Hindīyah, also known as **al-ḥisāb al-Hindī** or **ḥisāb al-Hind** – Hindu-Arabic numerical system used in the Mashriq (AN, 383; GA, 183).
al-arqām al-ghubārīyah, also known as **ḥisab** (or **ḥurūf**, **rasm**) **al-ghubār** – numerical system (also known as 'dust' or Toledan numerals) used in the Maghreb (EI, III, 468-9: AN, 387-388; GA, 183; KJ, no.3, 30).
rāqim, muraqqim – calligrapher, copyist (AC, 45; TE, 17; AW, 244; AM, no.76).
raqīm – inkwell (KM, IV, sifr 13, 5; IK, 82; SK, 106).
arqam, mirqam – reed pen, calamus (TE, 17; IR, 230; BA, III, 372; LL, I, 1140).
tarqīm – punctuation (AH, 147, 154).
tarqīm al-ṣafaḥāt – pagination.
tarqīm al-waraqāt – foliation.

رقن

raqn – compact writing (KM, IV, sifr 13, 5: raqana al-kitāb qariba bayna suṭūrih).

tarqīn 1. embellishing (a text, writing) (KM, IV, sifr 13, 5: tarqīn al-kitāb tazyīnuh) 2. calligraphy (FT, 394).

ركب

tarkīb 1. linking (joining) one letter with another; ligature (e.g. SA, III, 50, 60ff); composition of letters and words on the line (ER, IV, 681) 2. mounting (of leather on book covers and the covers on the textblock); boarding (TS, 24-27; AG, 109; ST, index, 14; MP, 58; HT, lin.73, 78) 3. preparing inks (by mixing two or more ingredients) (e.g. NW, 10: tarkīb al-alwān; IR, 236-237: al-aḥbār al-murakkabah), comp. ḥibr.
murakkab 1. (Turk. mürekkeb) – ink (DD, I, 389; UA, 393), comp. ḥibr 2. hybrid (of a script) (LM, 45).
al-ḥurūf al-murakkabah, murakkabāt – letters of the alphabet (written joined together, ligatured, on the line) (MY, 83).
al-ism al-murakkab – compound name, e.g. Muḥammad Ṣāliḥ.

ركز

markaz (pl. marākiz) – support (for reed pens) (UA, 393: li-mā ʿalay-hi yūḍaʿ ruʾūs al-aqlām liʾallā tuṣdaʿ).

ركع

rukūʿ , rakʿah – bowing (during the recitation of the Qurʾān), abbrev. ع, usually accompanied by numbers indicating rakʿah, juzʾ and āyah (CA, 36; EI, VIII, 406).

ركن

rukn (pl. arkān) 1. corner (on a book cover) (KR, 80) 2. wedged stamp (used for a corner piece) (TS, 30, 31; AG, 107) 3. corner piece itself (ST, index, 14; IB, 69).
mirkan – pitcher-shaped container (OM).

ركو

rakwah (pl. rikāʾ) – inkwell (KD, II, 703).

رم

ramm, tarmīm – repair, restoration (DM).
murammim – restorer.

رمج

tarmīj – smudging, obliteration (KM, IV, sifr 13, 7: ifsād al-suṭūr baʿda taswiyatihā wa-kitābatihā wa-yuqāl rammajahu bi-al-turāb ḥattá fasada).

رمز

ramz (pl. rumūz) 1. abbreviation; siglum (LC, 26; MH, 90, 99; EI, VIII, 428) 2. chronogram, chronosticon (EI, III, 468; WB, 55; TW, 159) 3. code, cypher; secret alphabet (EI, VIII, 427) 4. also **tarmīz** – marking the Qurʾānic text with the conventional reading signs (qirāʾāt), hence **marmūz** – provided with reading marks (DC, V, 209; KC, 33: akhar fī al-rubāʿī qadīm marmūz fī sifr).

رمض

Ramaḍān (al-mubārak, al-muʿaẓẓam) – the ninth month of the Muslim calendar, abbrev. ن / مض (OS, 89).

رمك

tarmīk see tazmīk.

رمل

tarmīl – sprinkling (of the freshly written text with sand) (TD, I, 127-136).
al-tarmīl al-dhahabī – gold sprinkling (TW, 86; TD, I, 135: **tarmīl bi-al-dhahab al-khāliṣ**).
mirmalah, ramlīyah – sand box; sand compartment in the writing case (dawāh) (SA, II, 478-480; AT, 133; SD, I, 559; DD, I, 389: ālah lil-raml al-aḥmar; UA, 393).

رود

mirwad (pl. marāwid) – little stick for the application of kohl, syn. mikḥāl (DD, I, 392: lil-iktiḥāl bi-hi; UA, 393; LL, I, 1186; DM).

روى

rāwin, rāwiyah (pl. ruwāh) – transmitter, link in the chain of transmission (TP, 53).
riwāyah 1. transmission, tradition (traditio); version (versio), recension (recensio) (LC, 26; EI, VIII, 545-547) 2. **riwāyat al-kitāb** – book ascription, also known as sanad (q.v.) (TP, 53; KF, II, 417-418 and 500-501) 3. variant reading, varia lectio (MR, 94).
ijāzat al-riwāyah – transmission certificate (MU, XII, 109-111).
marwiyah (pl. marwiyāt) – work transmitted through riwāyah (chain of transmitters) (EI, VIII, 545-547).

ريحان

(qalam) al-rayḥān – smaller version of al-muḥaqqaq (q.v.) script (AS, 146; JM, 73-77; LM, 43: wa-qāla Ibn al-Bawwāb wa-ammā al-rayḥān fa-huwa bi-al-qiyās ilá al-muḥaqqaq ka-al-ḥawāshī ilá al-naskh, qultu wa-ka-al-ghubār ilá al-riqāʿ, wa-al-farq bayna al-muḥaqqaq wa-al-rayḥān anna al-rayḥān yakūn iʿrābuhu bi-qalamih wa-yakūn iʿrābuhu mufattaḥ al-aʿyun wa-al-muḥaqqaq yakūn iʿrābuhu bi-ghayr qalamih).
rayḥānī – term used in the later Ottoman period and in modern publications either as a syn. of rayḥān or a type of muḥaqqaq script (EI, IV, 1123- in Persia, 1125- in Turkey).

ريش

rish(ah) – quill pen (UK, 144; MP, 38; MB, 100: al-aqlām al-rīshīyah).
(qalam) al-riyāshī see riʾāsī.

****

ز

زاج

zāj – vitriol, sulphuric acid or a sulphate (one of the components of ink, ḥibr, q.v.).

زبر

zabr, tazbīr 1. also **dhabr** – writing; inscription on stone (KM, IV, sifr 13, 4: al-zabr al-naqsh fī al-ḥajar) 2. copying, transcription (TE, 18; CI, I, 65: qad waqaʿa al-farāgh min zabr hādhihi al-Majālis al-Mustanṣirīyah…).
zabūr (pl. zubur) – composition, work (SA, II, 444; ND, 80; IK, 92).
zābir, zabūr – scribe, copyist (TE, 18; ND, 80; KK, 53: wa-yuqāl lil-kātib zābir wa-zabūr mithl ḍārib wa-ḍarūb).
mizbar or **midhbar** – reed pen, calamus (TE,18; SA, II, 444-465; IK, 85; IR, 230).

زبرج

zibrijah, zibrāj 1. elegant, embellished writing, copying (KK, 53: wa-yuqāl zabrajtu al-kitāb … idhā ḥassantuhu wa-zayyantuh; TE, 18) 2. polychrome illumination (TE, 18).

زخرف

zakhrafah 1. elegant, embellished writing, copying (KK, 53; TE, 18) 2. (pl. zakhārif) polychrome illumination (TE, 18) 3. arabesque or geometrical decoration (WR, 87).
muzakhrif – illuminator, decorator (WR, 80).

زر

zirr (pl. azrār, azirrah) – knob (of a clasp) (TS, 25, 34; AG, 110; KT, 135), comp. ʿurwah.

زركش

zarkashah – embellishment, decoration in gold and colours (LL, I, 1222).

زلج

zulayjah (**zalījah**, **zulāyjah**, see DC, V, 360) 1. ornamental tile (DM) 2. most probably a small, square format of a book (KC, passim: fī qālib al-zulāyjah; fī al-zulāyjah lil-kibar(?); ST, index, 19: in 12).

زلف

zulf (Pers./Turk., lit. 'hair lock', 'curl'), **zalf** (MN, 69) – serif-like stroke protruding from the head of the alif, lām, etc., comp. tarwīs (KH, 35; MN, 69; ER, IV, 682, 689).

زم

zamm – leather thong (for tying up a book); fastener (TS, 25; AG, 109).
zimām(ah) (pl. azimmah) 1. account book, register (IK, 95) 2. list, catalogue (SD, I, 601).
ḥurūf al-zimām – Graeco-Coptic alpha-numerical system used in early Arab administration records (AN, 383-385; GA, 181).
(al-khaṭṭ) al-zimāmī see musnad.

زمك

tazmīk – outlining (of a letter by means of a fine line in a colour different from it) (NC, 127; NA, pt.9, 222: al-tarmīk (!) huwa an yaḥbis al-ḥarf bi-lawn ghayr lawnih bi-qalam raqīq jiddan; TE, 18; AS, 145; MB, 101; KF, II, 315, 320), comp. taḥrīr, takḥīl.

زنجفر

zunjufr, zinjafr – cinnabar, vermillion ink (SA, II, 478).

زنفليجة

zanfalījah – case, box (DG, 91).

زهر

tazhīr – floral decoration, hence **muzahhar**, floriated (KJ, no.1, 38, 44; KR, 80: ʿamal al-muzahharāt wa-qaṣṣ al-waraq).

زوج

zawj (pl. azwāj) 1. bifolio (bifolium), diploma (TS, 13, 14, 15: fa-in kāna al-kitāb kulluh azwājan dūna mukarras; wa-dhālika anna azwāj al-kāghad akthar dalkihā fī al-awāsiṭ; TK, f.120b; AG, 107) 2. conjugate leaf (AG, 107).
muzdawij – urjūzah-type poem in which every two verses have the same rhyme (EI, VII, 825 and VIII, 376).
sarlawḥ muzdawij see sarlawḥ.

زود

mizwadah – small container (for making ink) (DD, I, 391).

زور

zawwār – painter (AD, 73).
tazwīr 1. also **tazwīrah** – elegant, embellished writing, copying (TE, 18) 2. forgery, falsification (UI, 6; AD, 73; EI, X, 408-409; GA, 283; ER, X, 90-100).
muzawwir – forger (EI, X, 409).

زوق

tazwīq (pl. tazāwīq) 1. elegant, embellished writing (KK, 53) 2. decoration, multi-colour illumination (HT, lin.102; WA, 11) 3. painting (with an admixture of quicksilver) (ME, 560) 4. writing, decorating (with colours other than gold) (KA, 105).
ziwāqah – art of illumination; miniature painting (WA, 12).
zawwāq – illuminator; miniature painter (ME, 560, n.4; MS, 4).

زوى

zāwiyah 1. corner; angle 2. square (an implement) (MB, 111; IA, 60, 62).

زيد

zāʾid(ah) (pl. zawāʾid) 1. superfluous, abbrev. ز ; written above a cancellation to indicate a dittographic error (TN, 52; MI, 127) 2. interpolation; addition (CM, 136).
ziyādah 1. dittography (TM, 184) 2. interpolation; addition (TP, 59; MH, 98) 3. post-scriptum (AD, 73).

زير

ziyār, ziyyār – bookbinder's press, also **takht al-ziyār** (ST, index, 9).
ziyār al-taqṣīṣ – press (for trimming) (ST, index, 9).
ziyār al-qarīṣ – ordinary screw press (ST, index, 9), comp. qarrāṣ.

زين

zīnah, tazyīn 1. elegant, embellished writing (SK, 119: ḥusn al-kitābah wa-zaynuhā) 2. embellishment, decoration (DM).

****

س

al-sīn al-muʿallaqah see muʿallaqah.

سال

suʾāl (pl. asʾilah) 1. quodlibet, abbrev. س (CI, II, xiv; MI, 128) 2. preamble to a fatwá, comp. jawāb.

سبح

sabḥalah, tasbīḥ 1. the doxological formula 'subḥāna Allāh' (MW, 108) used sometimes instead of the ḥamdalah (TP, 53, n.20; VA, nos. 461, 696, 1853, 3214) 2. the formula of glorification 'subḥāna wa-taʿālá', used after the word Allāh (TP, 54).

سبق

sabq(at) al-qalam – slip of the pen, lapsus calami (DM).

ستر

mistar – fore-edge flap (ST, index, 13; IB, 81, n.185).

سحق

al-dhahab al-masḥūq see dhahab.

سحى

siḥā'ah – piece, slip (of paper on which one writes a short sentence), piece (of poetry, etc.) (SD, I, 637).
tasḥiyah – binding (with thin leather, parchment) (IB, 11-12).

سختيان

sukhtiyān, sikhtiyān – morocco (leather) (DM).

سخم

sukhām – soot, smut (one of the ingredients of ink, midād, q.v.).

سد

sidād (pl. asiddah) – stopper, plug (in the inkwell) (IK, 83).
tasdīd – copying, transcription (TE, 17).

سر

surrah – center-piece, center-medallion (on a book cover) (FJ, 39, 40, 50: **al-surrah al-dāʾirīyah** – circular medallion, **al-surrah al-lawzīyah** – mandorla), comp. ṣurrah.

سراس

sirās, sīrās see shars, ashrās.

سرد

sard 1. awling, punching (SK, 122) 2. reading, recital; collation (of a text without linguistic or other analysis of it), hence **sārid** – reader, prelector (TP, 56, n.52).
sārid, sarrād – sewer of leather (LL, I, 1347).
misrad – awl, punch (SK, 122; KM, I, sifr 4, 115; LL, I, 1347).

سرلوح

sarlawḥ(ah) (Pers.) 1. headpiece (lawḥat ṣadr al-kitāb) 2. frontispiece; double-page frontispiece (**sarlawḥ muzdawij**) (LC, 27; MD, 127; AF, 36).

سرو

sarwah – lozenge-shaped element (with two sides longer than the others, resembling a cypress tree) in a Mamluk bookcover design, also known as **lawzah** (JL, 95, 97; KR, 82).

سطح

munsaṭiḥ – flat, horizontal stroke (UD, 11: huwa al-khaṭṭ al-mamdūd min yamīn al-kātib ilá yasārih aw bi-al-ʿaks ka-al-bāʾ wa-al-kāf wa-naḥwihimā; SA, III, 24).
al-qafāʾ al-musaṭṭaḥ see qafan.

سطر

saṭr (pl. asṭur, asṭār, suṭūr) – line (KD, II, 705: al-saṭr fī al-lughah al-athar al-mustaṭīl ʿalá istiwāʾ); line of writing.

ʿarsh al-saṭr see ʿarsh.
tasṭīr 1. ruling, lining; creating a line (of writing) (SA, III, 140: wa-huwa iḍāfat al-kalimah ilá al-kalimah ḥattá taṣīr saṭran muntaẓim al-waḍʿ ka-al-misṭarah) 2. writing, copying (TE, 17; TM, 174) 3. ruling (of folios), lineation (LC, 28; WS, 91; KA, 134) 4. number of lines per page (LC, 28) 5. geometrical design (polygonal interlace), as opposed to arabesque, tawrīq, tashjīr (ST, index, 22; IB, 83, n.256; LC, 28; WR, 86, 87).
sāṭir, musaṭṭir – amanuensis, syn. kātib; copyist, scribe (AA, 119; TE, 17).
misṭarah (pl. masāṭir) 1. ruler, straightedge (UK, 155; TS, 12; MB, 103, 104-105; TK, passim; SA, II, 482: ālah min khashab mustaqīmat al-janabayn yusaṭṭar ʿalayhā mā yaḥtāj min tasṭīrih min al-kitābah wa-mutaʿallaqatihā wa-akthar man yaḥtāj ilayhi al-mudhahhib) 2. lineation, (grid of) guidelines; number of lines per page (TK, ff.120a-b: faṣl fī ʿamal al-misṭarah; TS, 18; TA, 50; LC, 25) 3. threaded guideline board for ruling pages, ruling board (ST, index, 15; WA, 13; IN, I, 247) 4. stencil (AF, 48) 5. pasteboard (HT, lin. 73, 78, 113) 6. redaction, composition (AD, 77).
al-misṭarah al-ʿājīyah – ivory ruler, used for burnishing gold decoration or writing (KA, 104-105).
misṭarat al-rasm – ruler for drawing, designing (UK, 155; MB, 104; IA, 59).
misṭarat al-rīḥ – ruler for work with leather; folder (UK, 155; IB, 43).
misṭarat al-tabkīr – ruler for work with geometrical figures (MB, 104; IA, 59).
misṭarat al-taḥbīr – ruler for inking (UK, 155).
misṭarat al-takhṭīl – ruler for outlining (UK, 155).
misṭarat al-shughl – ‘work’ (heavy duty) ruler (UK, 155; MB, 105; IA, 59).

سعط

misʿaṭ, musʿuṭ – receptacle for saʿūt (snuff?, musk?) (IR, 230; LL, I, 1364; DM: snuff box).

سفر

sifr (pl. asfār) 1. textblock (ST, 15) 2. paper textblock (TS, 25; AG, 107) 3. book, codex, volume (bound in leather-covered pasteboards) (IK, 96: wa-qad jarat al-ʿādah fī al-akthar allā yuqāl al-sifr illā mā kāna ʿalayhi jild; MS, 16: al-maṣāḥif al-sifrīyah) 4. chapter, section in a book; pasteboards, binding (KC, passim: fī sifr, bi-dūn sifr).
sāfir (pl. safarah) – amanuensis, syn. kātib (KM, IV, sifr 13, 4; AA, 23-24: al-safarah al-katabah wāḥiduhum al-sāfir).
tasfīr 1. bookbinding (e.g. ST, index, 15) 2. (pl. tasāfīr) – book cover (MB, 97; TF, passim).
al-tasfīr al-Miṣrī – Egyptian-style binding characterized by a central medallion in the shape of an almond, lawzah (mandorla) (TS, 31; AG, 110).
musaffir, saffār – bookbinder (ST, index, 15; AD, 78).
al-nuskhah al-safarīyah see nuskhah.
al-maṣāḥif al-sifrīyah see muṣḥaf.

سفط

safaṭ (pl. asfāṭ) 1. small tool resembling a fish scale or a reed from a basket (TS, 11; AG, 109) 2. fibres (?) (in paper) (ID, 62: al-kāghad ajwaduh mā ṣafā lawnuh wa-naʿuma lamsuh wa-thaqula waznuh wa-jādat ṣiqālatuh wa-qallat asfāṭuh).

سفل

asfal (sufl) al-kitāb 1. tail (of the page); lower margin; end of a letter or book 2. spine (of a book) (UK, 158; HT, lin.115; MB, 109: thumma nazalta sufl al-kitāb mawḍiʿ al-khiyāṭah).

سفن

safan – coarse hide (used for polishing) (DM).
safīnah 1. oblong format (of a book) (MD, 106: al-ṣuḥuf al-safīnah; SD, I, 660; EI, IV, 742) 2. note-pad or commonplace book in oblong format in which the lines are usually written parallel with the spine (EI, VIII, 150).

سقط

saqṭ, saqaṭ (MU, XII, 238) 1. also **isqāṭ** – omission; haplography (TP, 58; MH, 87) 2. diamond-shaped element (in a Mamluk book cover design) (JL, 95, 97; KR, 88).
ghiṭāʾ al-saqṭ – hexagonal element (in a Mamluk book cover design, see above) (JL, 95, 97).
sāqiṭ 1. omission; haplography (MH, 94: kayfīyat takhrīj al-sāqiṭ fī al-ḥawāshī; TM, 186) 2. also **sāqiṭah** – envelope flap (MB, 107, 113: al-sāqiṭ wa-huwa al-raʾs, 118; IA, 60).

سقى

saqy al-waraq – sizing (of paper) (UK, 148; WS, 80), comp. ʿilāj.
misqāh, siqāh – water container (for diluting ink) (SA, II, 482; AT, 133; IR, 230).

سكن

sukūn 1. mark indicating vowellessness of a medial consonant, comp. jazmah 2. circle-like tool (HT, lin.133, 137).
sikkīn (pl. sakākīn) – knife; pen knife (IK, 90-91; SK, 103-104; SA, II, 465-466; AA, 115-117; IA, 60; UK, 76 and MB, 64: sikkīn al-bary, sikkīn al-qaṭṭ; KD, II, 711; LM, 31-33).
sikkīn al-kashṭ see kashṭ.

سلخ

salkh, insilākh, munsalakh – the last night of the month (SA, VI, 248).

سلسل

silsilah (pl. salāsil) 1. chainwork (in book cover design) (TS, 33; AG, 110; TF, passim) 2. spiritual genealogy (as found in diplomas, ijāzāt, especially in calligraphy) (EI, IX, 611).
silsilat al-nasab – stemma, stemma codicum (AL, I, 27).
(qalam) al-musalsal – relative of al-tawqīʿ script in which all letters are interlocked and the alif and lām look like links in a chain (AS,

146; KK, 47: ḥurūfuh muttaṣilah laysa fīhā shay' munfaṣil; JM, 58-63; EI, IV, 1124).

سلف

sulfah – soft leather (used for doublures) (TS, 15; AG, 107).

سلم

salām, **taslīm(ah)** – the formula of benediction "ʿalayhi al-salām' (YM, 5: al-muqaddimah fī al-taṣliyah wa-al-taslīmah), abbrev. عه / عسد / عم / ع / ع (TP, 54; VA, no.1830, 2211; CI, I, xiii; MI, 128).

سمر

mismār (pl. masāmīr) – nail, peg (part of a clasp) (BA, III, 372; TM, 171: kharīṭah dhāt ʿurwah wa-mismār).

سمع

samāʿ (pl. samāʿāt) 1. audition (of a text) (CT, 45) 2. audition note (statement, certificate), also known as **tasmīʿ** or **ṭabaqat al-samāʿ**, abbrev. ع (CW, 69; TP, 53; LC, 27; MU, X, 278; MU, XVII, 267; EI, VIII, 1019-1020).
ijāzat al-samāʿ – audition certificate (beginning with the words samiʿa, samiʿtu or balagha samāʿan) (e.g. TP, 53, n.25; KF, II, 485-493).
sāmiʿ – pupil attending a samāʿ-session, auditor.
tasmīʿ 1. auditing (MU, XIII, 85); writing down, recording a samāʿ (CT, 45) 2. audition note, certificate (JA, I, 268: wa-yaktub fī alladhī yalīhi al-tasmīʿ wa-al-ta'rīkh; MH, 100).
musammiʿ, **musmiʿ** – person (shaykh) conducting a samāʿ-session, audition leader (master); authoritative commentator, certifier (CT, 45).
masmūʿ (pl. masmūʿāt) – work transmitted through samāʿ, comp. maqrū'.

سمى

ism (pl. asmā', asāmin) 1. proper name (EI, IV, 179-181) 2. title of a book (**ism al-kitāb**).

ism al-jalālah see tajlīl.
al-Ism al-Aʿẓam see al-khātim al-Sulaymānī.
al-ism al-murakkab – compound name, such as Muḥammad Ṣāliḥ.
ism al-shuhrah see shuhrah.
tasmiyah 1. title (of a work) (LC, 28) 2. the expression 'sammaytuhu' (in a preface) (LC, 28; TP, 53, n.20) 3. the propitiatory formula otherwise known as basmalah (q.v.) (MH, 100).

سن

sinn (pl. asnān) – half-nib (of a calamus created by a slit, shaqq) (UK, 154: wa-sinnāhu ṭarafuhu al-mabrī; SK, 105: wa-lil-qalam sinnān); SA, II, 463; KK, 50; EI, IV, 471: **insī** – left side; **waḥshī** – right side, see also the article on insī in LL, I, 114).
misann or **ḥajar al-misann** – whetstone, hone (UK, 153; MB, 103; IA, 60: misann akhḍar, misann ṭulaylī (?); IR, 230; SA, II, 483; AT, 133; TS, 10; AG, 107; NH, 384: al-Rūmī, al-Ḥijāzī, al-Qawṣī).
misann al-misḥ – whetstone (for a misḥ, q.v.).
musannn al-aṭrāf – deckle-edged (paper) (DM).
musannanah – chevron (FT, 395).

سند

sanad (pl. asnād), also known as **isnād** and **riwāyat al-kitāb** – ascription (of a ḥadīth or work, indicating a chain of authorities going back to the author) (TP, 53, 56).
musnad – ḥadīth-work (not arranged thematically but on the basis of the first authority in the isnād) (SL, II, 2, 39; EI, VII, 705), comp. muṣannaf.
(qalam) al-musnad – Himyarite (ancient South Arabian) script, also known as **khaṭṭ Ḥimyar** (KM, IV, sifr 13, 5; FN, 8; RN, 2; EI, VII, 704-705).
al-Musnad al-imām see imām.
(al-khaṭṭ) al-musnad, also known as **(al-khaṭṭ) al-zimāmī** – Maghrebi chancery (secretarial) hand used primarily in legal documents and annotations (LT, 365; TW, 14, 47).
misnadah – copyist's book support made up of some dozen sheets of paper held together at the four corners and placed on the knee (SD, I, 692).
mustanad – closing phrases of a document including such statements

as bi-al-ishārah, ḥasaba al-amr and the like; in codices these statements indicate patronage and include bi-rasm, bi-ʿināyah, bi-himmah, ḥasaba al-ishārah, ḥasaba al-amr and the like) (SA, VI, 264-265; OS, 88; CM, 232).

سندس

sundus – silk brocade (NT, II, 143: wa-kusiya al-muṣḥaf al-ʿazīz bi-ṣiwān laṭīf min al-sundus al-akhḍar).

سنة

sanah (pl. sinūn, sanawāt) 1. year, often represented by a logograph consisting of a horizontal line with a downward curve at its end, and used predominantly in dates in non-Maghrebi manuscripts (SA, VI, 252), comp. ʿām. See also taʾrīkh 2. era.
al-sanah al-milādīyah (al-ʿĪsawīyah, al-Masīḥīyah) – Christian era (A.D.).
al-sanah al-qamarīyah (al-hilālīyah, al-hijrīyah) – Muslim era (DD, I, 384, 388).

سود

sawād 1. black ink (LC, 27; SK, 320; AI, 147-148: yanbaghī lil-ṭālib an yaktub al-ḥadīth bi-al-sawād thumma bi-al-ḥibr khāṣṣatan dūna al-midād li-anna al-sawād aṣbagh al-alwān wa-al-ḥibr abqāhā ʿalá marr al-duhūr wa-al-azmān) 2. also **musawwadah** – draft, rough copy (LC, 27; MU, VI, 161; MU, XIII, 126; MU, XV, 7: ʿathartu ʿalá al-musawwadah wa-bayyaḍtuhā; MU, XV, 23), comp. mubayyaḍah.
taswīd 1. preparation of a draft (TE, 18) 2. also **iswidād** (!) – writing, copying (TE, 18; AM, nos. 45, 50A) 3. marring (of a text), making it difficult to read (MH, 97, 98) 4. copying by an apprentice (TE, 18).
musawwid – copyist; calligrapher (AW, 237).
(al-khaṭṭ) al-Sūdānī see Ifrīqī.

سوس

sāyis (sāʾis) – catchword, vox reclamans (NZ, 65: wa-yuṭlaq ʿalayhā al-sāyis, wa-hiya al-ʿāmmīyah, fī al-katātīb al-Qurʾānīyah).
sūs(ah) (pl. sīsān) – woodworm.

taswīs – worming, damage caused by worms (LC, 28).
musawwas – worm-eaten.

سوى

taswiyah – aligning (of quires) and shaving, trimming the textblock (TS, 17-18).
istiwāʾ – straight (even) cut (of the point of the nib) (SK, 105; KK, 50; SA, II, 463; KD, II, 702), comp. taḥrīf.
al-qaṭṭ al-mustawī see qaṭṭ.

سياق

(khaṭṭ) al-siyāq(ah), khaṭṭ-i siyāqat, siyāqat – script and/or system of alphabetic abbreviations used in accountancy (EI, IV, 1124- in Persia, 1125- in Turkey; DR, 178-180; RA, 24-24). A variety of this script, used in Ottoman Egypt, was known as **qirmah** (GA, 183).

سير

sayr (pl. suyūr) 1. strip, narrow piece of leather (MB, 114; IA, 62) 2. endband (headband) strip (ST, index, 16; MB, 114; HT, lin.96).

سيف

sayf (pl. suyūf) – trimming sword, cutter (UK, 154; MB, 103, 104; IA, 60: sayf bi-niṣāb, sayf bi-niṣābayn, sayf ṣaghīr, sayf kabīr).

****

ش

شبك

shabīkah 1. endband (headband) (HT, lin.88-106, 115, 158: wa-al-ghilaẓ fī raʾs al-ibrah yashtariṭ ʿinda ṣināʿat al-shabīkah faqaṭ) 2. also **mushabbak** – lattice work (FT, 407; DH, nos. 33, 73).
tashbīk 1. preliminary endbanding (without silk) (TS, 19, 20) 2. (pl. tashābīk) – interlace (TF, passim).

al-khayṭ al-tashbīk see khayṭ.
mutashābikah – interlacing (FT, 406).

شباة

shabāt al-qalam – nib (of a calamus) (KD, II, 701: shabāt al-qalam ṭarafuhu al-mabrī; BA, III, 370: shabātuh ḥadduh), comp. jilfah.

شج

shajjah (pl. shijāj) – diacritic point (JA, I, 276: shijāj yaʿnī nuqaṭ).

شجر

shajar, līf al-shajar – paper pulp (OM).
shajarah – genealogical tree; stemma (AL, I, 27).
tashjīr 1. also **mushajjar** – foliated design, arabesque decoration (WR, 86, 87; DH, no.73) 2. creating a genealogical tree; stemma (SL, I, 14; EI, VII, 967) 3. composing a text in a schematic, tree-like way.
al-qalam al-mushajjar see qalam.

شحذ

shaḥdh – whetting, honing (of a knife) (KD, II, 711).
mishḥadh – whetstone, hone (DD, I, 390).

شحم

shaḥm(ah) – pith, white interior substance of the reed (IK, 86: wa-yuqāl li-bāṭinih al-shaḥmah wa-li-ẓāhirih al-līṭ; UD, 9; LM, 35-35).

شد

shaddah, tashdīd(ah) – doubling (of a consonant), doubling sign over a consonant (for various practices see GL, 14).

شدق

shidq (pl. ashdāq) 1. pasteboard (made of two or three pieces of paper and one piece of parchment), book cover; case binding (TS, 27;

AG, 109), comp. fakk 2. fore-edge flap (?) (NH, 369).

شرج

sharaj (pl. ashrāj) – plaited thong (al-sayr al-murassaʿ) placed beneath a ḥalqah in 'boxed books' (q.v.) (BA, III, 372).

شرح

sharḥ (pl. shurūḥ, shurūḥāt) 1. note, comment (LC, 27) 2. running (systematic) commentary, comprising the text commented upon (matn); comment-text book, also referred to as **al-sharḥ al-mamzūj** (bi-al-matn), **al-sharḥ al-mazjī**, abbrev. ش (LC, 27; CI, II, xiv; MI, 100; MM, 139; EI, IX, 397-320; EA, I, 174-175).
al-sharḥ al-kabīr (al-muṭawwal) – original, long commentary.
al-sharḥ al-wasaṭ – middle commentary.
al-sharḥ al-ṣaghīr (al-mukhtaṣar) – short commentary.
shāriḥ (pl. shurrāḥ) – commentator, abbrev. الشـ (CI, II, xiv).

شرس

shars – pasting, paste (MB, 109: sharastu (not sharshartu!) ʿalayhi bi-al-ashrās; KM, I, sifr 4, 100: wa-al-shars shaddat daʿk al-shayʾ).
ashrās – asphodelus paste (UK, 158; MB, 106-107; IA, 60; IB, 50-51), also **shirās**, **sirās** and **sīrās** (DM).

شرط

sharṭ(ah) (pl. shuraṭ) – line, stroke (DM).
sharīṭ (pl. sharāʾiṭ, ashriṭah) 1. rules, rule-border (LC, 27) 2. frame (on a book cover) (FJ, 41: wa-al-matn muḥāṭ bi-iṭār dhī thalāthat ashriṭah; FZ, 217; MD, 109) 3. decorative band (UI, 29) 4. fillet (in decoration) (FT, 401).
mishraṭ(ah) – knife, cutter (IA, 60; NH, 385; DD, I, 392: for opening sealed documents; OM).

شرف

al-ashraf – epithet of Najaf.
al-sharīf(ah) – epithet of the months of Shaʿbān, Shawwāl, Dhū al-

Qaʿdah and Dhū al-Ḥijjah (q.v.), as well as the words kitāb, khatmah, muṣḥaf, nuskhah and the like.

شرق

shurūq – the first hour of day (SA, VI, 250).
(al-khaṭṭ) al-Mashriqī – large size, ligatured Maghrebi script, sometimes referred to as **al-thuluth al-Maghribī**, used predominantly for titles and chapter headings (LT, 365; TW, 47, 322).

شزر

shayzarah – endband (headband) (FD, 54, 55), comp. shīrāzah.

شطب

shaṭbah, tashṭīb – erasure (by means of a pen stroke) (SD, I, 756); cancellation (LC, 28: IN, I, 251), comp. shaqq, ḍarb.
mishṭab – 1. duster, whisk (?); eraser (TS, 11; AG, 113) 2. burnisher, polisher (NH, 390).

شظى

shaẓīyah (pl. shaẓāyā) 1. side of the right half-nib; also **tashẓīyah** – line, stroke produced by the side of the right half-nib (either at the head of such letters as ḥā', ṭā', yā', ṣād, kāf, ghayn or at the tail of the alif (SA, III, 35, 40: wa-kull shaẓīyah fī awwal aw ākhir mithl subʿ alif khaṭṭihā; KU, 154: wa-shaẓīyatuh ṭaraf sinnih al-ayman; AA, 88; KH, 36: al-tashẓīyah, an yakūn aʿlá al-ḥarf ʿalá hayʾat al-shaẓīyah; UD, 13) 2. serif-like stroke (LM, 54: wa-ammā alif al-tawāqīʿ al-shabīhah bi-al-riqāʿ wa-al-ghubār fa-anta mukhayyar bayna al-shaẓyah ! wa-ʿadamihā; LM, 57, 97; UD, 13), comp. tarwīs.

شعب

Shaʿbān (al-muʿaẓẓam, al-mukarram, al-mubārak, al-sharīf) – the eighth month of the Muslim calendar, abbrev. شع / ش (OS, 89).

شعر

(qalam) al-sha'r see qalam.
shi'r (pl. ash'ār) – poetry, versification; scribal verse (see e.g. CI, I, no. 12; CI, II, nos. 81, 82, 116).
(qalam) al-ash'ār, (qalam) al-musha''ar, also known as **(qalam) al-mu'annaq** – allegedly a hybrid of either al-muḥaqqaq or al-thuluth or al-muḥaqqaq and al-naskh scripts (AS, 145; JM, 91-93; LM, 45, 47: wa-al-mu'annaq li-kitābat al-shi'r).
tash'īr 1. outlining; outline (KF, II, 321: bi-al-khaṭṭ al-muḥaqqaq bi-mā' al-dhahab al-musha''ar bi-al-aswad) 2. illumination in gold; design made up of thin lines and drawn in gold (HD, 104; IP, 144; AF, 50) 3. also **sha'rah** and **tash'īrah** – hairline (used for joining letters in the thuluth family of scripts) (NC, 127; NA, pt. 9, 222: tash'īrāt raqīqah taltaff 'alá al-ḥurūf; KH, 36: fī nihāyat al-'arāqāt; AS, 145; SA, III, 58).
al-alif al-musha''arah – the letter alif with its tail (foot) bent to the left (SA, III, 59; MJ, 224).
mish'ār – small tool (most probably for creating tendrils) (TS, 11; AG, 109).

شفر

shafrah 1. cutting edge (SK,104; AI, 161) 2. bookbinder's sword, trimmer (HT, lin.83; MB, 103, 112; IA, 59) 3. paring knife, parer, scraper (ST, index, 16; UK, 153, 161).
tashfīr – trimming, shaving (HT, lin.159).

شفق

shafaq – the first hour of night (SA, VI, 250).

شق

shaqq (pl. shuqūq) 1. line (drawn above a letter or word, e.g. **al-kāf al-mashqūqah**, i.e. the letter kāf with a line above the ascender to distinguish it from lām) (UD, 11-12: SK, 117: wa-yastaḥsinūn an takūn al-kāf ghayr mashqūqah) 2. cancellation mark (in the form of a line drawn across the top of the word) (TP, 59; MH, 97; IM, 171) 3. slit (of the nib); splitting of the nib to facilitate retention of ink (KU, 154: wa-shaqquhu farjah bayna sinnayh; SA, II, 460-462).

شك

mishakk – needle; awl, punch (UA, 393).

شكز

tashkīz – 1. sewing endbands (headbands); preliminary endbanding (IA, 62) 2. mounting (of leather on wooden book covers) (KJ, no.1, 43, 45: wa-al-tajlīd al-awwal al-Aghlabī yata'allaf min daffatayn min al-khashab al-mushakkazatayn bi-al-jild al-muṭarraz al-muzakhraf; KJ, no.3, 23: yujallidūn al-kutub wa-yubaṭṭinūnahā bi-al-khashab wa-yushakkizūnahā bi-al-jild).

شكسته

(khaṭṭ-i) shikastah (Pers.) – commonly used for **shikastah-nastaʿlīq**, a hybrid of two Persian scripts nastaʿlīq and taʿlīq developed in the 11/17th century. Unlike taʿlīq it has no tarwīs and the letter nūn is often written 'in reverse' (EI, IV, 1124; ER, IV, 699-702).
shikastah-taʿlīq – version of the taʿlīq script used for rapid writing (EI, IV, 1124; ER, IV, 694).

شكل

shakl(ah) (pl. ashkāl) 1. also **tashkīl** – vocalization, vowelization; vowel marks; orthographic (orthoepic) signs (e.g. IM, 150), hence **mushakkal** – vocalized, vowelized (for various practices see SA, III, 160-167; GL, 12) 2. diagram.
shākilah – lower end of the stem of a letter before the tail (SA, III, 59; KH, 36).
al-kāf mashkūlah – the letter kāf provided with a straight line above its stem (KU, 125; SA, III, 81), comp. shaqq.

شمر

shamrah, tashmīr – upward-curving tail of a letter (as in bā', dāl, nūn) (KH, 36; UD, 13, 14, 20).

شمس

shams(ah) (pl. shumūs) 1. circular, center-medallion (on a book cover) (UK, 156: wa-al-bīkār li-istikhrāj al-shumūs wa-hiya al-dawā'ir al-manqūshah allatī taqaʿ fī wasaṭ al-kitāb ; MB, 105) 2. circular illuminated medallion, rosette (LC, 27; AF, passim; PA, 116).

شمع

shamʿ(ah) – wax (AG, 110; MB, 118; IA, 63).
shamʿ al-ʿasal – beeswax (used for polishing threads for use in sewing quires) (FD, 51).
tashmīʿ – waxing (of leather or paper) (KA, 135).

شهد

shāhid 1. (pl. shuhūd, ashhād) witness; notary 2. (pl. shawāhid) – quotation (usually drawn from pre-Islamic poetry) serving as textual evidence (e.g. al-shawāhid al-Qurʾānīyah).
shāhidah (pl. shawāhid) – copy of a letter, document (DM).
shahādah, tashahhud – the doctrinal formula 'lā ilāha illā Allāh Muḥammad rasūl Allāh', also known as **kalimat al-tawḥīd** or **kalimatān** (TP, 53, n.20; EI, IX, 201 and X, 340-341); signed shahādah-statement (often on the front of the textblock): awdaʿtu fī hādhā al-kitāb shahādatan …).
ishhād – written attestation of a document (e.g. a waqfīyah, q.v.), usually beginning with the expression ashhadanī (he called upon me as a witness) (OS, 90).
Mashhad ʿAlī, al-Mashhad al-Gharawī – Najaf.
Mashhad (al-)Ḥusayn, Mashhad al-Ḥāʾir (al-Mashhad al-Ḥāʾirī) – Kerbela (Karbalāʾ).
al-Mashhad al-Muqaddas, al-Mashhad al-Riḍawī – Mashhad.

شهر

shahr (pl. shuhūr, ashhur) – new moon; month (LL, II, 1612).
al-shahr al-ḥarām – the Holy Month of Muḥarram (q.v.).
shuhrah, ism al-shuhrah – that part of a person's name under which he/she is best known, usually introduced by al-shahīr (al-mashhūr) bi, al-maʿrūf bi and the like (e.g. CI, II, 5).

شول

Shawwāl (al-mukarram, al-mubārak) – the tenth month of the Muslim calendar, abbrev. ش / ل (OS, 89).

شيأ

For the formula 'in shāʾa Allāh' see istithnāʾ and mashʾalah.

شيخ

mashyakhah (pl. of shaykh) – record of attested study consisting of a list of works and their transmitters (EI, VI, 725), comp. fihrist, fahrasah.

شيرازة

shīrāzah (Pers.) – endband (headband) (LA, pt.5, 386: wa-dhakara al-burshmān bi-maʿná mā yusammīhu mujallidū al-ʿIrāq al-shīrāzah; HD, 117; PA, 118).

****

ص

صب

al-aṣabb – epithet of the month of Rajab (q.v.).

صبح

ṣabāḥ – the last hour of night (SA, VI, 250).

صبع

iṣbaʿ (pl. aṣābiʿ) – ascender (upstroke of such letters as alif, lām and the like) (FN, 8; RN, 19-20; KH, 34: al-ḥurūf al-qāʾimah aw al-ṭāliʿah).

صبغ

ṣabghah, ṣibāgh – pigment, dye, tint (UK, 120-129; MP, 29-32; MB, 114-118; IA, 63; NH, 370: ṣabgh al-waraq; NW, 45-46: ṣibāgh al-waraq).
ṣibāghah – art of dyeing, tinting.
ṣabbāgh – dyer (EI, VIII, 671-672; QS, II, 267-268).

صح

ṣiḥḥah – soundness of the text (ant. maraḍ and saqam); attestation (of correctness in transcription); sic, thus (JA, I, 279: idh ra'ayta al-kitāb fīhi ilḥāq wa-iṣlāḥ fa-ishhad bi-al-ṣiḥḥah).
ṣaḥīḥ – correct, abbrev. صح (KG, 473; AR, 35; LE, 136; CT, 45).
taṣḥīḥ 1. correction; emendation 2. writing صح (sic) on or next to a word in the text (GA, 285; MH, 95-96: ammā al-taṣḥīḥ fa-huwa kitābat 'ṣaḥḥa' ʿalá al-kalām aw ʿindah) or at the end of omission, abbrev. ص (TP, 57, 58) 3. writing صح (placet) at the end of audition notes (TP, 53, n.25); signing (a document) 4. preparation of a critical edition, comp. taḥrīr, taḥqīq.
muṣaḥḥiḥ – corrector; editor.

صحب

ṣāḥib (pl. aṣḥāb) 1. author (**ṣāḥib al-kitāb**), abbrev. ص (MI, 133) 2. owner (OS).
istiṣḥāb – ownership, possession (OS).

صحف

ṣaḥīfah (pl. ṣuḥuf, ṣaḥā'if) 1. sheet of writing material, often leather, parchment, papyrus or paper (KD, II, 704: wa-yuqāl lil-ṣaḥīfah al-qaḍīm ayḍan; BA, III, 371: wa-al-ṣuḥuf mā kāna min julūd; SA, II, 485: al-qirṭās wa-al-ṣaḥīfah wa-humā bi-maʿnan wāḥid wa-huwa kāghad; WS, 43; EI, VIII, 834-835) 2. papyrus or parchment roll (SL, I, 22) 3. folio (folium), leaf (TC, 24); page (DM) 4. small pamphlet, notebook (SL, I, 22; IK, 95: al-kitāb wa-al-ṣaḥīfah fa-innahumā yaqaʿān ʿalá jamīʿ anwāʿih).
muṣḥaf, maṣḥaf, miṣḥaf (pl. maṣāḥif) 1. codex (either bound or unbound) (KM, IV, sifr 13,8: wa-al-muṣḥaf al-jāmiʿ lil-ṣuḥuf al-

maktūbah bayna al-daffatayn ka-annahu uṣḥifa ay jumiʿat fīhi al-ṣuḥuf bi-kasr al-mīm wa-ḍammihā wa-fatḥihā; SK, 320: fa-huwa muṣḥaf idhā ḍammat al-ṣuḥuf baʿḍuhā ilá baʿḍ) 2. parchment textblock (TS, 17, 25; AG, 107) 3. copy of the Qurʾān (**al-muṣḥaf al-sharīf**) (usually contained in one, sometimes two, volumes) (EI, VII, 668-669; KF, II, 316, n.4).
al-muṣḥaf al-imām see imām.
al-maṣāḥif al-sifrīyah – codices bound in pasteboards (TS, 17, 25; AG, 107; MS, 16).
al-maṣāḥif al-mulawwaḥah – codices bound in wooden boards (TS, 17; AG, 107; MS, 16).
(qalam) al-maṣāḥif – smaller version of al-muḥaqqaq script, but larger than al-rayḥān, used exclusively for the copying of the Qurʾān, hence its appellation (AS, 146; JM, 54-57).
muṣḥifī – calligrapher and decorator of the Qurʾān (MS, 4, 5).
taṣḥīf 1. distortion, error resulting from incorrect pointing or vocalization of a word or misplacing diacritical marks (e.g. جمرة / حمرة , خزم / حزم) (MQ, 641; SA, II, 485: wa-yusammá al-taṣḥīf taṣḥīfan lil-khaṭaʾ fī al-ṣaḥīfah), comp. taḥrīf, al-qalb al-makānī 2. mistake (in writing), syn. taḥrīf (q.v.) (EI, X, 347-348) 3. bookbinding (LA, pt.5, 385: wa-maʿnāhā al-tajlīd aw kamā yaqūl al-ʿIrāqīyūn al-taṣḥīf).
ṣaḥḥāf 1. also **muṣaḥḥif** – bookbinder (CI, II, 9; IB, 11, 13; HD, 118) 2. bookseller (QS, II, 269-270).

ص د ر

ṣadr (pl. ṣudūr), **ṣadārah** 1. also **taṣdīr** – incipit, preamble, preface (TP, 52, n.14; CM, no.73: qāla al-muṣannif fī ṣadr al-kitāb 'Bism Allāh al-Raḥmān al-Raḥīm'; FN, 351: wa-li-Abī Zayd al-Balkhī sharḥ ṣadr hādhā al-kitāb) 2. front of the textblock (TS, 24: fa-idhā jiʾta ilá ṣadr al-kitāb wa-huwa mā bayna al-udhn wa-al-tabṭīn) 3. recto of the first folio (LC, 27) 4. fore-edge (TS, 15) 5. fore-edge flap (TS, 16; AG, 107) 6. almond-shaped stamp (mandorla), known as **ṣadr al-bāz** (UK, 156; IB, 44; MB, 105; IA, 59).
ṣadr al-qalam – outer side of the nib, as opposed to inner side, wajh (SA, II, 464; MJ, 218).
ṣadārah see also lawḥ al-ṣadārah.

صدق

taṣdīq – the formula of attestation 'ṣadaqa Allāh al-ʿAẓīm' (placed usually at the end of the Qurʾān or a ḥadīth) (CA, 47); confirmation, certification (DM).

صر

ṣurrah – center-medallion, mandorla (FZ, 215-219: **al-ṣurrah al-wusṭá**, **al-ṣurrah al-lawzīyah**; JL, 83, 99; MD, 109, 110), comp. surrah.

صعد

ṣaʿd (pl. ṣuʿūd) – ascender (up-stroke of a letter) (AA, 50; TU, 34: wa-ḍāhá ṣuʿūduhu ḥudūrah).

صغر

taṣghīr – abbreviation (contraction, siglum) (TP, 58).

صفح

ṣafḥ(ah) – page (SJ, 371; FN, 227; KD, II, 703: wa-al-waraqah maʿrūfah wa-kull wajh minhā ṣafḥ).
ṣafḥat al-dībājah – opening page; verso of the first folio (LC, 27).
ṣafīḥah (pl. ṣafāʾiḥ) – slab (for tooling leather) (TS, 11, 30; AG, 107).
taṣfīḥ – catchword, vox reclamans (TT, 192).
taṣaffuḥ – examination, study (KF, II, 362: nuqila min dustūrih bi-khaṭṭih wa-ʿalayhi ʿalāmat al-taṣaffuḥ wa-al-muqābalah).

صفر

Ṣafar (al-khayr, al-ẓafar, al-muẓaffar, al-mubārak) – the second month of the Muslim calendar, abbrev. ص (OS, 89).
ṣifr (pl. aṣfār) – cancellation mark (in the form of a small circle) (IM,171; TP, 59).

صفو

miṣfāh (pl. maṣāfin) – filter, strainer, sieve (UA, 393: for ink).

صقل

ṣaql – polishing, burnishing (MB, passim; KA, 134).
ṣaqqāl, miṣqalah (pl. maṣāqil) – polisher, burnisher (for paper and gold) (UK, 142, 149, 156; IB, 44; MB, 99, 105; IA, 60: miṣqalah kabīrah, miṣqalah ṣaghīrah; TS, 11; AG, 107; AT, 133; SA, II, 482; DS, 181: al-miṣqalah wa-hiya allatī yuṣqal bi-hā al-waraq li-izālat mā fīhi min al-khushūnah wa-yuṣqal bi-hā al-dhahab baʿda al-kitābah li-taẓhar bahjatuhu; DD, I, 391: for polishing paper after erasure with a scraper).
maṣāqil al-zujāj – glass burnishers (UK, 149; OM)
al-waraq al-maṣqūl – see waraq.

صلب

ṣulb (pl. aṣlub, aṣlāb) 1. main body of the text, as distinguished from the margins, text-column (LL, II, 1712; LC, 27) 2. main, original text (LC, 27), comp. matn.
ṣalīb – cross (as a mark of two intersecting lines) (UK, 166; MB, 119).
taṣlīb 1. making pasteboards (MB, 110: taṣlīb al-daffatayn) 2. also **taṣlībah** – pasteboard (MB, 111; IA, 62) 3. bookbinding (IA, 62).
lawḥ al-taṣlīb – slab for making pasteboards (IA, 59).

صلح

iṣlāḥ 1. correction (FK, II, no.1209/1: qaraʾtu hādhihi al-kurrāsah wa-aṣlaḥtuhā; JA, I, 279) 2. repair, restoration (KC, 91, 94; TW, 135).
al-waraq al-maṣlūḥ see waraq.
iṣṭilāḥ, muṣṭalaḥ – abbreviation (contraction, suspension, siglum) (TP, 55-56; CI, II, no. 191; MM, 139: fa-bayān al-iṣṭilāḥ fī dībājat al-kitāb).

صلو

taṣliyah, ṣalwalah – the formula of supplication 'ṣallá Allāh ʿalayhi wa-sallam', also known as **al-ṣalāh wa-al-taslīm**, used after the name of the prophet Muhammad, abbrev. صلعم / صلَه / صلع صلم / صم / ص / صع (TP, 53, n.20; TP, 54; CI, I, xiii; EI, X, 358-359).

صم

al-aṣamm – epithet of the month of Rajab (q.v.).
ṣimām – plug, stopper (in the inkwell) (IK, 83).
taṣmīm – design, sketching (MO, 227: ittafaqa al-farāgh min taṣḥīfih wa-taṣmīmih wa-tadhhībih).

صندوق

ṣandūq, ṣundūq (pl. ṣanādīq) – wooden chest, box (for copies of the Qurʾān) (MD, 133; TB, 93-94).
ṣanduqī – keeper of the chest of the Qurʾān (CA, 35, 51).

صنع

ṣināʿah (pl. ṣināʿāt, ṣunaʿ); **ṣunʿ**, **ṣanʿah** – occupation of and production by artisans; art, craft (EI, IX, 625-626).
ṣanʿah – composition, work (as in ṣanʿat Abī Hilāl = by Abī Hilāl), comp. ʿamal.

صنف

taṣnīf (pl. taṣānīf) – composition, work (MU, III, 98: wa-lahu fī kull fann taṣānīf wa-majāmīʿ wa-tawālīf), comp. taʾlīf.
muṣannaf – compilation, work, often a thematically arranged ḥadīth compilation, as opposed to musnad (q.v.) (SL, II, 39; EI, VII, 662-663, 705).
muṣannif – author, compiler; often the author of the original text (matn), as opposed to a commentator (shāriḥ), abbrev. المصـ (CI, I, xi).

صوب

ṣawāb – correct, correctness; used in the expression 'ṣawābuhu kadhā', placed in the margin, abbrev. ص (LE, 136; TP, 57).
taṣwīb (pl. taṣwībāt) – correction, comp. taṣḥīḥ.
al-qaṭṭ al-muṣawwab see qaṭṭ.

صور

ṣūrah (pl. ṣuwar) 1. copy, transcript (e.g. ṣūrat ijāzah, ṣūrat ṭabaqat al-samāʿ) 2. exact copy, apograph (TP, 56) 3. example (JA, I, 268) 4. also **taṣwīrah** – miniature painting, painted illustration (EI, IX, 889-892 and X, 361; DH, no.212).
taṣwīr 1. miniature painting (MU, XV, 121; MU, XVI, 225; EI, X, 361-363) 2. microfilming.
muṣawwir – painter, illustrator (PA,141: 'portraitiste').

صون

ṣiwān (pl. aṣwinah) – case, box (NT, pt.2, 143; ME, 559), comp. ḥifāẓ.
ṣawn, ṣiyānah – conservation, preservation (DM).

****

ض

ضب

ḍabbah (pl. ḍibāb) 1. correction mark (in the shape of a 'door bolt' and resembling the initial form of the letter صـ), abbrev. ض (TP, 57; AR, 30) 2. sic, thus (TP, 57, n.64; MH, 95-96).
taḍbīb, also known as **tamrīḍ**, marking the word with a ḍabbah (TP, 57; MH, 95-96).

ضبر

iḍbarah (pl. aḍābīr)**, aḍbarah, ḍibārah** 1. a number of leaves or sheets put together; bundle of documents (IK, 95: al-ṣuḥuf tujmaʿ wa-tushadd; KM, IV, sifr 13, 8: al-ḥuzmah min al-ṣuḥuf) 2. quire

(consisting of sewn leaves) (DA, II, 5) 3. textblock (TS, 17, 18; AG, 112) 4. album (FT, 388).
taḍbīr 1. gathering (arranging) leaves together (IB, 11) 2. collation (of quires) (TS, 13; AG, 107) 3. binding (IB, 19, n.177).

ضبط

ḍabṭ – pointing and/or vocalization (SJ, 356: wa-ḍabaṭa al-naṣb bi-al-dhahab wa-ḍabaṭa al-rafʿ minhā bi-al-aḥmar wa-ḍabaṭa al-khafḍ minhā bi-al-lāzuward wa-al-akhḍar; KF, I, 222; MH, 90: kamā tuḍbaṭ al-ḥurūf al-muʿjamah bi-al-naqṭ ka-dhālika yanbaghī an tuḍbaṭ al-muhmalāt ghayr al-muʿjamah bi-ʿalāmat al-ihmāl; KF, II, 320: ḍabaṭa hādhihi al-khatmah al-sharīfah bi-al-shakl).
ḍābiṭ 1. specialist in ḍabṭ; orthographer (MH, 97) 2. (pl. ḍawābiṭ) – compass, (pair of) dividers (TS, 12, 16, 18, 26, 29; AG, 107; ST, index,16; IB, 44; TK, f.120a-b).

ضرب

ḍarb (pl. ḍurūb) – cancellation; erasure (MF, 606: wa-ajwad al-ḍarb allā yaṭmis al-maḍrūb ʿalayhi bal yakhuṭṭ min fawqih khaṭṭan jayyidan bayyinan yadull ʿalá ibṭālih wa-yaqraʾ min taḥtih mā khaṭṭa ʿalayh; KF, II, 347: wa-kānat fī ghāyat al-siqam kathīrat al-ḍurūb; for various methods of cancellation see TP, 59).
miḍrabah 1. small tool (resembling a drum stick; stalk?) (TS, 11; AG, 109) 2. mallet (LF, 62).

ضرس

ḍirs (pl. aḍrās, ḍurūs) 1. pallet-like tool (used in leather work) (TS, 12; AG, 109) 2. interlace (TS, 12: ḥadīd al-ḍirs wa-hiya sabʿah wa-tasmiyatuhā al-ḍirs wa-al-ṭawīl wa-al-ṣilah wa-al-takḥīlayn! aʿnī bi-himā takḥīl al-ḍirs wa-takḥīl al-ṭawīl wa-al-ḍafrah wa-al-nuqṭah; also TS, 32-33; AG, 109-110).

ضعف

ḍiʿf (pl. aḍʿāf), **taḍʿīf** (pl. taḍāʿīf) – space between lines; interline (LL, II, 1792; MU, XVII, 54: wa-qad alḥaqa bi-khaṭṭih fī taḍāʿīf al-suṭūr bi-khaṭṭ daqīq; LL, II, 1792; LC, 27).

ضغط

ḍaghṭ – stamping (KF, 44).
al-waraq al-maḍghūṭ see waraq.

ضفر

ḍafīrah (pl. ḍafāʾir) 1. plait, braid (FT, 413) 2. interlace (TF, passim).
ḍafrah – gouge-like tool (TS, 12, 33; AG, 110).
maḍfūr – plaited, interlaced (FZ, 217).
muḍaffarah – interlacing (FT,406).

ضلع

muḍallaʿ – polygonal; polygon.
al-ḥabk al-muḍallaʿ see ḥabk.

ضلف

miḍlaf – chisel-like implement (for work with wooden boards) (TS, 11; AG, 107).

ضوء

ḍawʾ (pl. aḍwāʾ) – counter, 'eye' (of a letter), e.g. ṣād, ṭāʾ, ʿayn, fāʾ (SA, III, 30, 32, 44, 45).

****

ط

طبع

ṭābiʿ, ṭābaʿ (pl. ṭawābiʿ), **miṭbaʿ** 1. seal, signet, stamp (IK, 96), comp. khātim 2. small tool (for leather work) (TS, 11, 26; AG, 109) 3. large stamp (for a center- medallion) (HT, lin.134: wa-ṭābiʿ ka-shakl ḥūt lil-wasaṭ).

طبق

ṭabaq (pl. aṭbāq, ṭibāq) 1. mould;. sheet of paper; roll (AJ, 144; WS, 87) 2. format (of a book) (SJ, passim: fī ṭabaq min al-kāghad, fī niṣf al-ṭabaq, fī rubʿ al-ṭabaq), comp. qaṭʿ and qālib 3. lid (of an inkwell) (KU, 154; DB, III, 2019) 4. center-medallion (on a book cover in the shape of a star) (DE, 979) 5. element of geometrical design (in Mamluk book cover decoration such as kindah, tirs, sarwah) (JL, 83, 95: al-aṭbāq al-najmīyah; KR, 81).
ṭabaqah (pl. ṭabaqāt, ṭibāq), **ṭabaqat al-samāʿ**, **ṭābiq** – group of auditors (auditors' circle); record of authorities (or those present at a reading session); audition note (EI, VIII, 1020; MZ, I, Taf.7; AD, 102).
ṭibāq – large sheets, leaves (of paper) (NH, 372).

طبل

ṭablah – fore-edge flap (MB, 107, 113; IA, 60).

طر

ṭurrah (pl. ṭurar) 1. edge; turn-in (TS, 21; AG, 109) 2. border (on a book cover) (TS, 33: wa-al-ṭurar takūn ʿalá anwāʿ minhā ṭurrah min bayt wāḥid; AG, 110) 3. margin (LC, 28; TK, f.120a) 4. marginal note, gloss; marginalia, abbrev. ط (TP, 59, n.84; AK, 352), comp. ḥāshiyah 5. head (upper) margin (TP, 58; ML, 46; SA, VI, 313; SD, II, 29) 6. address (ʿunwān) of a document, matter preceding the basmalah (MU, X, 57; TP, 58, n.67), comp. ṭughrá 7. illuminated headpiece (LC, 28) 8. 'title page' of a manuscript or recto of the first folio (LC, 28) 9. center-medallion on a book cover (LC, 28) 10. disc or roundel (serving as a text divider) (LC, 28) 11. ansa, palmette (LC, 28; KH, 36) 12. tailpiece (LC, 28) 13. serif-like stroke, comp. tarwīs and zulf (ER, IV, 682, 689).
al-ṭurrah al-suflá – lower margin (TK, f.120a).
al-ṭurrah al-ʿulyā – upper margin (TK, f.120a; HT, lin.85).
taṭrīr – glossing, annotation (WA, 16).
muṭarrar – glossed, annotated (WA, 16).

طرح

ṭarḥ (pl. ṭurūḥ), **taṭrīḥ** – sketch, outline (HD, 118; MB, 101; PA, 61, 69, 159: 'dessin, composition').
qalam al-ṭarḥ see mikhaṭṭ.
ṭarrāḥ 1. sketcher, draftsman (AB, 132; HD, 118; PA, 141: 'dessinateur, celui qui fait le tracé initial, ṭarḥ') 2. manuscript restorer; person who repairs parts of the manuscript damaged by humidity or worms by restoring the text (AD, 103).
ṭarḥah – mould (DG, 133).
al-waraq al-muṭarraḥ see waraq.

طرس

ṭirs (pl. ṭurūs, aṭrās) 1. palimpsest, i.e. writing surface or manuscript on which the original writing has been effaced to make room for a second writing (WS, 63-64; IW, 75-76; IK, 93; EI, VIII, 408; LL, II, 1840), comp. ṭils 2. sheet, leaf (of paper) (e.g. 'Kitāb al-khaṭṭ wa-ādābuh wa-waṣf ṭurūsih wa-aqlāmih' by Ibn al-ʿAdīm, d. 660/1262; OH, 140; LF, 79: **ṭirs mabshūr** or **ṭirs makshūṭ**: 'une feuille de papier (!) qui avait déjà servi, et dont on avait effacé l'écriture avec un grattoir, pour s'en servir encore une fois').
taṭrīs – obliteration, effacement (of the original writing) (KM, IV, sifr 13, 8; BA, III, 371).

طرف

ṭaraf (pl. aṭrāf) – key element (part) of a ḥadīth recorded on a slip of paper in order to later form an index (fihris) or dictionary (muʿjam) called **al-aṭrāf** (IM, 166; TH, 57, 87).

طرق

ṭarīq – fillet (in book cover design) (TS, 11, 30, 31, 38; AG, 109).
miṭraqah – mallet; hammer (TS, 11; AG, 107; IA, 60).
taṭrīq – pounding (of the spine) (TS, 15; AG, 107).

طرمس

ṭarmasah – obliteration, erasure (KM, IV, sifr 13, 7: ṭarmastu al-kitāb maḥawtuh).

طعم

ṭuʿmah – small tool (possibly in the shape of a calice) (TS, 11; AG, 109).
taṭʿīm – inlay, inlay work (AB, 134; FT, 406).

طغرى

ṭughrá, ṭughrāʾ (pl. ṭughrāʾāt, ṭughrāwāt) 1. address (of a document) (MU, X, 57: al-ṭughrāʾ hiya kalimah ʿajamīyah muḥarrafah min al-ṭurrah (q.v.) 2. signature of the Ottoman sultan (EI, X, 595-598) 3. headpiece (LC, 28) 4. decorative panel (on a book cover or in the text) (LC, 28).

طفو

al-tadhhīb al-muṭfá see tadhhīb.

طلب

ṭālibī – 'student' (medium) format (of a book) (MK, 83).

طلبق

ṭalbaqah – the formula of supplication, requiescat 'aṭāla Allāh baqāʾahu' (MG, I, 483).

طلح

ṭalḥ, ṭalaḥ – sheet, leaf (of paper) (TS, 27; UK, 147; WS, 92; AJ, 145; SD, II, 52).
ṭalḥīyah (pl. ṭalāḥīy) – sheet (of paper from the mould); roll (WS, 87: al-darj; SD, II, 52).
ṭalīḥah – ream (of paper) (DM).

طلخ

ṭalkh – obliteration, smudging (KM, IV, sifr 13, 7: ifsād al-kitāb wa-naḥwih).

طلس

ṭils – palimpsest (KM, IV, sifr 13, 7: wa-al-ṭils alladhī muḥiya thumma kutiba; NH, 373: **ṭals**; LL, II, 1866: 'written paper or the like; syn. ṣaḥīfah: or of which the writing has been obliterated; thus differing from ṭirs'), comp. ṭirs.
ṭalsah, taṭlīs – obliteration, erasure (ND, 63, 82; NH, 373: **ṭulsah**).

طلسم

ṭilsam, ṭilsim, ṭilsim (etc.) (pl. ṭalāsim) – talisman; magical combination of words (EI, X, 500-502).
ṭalāsim – cryptic characters (DM).

طلع

ṭāliʿ (pl. ṭawāliʿ) 1. ascender (of a letter), iṣbāʿ (q.v.) (KH, 36: al-ḥurūf al-ṭāliʿah, al-ḥurūf al-ṭawāliʿ) 2. also **ṭāliʿah** – head margin; beginning of the text; incipit (WA, 11; WB, 56); headpiece (TW, 258).
muṭālaʿah – reading or study note (usually beginning with the verbs ṭālaʿa, naẓara, waqafa) (LC, 26; OS, 90), comp. taqrīẓ, naẓar.

طلق

(al-khaṭṭ) al-muṭlaq – curvilinear script or a family of scripts using ligatures and hairlines for joining letters together (AS, 144; SA, III, 22: wa-ammā al-muṭlaq fa-huwa alladhī tadākhalat ḥurūfuh wa-ittaṣala baʿḍuhā bi-baʿḍ; RN, 29: 'common, popular class of scripts').
al-alif al-muṭlaqah – the letter alif with its tail (foot) slightly tapered (SA, III, 59; MJ, 224).
al-tawqīʿ al-muṭlaq see tawqīʿ.

طلى

ṭaly 1. daubing, coating, pasting (MB, passim) 2. gilding (SD, II, 58; DG, 136).
ṭilāʾ – coat of paste, gilt and the like (MB, 110).

طمس

ṭams 1. obliteration, erasure (JA, I, 278; KD, II, 710: ṭamastu al-kitāb ṭamsan idhā ʿammaytu khaṭṭahu ḥattá lā yuqraʾ) 2. filling in (inking in) (of the counters, 'eyes', of the letters such as ṣād, ṭāʾ ʿayn, fāʾ qāf, mīn, hāʾ and wāw) (SA, III, 46-47; IR, 242; KH, 36; AS, 144).
maṭmūs – closed ('blind'), as opposed to open (maftūḥ) (of the counter of a letter).

طنب

aṭnāb (sg. ṭunub) – ascenders (TU, 36: al-aṭnāb al-alifāt; MN, 6: al-alifāt wa-al-lāmāt).

طوق

ṭāqah 1. sheet (piece, layer) of paper (TS, 17, 35; AG, 109; MB, 111; IA, 62; TK, f. 120b) 2. strand (UK, 157; MB, 107; IA, 61).

طول

aṭāla Allāh ʿumrahu – formula of supplication for someone's longevity (placed after a person's name), abbrev. طره / طلع / طع / طع (CI, I, xviii).
aṭālah Allāh baqāʾahu see ṭalbaqah.
ṭawīl – long, pallet-like tool (used in the interlace) (TS, 31, 32; AG, 110), comp. ṣilah.
muṭawwal – original, unabridged work.
al-sharḥ al-muṭawwal see sharḥ.
mustaṭīl 1. rules, rule-border (LC, 26) 2. rectangular panel (AB, 135) 3. cartouche (LC, 26).

طومار

ṭūmār, ṭāmūr (pl. ṭawāmīr) 1. (Gr. tomarion) – 1/6th of the papyrus roll; papyrus, parchment or paper roll (IB, 31; AJ, 102; IK, 68: fī anṣāf al-ṭawāmīr) 2. sheet of paper or other writing surface (SA, VI, 189: thumma al-murād bi-al-ṭūmār al-waraqah al-kāmilah wa-hiya al-muʿabbar ʿanhā fī zamāninā bi-al-farkhah; KM, IV, sifr 13, 8: al-ṭāmūr wa-al-ṭūmār al-ṣaḥīfah).
(qalam) al-ṭūmār – one of the four ancient chancery scripts of a large size (FN, 11, 12). In the Mamluk period it was executed either using the rules of al-muḥaqqaq or al-thuluth (AS, 147: **al-ṭūmār al-kāmil**, **al-ṭūmār al-muʿtād**, **mukhtaṣar al-ṭūmār**). It was written with a reed pen, the nib of which was slit in three or more places (SA, III, 49-57).

طوى

ṭayy al-kāghad – fold (of a leaf of paper) (TK, f.120a).

طيب

ṭāba or **ṭayyba (Allāh) tharāhu** – requiescat, prayer for a deceased person, abbrev. طر / طه (MI, 142).
taṭyīb – scenting, perfuming (of ink, with camphor, kāfūr, and/or musk, misk) (e.g. MJ, 206, 212).
mustaṭāb(ah) – honorific (epithet) of kitāb, risālah, etc. (e.g. CI, II, 3; CM, 18).

طير

ṭayyārah – slip of paper used for additions and glossed and inserted between the sheets of the volume; inset (EM, 98; AH, 182).

****

ظ

ظرف

ẓarf (pl. ẓurūf) 1. receptacle, container (SA, II, 480) 2. case, box (LC, 29; LL, II, 1910; ME, 575).

ẓarrāf – seller of paper and boxes (cases) (QS, II, 495).

ظفر

al-ẓafar, al-muẓaffar – epithet of the month of Ṣafar (q.v.).
ẓufr (pl. aẓfār) – outline (surrounding the center-piece on a book cover) (LC, 29).
taẓfīr – ruling (of leaves by means of fingernails, usually the thumbnail) (TM, 172: fa-idhā ẓaffara fa-lā yakbis ẓufrah qawīyan; MM, 132).

ظل

taẓlīl (lit. 'shading') – outlining, outline (KJ, no.3, 28: wa-kataba bi-al-dhahab al-ḥaqīqī al-muḥaḍḍan bi-al-ḥibr al-thubūt lil-taẓlīl wa-al-īḥā' bi-maʿná al-burūz).

ظن

ẓann (pl. ẓunūn) – conjecture, abbrev. ظ (TP, 57, n.64; CI, I, xv; GA, 285), often expressed by the phrase 'aẓunnuhu', placed in the margin.

ظهر

ẓahr – back, verso, hair side (of parchment), comp. baṭn.
ẓahr al-waraqah – verso or recto (LC, 29).
ẓahr al-kitāb (al-nuskhah), ẓahrīyah 1. back of a document; blank reverse of a letter (LC, 29; SL, II, 59) 2. front of the textblock (LC, 29); title-page (ṣafḥat al-ʿunwān) 3. fly-leaf (SD, II, 88; ME, 553: 'la feuille de garde') 4. first page(s) of the textblock (KF, I, 8 and II, 473: wajh al-waraqah al-ūlá), comp. ghāshiyah.
ẓahr al-qalabbaq – tool resembling the back (shell) of a tortoise (TS, 11; AG, 109).
ẓāhir (lit. 'external, obvious, evident'; 'alleged, presumed') – word commonly used in the Persian/Indian context to indicate a conjecture, abbrev. ظ (KG, 473: wa-hiya ay al-ziyādah bayna al-ṣaḥīḥ wa-al-ẓāhir wa-al-badal wa-li-kull wāḥid minhā ramz al-awwal ṣḥ wa-al-thānī bi-hi ẓ wa-al-thālith bi-hi khl wa-qad yuktab al-ḥarf ẓ fī al-hāmish ayḍan ishāratan ilá kalimat al-ẓāhir; TP, 57, n.64; TN, 52).

****

ع

al-ʿayn al-muʿallaqah see muʿallaqah.

عتق

taʿtīq (al-waraq) – method of making paper look old using saffron or straw to give it a buff or light brown tint (UK, 148-149; MP, 40; AJ, 147; WS, 80-82).

عجز

ʿajz, ʿajuz (pl. aʿjāz) 1. the last word of a verse (DA) 2. conclusion, final part of a document or composition (work) (MU, V, 21-22; TP, 52, n.14).

عجل

ʿajjala Allāh farajahu – formula of supplication (used after the name of al-Imām al-Mahdī), abbrev. عج (MI, 146; RA, 26).
ʿujālah – (hastily prepared) short tract, treatise.

عجم

ʿajm, iʿjām, taʿjīm 1. diacritical pointing (of letters) (MH, 90; SA, III, 16: al-ʿajm al-naqṭ bi-al-sawād; MF, 608: aʿjamtu al-kitāb fa-huwa muʿjam lā ghayruh wa-huwa al-naqṭ) 2. diacritical point 3. vocalization (KM, IV, sifr 13, 5: shakaltu al-kitāb ashkuluhu shaklan aʿjamtuh).
muʿjam – record of attested study arranged alphabetically by name (SD, II, 98; EI, II, 743), comp. barnāmaj, thabat, mashyakhah.
al-ḥurūf al-muʿjamah – letters provided with diacritical points, pointed letters (TP, 57).
ḥurūf al-muʿjam – letters of the alphabet.

عرج

taʿrīj(ah) (pl. taʿārīj) – curve, curvature (of the descender) (SA, III, 29, 40, 45: mā huwa mutanāsib fī al-taʿrīj wa-huwa al-ʿayn wa-al-jīm wa-yajmaʿuhā qawluk ʿaj).
taʿarruj – scroll (in decoration) (UI, 30).

عرش

ʿarsh (pl. ʿurūsh) **al-saṭr** – base line (TW, 230: ʿalá ʿurūsh al-suṭūr).
ʿarīsh, taʿrīshah 1. trellis (FT, 423) 2. lattice-work (AB, 136).

عرض

ʿarḍ(ah), ʿirāḍ(ah), muʿāraḍah – collation of a text with the exemplar (usually in the presence of the teacher by means of recitation or reading) (LC, 25; TP, 56; MH, 92: afḍal al-muʿāraḍah an yuʿāriḍ al-ṭālib bi-nafsih kitābahu bi-kitāb al-shaykh maʿa al-shaykh fī ḥāl taḥdīthih iyyāhu min kitābih; MU, XVII, 78: ʿaraḍtu al-Qurʾān ʿalá Ibn ʿAbbās thalāthīn ʿarḍatan), abbrev. ع (for **ʿūriḍa**, JA, I, 202), comp. muqābalah.
ʿurḍ al-kitāb – outer or inner margin (IK, 94: fa-idhā naqaṣa min al-kitābah shayʾ fa-alḥiqhu bayna al-suṭūr aw fī ʿurḍ al-kitāb; IK, 101: fī asfal al-kitāb al-marfūʿ ilayh aw ʿalá ẓahrih aw fī ʿurḍih; LC, 29).
ʿarḍ al-qalam – left-side (of the) half-nib (of a reed pen) (MJ, 218; KU, 154: wa-ʿurḍuhu! al-jānib al-aysar; SA, II, 464; SA, III, 45).
muʿāriḍ – collator; reciter (CT, 45).

عرق

ʿarāqah, taʿrīqah (pl. taʿārīq), **muʿarraqah** – descender (terminal, sublinear stroke of a letter) (RN, 22; KH, 36, 37; SA, III, 11, 40, 50; KU, 125: **al-ḥurūf al-muʿarraqah** – sīn, ṣād, qāf, nūn, yāʾ , rāʾ, zāy, mīm, wāw), comp. muʿaqqaf.
(al-khaṭṭ) al-ʿIrāqī see muḥaqqaq.

عرم

ʿarrām – bookbinder (IB, 11).

عرو

ʿurwah (pl. ʿuran) – thong, leather fastener in the shape of a loop or noose (part of a clasp) (TS, 25, 34; AG, 110; KT, 135: al-muṣḥaf wa-lahu ʿuran wa-azrār; BA, III, 371: wa-fīhi [al-ghilāf] al-ʿurwatān).

عز

ʿazza wa-jalla – the formula of magnification (placed after the word Allāh), abbrev. عج / عج (CI, I, xiii).

عشر

ʿashr (pl. aʿshār), **ʿāshirah** (pl. ʿawāshir), **ʿāshirīyah** – mark, decorative disc or rosette indicating the end of a group of 10 verses of the Qurʾān (MS, 15, 28; KT, 138; LL, II, 2051; UI, 36; SD, II, 130).
al-ʿashr – the first 10 days of Muḥarram (DM).
taʿshīr 1. dividing a chapter of the Qurʾān into groups of 10 verses and marking them with the letter ع or ع 2. (pl. taʿshīrāt) the mark itself (MD, 126: wa-baʿda kull ʿashr āyāt tataḍamman al-dāʾirah raʾs ḥarf al-ʿayn wa-aṣbaḥat tusammá al-taʿshīrāt; KT, 139: kānū yakrahūn al-naqṭ wa-al-taʿshīr wa-iḥṣār al-suwar).
ʿushar 1. stamp with vegetal design (TS, 31: wa-al-ʿushar fī wasaṭ al-sifr wa-al-lawzah ḥawlah; AG, 109) 2. tool (used for the application of gold with the inside either engraved or not) (TS, 11; AG, 109).

عصر

ʿaṣr – pressing (MB, 108, 109).
ʿaṣṣārah – press (used for tanning leather) (MB, 116: ghaḍārah!).
miʿṣarah (pl. maʿāṣir) – bookbinder's press (UK, 154-155; SD, II, 134).
miʿṣarat dhāt ḥabl – rope press (UK, 154).
miʿṣarat al-maghāzil – screw press, also known as **laḥm Sulaymān** (UK, 154; IB, 42).

عطب

ʿuṭbah – cotton wad (tow) (in the inkwell) (KU, 155; IK, 84).

عطف

ʿaṭf (ah) 1. fold (of a leaf of paper or quire) (MB, 107: ʿaṭf al-kurrās; HT, lin.130) 2. curved line (used as a reference mark, signe de renvoi); caret (MR, 95: wa-qīla tamudd al-ʿaṭfah ilá awwal al-laḥaq thumma yuktab al-laḥaq qubālata al-ʿaṭfah fī al-ḥāshiyah; TP, 58) 3. rounding (of the end of descender or the tail of the alif) (KH, 37) 4. also **ʿalāmat al-ʿaṭf** or **maʿṭūfah** – conjunction, connection, abbrev. معط / عف / عط / ع (AR, 35, 36; MI, 145, 147; AM, introd.).

عظم

taʿẓīm – the formula of glorification, such as tabāraka, taqaddasa, ʿazza wa-jalla, subḥānahu, taʿālá (placed after the word Allāh) (MM, 132; MR, 93; TM, 176; TP, 54).
al-muʿaẓẓam – epithet of the months of Ramaḍān and Shaʿbān (q.v.).

عفص

ʿafṣ – galls, gall nuts (for making iron-gall or tannin inks, ḥibr) (MP, 16, 19).
ʿifāṣ – plug, stopper (in the inkwell) (IK, 83; LL, II, 2091).

عقب

ʿaqb, ʿaqib (pl. aʿqāb) – end of the text (matn) on a page; lower margin (ST, index, 17; ST, 8: wa-yanẓur fī ʿaqb al-waraqah wa-fī al-awwal allatī baʿdahā; MP, 62).
taʿqībah 1. note, comment (LC, 27) 2. catchword, vox reclamans (TN, 38: hiya al-kalimah allatī tuktab fī asfal al-ṣafḥah al-yumná ghāliban li-tadull ʿalá badʾ al-ṣafḥah allatī talīhā; KH, 37; NM, 683; SJ, 344).

عقد

ʿuqdah (pl. ʿuqad) 1. counter, ʿeyeʾ (of a letter) (SA, III, 46, 47, 58, 128: mufattaḥ al-ʿuqad; KH, 36) 2. knot-like tool (TS, 11; AG, 109).

عقف

ʿuqf(ah) – tail of the alif curved to the right (KH, 37).
muʿaqqaf – letter (such as jīm and ʿayn) having its tail or descender curved to the right) (KU, 126), comp. taʿrīq.

عل

ʿallahu, laʿallahu (lit. 'perhaps, maybe') – used in the expression 'laʿallahu kadhā' (perhaps thus), to indicate a conjecture, abbrev. ع or عه (TN, 52; MI, 145).

علج

ʿilāj – sizing (of paper) (AB, 90; WS, 80: ṣifat saqy al-kāghad wa-huwa al-musammá fī muṣṭalaḥ al-nās al-ān al-ʿilāj), comp. saqy.

علق

taʿlīq 1. writing, composition; transcription, copying (TE, 15) 2. copy, transcript (AD, 119) 3. ligature (KU, 124); script, hand (using an unconventional way of joining letters) (MM, 133: huwa khalṭ al-ḥurūf allatī yanbaghī tafriqatuhā;TP, 55; MA, IV, 84) 4. dictation session (in Shāfiʿī circles) (KF, I, 86) 5. also **taʿlīqah**, abbrev. ه / ت (MI, 107) (pl. taʿālīq, taʿlīqāt) – marginal gloss, comment; scholium, explication (TE, 15; LC, 27; MU, IX, 71; EI, X, 165) 6. insertion/ omission (written in the margin) (SD, II, 162).
(khaṭṭ) al-taʿlīq 1. (also known as **taʿlīq-i qadīm** or **taʿlīq-i aṣl**) – Persian chancery hand and later also (though less frequently) a book hand which emerged in its definite form in the 7/13th century. It is characterized by numerous ligatures, the **tarwīs** protruding to the left and the tail (foot) of the alif bent leftward and often joined with the following letter (EI, IV, 1124; ER, IV, 694-696) 2. name often given, in the Turkish/Arabic context, to the script which is properly known as **nastaʿlīq** (q.v.).
muʿalliq – glossator (MI, 26).
muʿallaqah – strip of parchment (used for lining the spine of the textblock before covering); hinge (guard) (TS, 17: ammā al-maṣāḥif al-mulawwaḥah fa-innamā takūn lahā muʿallaqāt min al-raqq mud-

khalah bayna al-lawḥ wa-al-muṣḥaf; also TS, 26, 28; AG, 104), comp. rājiʿ.
al-ʿayn al-muʿallaqah – syn. **al-ʿayn al-maṭmūsah**, closed ('blinded') form of the letter ʿayn (SA, III, 77).
al-sīn al-muʿallaqah – the letter sīn without 'teeth' (SA, III, 72).
miʿlāq – fastener (part of a clasp) (BA, III, 371, 372: wa-huwa khayṭ aw sayr yushadd ilá ʿurāhā).

علم

ʿalam (pl. aʿlām) – decorated border (LL, II, 2140).
ʿalāmah – 1. mark, book mark (e.g. to mark centers of quires when rebinding, TS, 27) 2. abbreviation (siglum) (MU, XII, 138: wa-qad aʿlama ʿalayhi ʿayn wa-hiya ʿalāmah li-nafsih) 3. motto, signature (SD, II, 164; EI, I, 352) 4. autograph (LC, 22).
al-ʿalāmah al-māʾīyah – watermark (HN, 381).
ʿalāmat al-ʿaṭf see ʿaṭf.
ʿalāmat al-balāgh see balāgh.
ʿalāmat al-iḥālah see iḥālah.
ʿalāmat al-ihmāl see ihmāl.
ʿalāmat al-rajʿ see rajʿ.
ʿalāmat al-taḍbīb see ḍabbah.
ʿalāmat al-takhrīj see takhrīj.
ʿalāmat al-tamrīḍ see ḍabbah.
ʿalāmat al-taṣḥīḥ see taṣḥīḥ.
ʿalāmat al-waqf see waqf.
taʿlīm 1. marking; marking quires before sewing (ST, index, 18) 2. signing a document (AA, 135; SD, II, 164); also possibly the textual closing formula 'wa-Allāh aʿlam (bi-al-ṣawāb)'.

علو / على

ʿilāwah – upper book cover (BA, III, 372).
aʿlá Allāh maqāmahu – the formula of supplication, abbrev. اع (MI, 100).
al-muʿallá – epithet of Kerbela (Karbalāʾ) (CM, no.39).
taʿālá – the formula of glorification placed after the word Allāh or qawluhu (introducing a Qurʾānic quotation), abbrev. تعـ or تع (TP, 54).

عمد

ʿamūd al-kitāb – text-column (as opposed to the margins) (LL, II, 2153: ‘text of the book’).
al-nuskhah al-muʿtamadah see nuskhah.

عمل

ʿamal (pl. aʿmāl) 1. composition, compilation (MU, VII, 256: ʿamaltu bi-idhn Allāh kitāban), comp. ṣanʿah 2. also **ʿamalīyah** – execution, i.e. writing, colouring, painting, etc. (SJ, passim: min ʿamal ḥasan jiddan, mukhtalifat al-ʿamal, laṭīf al-ʿamal; TC, 30) 3. main work of a painter (PA, 61: le ‘gros’ de l’oeuvre, used in opposition to ṭarḥ, q.v.).

عمى

taʿmiyah 1. ‘blinding’ of the ‘eyes’ (counters) of letters (KU, 123), comp. taʿwīr 2. also **muʿammá** – cryptography, cryptogram; chronosticon (TI, 47-48; SA, IX, 229; EI, VII, 257-258).
al-taʿmiyah bi-al-naqṣ see taʾrīkh.
al-taʿmiyah bi-al-ziyādah see taʾrīkh.

عن

ʿanʿanah – the formula “ʿan fulān’ (on the authority of, by), abbrev. ع (used in the isnād and indicating an indirect transmission of a text) (MW, 110; PK, 211; SL, I, 16; EI, VII, 260-261).

عنون

ʿunwān (pl. ʿanāwīn) 1. address (in diplomatic: min fulān ilá fulān); the matter preceding the basmalah (LC, 29; EI, X, 870), comp. tarjamah 2. title (of a book) (LC, 29; EI, X, 871-872) 3. illuminated headpiece or frontispiece (sometimes containing the title of the work) (AF, 36; PA, 66, 116; EI, X, 870-871) 4. chapter, section heading (LC, 29).

عهد

ʿuhdah – faulty formation of letters (fī khaṭṭih ʿuhdah) (LL, II, 2183).

عوج

ʿāj – ivory (EI, I, 200-203).
al-misṭarah al-ʿājīyah see misṭarah.
iʿwijāj – curvature, hence **muʿawwaj** – crooked, curved (of a line, stroke) (KU, 126: curvature of the tail of jīm and ʿayn; UD, e.g. 13, 14).

عود

ʿūd al-nasākhah – copyist's book support (WA, 12; IN, I, 230).
iʿādah – reiteration of dictation; collation session (MF, 74).
muʿīd – transmitter's clerk (famulus); collation master, repetitor (EI, VII, 726).

عوذ

taʿawwudh, istiʿādhah – the formula of protection 'aʿūdhu bi-Allāh' (EI, X, 7).
taʿwīdhah (pl. taʿāwīdh) – talisman, amulet (DT, 69).

عور

taʿwīr – filling in (inking in) (of the counters, 'eyes', of letters) (AP, 95; KU, 114, 123-124), comp. ṭams.

عوم

ʿām (pl. aʿwām) – year (word used predominantly in dates in Maghrebi manuscripts) (SA, VI, 252-253), comp. sanah.

عين

ʿayn (pl. ʿuyūn, aʿyun) – counter ('eye' of a letter) (MJ, 194; LM, 43), comp. ʿuqdah.

****

غ

غبر

(qalam) al-ghubār – the smallest curvilinear script, also known as **(qalam) al-janāḥ**, **(qalam) al-baṭāʾiq** (AS, 145), as well as **ghubār** (or **qalam**) **al-ḥalbah** or **al-ḥilyah** (KK, 47; IK, 88; MP, 41, n.289: ghabār al-ḥulbah!; JM, 58-63; AS, 145; EI, IV, 1124).
al-khamsah al-ghubārīyah see khams.
rasm al-ghubār, **al-arqām al-ghubārīyah** see raqm.
ghubrah – mixture of white, red and black colours (SD, II, 199).

غر

ghurrah – the first night of the month (SA, VI, 244).
ghurar – the first three nights of the month (SA, VI, 250).

غرا

gharan, ghirāʾ (pl. aghriyah) – paste, adhesive (TS, 12-13; AG, 107; HT, lin.60-72; NW, 45-47).
ghirāʾ al-ḥalazūn – snail paste (UK, 141; MB, 97; MP, 37; IB, 73).
ghirāʾ al-ḥūt – whitefish paste (ST, 19-23; IB, 74).
ghirāʾ al-samak – fish paste (UK, 141; MB, 97; MP, 37; IB, 74; NW, 47).
taghriyah 1. pasting (ST, index,18) 2. sizing (of paper) (AB, 90; NW, 46: taghriyat al-waraq).

غرب

ghurūb – the last hour of day (SA, VI, 250).
(al-khaṭṭ) al-Maghribī – generic name for a host of 'non-proportioned' scripts which originated from the category currently known as the 'Abbasid bookhand' and which were used throughout Andalusia, North Africa, and sub-Saharan Africa (DQ, 233; OD; DW, 32-34, 42-45), comp. Ifrīqī.

غزل

jild (raqq) ghazāl see jild.
miʿṣarat al-maghāzil see miʿṣarah.

غشى

ghishāʾ (pl. aghshiyah) 1. book cover; covering of the board, binding (TS, 35, 36; ME, 554, 564) 2. case, box (SD, II, 214; KC, passim).
ghāshiyah (pl. ghawāshin) 1. book cover; inner cover, paste-down end paper or recto of the first folio (TM, 182: wa-yajʿalu ruʾūs ḥurūf hādhihi al-tarjamah ilá al-ghāshiyah allatī min jānib al-basmalah; CD, III, pl. 71: samiʿa al-juzʾ kullah wa-mā fī ghāshiyatih; qaraʾtuh wa-mā ʿalá ghāshiyatih) 2. last page(s) of the textblock; area around the tail of the text and the colophon (KF, I, 8: al-ṣafaḥāt al-akhīrah; KF, II, 473).
taghshiyah – book covering, binding (IN, I, 257).

غفر

istighfār(ah) 1. the formula of forgiveness 'astaghfiru Allāh' (SD, II, 217) 2. prayer (in verse) on the theme of forgiveness.

غفل

ghufl – anonymous (BA, III, 371: hādhā kitāb ghufl ... idhā lam yakun mawsūman).

غلط

ghalaṭ (pl. aghlāṭ), **ghalṭah** – error, mistake, abbrev. غ (written above a word) (MI, 150).

غلظ

ghilaẓ, ghilẓah, ghilāẓah – boldness (of letters); bold character, letter (SK, 105; TB, 95: in kāna al-Qurʾān bi-khaṭṭ mutamayyiz bi-ghilaẓ aw ḥumrah aw ghayrihā ḥaruma).
taghlīẓ – writing in bold letters (TM, 192).

غلف

ghilāf (pl. aghlifah, ghilāfāt) – book cover (MD, 108).
mughallif – bookbinder (DG, 157).
taghlīf – book covering; binding (FZ, 213, 214; AB, 132).

غلق

ghāliqah (pl. ghawāliq) – tailpiece (KF, II, 320: hādhihi al-fawātiḥ wa-al-ghawāliq min idʿān al-ʿabd ... Ṣandal).

****

ف

فافير

fāfīr – papyrus (EI, VIII, 261).

فتح

fatḥ – opposite of ṭams (q.v.); **mufattaḥ al-ʿuqad** – letters with open counters (KU, 114; SA, III, 46, 47, 128), comp.ʿuqdah.
fātiḥah (pl. fawātiḥ) 1. also **iftitāḥ**, **istiftāḥ** – opening lines (of a composition); incipit (MU, XVII, 92: kull mujallad lahu fātiḥah bi-khuṭbah; LC, 23) 2. preface, prologue, proem (MU, XV, 8: kull mujallad lahu fātiḥah wa-khātimah; TP, 52, n.14; LC, 23) 3. heading (e.g. **fawātiḥ al-suwar**, LC, 23) 4. headpiece (KF, II, 320: al-fawātiḥ wa-al-ghawāliq).
miftāḥ al-qarrāṣ see qarrāṣ.
muftataḥ – the first day of the month (SA, VI, 245).

فتل

fatīlah 1. also **maftūl** – endband (headband) strip (MB, 114: wa-yusammá hādhā al-sayr al-maftūl al-fatīlah; IA, 62; TS,18; AG, 109) 2. press screw (MB, 104; IA, 59).

فرخ

farkhah – sheet, leaf (of paper) (SA, VI, 189; SD, II, 249), comp. ṭūmār.

فرد

fard(ah) (pl. afrād) – one of a pair; one half of a piece of leather (TS, 28); conjugate leaf.
al-fard – epithet of the month of Rajab (q.v.).
farīdah – quire (of paper) (DM).
al-nukhah al-farīdah see nuskhah.
ifrād – letter in its isolated, as opposed to linked (ligatured) form, tarkīb (q.v.) (SA, III, 50).
al-ḥurūf al-mufradah, mufradāt – letters of the alphabet written individually (in their isolated forms) (e.g. SA, III, 60; MY, 83).

فرش

mifrash(ah) – piece of cotton or wool (used as lining for pens in a writing case) (SA, II, 481; AT, 133; IR, 230; DD, I, 390).

فرض

farḍ al-qalam – syn. shaqq (q.v.) (KU, 154).
furḍah (pl. furaḍ) – place in the writing case (dawāh) where the ink is kept; perhaps syn. of jūnah (q.v.) (LL, II, 2374).

فرط

mifraṭ – cutter (ST, index,18), most probably a variant of **miqrāḍ**, **miqrāṭ** and **miqrāẓ**.

فرع

farʿ (pl. furūʿ) 1. also **al-nuskhah al-farʿ** – copy, apograph; witness (MR, 94: wa-yakfī muqābalatuh bi-farʿ qūbila bi-aṣl al-shaykh; LC, 23) 2. note, annotation (TM, 191: wa-lā yusawwiduh bi-naql al-masāʾil wa-al-furūʿ al-gharībah; KZ, 95: kāna ʿalá al-aṣl al-manqūl minhu hādhā al-farʿ mā ṣūratuh…) 3. script derived from the original

(principal) script (aṣl, q.v.) (UD, 15; SM, 269) 4. argument resulting from a legal point, aṣl; application as opposed to theory, abbrev. ع (AD, 131).
tafrīʿ – interlacing, scroll (FI, 87, 88; JL, 93; KR, 82).

فرغ

farāgh (pl. farāghāt) 1. also **tafrīgh** (MO, 41) – end, completion, execution; one of the standard words introducing a colophon (tail of the text), e.g. kāna or waqaʿa or wāfaqa al-farāgh, faragha min tafrīgh 2. also **qayd al-farāgh** – colophon (LC, 23, 26; GA, 289) 3. blank, lacuna (LC, 23).

فرك

farkah (MN, 116) – thinner part of a letter (stoke) at its bend (JM, 17: al-qaṭṭ al-muḥarraf yuẓhir al-farakāt fī al-kitābah wa-al-farkah riqqat al-zāwiyah; KH, 37; LM, 42).

فسر

tafsīr (pl. tafāsīr) 1. explication, comment; commentary on a given work (usually but not necessarily relating to the text of the Qurʾān) (FN, 350: fassarahā fī thalāth maqālāt), comp. sharḥ 2. commentary and/or translation, e.g. from Greek into Arabic (EI, X, 83).
mufassir – commentator.

فص

faṣṣ (pl. fuṣūṣ) – lobe (in design) (JL, 103: buḥur mustaṭīlah dhāt fuṣūṣ fī nihāyatihā; MD, 128: dāʾirah min fuṣūṣ – scalloped circle).

فصل

fāṣil(ah) (pl. fawāṣil) – mark (such as a circle, letter hāʾ, disc, three dots, three 'inverted commas') used as a textual divider; paragraph mark (TP, 55; LC, 23; AK, 351; MS, 28: **fawāṣil al-khams**, **fawāṣil al-ʿashr**; SA, III, 146: fa-al-nussākh yajʿalūn li-dhālik dāʾirah tufaṣṣil bayna al-kalāmayn; IR, 245).

faṣl (pl. fuṣūl), **tafṣīl** 1. word division (in a text); space between words or passages; spacing (TP, 55; MM, 134, 138; SA, III, 145-146) 2. division of a composition into fuṣūl (FK, I, no.546: wa-qad faraghtu min hādhā al-kitāb wa-taḥṣīlih wa-tafṣīlih) 3. chapter (SD, II, 271).
faṣl al-khiṭāb – (in epistolography and diplomatic) conclusion of the formal greetings by the words 'amma baʿdu'; place separating the doxological and doctrinal formulae from the preface proper (AA, 37; TP, 53, n.20), comp. baʿdīyah.

فض

fiḍḍah – silver, silver-based ink (UK, 130-133; MB, 92; MP, 33).

فضح

(qalam) al-faḍḍāḥ, or **faḍḍāḥ al-naskh** see matn.

فضل

faḍl – inner or outer margin (SA, III, 50: an yakūn al-faḍl min jānibay al-qirṭās mutasāwiyan fī al-miqdār).

فقر

fiqrah (pl. fiqar) – passage, section of a text, paragraph (LC, 23; AK, 351).

فقط

tafqīṭ – writing the word **faqaṭ** 'only' (closing formula found at the end of colophons and marginal glosses), abbrev. ط (often represented in the form of a logograph) (CI, I, xiii; SD, II, 273; DM), comp. taʾmīn, tatmīm.

فك

fakk (pl. fukūk) – book cover (HN, 385; BA, III, 372: wa-huwa mā yastur al-awrāq min jānibayh), comp. shidq.

mafkūk, mufakkak – loose, disbound (e.g. **al-nuskhah al-mufakkakah**).

فنق

fanīq (pl. funuq) – case, box (KC, 45).

فهرس

fihris, fihrist (pl. fahāris) 1. table of contents (LC, 23) 2. record of attested study 3. list, catalogue (SD, II, 286; EI, II, 743-744) 4. bibliography.
fahrasah 1. record of attested study, comp. mashyakhah 2. cataloguing.

فيد

fā'idah (pl. fawā'id) 1. digressional remark (in a text) (SD, II, 293) 2. marginal note, gloss; nota bene (notabilia), abbrev. ف or فيه (CM, 52, 66, 149, 207; LC, 23; AR, 36), also **fā'idat al-aṣl**, abbrev. فصـ or فصل (CA, 49, 50).

****

ق

قانون

qānūn (pl. qawānīn) – trapezium-shaped instrument (used for creating compartments and frames, tabyīt, on book covers) (TS, 32; AG, 107).

قب

Qubbat al-Islām – epithet of the city of Basra.
Qubbat al-Ṣakhrah – the Dome of the Rock (the Mosque of ʿUmar in Jerusalem).
taqbīb – rounding (backing) the spine (of a book) (TS, 15).
al-qafā' al-muqabbab see qafan.

قبر

qubūr (sg. qabr, lit.'grave') – pen box (EI, IV, 471).

قبطال

qubṭal, qubṭāl (qabāṭil) – ruler, straightedge (TS, 12: wa-yaḥtāj qubṭālan wa-hiya misṭarah; AG, 107; SD, II, 302).

قبل

qabla – before, abbrev. ق (when used for a transposed word) (LE, 137), see also taqdīm.
muqābalah – 1. collation (of the text with the exemplar either in the presence of the shaykh or not) (MR, 94: afḍal al-muqābalah an yamsik huwa wa-shaykhuh kitābayhimā ḥāla al-samāʿ; MH, 92: ʿalá al-ṭālib muqābalat kitābih bi-aṣl samāʿih;TP, 56, n.52; EI, VII, 490-492), comp. muʿāraḍah 2. collation note (statement).
muqābil – collator; corrector.

قحم

iqḥām – interpolation (LL, II, 2985: **ḥarf muqḥamah**, letter inserted without reason; AD, 138), comp. zāʾidah.

قد

qadd, taqdīd – cutting (of leather, etc.) into strips (lengthwise) (KD, II, 701; AA, 109), comp. qaṭṭ.
qidd (pl. aqudd) – strip (of leather).
miqaddah – crescent-shaped trimming knife (TS, 10, 11, 18, 24; AG, 107).

قدس

taqdīs – the formula of benediction 'qaddasa Allāh sirrahu (rūḥahu)', abbrev. س / ق / ق س / قس / قده / قد (TP, 54, n.37; CI, I,xiii; CI, II, xiv).

قدم

muqaddam – fore-edge; fore-edge flap (TS, 16: al-muqaddam wa-huwa al-ṣadr; also TS, 17, 26, 27: ṭurrat al-muqaddam wa-al-udhn; TS, 28: min nāḥiyat al-ḥabk wa-al-muqaddam; AG, 107).
muqaddimah – forward, preface, introduction (EI, VII, 495-496).
al-taqdīm wa-al-taʾkhīr – transposition (of words), abbrev. ق or م for taqdīm or muqaddam and خ for taʾkhīr or muʾakhkhar or م م for both muqaddam and muʾakhkhar; م خ for muʾakhkhar muqaddam; خ م for muqaddam muʾakhkhar (TN, 52; TP, 59; MI, 120, 173), comp. al-qalb al-makānī.

قر

taqrīr (pl. taqārīr) – marginal note, gloss; collection of glosses, commentary (AD, 139).

قرأ

qāriʿ (pl. qurrāʾ) – reader, prelector; reciter.
qirāʾah 1. reading, recitation (LC, 26) 2. manner of recitation, punctuation and vocalization of the Qurʾānic text (DM; EI, V, 127-129) 3. variant reading (varia lectio), lection (especially relating to the text of the Qurʾān) (AL, I, 26; TP, 51), comp. ḥarf.
ijāzat al-qirāʾah – audition (recitation) certificate (beginning with the word qaraʾa, quriʾa or qaraʾtu) (e.g. TP, 53, n.25; KF, II, 494-498), comp. samāʿ.
maqrūʾah (pl. maqrūʾāt) – work for which an ʻijāzat al-qirāʾahʼ was granted (LM, 78: min maqrūʾātih wa-masmūʿātih).

قرب

qirāb (pl. aqribah) 1. sheath (SK, 104; SA, II, 466) 2. sleeve case (TS, 35-36; AG, 110).
al-qirāb al-mabnī – case or box (built around a form) (TS, 36; AG, 110).
al-qirāb al-makhrūz – sewn case or box (TS, 36; AG, 110).

قرص

qurṣ (pl. aqrāṣ) disc (in decoration) (ZM, 47).
qarṣ, qarīṣ – pressing, putting something into a press (ST, index,19; MP, 63).
qarrāṣ – bookbinder's press; screw press (MB, 103: miqrāḍ (!), elsewhere, qarrāḍ and qarrāṣ; IA, 59).
miftāḥ al-qarrāṣ – press screw (IA, 60).

قرصع

qarṣaʿah – fine, compact writing (KM, IV, sifr 13, 5: qarṣaʿtu al-kitāb qarmaṭtuh; IK, 94).

قرض

miqrāḍ (pl. maqāriḍ) – (pair of) scissors (TS, 10, 21; AG, 107; ST, index, 19; IK, 91-92; IB, 44; QS, II, 417).
qurāḍah – slip (of paper) (UI, 20).

قرطبون

qarṭabūn – square (an instrument) (TS, 18; AG, 107; ST, index, 19; MP, 63; IB, 44).

قرطس

qirṭās, qurṭās, qarṭās (Gr. khartes) (pl. qarāṭis, qarāṭīs) – sheet or roll of papyrus (EI, V, 173-174; EI, VIII, 261; AE, 66-93; WS, 66-76; IW, 82-91), parchment (AE, 108; EI, VIII, 407) or paper (SA, II, 485: al-qirṭās wa-al-ṣaḥīfah wa-humā bi-maʿnan wāḥid wa-huwa kāghad; KK, 50; AE, 98; UD, 11: wa-l-yakun al-qirṭās fī ḥāl al-kitābah ʿalá al-rukbah al-yumná), comp. ṣaḥīfah.
qarāṭīsī – papyrus maker (KF, I, 17).

قرظ

taqrīẓ(ah) (pl. taqārīẓ, taqrīẓāt) – approbation (appreciation) note or statement attached to a manuscript, often in the form of laudatory verses or encomia for the promotion of a newly composed work;

blurb (SA, XIV, 335-340: taqrīḍāt (!); BL; AM, nos. 4, 34, 83, 112, 122, 136, 143, 313), comp. muṭālaʿah.
muqarriẓ – blurb-writer (BL, 182, 186).

قرمد / قرمط

qarmadah, qarmaṭah – fine, compact writing (KM, IV, sifr 13, 5: al-qarmadah wa-al-qarmaṭah diqqat al-kitābah; TP, 55; SK, 120: fa-in jamaʿa al-ḥurūf wa-qāraba al-suṭūr baʿḍahā min baʿḍ qīla qarmaṭahā).

قرمه

qirmah see **siyāq**.

قرن

qurnah – corner (MB, 112: al-qurnah al-yumná, al-qurnah al-yusrá).
(qalam) al-muqtarin – script derived from al-riqāʿ, the main characteristic of which is that it is executed in lines grouped in twos with a large interline spacing between each group (AS, 146; JM, 41).

قسم

miqsam(ah) (lit. 'divider') – tool (most probably a compass) used in leather work (lil-naqsh) (IA, 60, see also UA, 393: not defined).

قص

qaṣṣ, taqṣīṣ – shaving, trimming (ST, index,19; HT, 80).
miqaṣṣ (pl. maqāṣṣ) – (pair of) scissors (UK, 153; IB, 42; DS, 181; MB, 103; IA, 59; IK, 91-92: wa-yuqāl huwa al-miqaṣṣ wa-al-miqṭaʿ wa-al-miqrāḍ wa-al-jalam).

قصب

qaṣab(ah) – reed; reed pen (IK, 86; EI, IV, 682; EI, IV, 471: **baḥrī** – reeds from a seashore and **ṣukhrī** – reeds from a rocky ground; AA, 69).

قصدير

qaṣdīr – tin, tin-based ink (UK, 130; MP, 32).

قصم

qaṣamah, quṣāmah – a shaving (from a reed) (KU, 154).
miqṣamah – plaquette (for nibbing a calamus) (KU, 153), comp. miqaṭṭ.

قضم

qaḍm – syn. qaṭṭ (nibbing) (IK, 86).
qaḍīm(ah) – white hide, leather (IW, 72-74; KM, I, sifr 4, 102; IK, 93).

قط

qaṭṭ(ah) – cutting (of the point of the nib), nibbing; the point itself; cutting (of leather, etc.) breadthwise (KD, II, 701: wa-kull qaṭʿ ʿarḍan qaṭṭ; AA, 109-110; KK, 50; KU, 153; qaṭaṭtu al-qalam qaṭṭan idhā qaṭaʿtu min ṭarafih al-mabrī li-yastawī; SA, II, 462-463; LM, 39: wa-qad ikhtalafa al-kuttāb fī qaṭṭ al-qalam ʿalá khamsat madhāhib).
al-qaṭṭ al-muḥarraf – oblique point of the nib (SA, II, 462; LL, I, 551: muḥarraf – 'reed pen nibbed bliquely; having the right 'tooth' of the nib higher, i.e. longer than the left'; LM, 39: fa-ṭāʾifah taquṭṭ muḥarrafan fī jamīʿ al-aqlām wa-huwa ikhtiyār Yāqūt al-Mustaʿṣimī; LM, 42: fa-ammā al-muḥarraf fa-yakhtaṣṣ bi-al-muḥaqqaq wa-al-rayḥān, wa-al-muḥarraf yuraqqiq al-muntaṣibāt ka-al-alif wa-raʾs al-lām).
al-qaṭṭ al-muṣawwab – 'nibbing in which the exterior of the writing-reed is made to extend beyond the pith, opposed to qāʾim' (LL, II, 1742; MJ, 217).
al-qaṭṭ al-mustawī – even, straight point of the nib (SA, II, 462); see also istiwāʾ.
al-qaṭṭ al-qāʾim – 'nibbing in which the pith and the exterior of the reed are made of equal length, opposite to muṣawwab' (LL, II, 2996; MJ, 217).
quṭāṭah – a shaving (from a reed) (KU, 154).
miqaṭṭ(ah) (pl. miqāṭṭ) – nibbing plaquette (made of wood, ivory,

etc. for nibbing a calamus) (UK, 76; MB, 65; SA, II, 468; ND, 54, 62; SK, 105: maqaṭṭ; AT, 133).

قطع

qaṭʿ (pl. aqṭāʿ) – format (of a sheet or codex) (EI, IV,742; IP, 45; MK, 83: qaṭʿ niṣf al-waraqah, niṣf al-waraqah al-kabīrah, thulth, rubʿ, thumn al-waraqah al-kabīrah, niṣf al-thumn; LS, 70: qaṭʿ al-kāmil, al-kāmil al-kabīr, qaṭʿ al-niṣf, qaṭʿ al-rubʿ, qaṭʿ al-thumn; MM, 131: al-qaṭʿ al-kabīr, al-qaṭʿ al-ṣaghīr), comp. qālib.
qāṭiʿ – artist skilled in the art of paper cutting, decoupage (ER, VI, 475).
al-qāṭiʿ wa-al-maqṭūʿ – 'cutting and the cut', principle of the interlace, ḍirs (AG, 110).
qiṭʿah 1. piece of something (e.g. piece of poetry) 2. piece of calligraphy, calligraph (AC, 42: adhantu bi-waḍʿ al-kitbah li-muḥarrir hādhihi al-qiṭʿah al-mubārakah; NI, 180); piece of calligraphic decoupage (ER, VI, 475).
qiṭʿat al-taʾrīkh see taʾrīkh.
miqṭaʿ (pl. maqāṭiʿ) 1. (pair of) scissors (IK, 91); cutting instrument (DM) 2. instrument for fixing or removing decoration from book covers (TS, 11; AG, 107), comp. mishraṭ.
taqṭīʿ 1. splitting (of a word at the end of the line) (MS, 21) 2. tear(s) (SJ, no.36: fīhā kharm wa-taqṭīʿ; SJ, no.46: awrāq muqaṭṭaʿah) 3. format (of a book) (TL, 85: wa-yanbaghī an yakūn taqṭīʿ al-kitāb murabbaʿan fa-innahu taqṭīʿ Abī Ḥanīfah wa-huwa aysar ʿalá al-rafʿ wa-al-waḍʿ wa-al-muṭālaʿah; WS, 90) 4. also **qaṭʿah** – art of paper cutting, papercut(s); collage, decoupage, filigree work (IP, 144; PA, 60; ER, VI, 475; HD, 120, 127: qāṭiʿ, muqaṭṭaʿ).
muqaṭṭaʿāt – disjoined, mysterious letters at the beginning of 26 chapters of the Qurʾān (EI, VII, 509).

قعد

Dhū al-Qaʿdah (al-sharīfah, al-ḥarām) – the eleventh month of the Muslim calendar, abbrev. ذا / قع (OS, 89).

قفل

qufl (pl. aqfāl, qufūl) – clasp (for fastening bookbindings) (NH, 377).

قفو

qafan, qafā' – spine (back of a codex) (TS, 14, 15; AG, 107; ST, index, 20).
al-qafā' al-muqabbab – round back (TS, 15; AG, 107).
al-qafā' al-musaṭṭaḥ – straight, flat back (TS, 15; AG, 107).
taqfiyah – backing (TS, 15-17; AG, 107).

قلب

qalb, al-qalb al-makānī – transposition (of letters) (MQ, 641), comp. taḥrīf.
qālib, qālab (pl. qawālib) 1. mould (UK, 147, 148) 2. format (of a sheet or book) (TS, 14, 26; LC, 26; ST, index,19; MK, 83: mujalladah ṣaghīrat al-qālib; AD, 145: qālib al-kāmil – in folio, qālib al-niṣf – in quarto; KC, passim: fī al-qālib al-kabīr; fī qālib rubāʿī, fī al-rubāʿī, fī al-rubāʿī lil-ṣighar, fī al-thumānī; HT, lin.123: al-ribāʿ wa-al-thimān; KJ, no.3, 28-29: qālib al-thumn, qālib al-thumn al-ṣaghīr, qālib al-thumn al-kabīr, qālib al-rubʿ al-kabīr), comp. qaṭʿ 3. stamp (for book cover design) (IA, 59; FI, 88; FZ, 214; JL, 93) 4. folder (IB, 43).
miqlab (pl. maqālib) (Turk. mikleb) – envelope flap (MT, 202-203).

قلد

qilādah (pl. qalā'id) – round center-piece (on book covers) (LC, 26).
taqlīd – imitation of the master calligrapher's work by reproducing it from memory (MY, 83; DW, 68).

قلم

qalam (pl. aqlām, qilām) 1. piece of wood (KK, 49; TS, 37) 2. calamus, reed pen; also **qalam al-qaṣab**, as opposed to **qalam al-nuḥās**, i.e. copper pen, see TW, 232; TC, 13 (AA, 69: **al-aqlām al-qaṣabīyah**; IK, 45-87; SA, II, 44-465; KU, 153: al-qalam al-unbūb min al-qaṣab wa-al-qinnā (?); KK, 49-50; AT, 133-134; UK, 71-75; MB, 59-64; EI, IV, 471) 3. script; hand, handwriting; ductus.
qalam al-rīsh see rīsh.
qalam al-shaʿr – brush pen (UK, 144, 356; MP, 38-39; MB, 100).
al-qalam al-Fāsī (al-Rūmī) see khaṭṭ.
al-aqlām al-mabsūṭah (al-yābisah) see mabsūṭ, yābis.

al-aqlām al-murattabah (al-layyinah, al-muqawwarah) see tartīb, layyin, muqawwar.
al-qalam al-mushajjar – cryptographic script, otherwise known as the alphabet of Dioscorides, used in talismans and amulets (IT, I, 335).
al-aqlām al-mawzūnah – 'weighed scripts', an appellation given by Ibn al-Nadīm to some 24 ancient scripts used in the early centuries of Islam (FN, 11-12).
al-aqlām al-sittah – the six main calligraphic scripts based on the principle of proportionality (tanāsub): al-muḥaqqaq, al-rayḥān, al-naskh, al-thuluth, al-tawqīʿ and al-riqāʿ, and used extensively in the main Arab lands, Iran and Turkey throughout the medieval and post-medieval periods (AS, 144).
al-aqlām al-uṣūl – principal scripts from which other scripts are derived (AS, 145).
qulāmah – a shaving (from a reed) (KU, 153; IK, 85).
miqlam(ah) (pl. maqālim) 1. pen box (case) (IK, 85; AI, 160: fī al-sikkīn wa-al-miqaṭṭ ijtimāʿuhumā maʿa al-aqlām fī al-miqlamah; SA, II, 465: sawāʾan kāna min nafs al-dawāh aw ajnabiyan ʿanhā; IA, 63, n.18) 2. compartment for reed pens in the writing case (dawāh) (DS, 179: al-miqlamah wa-hiya al-jūnah allatī takūn fīhā al-aqlām wa-naḥwihā min ālāt al-dawāh; AT, 132).
taqlīm – paring, trimming (a reed), hence **miqlam**, a knife for taqlīm (IK, 85).

قمح

qamḥah – small tool (resembling a wheat grain) (TS, 11; AG, 109).

قمطر

qimṭar(ah) (pl. qamāṭir) – container (made of reeds woven together for storing books); chest (LL, II, 2565). For a list of words used for such containers see SL, II, 43, 49-51.

قنطرة

qanṭarat al-lisān – fore-edge flap (KF, I, 43; KR, 79).

قور

taqwīr – rounding (of letters) (AS, 144), comp. tarṭīb, taqwīs.
al-aqlām al-muqawwarah (al-muraṭṭabah, al-layyinah) – curvilinear scripts such as al-thuluth, al-tawqīʿ and al-riqāʿ (SA, III, 11; AS, 144).

قوس

taqwīs – syn. taqwīr, tadwīr, rounding (of letters, especially descenders) (KH, 37).
muqawwas – sublinear stroke (line) forming an arch of the circle, as in sīn, qāf and nūn (UD, 11; LM, 49: wa-al-muqawwas huwa alladhī lā yumkin an yufraḍ ʿalayhi thalāth nuqaṭ ʿalá samt wāḥid ka-dawr al-nūn wa-al-sīn wa-al-qāf wa-naḥwihā).

قول

qawl (pl. aqwāl) – quotation, passage; in commentaries and glosses usually introduced by qāla or qawluhu, abbrev. ق / قه , as well as fa-qāla, yuqāl, fa-yuqāl, abbrev. فق / يق / فيق respectively (CI, II, xiv; TP, 55; MI, 154, 155, 190; MU, XII, 238).
maqālah 1. short composition, treatise, tract 2. chapter in a composition (such as in the *Fihrist* of Ibn al-Nadīm).

قولب

qawlabah – moulding (of paper) (AB, 90; DM), comp. qālib.

قوم

qāʾimah (pl. qawāʾim) – leaf, folio (folium) (MK, 82, 83, 86; DF, III, 190, 283, 327, 377; KF, I, 222: wa-kaʾannahu matá fasada maʿahu shayʾ abṭala tilka al-qāʾimah; KF, I, 90: yaktub al-mustamlī awwal al-qāʾimah 'majlis amlāhu shaykhunā fulān').
al-qaṭṭ al-qāʾim see qaṭṭ.
mustaqīm – upright, erect; rectilinear (of letters and scripts) (e.g. RN, 22), comp. mabsūṭ.

قوى

taqwiyah (pl. taqāwin) – endpaper (UK, 159: ammā al-ʿIrāqīyūn fa-innahum yalziqūn al-kitāb bi-waraqah minhu bilā hādhihi al-baṭā'in wa-tusammá al-taqāwī; MP, 43).
al-waraq al-muqawwá see waraq.

قيد

qayd (pl. quyūd) – note, statement.
qayd al-tamalluk see tamalluk.
qayd al-farāgh see farāgh.
taqyīd 1. committing something to writing; composition (TE, 17; TP, 51: taqyīd bi-al-kitāb; SD, II, 430: 'ce qu'on note, ce qu'on couche par écrit'), comp. tadwīn 2. copying, transcription (TE, 17) 3. tying, binding; sewing endbands (headbands) (MB, 113; IA, 62) 4. diacritical pointing (of letters) (BA, III, 371: naqaṭtu al-kitāb wa-aʿjamtuhu wa-shakaltuhu wa-qayyadtuh; IK, 87: **muqayyadah** – pointed; LL, II, 2576) 5. (pl. taqāyīd, taqyīdāt) – marginal note, gloss (LC, 27).
muqayyid 1. author 2. glossator (AM, no.187).

****

ك

al-kāf al-mashkūlah (al-mashqūqah) see shakl and shaqq.

كازن

kāzan – mallet (UK, 153; IB, 43).

كاغد

kāghad, kāghid, kāghadh (pl. kawāghid, kawāghīd, kughūd, AJ, 136), **kāghiṭ, kāghīṭ** (ST, passim) (pl. kawāghīṭ, WS, 77) – paper (EI, IV, 419-420; AE, 98-105; WS, 77-85), comp. waraq.
al-kāghad al-Islāmī, al-Rūmī, al-Ṭalḥī, etc. see waraq.
kāghidah – sheet, leaf (of paper) (AJ, 136).

kaghghād, kāghidī, kawāghidī – paper maker (AJ, 136; WS, 85-86).
ṭayy al-khāghad see ṭayy.
kāghadkhānah – paper mill (HN, 374).

كب

kubbah (pl. kubab) – ball (of fibre, in papermaking) (OM).
munkabb – inclined, downward sloping curved stroke (from right to left or vice versa, as in the beginning of wāw) (UD, 11; LM, 49), comp. munḥanin.

كبس

mikbas, makbas – bookbinder's press (QS, II, 416; SD, II, 440; UA, 393).
takbīs – pressing (QS, II, 416).

كبيكج

kabīkaj 1. Ranunculus asiaticus, Asiatic crowfoot (bot.) 2. talismanic word (used as an invocation against worms and insects, known in the Maghreb as kaykataj, q.v.) (US, 49-53; TS, 40; AG,107; KL, 43: iḥbas yā kabīkaj al-araḍah yā ḥafīẓ yā Allāh yā Allāh yā Allāh; CM, 88: yā kabīkaj yā kabīkaj yā kabīkaj huwa al-ḥāfiẓ huwa huwa faqaṭ; CM, 169).

كتب

katb, kitbah (MH, 91; TH, 21: naskh al-kitāb: TH, 27), **kitāb, kitābah** – writing, composition; copying, transcription.
kitbah – the word 'kataba' or 'katabahu/hā' (abbrev. كه / ك , TE, 16) used as part of the signature or autograph of the writer (copyist, calligrapher) (HI, 90, 91: ajāza lahu bi-al-kitbah; NI, 183: al-ijāzah bi-al-kitbah; wa-ajaztu lahu an yaktub fī kitābatih al-kitbah; CT, 45: 'hence katabah, Turkish **ketebehü**, becomes a term equivalent to colophon').
kātib (pl. kuttāb, katabah) 1. secretary, amanuensis (EI, IV, 554-760); scribe, scrivener 2. fully-fledged (licensed) calligrapher (NI, 180), comp. muḥarrir.

kitāb – writing; piece of writing; letter, document; book, booklet; chapter in a book (SL, I, 23; IK, 95: wa-yuqāl lil-kitāb ayḍan mawaddah, wa-majallah wa-waḥy; EI, V, 207-208).
kitābkhānah, kutubkhānah – library.
asfal (sufl) al-kitāb 1. tail (of a book or document) 2. spine (of a codex) (HT, lin.115).
aʿlá (ʿulw) al-kitāb – head (of a book or document).
al-kitāb al-awwal – ʿUthmanic canon, codex (MA, IV, 86); archetype.
al-kitāb al-mukarras see kurrās.
al-kitābah al-mansūbah – see khaṭṭ.
kutubī – bookseller (KF, I, 165, 166: sūq al-kutubīyīn; QS, II, 383-384).
maktab – place designated for writing, copying (KK, 53; KD, II, 705; NH, 388: **mukattab**).
maktabah – library (EI, VI, 197-200).
maktūb (pl. maktūbāt) – piece of calligraphy, calligraph (DP, 53).
muktib, mukattib (e.g. Ibn al-Ṣāʾigh al-Mukattib) – teacher of calligraphy; master calligrapher (KK, 51; KM, IV, sifr 13, 4; KD, II, 705).
istiktāb – copying on request (for a patron) (KM, IV, sifr 13, 4: idhā amartuhu an yaktub laka aw ittakhadhtuhu kātiban; KK, 51; OS, 88).

كثر

kathīrāʾ – tragacanth, paste obtained from tragacanth (DM).
miktharah – receptacle (for paste) (DD, I, 391: ka-al-minshāh; UA, 393).

كحل

kuḥl – antimony; kohl.
akḥal – dark-blue ink (or black with bluish luster) (DG, 187).
mikḥalah (pl. makāḥil), **mukḥul** – kohl container (UA, 393; IR, 230).
mikḥāl see mirwad.
takḥīl 1. pointing (of a wall) (FT, 414) 2. outlining, outline (of letters) (DH, no.383: ʿiddat khatamāt bi-khaṭṭihimā maktūbah bi-al-dhahab al-mukaḥḥal bi-al-lāzuward); outlining, outline (of designs on book covers) (IB, 68), comp. misṭarat al-takḥīl 3. fine (thin) lines (in

writing) (UK, 142: al-diqqah fī rasm al-ḥurūf) 4. small, pallet-like tool (used in the interlace) (TS, 12, 33; AG, 110: takḥīl al-ḍirs, takḥīl al-ṭawīl).

كحلبون

kaḥlibūn – screw press (UK, 154; IB, 42).

كذا

kadhā – thus, sic, abbrev. ک (MI, 161; TN, 52: wa-tūḍaʿ k fī baʿḍ al-hawāmish ishāratan ilá annahu 'kadhā fī al-aṣl'); for the use of 'ṣawābuhu kadhā' and 'laʿallahu kadhā' see TP, 57).
takdhīyah – the kadhā-statement (MI, 48, 162).

كر

tikrār, **mukarrar** (or **al-ḥarf al-mukarrar**), **takarrur** – dittographic error, dittography (e.g. TM, 184).

كرس

kurrās(ah) (Syr.) (pl. karārīs) 1. also **al-kitāb al-mukarras** – codex form of a book (AB, 131; TS, 14; AG, 107) 2. quire (gathering), abbrev. ک / ك (KM, IV, sifr 13, 8: summiyat bi-dhālika li-takarrusihā ay inḍimām baʿḍihā ilá baʿḍ; TS, passim; CI, II, x; SK, 321: al-kurrāsah li-annahā ṭabaqah ʿalá ṭabaqah; SL, II, 60).
takrīs – collation (of quires) (HT, lin.92).
kursī – book cradle, reading stand (MD, 132), comp. raḥl.
kursī al-ḥajar – support (for a stone slab) (IA, 60).

كرسف

kursuf(ah) – tow (wad of raw cotton or wool used in an inkwell) (KK, 48; IK, 84; AA, 100; SA, II, 468-471; KU, 154: wa-huwa jawf al-quṭn wa-yuqāl lahā al-ʿuṭbah; KD, II, 700).

كرش

kirsh (pl. kurūsh), **takrīsh** – letter-head or serif in the shape of a barb or dot (blob) (KJ, no.1, 39, 41), comp. tarwīs.

كرم

karīm, mukarram – honorific (epithet) of muṣḥaf, Qur'ān, khatmah.
takrīm – the formula of benediction 'karrama Allāh wajhahu' (used after the name of the Imām ʿAlī ibn Abī Ṭālib).
al-mukarram – epithet of the months of Shawwāl and Shaʿbān (q.v.).

كرة

kurah – wooden ball (for burnishing paper) (NH, 363).

كسر

miksar (pl. makāsir) – fold (in a leaf of paper) (OM).
al-ta'rīkh bi-al-kusūr see ta'rīkh.

كشد

kashīdah – long line or stroke (like a long fatḥah) used to embellish the script (MN, 128).

كشط

kashṭ – erasure (by means of a pen knife or scraper) (MM, 137; TP, 58); syn. of bashr (LF, 79; IR, 237: bi-al-ṣadr lā bi-al-sinn kashṭ fī al-waraq).
mikshaṭ, sikkīn al-kashṭ – scraper, knife (for making erasures) (IR, 274; NH, 389; DD, I, 391).

كشكول

kashkūl – commonplace book, comp. tadhkirah, kunnāsh.

كعب

kaʿb (pl. kuʿūb) – spine (back of a codex) (MB, passim; IA, 61; JL, 84, 90).
al-kaʿb al-muhallal – round back (MB, 109).
al-kaʿb al-murabbaʿ – straight, flat back (MB, 109).

كف

kaff(ah), kaff al-waraq – quire (Fr. main de papier), usually 25 sheets (PT, 39; AJ, 145; AB, 92; WS, 92, 94), comp. dast, rizmah.

كفت

takfīt – inlaying, inlay (SA, II, 442; FT, 406).

كلب

kallābah, kullābah – (pair of) pincers, tongs (MB, 109; DM).

كندة

kindah – sexagonal element (in a Mamluk book cover design) (JN, 95, 97; DE, 977; KR, 82).

كنش

kunnāsh(ah) (pl. kanānīsh) – 1. commonplace book (LC, 25; HB, 233), comp. tadhkirah, kashkūl 2. syn. of barnāmaj or fahrasah (in the Maghreb).

كنى / كنو

kunyah (pl. kunan) – patronymic, consisting of abū or umm followed by the name of the son/daughter (EI, V, 395-396).
mukannan – named by (known by) his/her kunyah.
al-taʾrīkh al-kināʾī see taʾrīkh.

كوفي

(al-khaṭṭ) al-Kūfī 1. originally and properly speaking, an early script asscociated with the scribal circles of Kūfah (FN, 8: fa-awwal al-khuṭūṭ al-ʿArabīyah al-khaṭṭ al-Makkī wa-baʿdahu al-Madanī thumma al-Baṣrī thumma al-Kūfī) 2. generic name used loosely for a host of early Arabic 'non-proportioned scripts' currently distinguished as the 'Ḥijāzī scripts', 'Early Abbasid scripts', 'New Abbasid style' and the 'Abbasid bookhand' (see e.g. AV, 27ff; MV, 363; FN, 8-9, 11-13; OD), comp. Ḥijāzī.

كيكتج

kaykataj – talismanic word (used in the Maghreb as an invocation against worms and insects) (TS, 40; AG, 107; US, 49), comp. kabīkaj.

****

ل

لازورد

lāzuward, lāzaward – lapis lazuli, ultramarine; azure ink, paint (UK, 114, 119; MP, 27, 29; SA, II, 478).

لألأ

(qalam) al-luʾluʾī – script akin to al-thuluth al-khafīf (i.e. probably al-tawqīʿ) in which vertical and flat strokes are less than five dots in length (AS, 145; JM, 85).

لبس

talbīs – sizing (of paper) (OH, 139).

لحق

laḥaq (pl. alḥāq, liḥāq), **ilḥāq**, **mulḥaq** – omission; insertion (TP,

58; IK, 94: idhā naqaṣa min al-kitābah shay' fa-alḥaqahu bayna al-suṭūr aw fī ʿurḍ al-kitāb wa-huwa al-laḥaq; TM, 185; LC, 24; JA, I, 279).

لحم

laḥm Sulaymān – screw press (UK, 154; IB, 42).

لزق

lizāq – paste, adhesive (KD, II, 703), comp. liṣāq.

لزم

lazm – pressing (TS,14).
milzam(ah) (pl. malāzim) 1. bookbinder's press (UK, 155; TS, 10, 11, 14, 15; AG, 107; SA, II, 481) 2. large paper clip (made of copper or other metal to hold the head of a leaf or roll or quire in place while copying) (AT, 133; SA, II, 481; IR, 230, n.24; DD, I, 390) 3. copyist's book support; book cradle (TW,169; WA, 12: ʿūd al-nasākhah or maḥmal min khashab yaftaḥ wa-yaṭwī fa-yuḍaʿ ʿalayhi a-kitāb al-muntasakh minhu ḥattá yartafiʿ ʿan al-arḍ wa-yastanid jānibāhu ilá lawḥatay al-malzam).
malzamah (pl. malāzim) 1. quire (often encountered in Maghrebi lithographed books, where each gathering is numbered separately), abbrev. م (LC, 25; LE, 137) 2. sheet, leaf (of paper) (AD, 157; LE, 137) 3. large size bifolio (bifolium) (TC, 25).

لسن

lisān (pl. alsinah) – envelope flap (ST, index, 20; ST, 13; HT, lin.109, 119; LC, 25; JL, 90; MM, 132).
qanṭarat al-lisān see qanṭarah.

لشى

mutalāshin – worn, damaged (TW, 55: fī sifr mutalāshin).

لصق

liṣāq (pl. alṣiqah) – paste, adhesive (SA, II, 480; SD, II, 530), comp. lizāq.

لعن

laʿnah – curse, malediction; the formula of malediction 'laʿanahu Allāh' or 'laʿnat Allāh ʿalayhi' , abbrev. لعـ or ع لله (MI, 145, 167; RA, 26).

لف

laffah, lifāfah (pl. lafāʾif) – roll (of parchment or paper) (AB, 131; DM).
milaff 1. spool (DS, 181; DD, I, 391; IR, 230) 2. wrapper (DM).

لفح

lafḥ – tooling, stamping (HT, lin.166).

لفق

mulaffaq, al-nuskhah al-mulaffaqah – made-up copy (KC, passim).

لقب

laqab (pl. alqāb) – nickname; honorific title (EI, V, 618-631).
mulaqqab bi – known by (referred to) his/her laqab.

لقط

milqaṭ, milqāṭ (pl. malāqīṭ) 1. (pair of) tongs, pincers, tweezers (MB, 109) 2. implement for collecting shavings (small fragments) after erasure (UA, 393: limā shāna al-qalam; DD, I, 391: yalquṭ baqāyā mā yaẓhar bi-al-waraq min athar al-kashṭ).

لقم

talqīm – inlaying, inlay (FT, 406).

لقى

mustalqin – line, stroke sloping (descending) from right to left and vice versa (as in the beginning of kāf, ṣād, yāʾ and rāʾ) (UD, 11; LM, 49).

لك

lak, lakk (or lāk, DG, 194) 1. lac, crimson red pigment or ink (MS, 5: wa-al-lak lil-ḍammāt wa-al-fatḥāt wa-al-kasrāt; MB, 84-86) 2. lacquer, varnish (AB, 140).

لمع

lammāʿ – glossy, glazed, burnished (e.g. al-tadhhīb al-lammāʿ, q.v.).

لمق

lamq – elegant writing, copying (TE, 16), comp. namq.

لملم

lamlīmah – small tool (resembling an elephant's tusk ?) (TS, 11; AG, 109).

لوح

lawḥ(ah) (pl. alwāḥ, lawḥāt) 1. tablet (of any hard-surfaced material) (SL, II, 58-59) 2. wooden board (TS, 11, 24; HT, lin.123, 124) 3. wooden tablet (for burnishing gold or paper) (UK, 142-143; MB, 99; OM) 4. pasteboard (ST, 5) 5. panel (in decoration); illuminated piece (such as frontispiece, head- or tailpiece) (LC, 25; MS, 29, 31) 6. (Turk. levha) large panel (of calligraphy, usually framed).
lawḥ al-ṣadārah – frontispiece, headpiece (FT, 402).
lawḥ al-taṣlīb – see taṣlīb.
lawwāḥ – master decorator, illuminator (HD, 125).
talwīḥ – marginal note, gloss (DM).
al-maṣāḥif al-mulawwaḥah see muṣḥaf.

لوز

lawzah 1. oval figure 2. almond-shaped tool or stamp (UK, 156; IB, 44; TS, 11, 31; AG, 109; MB, 105; IA, 59, 60: lawzah wa-niṣf, ra'ʾs al-lawzah; see also nuqṭah) 3. central medallion (on a book cover), mandorla 4. lozenge-shaped element (in a Mamluk book cover design), also known as sarwah (q.v.).
talwīz – rounding ('giving an almond shape to') of the initial stroke of such letters as ṣād, ṭāʾ and ḥāʾ (KH, 38).

لوق

milwāq (pl. malāwiq) – spatula, stirrer (for mixing ink) (SA, II, 478; AT, 133; IR, 230; IB, 45; MJ, 208).

لون

lawn (pl. alwān) – colour; pigment, tint (EI, V, 698-707; AI, 148; JA, I, 250; NW, 10: tarkīb al-alwān).
talwīn 1. polychrome illumination (WA, 11; LC, 27) 2. tinting (of paper).

ليط

līṭ(ah) – bark (skin) of the reed (BA, III, 370: qishr al-qaṣab; IK, 86; see also the quotation under shaḥm).
talyīṭ 1. shaving off the bark of the reed (IK, 86: layyaṭtu min al-qalam līṭah qashartuhu) 2. placing a līṭah in the slit of the nib to increase the intake of ink (KD, II, 702; BA, III, 370).

ليف

līf al-shajar – bast fibres, paper pulp (OM).

ليق

līqah (pl. liyaq) 1. also **milāq** (UA, 393) tow (wad, tuft of unspun silk, wool or cotton used in an inkwell) (ST, index, 20; MP, 13, n. 55, 26-29; IK, 84; MJ, 203) 2. colour, tint (AD, 160) 3. coloured ink (SA, II, 477-478; UK, 111-119; MB, 79-84; MP, 26-29; AT, 133).

malīq (pl. amliqah) 1. also **milāqah** (BA, III, 370) – compartment for ink (KD, II, 700: al-nuqrah allatī yujʿal fīhā al-midād wa-al-ṣūf; AT, 133), comp. jūnah. 2. tow (of cotton or wool) (BA, III, 370).

لين

layyin – curvilinear (of a letter or script) (AS, 144; KH, 38: al-khaṭṭ al-layyin huwa alladhī fīhi al-tadwīr).
al-aqlām al-layyinah – curvilinear scripts, such as al-thuluth, al-tawqīʿ and al-riqāʿ, comp. muraṭṭab, muqawwar.

****

م

متن

matn (pl. mutūn) 1. content (text) of a ḥadīth (as distinguished from the chain of transmitters who handed it down) (SL, II, 1; EI, VI, 843) 2. main body of the text (as opposed to margins); text-column (MU, V, 111: al-matn al-ṭarīqah al-mumtaddah min yamīn al-ṣulb wa-shamālih; DF, V, 456: al-maktūbah fī matn al-kitāb ʿadā al-ḥāshiyah; MH, 89: yaḍbiṭuhā fī matn al-kitāb thumma yaktubuhā qubālata dhālik fī al-ḥāshiyah; AD, 161) 3. original (main) text (as opposed to a commentary, sharḥ or gloss, ḥāshiyah), abbrev. م (VA, no. 2828; MM, 139: wa-lahu fī kitābat sharḥ mamzūj bi-al-matn an yumayyiz al-matn bi-kitābatih bi-al-ḥumrah; EI, VI, 843) 4. central panel (on a book cover) as opposed to the border (FZ, 214; MD, 109; LC, 25).
(qalam) al-matn, also known as **faḍḍāḥ al-naskh**, **al-naskh al-faḍḍāḥ** and **al-waḍḍāḥ** – larger version of al-naskh (NA, IX, 222: wa-qalam al-naskh yatafarraʿu ʿanhu qalam al-matn wa-huwa ghalīẓuh wa-qalam al-ḥawāshī wa-huwa khafīfuh; AS, 146; JM, 64-66).
ḥard al-matn (HN, 251-252) or **jard** (?) **al-matn** – colophon (LC, 24; TP, 53).
mātin – author of the original composition, matn (as opposed to a commentator, shāriḥ) (JN, 1; SD, II, 568).

مثل

mithāl (pl. amthilah) – copy, transcript, apograph (CD, IV, pl.115: mithāl al-samāʿ), comp. ṣūrah.

مجمج

majmajah – scribbling (KM, IV, sifr 13, 7: takhlīṭ al-kitāb wa-ifsāduhu bi-al-qalam; BA, III, 371).

محر

tamḥīr – polishing (burnishing) with an oyster shell, **maḥārah** (q.v.) (KF, I, 30: fī ṣināʿat tajhīz al-raqq wa-ṣaqlih wa-tamḥīrih wa-ṣabghih).

محط

tamḥīṭ 1. process of softening leather (making it flexible, supple) (by rubbing it with a piece of wood) (ST, index, 21; KR, 79: dalk) 2. blind tooling, hence **mumaḥḥaṭ** – blind tooled (FI, 86; JL, 90), comp. ḥaṭṭ.
tamḥīṭ bi-al-dhahab – gold tooling (FI, 89).

محو

maḥw – ink removal; erasure, obliteration (by means of a cloth, khirqah, or licking) (TP, 58; UK, 138-140; MP, 36-37).
al-waraq al-māḥī see waraq.

مد / مط

madd, istimdād, maṭṭ, tamṭīṭ – elongation (of letters) (KU, 121-122; TP, 55; KH, 38; MJ, 238).
midād (pl. amiddah) – soot ink; ink (in general) (SK, 320: summiya al-midād midādan li-annahu yamudd al-qalam; SA, II, 471-477; UK, 79-90, MB, 67-71; MP, 13, n.52, 15-18; AT, 134-135; AE, 127-131; EI, VI, 1031), comp. ḥibr.
istimdād – the manner of dipping the pen in the inkwell (SA, III, 38; MJ, 216).

مدن

al-Madīnah (al-munawwarah), also known as **Madīnat al-Nabī** – Medina.
Madīnat al-Salām – Baghdad (DM).
(al-khaṭṭ) al-Madanī see Ḥijāzī and Kūfī.

مدى

mudyah (madyah, midyah) (pl. mudan, midan) – knife, pen knife (SA, II, 465-467; SK, 103-104; UA, 393; IR, 230, 231), comp. sikkīn.

مر

marrah – spatula (for mixing paper pulp) (OM).

مرض

tamrīḍ see ḍabbah, taḍbīb.

مزج

al-sharḥ al-mazjī (al-mamzūj) see sharḥ.

مسح

masḥ – rubbing, wiping (MB, 110, 114).
misḥ 1. sword (for rubbing leather) (UK, 166; IA, 60: misann al-misḥ) 2. coarse haircloth, sackcloth (DG, 202).
mimsaḥah – pen wiper (IR, 230; SA, II, 481-482; AT, 133; DD, I, 391).

مشألة

mashʾalah – the formula of submission to the will of God 'mā shāʾa Allāh' (MG, I, 484), comp. istithnāʾ.

مشط

misht, musht – comb (IA, 60; IR, 230).

مشق

mashq 1. elongation (of letters) (JA, I, 262: al-mashq huwa madd al-ḥurūf fī al-kitābah; TM, 194; SK, 116: wa-yastaḥsinūn al-mashq fī al-sīn wa-al-shīn illā fī awākhir al-kalām; SA, III, 146: al-jamʿ wa-al-mashq; SK, 116-117; AA, 55) 2. copying, transcription (TE, 16) 3. hasty, inelegant hand; scribbling (MM, 133: wa-al-mashq fa-huwa surʿat al-kitābah maʿa baʿtharat al-ḥurūf; MH, 89: sharr al-kitābah al-mashq; AA, 123: mashaqa ... idhā asraʿa al-kitābah; TP, 55; TE, 16) 4. calligraphic exercise; copying from a model (TE, 16; MY, 83) 5. calligraphic model (AD, 164) 6. elegant, calligraphic hand (CM, 151).
(khaṭṭ) al-mashq – one of the ancient scripts (?) used originally by the scribes in the city of al-Anbār and characterized as light, having a slanted alif and, according to some opinions, unsuitable for the copying of the Qurʾān (FN, 9, 10: fa-ammā al-warrāqūn alladīna yaktubūn al-maṣāḥif bi-al-khaṭṭ al-muḥaqqaq wa-al-mashq...; IK, 89: al-mashq huwa al-khaṭṭ fīhi al-khiffah; KK, 48; KT, 134: ʿan Ibn Sīrīn annahu kariha an tuktab al-maṣāḥif mashqan...li-anna fīhi naqṣ, a lā tará al-alif kayfa yugharriquhā yanbaghī an turadd; see also AV, 12: 'Mashq, for example, is a technique that can be applied to any kind of script and is not an independent style of its own.').
mashqah 1. fine elongation, fine elongated stroke (SK, 320: al-mashqah al-maddah al-daqīqah wa-al-khaṭṭ al-mamshūq huwa al-mamdūd) 2. tail of the letter mīm (LM, 66: illā anna mashqatahu fī al-naskh qaṣīrah).
māshiq – calligrapher (NI, 183).
mushāq ḥarīr – silk tow (wad) (DD, I, 389), comp. līqah.

مضى

imḍāʾ 1. signing; signature, autograph (DM) 2. signed attestation/reading statement (OT, 46: lammā ʿuriḍa hādhā al-kitāb ilayya naẓartu wa-taʾammaltu bi-mā yaḥwīhi fa-wajadtuhu muṭābiqan lil-ṣawāb fa-ḥakamtu bi-ṣiḥḥatih wa-amḍaytuhu nammaqahu... Aḥmad al-Qāḍī bi-madīnat Nīkdah), comp. naẓar 3. execution statement (containing the calligrapher's name) (MN, 8).

مغرة

maghrah – ochre pigment (FT, 411).
al-maghrah al-ʿIrāqīyah – reddish brown ink (SA, II, 478).

مكة

Makkah (al-mukarramah, al-musharrafah, al-muʿaẓẓamah) – Mecca.
(al-khaṭṭ) al-Makkī see Ḥijāzī and Kūfī.

ملس

mimlasah 1. plane-like instrument (TS, 11; AG, 107) 2. also **malasah** – burnisher, polisher (NH, 390; TS, 11, 31; AG, 107).

ملك

milk – ownership (OS, 88; EI, VII, 60-61).
milkīyah, tamlīk, tamalluk – ownership note or statement (such as ex-libris, ex-dono, ex-library, etc.), also referred to as **qayd al-tamalluk** (OS, 88; LC, 25; LC, 27). For various expressions used in ownership statements see OS.

ملو

imlāʾ (pl. amālin) 1. dictation (AI, passim; WS, 10-13; KF, I, 85-94) 2. work (known as al-amālī) produced through dictation.
mumlin – dictation master (AI, passim; SL, II, 48).
istimlāʾ – repetition of a dictation by a specially appointed famulus; writing down (of a dictated text) (EI,VII, 725-726).
mustamlin – tradition transmitter's clerk; famulus (AI, passim; EI, VII, 725-726; GA, 287: Vermittler – muballigh, mulqī, muktib).

مهر

muhr – seal, signet, stamp (EI, VII, 472-473), comp. khātam.
tamhīr – sealing, stamping (EI, VII, 472-473).

مهرق

muhraq (pl. mahāriq) 1. glazed cloth, silk (used as a writing surface) (IW, 79-82; KM, IV, sifr 13, 8-9; AE, 105-106; WS, 50-52) 2. sheet, leaf (of any writing material) (KD, II, 704: wa-al-qirṭās wa-al-ṣaḥīfah wa-al-sifr wa-al-muhraq sawāʾ) 3. sheet, leaf (of paper) (SA, II, 472, 482: al-muhraq wa-huwa al-qirṭās).

موزة

mawzah – burnisher, polisher (IA, 60, 63).

موس

mūsá (pl. mawāsin, amwās) – pen knife; trimmer (TW, 169: li-bary qalam al-qaṣab wa-iṣlāḥ al-kitābah; IA, 60: **maws**; UD, 16: al-maws al-Shīrāzī).

موه

māʾ al-dhahab – gold ink (MU, V, 226; LC, 25).
māʾ al-ward – rose water (MP, 64).
mimwah, māwardīyah – water container (for diluting ink) (SA, II, 482; NH, 390; DD, I, 390: mimwah ālah ...wa-tāratan takūn min al-nuḥās wa-min al-ḥalazūn wa-ghayrih), comp. misqāh.
tamwīh 1. inlaying (SA, II, 442) 2. coating; gilt (SD).
tamwīh bi-al-ṭalāʾ (al-dhahab) – gilt (FT, 403).

ميل

imālat al-qalam – tilting of the pen; slanting (of the line, script) (UD, 12; SA, II, 45), hence **māʾil** – inclining, tilting (of a script).

****

ن

نبق

nabq, tanbīq – elegant writing, copying (TE, 16; KM, IV, sifr 13, 5: nabaqtu al-kitāb wa-nabbaqtuhu saṭṭartuhu wa-katabtuh).

نبه

tanbīh – note, remark (in the body of a composition); nota bene, marginal annotation (DM; TH, 28: tanbīh ʿalá al-ghalaṭ).

نثر

(qalam) al-manthūr – naskh or riqāʿ/naskh-based script (characterised by large spaces between words) (AS, 146; JM, 40).

نجذ

nawājidh (sg. nājidh) – letters such as bāʾ and tāʾ (TU, 36).

نجم

minjam – mallet (ST, index, 21; IB, 43: **mījamah**).

نحت

naḥt 1. paring, trimming (of a reed) (IR, 232; UD, 9: wa-al-naḥt naḥtān naḥt baṭnih wa-naḥt jawānibih) 2. abbreviation of the type called contraction in which two or three words are fused into one portmanteau word, e.g. basmalah, ḥamdalah, etc. (MG, I, 482).

نحس

nuḥās – copper, copper-based ink (UK, 133-134; MP, 35).

نخب

nakhb, intikhāb, muntakhab 1. selected passage 2. (pl. intikhābāt, muntakhabāt) – anthology (EA, I, 94-95).
muntakhib – compiler, selector (DF, II, 384).

نخل

munkhul – sieve (IR, 230; DM).

نرجسة

narjasah – y-shaped nonagonal or decagonal element (in a Mamluk book cover design) (JL, 95, 97; KR, 82).

نسب

nasab (pl. ansāb) – lineage, genealogy, pedigree (EI, VII, 967-968).
nisbah (pl. nisab) – descriptive adjective (adjective of relation) indicating an individual's birthplace, tribe, religious sect or school, etc. ending in ى – (EI, VIII, 53-56).
al-khaṭṭ (al-kitābah) al-mansūb(ah) see khaṭṭ.
munāsabah – collation (of quires) (ST, index, 21).

نستعليق

(khaṭṭ) al-nastaʿlīq – hybrid of **naskh** and **taʿlīq** (thus properly known as **naskh-i taʿlīq**, **naskh-taʿlīq**), a script which emerged in the 8/14th century in Persia and later was used extensively in Turkey and India (EI, IV, 1124 (in Persia), 1126 (in Turkey), 1127 (in Muslim India); ER, IV, 696-699). In Turkey this script was often (but incorrectly) known under the name of **taʿlīq**.

نسخ

naskh 1. also **naskhah, tansīkh, nasākhah, intisākh, istinsākh** – copying, transcription (TE, 17; KM, IV, sifr 13,5; KK, 57) 2. **(qalam) al-naskh** – book hand, par excellence, which according to the Mamluk tradition, belonged to the muḥaqqaq family of scripts. The Mamluk naskh was written sans serif, tarwīs, while the Ottoman naskh and the Persian naskh of the 10/16th century and later often featured the serif on the letter lām of the definite article. The serif of this letter in the Ottoman naskh was often right-sloping, while the serif in the Persian naskh was mostly left-sloping (AS, 146; LM, 47: wa-al-naskh lil-ḥadīth wa-al-tafsīr wa-naḥwihimā; LM, 44: al-naskh iʿrābuhu aqall min al-rayḥān wa-fīhi taʿlīq wa-ṭams fa-qaruba min al-riqāʿ; LM, 45: wa-min al-rayḥān al-naskh; LM, 54: ammā qalam al-naskh wa-al-waḍḍāḥ wa-al-ḥawāshī wa-al-manthūr fa-asqiṭ minqārah; KL, no.12: **rafīʿ al-naskh**, **al-naskh al-muʿtād**; CA, 36, 47; EI, IV, 1123- in Persia, 1125- in Turkey, 1127- in Muslim India).

al-naskh al-faḍḍāḥ see matn.

al-naskh al-sādah – regular naskh hand (HI, 89).

al-naskh al-waḍḍāḥ see matn.

naskhī 1. properly 'pertaining to naskh'; commonly, but erroneously, used as a synomym of **al-naskh** proper (NC, 128, n.12) 2. **naskh**-based (related) hand of an idiosyncratic (informal, personal) nature (CI, I, xiv).

nuskhah (pl. nusakh) 1. transcript, copy (EI, VIII, 149) 2. version, recension (MU, XVI, 106: wa-kitāb 'al-Bayān wa-al-tabyīn' nuskhatān ūlá wa-thāniyah wa-al-thāniyah aṣaḥḥ wa-ajwad) 3. variant reading (varia lectio), abbrev. خه / نخـ / نخ / ن / خـ / خ (AR, 37; AK, 352; MI, 182; LE, 138; CI, I, xv; CM, 123, 141; MZ, II, 412: خ ل – nuskhah-aṣl, comp. badal) 4. list, catalogue (AD,171).

al-nuskhah al-aṣl (al-nuskhah al-muʿtamadah, CD, IV, pl.131: balagha qirāʾatan wa-muqābalatan wa-taṣḥīḥan ʿalá nuskhah muʿtamadah) – exemplar; archetype (LC, 26).

al-nuskhah al-dustūr see dustūr.

al-nuskhah al-farʿ see farʿ.

al-nuskhah al-mufakkakah see mafkūk, mufakkak.

al-nuskhah al-mulaffaqah see mulaffaq.

al-nuskhah (al-kutub, al-makhṭūṭāt) al-safarīyah – 'pocket book' (small size manuscript produced for travelers) (TC, 26).

al-nuskhah al-umm – holograph; archetype (LC, 26).

al-nuskhah al-waḥīdah (**al-farīdah**) – single surviving copy, unicum.

nāsikh (pl. nussākh), **nassākh** (pl. nassākhah), **muntasikh** – copyist, scribe (TE, 17; WB, 47).

mansūkh, muntasakh – manuscript (AK, 348; MA, 16; TW, passim).

ʿūd al-nasākhah see ʿūd.

نسق

nasaq, tansīq – text arrangement; layout (mise en page) (FK, I, no. 1014/2: faragha min taḥrīrih ʿalá hādhā al-nasaq).

نشأ

inshāʾ – construction, style or composition, e.g. of letters, documents or state papers; letter-writing, epistolography (EI, III, 1241-1244).
munshiʾ 1. secretary, amanuensis (EI, VII, 580), comp. kātib 2. author (usually referring to poetry) (SS, 67).

نشر

nashr, **tanshīr**, **tawshīr** – sprinkling of a freshly copied text with sawdust, nushārah.
nushārah (also **ushārah, wushārah**) – sawdust (for drying ink) (JA, I, 278; IK, 94; AI, 173; TD, I, 134, 136).
minshar, minshār (pl. manāshīr) – saw (for work with wooden boards) (TS, 11, 18; AG, 107; IA, 60: minsharah kabīrah, minsharah ṣaghīrah; UA, 393: for cutting reeds).
minsharīyah – chevron (FT, 395).
raqq manshūr see raqq.

نشف

nashshāf – blotting paper (DM).
minshafah – blotter (TD, I, 136).

نشى

nashan – wheat starch, starch paste (TS, 12, 13; ST, index, 21; IB, 50; MB, 106; IA, 60; SA, II, 480: al-nashā al-muttakhadhah min al-burr aw al-kathīrāʾ); starch paste (made of sorghum, dhurah) (OM).
tanshiyah – pasting (ST, index, 21).
minshāh – paste-receptacle; compartment for paste (in a writing case) (SA, II, 480; AT, 133; OM; DD, I, 390; IR, 230: **minshaʾah**).

نصب

naṣb 1. straight line, stroke; the letter alif (IR, 239: al-madd ka-al-naṣb wa-ka-al-naṣbayn, 240, 241, 249, 269: al-lām naṣb thumma bāʾ al-khaṭṭ) 2. pallet-like tool (HT, lin.133, 137).
niṣāb 1. handle (SK, 103: niṣāb al-sikkīn; SA, II, 466; IK, 90) 2. folder (instrument used for folding sheets of paper when binding) (UK, 156; IB, 43, 47; MB, 103; IA, 59) 3. also **niṣāb al-dalk** – burnisher (IA, 59).
muntaṣib – ascender, up-stroke (SA, III, 101; UD, 11; LM, 49: fa-al-muntaṣib huwa alladhī yusāmit qāmat al-kātib).

نصل

tanṣīl – elongation (of letters) (SA, III, 140: wa-huwa mawāqiʿ al-maddāt al-mustaḥsanah min al-ḥurūf al-muttaṣilah).

نطق

minṭaqah (pl. manāṭiq) – decorative element, e.g. medallion, panel and the like (in illumination and book cover design) (FI, 88; FZ, 217, 218; JL, 93; ZM, 43).

نظر

naẓar – study note, reading note, statement (usually introduced by 'naẓara fī') (AH, 97; KF, I, 243; CM, no.141/1: naẓara fīhi wa-taʾam-mala maʿānīh wa-daʿā li-mālikih), comp. muṭālaʿah.
unẓur – 'see', abbrev. ظ (used in the margin for notabilia, nota bene, along with the word qif, see tawqīf).
nāẓir (pl. nuẓẓār) 1. administrator of a waqf 2. curator.
fīhi naẓar – 'phrase (syn. fīhi taʾammul) implying doubt and insinuating politely that the words to which it relates are false or wrong' (LL, II, 2812).

نظم

naẓm, tanẓīm – composition (in verse or prose) (AM, no.170); versification, comp. shiʿr.

نفخ

nafkh – gaufrage (KJ, no.3, 23).

نفذ

nafdh – punching, awling (MB, passim).
minfadh – punch, awl (SA, II, 481; IR, 230; AT, 133; MJ, 208; DD, I, 391: for sewing of quires).

نفط

nafaṭ (sg. nafṭah) – pockets of air, bubbles (between the doublures and the cover board) (NH, 392).
al-waraq al-nafṭī see waraq.

نقح

tanqīḥ, **tanaqquḥ** – correction; revision (KF, II, 503: ṣuḥḥiḥat wa-tunuqqiḥat).

نقر

naqr – inscription, engraving (on stone), epigraphy (KM, IV, sifr 13, 5: al-kitāb fī al-ḥajar).
naqqār – carver, engraver (KM, IV, sifr 13, 5).
minqār – serif-like stroke, syn. tarwīs (q.v.) (LM, 54).

نقس

niqs (pl. anqās, nuqūs) – ink (KK, 49; SA, II, 469, 471; IK, 84; KM, IV, sifr 13, 5).

نقش

naqsh (pl. nuqūsh), **niqāshah** 1. inscription, engraving, epigraphy (FT, 400), comp. naqr 2. tooling or stamping (of leather) (UK, 156; TS, 29-32; MB, 105; IA, 63) 3. painting, illumination (EI, VII, 931).
minqāsh (pl. manāqish, manāqīsh) bookbinder's tool (UK, 156; MB, 105; IA, 59).

naqqāsh 1. carver, engraver (KM, IV, sifr 13, 5) 2. miniature painter, designer, illuminator (PA, 141, 155, 159).
naqqāsh'khānah – Ottoman imperial painting atelier (workshop) (EI, VII, 931-932).
nāqish – calligrapher (AW, 266).
tanqīsh – writing, copying (FK, III, 304: wa-qad waqaʿa al-farāgh min tanqīsh hādhā al-kitāb).

نقص

naqṣ, nuqṣān, naqīṣah (pl. naqāʾiṣ) – omission; haplographic error, haplography (TP, 58).

نقط

naqṭ 1. vocalization (by means of dots) (SA, III, 16: al-naqṭ qad yakūn bi-maʿná al-shakl; SA, III, 160; TE, 16-17) 2. letter-pointing (TE, 16-17; SA, III, 151; KH, 38).
nuqṭah (pl. nuqaṭ) 1. diacritical point, dot (HI, 81: qāla Ibn Muqlah: wa-al-naqṭ ṣūratān aḥaduhumā shakl murabbaʿ wa-al-akhar shakl mustadīr) 2. small tool, point (for creating dots on leather) (TS, 12, 33; HT, 133, 137; MB, 105; IA, 59: nuqaṭ mudawwarah; IA, 60: nuqṭat al-lawzah, nuqṭah lil-tadhhīb, nuqṭah kabīrah li-buyūt al-lawzah).
nāqiṭ (pl. nuqqāṭ), **naqqāṭ** – vocaliser; orthographer (LT, 368).

نقل

naql 1. transmission, tradition; exemplar (FK, I, no.729: qūbila Rawḍat al-murīdīn maʿa naqlih fa-ṣaḥḥa) 2. quoting, citing; extract, quotation 3. copying, transcription (MU, XII, 138: naqaltuhu min khaṭṭih; TE, 16) 4. exact copy (apograph), 'facsimile' of the master calligrapher's work (DW, 68) 5. translation.
nāqil (pl. naqalah) 1. copyist; calligrapher (TE, 16; AW, 218) 2. translator.

نمر

numrah, nimrah – number, figure, abbrev. ره (often represented by a horizontal line for rāʾ with a loop at its end representing hāʾ used

among other things as a reference mark, written over the word in the text and repeated above the relevant gloss in the margin and bearing a superscript number) (RA, 45; AM, 53, 62, 91).
tanmīr – marking (providing) with numbers, numbering.

نمق

namq, tanmīq – elegant, embellished writing, copying (TE, 16; KK, 53; SK, 119: ḥusn al-kitābah namquh; WR, 87); elegant composition (of a text) (DM).
nāmiq, munammiq – calligrapher (AC, 45; NI, 180: adhantu li-nāmiq hādhihi al-qiṭʿah al-marghūbah; TE, 16).
namīqah – piece (of calligraphy); calligraph, calligraphic composition (NI, 181; AW, 237).

نمل

tanmīl – compact writing, copying (KH, 38).

نمنم

namnamah 1. elegant, embellished writing, copying (SK, 119; AA, 105) 2. compact writing (KM, IV, sifr 13, 5: namnamtu al-kitāb qarmaṭtuhu).
munamnamah – miniature (figurative) painting, painted illustration (KF, II, 369, n.1).

نور

nuwwār (pl. nawāwīr) – floral design, arabesques (on book covers) (LC, 26; IB, 69).
nawārah – corner stamp (smaller than turunjah, used in the decoration of an envelope flap) (ST, index, 22; IB, 44).
al-munawwarah – epithet of Medina.
munīr – syn. of mufattaḥ, having an open counter (ant. of maṭmūs, q.v.) (LM, 43).

نول

munāwalah, ijāzat al-munāwalah – authorisation note or statement (allowing the transmission of a work by means of handing over the shaykh's copy to the student) (MF, 86-87: nāwaltu hādhā al-kitāb kāmilan wa-huwa sabʿat ajzāʾ; KF, II, 498-450; EI, III, 27).

نون

nūn (pl. anwān, nīnān) – inkwell (SK, 106; KD, II, 700; IK, 82: wa-yuqāl hiya al-dawāh wa-al-nūn wa-al-raqīm).

نهى

intihāʾ – end, termination, used as a paragraph mark or textual divider, abbrev. هى / ﻫ / ه / اه (for intahá) (MW, 110; CI, I, xiii; CI, II, xi; SL, II, 87; GA, 285).
inhāʾ (pl. inhāʾāt) – collation statement and/or ijāzah (beginning with the word 'anhāhu') (IH, 7, 15: fa-kataba lahu inhāʾan fī ākhir kitāb al-zakāh minhu).

****

ه

هد ب

ahdāb (sg. hudb, hudub) – letters such as rāʾ and zāʾ (TU, 36).

هد هد

hudʹhud (pl. hadāhid) – hoopoe (see tabkhīr).

هدى

ihdāʾ – dedication (FN, 17: katabtu ʿalá ẓahr juzʾ ahdaytuh ilá ṣadīq lī; MU, XIII, 98: wa-hiya al-nuskhah allatī ahdāhā ilá Sayf al-Dawlah).

هذ ب

tahdhīb 1. correction, revision (DM) 2. abridgement, epitome (EA, I, 23).

muhadhdhib 1. author, compiler (SS, 69, 72, 73) 2. abridger, epitomist.

هل

al-waraq al-hilālī see waraq.
tahlīl 1. also **haylalah** – the doctrinal formula 'lā ilāha illá Allāh' (AD, 181; MG, I, 483; EI, X, 108) 2. rounding (of the spine), backing (MB, 109; IA, 61).
al-kaʿb al-muhallal see kaʿb.
muhall, mustahall – the first night of the month, e.g. fī muhall (mustahall) shahr kadhā (SA, VI, 244).

همش

hāmish (pl. hawāmish) 1. margin (DF, III, 180, 190, 210) 2. marginal note, gloss, abbrev. ﻫ (LC, 24; MI, 185).
hāmishah – interline (BA, III, 371: yuqāl ajābahu fī hāmishat kitābih idhā kataba bayna al-saṭrayn).
tahmīsh 1. glossing, annotation (TT, 193: hammasha al-kitāb ʿallaqa ʿalá hāmishih) 2. marginal note, gloss (AK, 352).
muhammash – glossed, annotated (TW, 102: sifr muhammash bi-taʿālīq muhimmah).

همل

ihmāl, ʿalāmat al-ihmāl – mark distinguishing an unpointed letter from its pointed counterpart (for various practices see TP, 57; GL, 4; IR, 244).
al-ḥurūf al-muhmalah, al-muhmalāt – letters without diacritical points, unpointed letters (TP, 57; MH, 90).

هوم

hāmah – head (of a letter), syn. raʾs (e.g. SA, III, 60: hāmat al-alif).

****

و

وجز

ījāz, mūjaz – abridgement, epitome (DM).

وجه

wajh(ah) 1. face, upper part (of a document or textblock) (TS, 25) 2. upper cover (TS, 25, 31) 3. recto (of a document or leaf) 4. page (MU, IV, 182: mujalladah ḍakhmah taḥtawī ʿalá ʿishrīn kurrāsatan fī kull wajhah ʿishrīn saṭran; DF, III, 239, 283: fī sabʿ qawāʾim wa-wajhah wāḥidah).
ʿalá al-wajh – copying, transcription in full; making a complete copy (of a manuscript or collection) (SL, II, 31, 43-45).
wajh al-hirr (lit. 'tomcat's face') – the letter hāʾ in the form of a rounded (as opposed to 'almond shaped' – mulawwaz) double loop (ه) (SA, III, 91-92).
wajh al-kitāb – upper cover (AG, 109).
al-wajh al-awwal (al-wajhah al-ūlá) – recto (of a leaf) (LC, 29; MK, 82).
al-wajh al-thānī (al-wajhah al-thāniyah) – verso (of a leaf) (LC, 29; MK, 82).
wajh al-qalam – inner side of the nib (KU, 154: wa-wajhuhu bāṭin sinnayh; SA, II, 464; MJ, 218).
wajh al-waraqah see waraqah.

وحش

waḥshī see sinn.

وحى

waḥy – writing; piece of writing (in an unspecified form) (IK, 95: wa-yuqāl lil-kitāb ayḍan mawaddah wa-majallah wa-waḥy; KM, IV, sifr 13, 5; KK, 53).

ود

mawaddah – writing; piece of writing (see waḥy above) (IK, 95; DA).

ورخ

tawrīkh see ta'rīkh.

ورد

wardah – rosette, lobed medallion (DH, no.73).
muwarrad – floriated (of design) (DH, no.73).

وزن

al-aqlām al-mawzūnah see qalam.

ورق

waraq (pl. awrāq) 1. paper (for various types of paper, such as al-waraq al-Samarqandī, al-Baghdādī, al-Khurāsānī, al-Shāmī, al-Misrī, al-Tihāmī, al-Maghribī, al-Andalusī, see e.g. SA, VI, 189-195; WS, 85-104), comp. kāghad 2. parchment (AE, 108).
waraqah 1. piece (of paper, parchment or leather) 2. leaf, folio (folium), abbrev. ق / و (AR, 36, 37) 3. small tool (resembling a vine leaf) (TS, 11; AG, 109).
khalf al-waraqah – verso (of a leaf) (LC, 25).
wajh al-waraqah – recto (of a leaf) (LC, 29).
al-waraq (al-kāghad) al-Islāmī – 'Islamic paper' (paper produced by Muslims) (WM, I, 85).
al-waraq (al-kāghad) al-Rūmī 1. European (usually watermarked) paper (WM, I, 75, 77) 2. French paper (PT, 31).
al-waraq al-ʿādim – waste paper (HN, 378).
al-waraq (al-kāghad) al-baladī – local paper (as opposed to imported) (PT, 30; SA, VI, 193; OM).
waraq damghah (tamghah) – stamped paper (DM), paper bearing an imitation watermark.
al-waraq al-hilālī – Venetian paper (bearing a crescent watermark, Tre Lune) (PT, 31).

al-waraq al-khām – unglazed paper (PT, 32).
al-waraq al-maṣlūḥ (al-maṣqūl) – glazed paper (PT, 32; SA, II, 487; WS, 82).
al-waraq al-madghūṭ – papier maché (FI, 88; JL, 84).
al-waraq al-māḥī – wove paper (HN, 380).
al-waraq al-muqawwá 1. pasteboard (JL, 87; MS, 35; MD, 107; WS, 104) 2. cardboard (FT, 394).
al-waraq al-mujazzaʿ **(al-nafṭī** or **waraq al-abrū)** – marbled paper (DM; MN, 161).
al-waraq al-muṭarraḥ – laid paper (HN, 380).
al-waraqah al-wusṭá – middle leaf (of a quire) (ST, index, 22; MP, 65).
warrāq, muwarriq – papermaker, stationer, bookseller; professional copyist, scribe (SL, II, 16; IK, 66: fa-kātib al-khaṭṭ huwa al-warrāq wa-al-muḥarrir); bookbinder (QS, II, 495).
(al-khaṭṭ) al-warrāqī see muḥaqqaq.
al-lām alif al-warrāqīyah see lām alif.
wirāqah 1. profession of the warrāq 2. culture of the handwritten book.
warrāqah – paper-mill (MA, IV, 81, 82; WS, 94).
tawrīq 1. copying, transcription (WS, 9, 14; KF, I, 148) 2. foliation (as opposed to pagination) 3. vegetal (curvilinear) decoration; foliated arabesque design (ST, index, 22; IB, 69; FI, 88; LC, 28; JL, 93; WR, 87; EI, I, 558-561).

وسم

maysam (pl. mayāsim) – tool, stamp (AB, 135).
mawsim (pl. mawāsim) – feast, festival. For dating by feasts see taʾrīkh.
mawsūm bi – entitled (e.g. CI, II, 10).

وشح

washḥ – decorating, decoration (of book covers by impression and stamping) (ST, index, 22; MP, 65).

وشر

wushārah see nushārah.

وشم

washm 1. writing, drawing (AD, 186) 2. diacritical pointing (of letters) (IK, 93) 3. also **tawshīm** – tooling, stamping (of leather) (HT, lin.125, 164), comp. rashm, tarshīm.
mawshim (pl. mawāshim) – pattern (created by tooling); stamp (HT, lin.126).

وشى

washy, tawshiyah – polychrome illumination (TE, 18; UK, 147: al-tawshiyah al-naqsh wa-al-zakhrafah).

وصل

waṣl, wiṣl, wuṣl (pl. awṣāl, waṣlāt) 1. straight line (drawn with a ruler) (SD, II, 812; SA, VI, 195: fa-qaṭʿ al-Baghdādī yutrak fīhi sittat awṣāl bayāḍan wa-tuktab al-basmalah fī awwal al-sābiʿ) 2. connection (between two sheets when pasted side by side) (MB, 110); line of paste (kollesis) (AJ, 144) 3. piece, leaf (of parchment or paper forming an integral part of a roll, darj), collema (kollema) (WS, 10, 88, 90).
waṣlah 1. also **wāṣilah** – catchword, vox reclamans (NM, 683; HB, 234; NZ, 65) 2. knife (used by the waṣṣāl) (AD, 187).
waṣṣāl – manuscript decorator (who cuts the margins of leaves, replaces them with coloured papers and draws lines to cover the joints) (AD, 187; PA, 161: person involved in 'reparation et montage des marges').
ṣilah – pallet-like connecting tool (used in the interlace) (TS, 12, 31-32), comp. ṭawīl.

وضح

(qalam) al-waḍḍāḥ see matn.

وضع

waḍʿ (pl. awḍāʿ) – composition, arrangement (of a text) (MU, VI, 62; KF, I, 222: ḥusn al-waḍʿ wa-riʿāyat al-marsūm).
wāḍiʿ – compiler, author (DF, IV, 376).

وطأ

tawṭiʾah – preface, prologue, proem (DM).

وعد

mīʿād, mawʿid (pl. mawāʿīd) – collation session (TP, 56; TM,192: fa-in kāna dhālik fī samāʿ al-ḥadīth kataba ʻbalagha fī al-mīʿād al-awwal aw al-thānīʼ; AI, 39, 41).

وعى

wiʿāʾ (pl. awʿiyah) – 1. case, box (MS, 16, 19; ME, 575) 2. container (OM).

وفع

wafīʿah – pen wiper (IK, 87: **waqīʿah**; DA).

وفق

wifq (pl. awfāq) – talismanic seal (in the form of a square) (DT, 69, 100, 108).
mīfaq – seal, stamp (IK, 96).

وقب

waqabah see jūnah.

وقع

waqīʿah see wafīʿah.
tawqīʿ 1. writing something down, taking something down in writing (SL, I, 10) 2. royal edict, decree (EI, X, 392-393) 3. motto; autograph, signature (EI, X, 392; LC, 28; KM, IV, sifr 13, 6: al-tawqīʿ an yulḥiq fī al-kitāb shayʾan baʿda al-farāgh minhu; FK, II, no.1393/5: naqaltu min khaṭṭ al-muṣannif wa-waqqaʿa ʿalayhi bi-khaṭṭih hādhā ṣaḥīḥ; KF, I, 124, 125) 4. gloss, apostil (usually signed) (AD, 189; LC, 28; AD, 189).
(qalam) al-tawqīʿ, al-tawāqīʿ, al-tawqīʿāt – smaller version of the

thuluth script (characterised by a liberal use of hairlines, tashʿīrāt) (AS, 146; JM, 43-46, 73-77; LM, 47: wa-al-tawāqīʿ yuktab bi-hi al-tawāqīʿ al-kibār allatī lil-umarāʾ wa-al-quḍāh wa-al-akābir; EI, IV, 1123- in Persia, 1125- in Turkey).
al-tawqīʿ al-muṭlaq – regular size tawqīʿ script (SA, III, 100; AS, 146).
(qalam) al-tawāqīʿ al-riqāʿīyah – smaller version of tawqīʿ script (AS, 146; LM, 69).
(qalam) al-tawāqīʿ al-thuluthīyah – larger version of tawqīʿ script (AS, 146; LM, 63).

وقف

waqf 1. also **ʿalāmat al-waqf** – pause-mark or abbreviation (written above the line in the text of the Qurʾān, e.g. م = lāzim, ج = jāʾiz) (KH, 38) 2. endowment, wakf 3. reading, perusal (from waqaftu ʿalá – 'I have read'), a standard opening phrase of reading notes and blurbs, taqrīẓ (q.v.) (BL, 187).
waqfīyah, **tawqīf** (KF, II, 473) – endowment certificate or statement; bequest note (OS, 90; LC,29; KF, II, 428-442).
wāqif – donor (of a wakf) (e.g. KF, II, 441).
mawqūf 1. unfinished stroke (e.g. al-bāʾ al-mawqūfah, see SA, III, 61; KH, 38) 2. **al-mawqūf** – object of the endowment (e.g. number of volumes and titles of the books) (OS, 90).
al-mawqūf ʿalayhi – beneficiary or usufructuary (of a wakf).
tawqīf (pl. tawqīfāt) 1. marginal note, side-head (preceded by the word 'qif' (also qif ʿalá) or its stylised form, logograph, which resembles two unpointed bāʾs or tāʾs. It was used extensively in Maghrebi manuscripts for notabilia.) (LC, 28), comp. taʾammul 2. overlining (TP, 55).

وكت

wakt – letter pointing (KM, IV, sifr 13, 6: wakata al-kitāb waktan naqaṭahu).

وهم

wahm – mistake, error (IK, 95; AA, 122).
īhām – omission (IK, 95; AA, 123).

****

لا

al-lām alif al-muḥaqqaqah – the lām alif ligature characterized by a loop at the base (SA, III, 95-96; SA, III, 58: wa-al-lām alif al-muḥaqqaqah kulluhā mufattaḥah lā yajūz fīhā al-ṭams bi-ḥāl; AS, 146).
al-lām alif al-mukhaffafah – the lām alif ligature characterized by joining the foot of the alif to the extremity of lām on the base line (SA, III, 96).
al-lām alif al-warrāqīyah – the lām alif ligature characterized by its triangular base (ﻻ) and used in the Mamluk period exclusively in the rectilinear family of scripts (muḥaqqaq, maṣāḥif, rayḥān, naskh) (SA, III, 97: wa-lā yakūn hādhā al-shakl illā fī qalam al-naskh wa-mā shākalahu wa-fī qalam al-muḥaqqaq wa-mā shābahah; MJ, 236; AS, 146).

****

ى

al-yāʾ al-rājiʿah see rājiʿah.

يبس

yābis – rectilinear, ant. of raṭb (of a letter or script) (AS, 144).
al-aqlām al-yābisah – rectilinear scripts (such as al-muḥaqqaq and al-rayḥān) (SA, III, 11; UD, 19; AS, 144; LM, 45), comp.mabsūṭ.

يد

yad (pl. aydin, ayādin) – hand; used in the expressions such as **ʿalá yad**, **fī yad**, **bi-yad** and **ʿan yad** (copied by, in the hand of) (OT, 42), comp. yamīn and khaṭṭ.

يرع

yarāʿ(ah) – reed; reed pen (IK, 86; UA, 393; DM; KD, II, 701: fa-idhā lam yakun mabrīyan fa-huwa yarāʿah wa-al-jamʿ yarāʿ).

يمن

yamīn – right hand (e.g. CM, no.39: katabahu mu'allifuhu bi-yamīnihi al-dāthirah).
maymūn(ah) – one of the honorifics (epithets) of the words kitāb, risālah, nuskhah and the like (CI, II, 65: al-nuskhah al-mubārakah al-maymūnah).

ABBREVIATIONS

1. Sources/References

- A -

AA = Muḥammad ibn Yaḥyá al-Ṣūlī. *Adab al-kuttāb*, ed. Muḥammad Bahjah al-Atharī. Baghdad/Cairo, 1341 A.H.

AB = Johannes Pedersen. *Al-Kitāb al-ʿArabī mundhu nashʾatih ḥattá ʿaṣr al-ṭibāʿah*, transl. Ḥaydar Ghaybah. Damascus, 1989.

AC = Adam Gacek. "Arabic calligraphy and the 'Herbal' of al-Ghāfiqī: a survey of Arabic manuscripts at McGill University". *Fontanus: from the collections of McGill University*, 2 (1989): 37-53.

AD = E. Fagnan. *Additions aux dictionnaires arabes*. Algiers, 1923.

AE = Adolf Grohmann. *Arabische Paläographie*. Vol.1. Wien, 1967.

AF = Oleg F. Akimushkin and Anatol. A. Ivanov. "The art of illumination". *The arts of the book in Central Asia*, ed. B. Gray. Paris/London, 1979: 35-57.

AG = Adam Gacek. "Arabic bookmaking and terminology as portrayed by Bakr al-Ishbīlī in his 'Kitāb al-taysīr fī ṣināʿ at al-tasfīr'". *Manuscripts of the Middle East*, 5 (1990-91): 106-113.

AH = ʿĀbid Sulaymān al-Mashūkhī. *Anmāṭ al-tawthīq fī al-makhṭūṭ al-ʿArabī fī al-qarn al-tāsiʿ ʿashar*. Riyad, 1414/1994.

AI = ʿAbd al-Karīm ibn Muḥammad al-Samʿānī. *Adab al-imlāʾ wa-al-istimlāʾ*, ed. Max Weisweiler. Beirut, 1981.

AJ = J. von Karabacek. "Das arabische Papier". *Mittheilungen aus der Sammlung der Papyrus Erzherzog Rainer*, 2-3 (1887): 87-159.

AK = Muḥammad al-Manūnī. "ʿAlāmat al-kitābah al-ʿArabīyah fī al-makhṭūṭāt: al-naqṭ wa-al-shakl wa-ishārāt ukhrá". *Al-Maṣādir al-ʿArabīyah li-taʾrīkh al-Maghrib: al-fatrah al-muʿāṣirah 1790-1930*, by Muḥammad al-Manūnī. Rabat, 1989: 2, 349-360.

AL = *Kitāb alf laylah wa-laylah*, ed. Muḥsin Mahdī. Leiden, 1984.

AM = Adam Gacek. *Arabic lithographed books in the Islamic Studies Library, McGill University. Descriptive catalogue*. Montreal, 1996.

AN = Richard Lemay. "Arabic numerals". *Dictionary of the Middle Ages*. New York, 1982: 1, 382-398.

AO = Adrian Brockett. "Aspects of the physical transmission of the Qurʾān in 19th-century Sudan: script, decoration, binding and paper". *Manuscripts of the Middle East*, 2 (1987): 45-67.

AP = Nabia Abbott. "Arabic paleography: the development of early Islamic scripts". *Ars Islamica*, 8 (1941): 65-104.

AQ = David James. *After Timur: Qurʾans of the 15th and 16th centuries A.D.* London/Oxford, 1992.

AR = Ḥusayn ʿAlī Maḥfūẓ. "Al-ʿAlāmāt wa-al-rumūz ʿinda al-muʾallifīn al-ʿArab qadīman wa-ḥadīthan". *Al-Turāth al-shaʿbī*, 1, nos.4-5 (1963-4): 22-37 [436-451].

AS = Adam Gacek. "Arabic scripts and their characteristics as seen through the eyes of Mamluk authors". *Manuscripts of the Middle East*, 4 (1989): 144-149.

AT = Niḍāl ʿAbd al-ʿAlī Amīn. "Adawāt al-kitābah wa-mawādduhā fī al-ʿuṣūr al-Islāmīyah". *Al-Mawrid*, 15, no.4 (1986): 131-137.

AV = François Déroche. *The Abbasid tradition: Qurʾans of the 8th to the 10th centuries AD*. London/Oxford, 1992.

AW = Nabil F. Safwat. *The art of the pen: calligraphy of the 14th to 20th centuries*. London/Oxford, 1996.

- B -

BA = Maḥmūd Shukrī al-Ālūsī al-Baghdādī. *Bulūgh al-arab fī maʿrifat aḥwāl al-ʿArab*. Beirut, Dār al-Kutub al-ʿIlmīyah, [198?].

BL = Franz Rosenthal. "'Blurbs' (taqrīẓ) from fourteenth-century Egypt". *Oriens*, 27-28 (1981): 177-196.

- C -

CA = Adam Gacek. "A collection of Qurʾanic codices". *Fontanus: from the collections of McGill University*, 4 (1991): 35-53.

CD = Arthur J. Arberry. *The Chester Beatty Library. A handlist of the Arabic manuscripts*. Dublin, 1958.

CI = Adam Gacek. *Catalogue of Arabic manuscripts in the library of the Institute of Ismaili Studies*. London, 1984-85.

CL = Jan Just Witkam. *Catalogue of Arabic manuscripts in the Library of the University of Leiden and other collections in the Netherlands*. Leiden, 1982 - .

CM = Adam Gacek. *Arabic manuscripts in the Libraries of McGill University: union catalogue*. Montreal, 1991.

CT = Pierre A. MacKay. "Certificates of transmission on a manuscript of the 'Maqāmāt' of Ḥarīrī (MS.Cairo,Adab 105)". *Transactions of the American Oriental Society*, N.S. 61, no.4 (1971).

CW = A.Z. Iskandar. *A catalogue of Arabic manuscripts on medicine and science in the Wellcome Historical Medical Library*. London, 1967.

- D -

DA = A. De Biberstein Kazimirski. *Dictionnaire arabe-français*. Paris, 1960.

DB = R. Blachère, M. Chouémi and C. Denizeau. *Dictionnaire* *arabe-français-anglais: langue classique et moderne*. Paris, 1967- .

DC = A.-L. de Premare. *Dictionnaire arabe-français*. Paris, 1993 - .

DD = ʿAbd al-Qādir ibn Muḥammad al-Anṣārī al-Jazīlī. *Al-Durar al-farāʾid al-munaẓẓamah fī akhbār al-ḥājj wa-ṭarīq Makkah al-Muʿaẓẓamah*, ed. Ḥamd al-Jāsir. Riyad, Dār al-Yamāmah, 1983.

DE = Martin Hinds and El-Said Badawi. *A dictionary of Egyptian Arabic: Arabic-English*. Beirut,1986.

DF = Muḥammad ibn Sayf al-Dīn Aydamur. *Al-Durr al-farīd wa-al-bayt al-qaṣīd*. Frankfurt, 1989.

DG = Werner Diem. *A dictionary of the Arabic material of S.D. Goitein's 'A Mediterranean society'*. Wiesbaden, 1994.

DH = Aḥmad ibn al-Rashīd ibn al-Zubayr. *Kitāb al-dhakhāʾir wa-al-tuḥaf*. Kuwait, 1984.

DM = Hans Wehr. *A dictionary of modern written Arabic*, ed. J.M. Cowan, 4th ed. Ithaca, NY, 1994.

DP = Adam Gacek. "The diploma of the Egyptian calligrapher Ḥasan al-Rushdī". *Manuscripts of the Middle East*, 4 (1989): 44-55.

DQ = François Déroche. "Deux fragments coraniques maghrébins anciens au Musée des arts turc et islamique d'Istanbul". *Revue des études islamiques*, 59 (1991): 229-235.

DR = Donald P. Little. "Documents related to the estates of a merchant and his wife in late fourteenth century Jerusalem". *Mamlūk studies review*, 2 (1998): 93-193.

DS = Aḥmad ibn ʿAlī al-Qalqashandī. *Ḍawʾ al-ṣubḥ al-musaffar*, ed. Maḥmūd Salāmah. Cairo, 1906.

DT = Tawfik Canaan. "The decipherment of Arabic talismans". *Berytus. Archeological studies*, 4, fasc.1 (1937): 69-110; 5, fasc.2 (1938): 141-151.

DW = Manijeh Bayani, Anna Cantadini and Tim Stanley. *The decorated word: Qur'ans of the 17th to 19th centuries.* Part 1. London/ Oxford, 1999.

- E -

EA = J.S. Meisami and P. Starkey, eds. *Encyclopedia of Arabic literature.* New York, 1998.

EI = *The Encyclopaedia of Islam.* New ed. Leiden, 1960 - .

EM = Ayman Fu'ād Sayyid. "Early methods of book composition: al-Maqrīzī's draft of the 'Kitāb al-khiṭaṭ'". *The codicology of Islamic manuscripts.* London, 1995: 93-101.

EP = François Déroche. "L'emploi du parchemin dans les manuscrits islamiques: quelques remarques liminaires". *The codicology of Islamic manuscripts. Proceedings of the second Conference of al-Furqān Islamic Heritage Foundation, 1993.* London, 1995: 17-57.

ER = *Encyclopaedia Iranica*, ed. E. Yarshater. London (later Costa Mesa, Calif.), 1982 - .

- F -

FD = Ibrāhīm Ibrāhīm Murūwah. *Fī al-makhṭūṭāt al-ʿArabīyah: qarāʾāt taṭbīqīyah.* Beirut/Damascus, 1997.

FI = M.S. Dimand. *Al-Funūn al-Islāmīyah*, transl. Aḥmad Muḥammad ʿĪsá. Cairo, n.d.

FJ = Iʿtimād Yūsuf al-Quṣayrī. *Fann al-tajlīd ʿinda al-Muslimīn.* Baghdad, 1979.

FK = Ramzan Şeşen et al. *Catalogue of manuscripts in the Köprülü Library.* Istanbul, 1986.

FM = Ibrāhīm Zāhidah. "Fahrasat al-makhṭūṭāt". *Al-Mawrid*, 5 (1976): 164-168.

FN = Ibn al-Nadīm. *Fihrist lil-Nadīm*. Beirut, Dār al-Maʿrifah, 1978 (reprint of the Cairo edition of 1929).

FT = Oktay Aslanapa. *Funūn al-Turk wa-ʿamāʾiruhum*, transl. Aḥmad Muḥammad ʿĪsà. Istanbul, 1987.

FZ = Muḥammad ʿAbd al-ʿAzīz Marzūq. *Al-Funūn al-zakhrafīyah al-Islāmīyah fī al-ʿaṣr al-ʿUthmānī*. Cairo, 1987.

- G -

GA = *Grundriss der arabischen Philologie*. Band I: *Sprachwissenschaft*, herausgegeben von W. Fischer. Wiesbaden, 1982.

GL = W. Wright. *A Grammar of the Arabic language*. 3rd ed. Cambridge, 1967.

- H -

HB = Ahmed-Chouqui Binebine. *Histoire des bibliothèques au Maroc*. Rabat, 1992.

HD = A.U. Kaziev (Gaziev). *Khudozhestvenno-tekhnicheskie materialy i terminologiia srednovekovoi knizhnoi zhivopisi, kalligrafii i perepletnogo iskustva*. Baku, 1966.

HI = Muḥammad Murtaḍá al-Zabīdī. "Ḥikmat al-ishrāq ilá kuttāb al-āfāq". *Nawādir al-makhṭūṭāt*, ed. ʿAbd al-Salām Hārūn. Cairo, 1954: 5, 50-99.

HN = ʿĀyidah Ibrāhīm Naṣīr. *Ḥarakat nashr al-kutub fī Miṣr fī al-qarn al-tāsiʿ ʿashar*. Cairo, 1994.

HT = Adam Gacek. "Ibn Abī Ḥamīdah's didactic poem for bookbinders". *Manuscripts of the Middle East*, 6 (1991): 41-58.

- I -

IA = Adam Gacek. "Instructions on the art of bookbinding attributed to the Rasulid ruler of Yemen al-Malik al-Muẓaffar". *Scribes et manuscrits du Moyen-Orient*, ed. F. Déroche and F. Richard. Paris, 1997: 57-63.

IB = G. Bosch, J. Carswell and G. Petherbridge. *Islamic bindings and bookmaking: a catalogue of an exhibition, The Oriental Institute, Univ. of Chicago, May 18 - August 18,1981*. Chicago, 1981.

ID = Jaʿfar ibn ʿAlī al-Dimashqī. *Al-Ishārah ilá maḥāsin al-tijārah*, ed. Fahmī Saʿd. Beirut, 1983.

IH = Aḥmad al-Ḥusaynī. *Ijāzāt al-ḥadīth allatī katabahā Muḥammad Bāqir al-Majlisī al-Iṣbahānī*. Qum, 1401 AH [1989 or 1990].

IJ = Jan Just Witkam. "Human element between text and reader: the ijāza in Arabic manuscripts". *The codicology of Islamic manuscripts*. London, 1995: 123-136.

IK = ʿAbd Allāh ibn Muḥammad ibn al-Sīd al-Baṭalyawsī. *Al-Iqtiḍāb fī sharḥ adab al-kuttāb*. Beirut, 1973.

IM = ʿIyāḍ ibn Mūsá al-Yaḥṣubī. *Al-Ilmāʿ ilá maʿrifat uṣūl al-riwāyah wa-taqyīd al-samāʿ*, ed. Aḥmad Ṣaqr. Cairo/ Tunis, 1389/1970.

IN = Aḥmad ibn Maʾmūn al-Balghīthī. *Al-Ibtihāj bi-nūr al-Sirāj*. Cairo, 1319 A.H.

IP = Ḥusayn ʿAlī Maḥfūẓ. "ʿIlm al-makhṭūṭāt". *Al-Mawrid*, 5 (1976): 144-145.

IR = Shaʿbān ibn Muḥammad al-Ātharī al-Qurashī. "Al-ʿInāyah al-rabbānīyah fī al-ṭarīqah al-Shaʿbānīyah", ed. Hilāl Nājī. *Al-Mawrid*, 8, no.2 (1979): 221-284.

IT = Muḥammad Marāyātī. *ʿIlm al-taʿmiyah wa-istikhrāj al-muʿammá ʿinda al-ʿArab*. Damascus,1987? - .

IW = Muhammad Faris Jamil. "Islamic wiraqah 'stationery' during the early Middle Ages". Ph.D., University of Michigan, 1985.

- J -

JA = al-Khaṭīb al-Baghdādī. *Al-Jāmiʿ li-akhlāq al-rāwī wa-ādāb al-sāmiʿ*. Riyad, 1983.

JL = ʿAbd al-Laṭīf Ibrāhīm. "Jildat muṣḥaf bi-Dār al-Kutub al-Miṣrīyah". *Majallat Kullīyat al-Ādāb* (Cairo), 20, no.1 (1958): 81-106, 6 pl.

JM = Muḥammad ibn Ḥasan al-Ṭībī. *Jāmiʿ maḥāsin kitābat al-kuttāb*, ed. Ṣalāḥ al-Dīn al-Munajjid. Beirut, 1962.

JN = Jamāl al-Dīn ibn al-Muṭahhar al-Ḥillī. *Al-Jawhar al-naḍīd fī sharḥ manṭiq al-Tajrīd*. Qum, 1363 [1984].

- K -

KA = Suhaylah Yāsīn al-Jubūrī. *Al-Khaṭṭ al-ʿArabī wa-taṭawwuruh fī al-ʿuṣūr al-ʿAbbāsīyah*. Baghdad, 1962.

KB = Aḥmad ibn al-Ḥājj al-ʿAyyāshī Sukayrij. *Kashf al-ḥijāb ʿamman talāqá maʿa al-Shaykh al-Tijānī min al-aṣḥāb*. S.l., s.n.,1961.

KC = Muḥammad al-Manūnī. "Al-Khizānah al-Maghribīyah fī ʿaṣr al-Sulṭān al-Ḥasan al-awwal". *Al-Manāhil*, 38 (1989): 7-103.

KD = Abū Hilāl al-ʿAskarī. *Kitāb al-talkhīṣ fī maʿrifat asmāʾ al-ashyāʾ*, ed. ʿIzzat Ḥasan. Damascus, 1969.

KF = Ayman Fuʾād Sayyid. *Al-Kitāb al-ʿArabī al-makhṭūṭ wa-ʿilm al-makhṭūṭāt* (= *Le manuscrit arabe et la codicologie*). Cairo, 1997.

KG = Jaʿfar ibn Khiḍr al-Janāḥī. *Kashf al-ghiṭāʾ*. [Tehran?], 1317 [1889] (lithographed).

KH = Muḥammad ibn Saʿīd Sharīfī. *Khuṭūṭ al-maṣāḥif ʿinda al-Mashāriqah wa-al-Maghāribah min al-qarn al-rābiʿ ilá al-ʿāshir al-hijrī*. Algiers, 1982.

KI = Zakī Muḥammad Ḥasan. "Al-Kitāb qabla ikhtirāʿ al-ṭibāʿah". *Al-Kitāb*, 2 (1946): 9-18.

KJ = ʿUthmān al-Kaʿʿāk. "al-Khiṭāṭah al-Tūnisīyah". *Majallat al-maktabah al-ʿArabīyah* (Cairo), 1, no. 1 (1963): 26-48; 1, no.3 (1964): 19-33.

KK = Abū al-Qāsim ʿAbd Allāh al-Baghdādī. "Kitāb al-kuttāb wa-ṣifat al-dawāh wa-al-qalam wa-taṣrīfuhā", ed. Hilāl Nājī. *Al-Mawrid*, 2, no.2 (1973): 43-78.

KL = G. Fehervari and Y.H. Safadi. *1400 years of Islamic art: a descriptive catalogue*. London, 1981.

KM = ʿAlī ibn Ismāʿil ibn Sīdah. *Kitāb al-mukhaṣṣaṣ*. Cairo, 1316-21 A.H.

KN = ʿUthmān ibn Saʿīd al-Dānī. *Al-Muqniʿ fī rasm maṣāḥif al-amṣār*, ed. Muḥammad Ṣādiq Qamḥāwī. Cairo, 1978.

KR = Sihām Muḥammad al-Mahdī. *Dirāsāt al-makhṭūṭāt al-Islāmīyah bayna iʿtibārāt al-māddah wa-al-bashar: aʿmāl al-Muʾtamar al-Thānī li-Muʾassasat al-Furqān lil-Turāth al-Islāmī*, ed. Rashīd al-ʿInānī. London, 1997: 77-91.

KS = Yūsuf al-Kattānī. "Khatamāt al-Ṣaḥīḥ al-Bukhārī". *Daʿwat al-ḥaqq*, no.240 (1984): 61-68.

KT = ʿAbd Allāh ibn Abī Dāʾūd al-Sijistānī. "Kitāb al-maṣāḥif". *Materials for the history of the text of the Qurʾān*, by Arthur Jeffery. Leiden, 1937: 125-161.

KU = ʿAbd Allāh ibn Jaʿfar ibn Durustūyah (Durustawayh). *Kitāb al-kuttāb*, ed. Ibrāhīm al-Samarrāʾī and ʿAbd al-Ḥusyan al-Fatlī. Kuwait, 1977.

KZ = Asad ibn Mūsá. *Kitāb al-zuhd*, ed. Raif Georges Khoury. Wiesbaden, 1976.

- L -

LA = *Lughat al-ʿArab*. Baghdad, 1911-1931.

LB = Jan Just Witkam. "Lists of books in Arabic manuscripts". *Manuscripts of the Middle East*, 5 (1990-91): 123-136.

LC = Adam Gacek. "The language of catalogues of Arabic manuscripts". *MELA Notes*, 48 (1989): 21-29.

LD = P.S. van Koningsveld and Q. Samarrai. *Localities and dates in Arabic manuscripts. Descriptive catalogue of a collection of Arabic manuscripts in the possession of E.J. Brill*. Leiden, 1978 (catalogue no.500).

LE = M. Ben Cheneb. "Liste des abréviations employées par les auteurs arabes". *Revue africaine*, 302-303 (1920): 134-138.

LL = Edward William Lane. *Arabic-English lexicon*. Rev. ed. Cambridge, 1984.

LM = Ḥusayn ibn Yāsīn ibn Muḥammad al-Kātib. *Lamḥat al-mukhtaṭif fī ṣināʿat al-khaṭṭ al-ṣalif*, ed. Hayā Muḥammad al-Dawsarī. Kuwait, 1992.

LS = Frederick de Jong and Jan Just Witkam. "The library of šayḵ Ḵālid al-Šahrazūrī al-Naqšabandī .....". *Manuscripts of the Middle East*, 2 (1987): 68-87.

LT = Muḥammad al-Manūnī. "Lamḥat ʿan taʾrīkh al-khaṭṭ al-ʿArabī fī al-gharb al-Islāmī ilá al-qarn 19". *Al-Maṣādir al-ʿArabīyah li-taʾrīkh al-Maghrib: al-fatrah al-muʿāṣirah, 1790-1930*, by Muḥammad al-Manūnī. Rabat, 1989: 2, 361-382.

- M -

MA = Muḥammad ibn Muḥammad ibn al-Ḥājj al-ʿAbdarī al-Fāsī. *Al-Madkhal*. Cairo, 1929.

MB = al-Malik al-Muẓaffar Yūsuf ibn ʿUmar al-Ghassānī. *Al-Mukh-*

tara' fī funūn min al-ṣuna', ed. Muḥammad 'Īsá Ṣāliḥīyah. Kuwait, 1989.

MC = Nājī Zayn al-Dīn. *Muṣawwar al-khaṭṭ al-'Arabī*. Beirut, 1980.

MD = Muḥammad 'Abd al-'Azīz Marzūq. "Al-Muṣḥaf al-sharīf: dirāsah fannīyah". *Majallat al-Majma' al-'Ilmī al-'Irāqī*, 20 (1970): 88-137.

ME = A. Lamare. "Le muṣḥaf de la Mosquée de Cordoue". *Journal asiatique*, 230 (1938): 551-575.

MF = al-Ḥasan ibn 'Abd al-Raḥīm al-Rāmahurmuzī. *Al-Muḥaddith al-fāṣil bayna al-rāwī wa-al-wā'ī*, ed. Muḥammad 'Ajjāj al-Khaṭīb. Beirut, 1391/1971.

MG = Jalāl al-Dīn 'Abd al-Raḥmān al-Suyūṭī. *Al-Muzhir fī 'ulūm al-lughah wa-anwā'ihā*, ed. Muḥammad Aḥmad Jād al-Mawlá. Cairo, n.d.

MH = 'Uthmān ibn al-Ṣalāḥ al-Shahrazūrī. *Muqaddimat Ibn al-Ṣalāḥ fī 'ulūm al-ḥadīth*. Damascus, 1972.

MI = Muḥammad Riḍá al-Māmaqānī. *Mu'jam al-rumūz wa-al-ishārāt*. Beirut, 1992.

MJ = Muḥammad ibn Aḥmad al-Ziftāwī. "Minhāj al-iṣābah fī ma'rifat al-khuṭūṭ wa-ālāt al-kitābah", ed. Hilāl Nājī. *Al-Mawrid*, 15, no.4 (1986): 185-248.

MK = Etan Kohlberg. *A medieval Muslim scholar at work: Ibn Ṭāwūs and his library*. Leiden, 1992.

ML = 'Abd al-Raḥīm ibn 'Alī ibn Shīth al-Qurashī. *Ma'ālim al-kitābah wa-maghānim al-iṣābah*. Beirut, 1913.

MM = 'Abd al-Bāsiṭ al-'Almawī. *Al-Mu'īd fī adab al-mufīd wa-al-mustafīd*. Damascus, 1349 [1930].

MN = 'Afīf al-Bahnassī. *Mu'jam muṣṭalaḥāt al-khaṭṭ al-'Arabī wa-al-khaṭṭāṭīn*. Beirut, 1995.

MO = David James. *The master scribes: Qur'ans of the 11th to 14th centuries*. London/Oxford, 1992.

MP = Martin Levey. "Mediaeval Arabic bookmaking and its relation to early chemistry and pharmacology". *Transactions of the American Philosophical Society*, N.S., 52, pt.4 (1962).

MQ = Aḥmad Rizq Muṣṭafá al-Sawāḥilī. "Min qaḍāyā al-ḥarf al-ʿArabī: al-taṣḥīf wa-al-taḥrīf". *ʿĀlam al-kutub*, 14, no.6 (1993): 641-649.

MR = Badr al-Dīn Muḥammad ibn Jamāʿah al-Kinānī. *Al-Manhal al-rāwī fī mukhtaṣar ʿulūm al-ḥadīth al-nabawī*, ed. Muḥyī al-Dīn ʿAbd al-Raḥmān Ramaḍān. Damascus, 1986.

MS = Muḥammad al-Manūnī. "Taʾrīkh al-muṣḥaf al-sharīf bi-al-Maghrib". *Majallat Maʿhad al-Makhṭūṭāt al-ʿArabīyah*, 15, no.1 (1969): 3-47.

MT = Adam Gacek. "Makhṭūṭāt ṭibbīyah ʿArabīyah fī Maktabat al-Dirāsāt al-Sharqīyah al-Ifrīqīyah", transl. ʿAdnan Jawwād al-Ṭumʿah. *Al-Mawrid*, 18, no.2 (1989): 201-203.

MU = Yāqūt ibn ʿAbd Allāh al-Ḥamawī. *Muʿjam al-udabāʾ*. Cairo, 1936-38.

MV = François Déroche. "Les manuscrits arabes datés du IIIe/IXe siècle". *Revue des études islamiques*, 55/57 (1987/89): 343-379.

MW = Ibrāhīm al-Samarrāʾī. "Al-Mukhtaṣarāt wa-al-rumūz fī al-turāth al-ʿArabī". *Majallat Majmaʿ al-Lughah al-ʿArabīyah al-Urdunī*, 32 (1987): 105-114.

MY = François Déroche. "Maîtres et disciples: la transmission de la culture calligraphique dans le monde musulman". *Revue du monde musulman et de la Méditerranée*, 75/76 (1995): 81-90.

MZ = Rudolf Sellheim. *Materialien zur arabischen Literaturgeschichte*. Wiesbaden/ Stuttgart, 1976-87.

- N -

NA = Aḥmad ibn ʿAbd al-Wahhāb al-Nuwayrī. *Nihāyat al-arab fī funūn al-adab*. Cairo, 1342/1923 - .

NC = Adam Gacek. "Al-Nuwayrī's classification of Arabic scripts". *Manuscripts of the Middle East*, 2 (1987): 126-130.

ND = J. Sadan. "Nouveaux documents sur scribes et copistes". *Revue des études islamiques*, 45 (1977): 1-87.

NH = Ibrāhīm Shabbūḥ. " Naḥwa muʿjam taʾrīkhī li-muṣṭalaḥ wa-nuṣūṣ funūn ṣināʿat al-makhṭūṭ al-ʿArabī". *Ṣiyānah wa-ḥifẓ al-makhṭūṭāt al-Islāmīyah: aʿmāl al-Muʾtamar al-Thālith li-Muʾassasat al-Furqān lil-Turāth al-Islāmī, 18- 19 Nūfimbir 1995*, ed. Ibrāhīm Shabbūḥ. London, 1418/1998: 341-393.

NI = ʿAbbās al-ʿAzzāwī. "Nuṣūṣ fī ijāzāt al-khaṭṭāṭīn". *Al-Mawrid*, 1, nos.3-4 (1971-72): 180-186.

NM = ʿAbd al-ʿAzīz al-Ṣāwirī. "Nadwah: al-makhṭūṭ al-ʿArabī wa-ʿilm al-makhṭūṭ al-ʿArabī". *ʿĀlam al-kutub*, 13, no.2 (1992): 679-683.

NO = Dimitri Gutas. "Notes and texts from Cairo manuscripts, II: texts from Avicenna's library ... ". *Manuscripts of the Middle East*, 2 (1987): 8-17.

NS = S.A. Bonebakker. "Notes on some old manuscripts of the 'Adab al-kātib' of Ibn Qutaybah, the 'Kitāb aṣ-ṣināʿatayn' of Abū Hilāl al-ʿAskarī and the 'Maṯal as-sāʾir' of Ḍiyāʾ al-Dīn ibn al-Aṯīr". *Oriens*, 13-14 (1960-61): 159-194.

NT = Aḥmad ibn Muḥammad al-Maqqarī. *Nafḥ al-ṭīb min ghuṣn al-Andalus al-raṭīb*. Cairo, 1367/1949.

NW = Muḥammad ibn Abī al-Khayr al-Ḥasanī al-Dimashqī. *Al-Nujūm al-shāriqāt fī dhikr baʿḍ al-ṣanāʾiʿ al-muḥtāj ilayhā fī ʿilm al-mīqāt (!)*. Damascus, 1928.

NZ = Aḥmad Shawqī Binbīn. "Niẓām al-taʿqībah". *Fann fahrasat al-*

makhṭūṭāt: madkhal wa-qaḍāyā, by Fayṣal al-Ḥafyān. Cairo, 1999: 65-72.

- O -

OD = François Déroche. "O. Houdas et les écritures maghrébines". *Al-Makhṭūṭ al-ʿArabī wa-ʿilm al-makhṭūṭāt (= Le manuscrit arabe et la codicologie)*. Rabat, 1994 : 75-81.

OH = J. Derek Latham. "Observations on the text and translation of al-Jarsīfī's Treatise on 'Hisba'". *Journal of Semitic studies*, 5 (1960): 124-143.

OM = Adam Gacek. "On the making of local paper: a thirteenth century Yemeni recipe". *Revue des mondes musulmans et de la Méditerranée* (forthcoming).

OS = Adam Gacek. "Ownership statements and seals in Arabic manuscripts". *Manuscripts of the Middle East*, 2 (1987): 88-95.

OT = Adam Gacek and Ali Yaycioğlu. "Ottoman-Turkish manuscripts in the Islamic Studies Library and other libraries of McGill University". *Fontanus: from the collections of McGill University*, 10 (1998): 41-63.

- P -

PA = Yves Porter. *Peinture et arts du livre: essai sur la littérature technique indo-persane*. Paris/Teheran, 1992.

PK = S.H. Alič. "Problem kratica u arapskim rukopisima sa spiskom arapskih kratica iz 16 vjeka". *Prilozi Orientalnu Filologiju*, 26 (1976): 199-212.

PT = Terence Walz. "The paper trade of Egypt and the Sudan in the eighteenth and nineteenth centuries". *Modernization in the Sudan: essays in honour of Richard Hill*, ed. M.W. Daly. New York, 1985: 29-48.

- Q -

QF = Ṣalāḥ al-Dīn al-Munajjid. *Qawāʿid fahrasat al-makhṭūṭāt al-ʿArabīyah.* Beirut, 1973.

QS = Muḥammad Saʿīd al-Qāsimī. *Qāmūs al-ṣināʿāt al-Shāmīyah.* Paris, 1960.

- R -

RA = William L. Hanaway and Brian Spooner. *Reading nastaʿliq: Persian and Urdu hands from 1500 to the present.* Costa Mesa, 1995.

RI = W. Bull. "Rebinding Islamic manuscripts, a new direction". *Bookbinder*, 1 (1987): 21-38.

RN = Nabia Abbott. *The rise of the North Arabic script and its ḳurʾānic development.* Chicago, 1938.

- S -

SA = Aḥmad ibn ʿAlī al-Qalqashandī. *Ṣubḥ al-aʿshá fī ṣināʿat al-inshāʾ.* Cairo, 1383/1963 (reprint of 'al-Ṭabʿah al-Amīrīyah', 1913-1920).

SD = R. Dozy. *Supplément aux dictionnaires arabes.* 3rd ed. Paris, 1967.

SJ = Ibrāhīm Shabbūḥ. "Sijill qadīm li-Maktabat Jāmiʿ Qayrawān". *Majallat Maʿhad al-Makhṭūṭāt al-ʿArabīyah*, 2 (1956): 339-372.

SK = Abū Jaʿfar Aḥmad ibn Muḥammad al-Naḥḥās. *Ṣināʿat al-kuttāb*, ed. Badr Aḥmad Ḍayyif. Beirut, 1410/1990.

SL = Nabia Abbott. *Studies in Arabic literary papyri.* Chicago, 1957-72.

SM = Ibn al-Baṣīṣ. "Sharḥ al-manẓūmah al-mustaṭābah fī ʿilm al-kitābah", ed. Hilāl Nājī. *Al-Mawrid*, 15, no.4 (1986): 259-270.

SS = Aḥmad Khān. "Samāʿāt muʾallafāt al-Ṣaghānī al-lughawīyah". *Majallat Maʿhad al-Makhṭūṭāt al-ʿArabīyah*, 41, no.1 (1997): 55-90.

ST = Aḥmad ibn Muḥammad al-Sufyānī. *Ṣināʿat tasfīr al-kutub wa-ḥall al-dhahab*, ed. P. Ricard. Paris, 1925.

- T -

TA = Yvette Sauvan. "Un traité à l'usage des scribes à l'époque nasride". *Les manuscrits du Moyen Orient*, ed. François Déroche. Paris/Istanbul, 1989: 49-50.

TB = Yaḥyá ibn Sharaf al-Nawawī. *Al-Tibyān fī ādāb ḥamlat al-Qurʾān*. Damascus, 1965.

TC = Muḥammad al-Manūnī. "Taqnīyāt iʿdād al-makhṭūṭ al-Maghribī". *Al-Makhṭūṭ al-ʿArabī wa-ʿilm al-makhṭūṭāt (= Le manuscrit arabe et la codicologie)*. Rabat, 1994: 11-32.

TD = ʿAbd al-Ḥayy al-Kattānī. *Kitāb al-tarātīb al-idārīyah wa-al-ʿamālāt wa-al-ṣināʿāt wa-al-matājir wa-al-ḥālah al-ʿilmīyah*. Rabat, 1346-49 A.H.

TE = Adam Gacek. "Some technical terms relative to the execution of Arabic manuscripts". *MELA notes*, 50-51 (1990): 13-18.

TF = Murād al-Rammāḥ. "Tasāfīr Maktabat al-Qayrawān al-ʿatīqah". *Dirāsāt al-makhṭūṭāt al-Islāmīyah bayna iʿtibārāt al-māddah wa-al-bashar: aʿmāl al-Muʾtamar al-Thānī li-Muʾassasat al-Furqān lil-Turāth al-Islāmī*, ed. Rashīd al-ʿInānī. London, 1997: 135-150.

TH = Aḥmad Shākir. *Taṣḥīḥ al-kutub wa-ṣunʿ al-fahāris al-muʿjamah wa-kayfīyat ḍabṭ al-kitāb wa-sabq al-Muslimīn wa-al-Ifranj fī dhālik*. Beirut, 1995.

TI = Ṭāhir ibn Ṣāliḥ al-Jazāʾirī. *Tashīl al-majāz ilá fann al-muʿammá wa-al-alghāz*. Damascus, 1303 A.H.

TK = Muḥammad ibn Muḥammad al-Qalalūsī. *Tuḥaf al-khawāṣṣ fī ṭuraf al-khawāṣṣ*. MS (Paris, Bibliothèque nationale, arabe 6844).

TL = Burhān al-Dīn al-Zarnūjī. *Taʿlīm al-mutaʿallim ṭarīq al-taʿallum*, ed. Marwān Qabbānī. Beirut, 1981.

TM = Badr al-Dīn Muḥammad ibn Jamāʿah al-Kinānī. *Tadhkirat al-sāmiʿ wa-al-mutakallim fī adab al-ʿālim wal-mutaʿallim*. Hyderabad, 1353/1934.

TN = ʿAbd al-Salām Hārūn. *Taḥqīq al-nuṣūṣ wa-nashruhā*. Kuwait, n.d.

TP = Adam Gacek. "Technical practices and recommendations recorded by classical and post-classical Arabic scholars concerning the copying and correction of manuscripts". *Les manuscrits du Moyen Orient*, ed. F. Déroche. Paris/Istanbul, 1989: 51-60, pl. xx-xxxii. [Includes a facsimile of Chapter 6 from 'al-Durr al-naḍīd fī ādāb al-mufīd wa-al-mustafīd' by Badr al-Dīn al-Ghazzī.]

TQ = al-Khaṭīb al-Baghdādī. *Taqyīd al-ʿilm*, ed. Yūsuf al-ʿIshsh. Damascus, 1949.

TS = Bakr ibn Ibrāhīm al-Ishbīlī. "Kitāb al-taysīr fī ṣināʿat al-tasfīr", ed. ʿAbd Allāh Kannūn. *Revista del Instituto de Estudios Islámicos en Madrid*, 7-8 (1959-60): 1-42.

TT = ʿAbd al-Hādī al-Faḍlī. *Taḥqīq al-turāth*. Jedda, 1982.

TU = ʿAbd al-Raḥmān ibn Yūsuf ibn al-Ṣāʾigh. *Tuḥfat ūlī al-albāb fī ṣināʿat al-khaṭṭ wa-al-kitāb*, ed. Hilāl Nājī. Tunis, 1967.

TW = Muḥammad al-Manūnī. *Taʾrīkh al-wirāqah al-Maghribīyah: ṣināʿat al-makhṭūṭ al-Maghribī min al-ʿaṣr al-wasīṭ ilá al-fatrah al-muʿāṣirah*. Rabat, 1991.

- U -

UA = Nūr al-Dīn al-ʿUsaylī. "Urjūzah fī ālāt dawāt al-kātib". *Al-Durar al-farāʾid al-munaẓẓamah fī akhbār al-ḥājj wa-ṭarīq Makkah al-Muʿaẓẓamah*, by ʿAbd al-Qādir ibn Muḥammad al-Anṣārī al-Jazīlī, ed. Ḥamd al-Jāsir. Riyad, Dār al-Yamāmah, 1983: 1, 392-393.

UD = ʿAbd Allāh al-Hītī. *Al-ʿUmdah: risālah fī al-khaṭṭ wa-al-qalam*, ed. Hilāl Nājī. Baghdad, 1970.

UI = *The unique Ibn al-Bawwab manuscript: complete facsimile edition of the earliest surviving naskhi Qurʾan, Chester Beatty Library, Dublin*. Graz, 1983.

UK = al-Muʿizz ibn Bādīs. "ʿUmdat al-kuttāb wa-ʿuddat dhawī al-albāb", ed. ʿAbd al-Sattār al-Ḥalwajī and ʿAlī ʿAbd al-Muḥsin Zakī. *Majallat Maʿhad al-Makhṭūṭāt al-ʿArabīyah*, 17 (1971): 43-172.

US = Adam Gacek. "The use of 'kabīkaj' in Arabic manuscripts". *Manuscripts of the Middle East*, 1 (1986): 49-53.

- V -

VA = Wilhelm Ahlwardt. *Verzeichnis der arabischen Handschriften*. Hildesheim/New York, 1980.

- W -

WA = Muḥammad al-Manūnī. "Al-Wirāqah al-ʿAlawīyah ʿabra sabʿat ʿuqūd min al-miʾah al-hijrīyah al-thālithah ʿashrata". *Daʿwat al-ḥaqq*, 23, no.4 (1982): 10-24.

WB = Muḥammad al-Manūnī. "Al-Wirāqah al-Maghribīyah fī ʿahd al-Sulṭān al-ʿAlawī Muḥammad al-Thālith". *Daʿwat al-ḥaqq*, 18, no.2 (1977): 45-56.

WM = Aḥmad ibn Yaḥyá al-Wansharīsī. *Al-Miʿyār al-muʿrib wa-al-jāmiʿ al-mughrib*. Beirut, 1981-83.

WR = Muḥammad al-Manūnī. "Al-Wirāqah al-Maghribīyah fī ʿaṣr al-ʿAlawī al-awwal". *Daʿwat al-ḥaqq*, 16, no.10 (1975): 80-92.

WS = Ḥabīb Zayyāt. *Al-Wirāqah wa-ṣināʿat al-kitābah wa-muʿjam al-sufun*. Beirut, 1992.

- Y -

YM = Sulaymān al-Balkhī. *Yanābīʿ al-mawaddah li-dhī al-qurbá*. Tehran, 1308 [1890-1] (lithographed).

- Z -

ZM = Farīd Shāfiʿī. "Zakhārif muṣḥaf bi-Dār al-Kutub al-Miṣrīyah". *Majallat Kullīyat al-Ādāb* (Cairo), 17, no.1 (1955): 43-48, 6 pl.

2. Technical terms in the glossary

اع = aʿlá Allāh maqāmahu
الخ = ilá ākhirih
لم / ام = āmīn
انشه / انشـ = in shāʾa Allāh (istithnāʾ)
اه = intahá
ب = baʿdu; bāb; bayān; Rajab
ت = taʿlīqah
تع / تعـ = taʿālá
ث = tathlīth
جـ / ١ج / جا = Jumādá al-Ūlá
ج / ٢ج = Jumādá al-Ākhirah
ج / جـ = juzʾ; jazmah; jawāb; jāʾiz (see under waqf)
جش = jalla shaʾnuh (tajlīl)
ح = ḥāʾil (taḥwīl, ḥaylūlah)
حـ / حر = ḥasbunā Allāh (ḥasbalah)
حشـ / حـ = ḥāshiyah
خ = taʾkhīr (muʾakhkhar); nuskhah (ukhrá)
خه / خـ = nuskhah (ukhrá)
خ د = nuskhah-badal
خ ل = nuskhah-badal; nuskhah-aṣl
خف = mukhaffaf
ذ = Dhū al-Ḥijjah
ذا = Dhū al-Qaʿdah
ر = Rabīʿ al-Thānī, Rajab
١ر = Rabīʿ al-Awwal
٢ر = Rabīʿ al-Thānī
رضه / رض / ر = raḍiya Allāh ʿanhu (tarḍiyah)
ره = raḥimahu Allāh (tarḥīm); raḍiya Allāh ʿanhu (tarḍiyah); numrah
رحه / رم = raḥimahu Allāh (tarḥīm)
ز = zāʾidah
س = qaddasa Allāh sirrahu or rūḥahu (taqdīs); suʾāl
الشـ = al-shāriḥ
ش = sharḥ; Shaʿbān; Shawwāl
شا = in shāʾa Allāh (istithnāʾ)
شع = Shaʿbān
ص = aṣl; ṣaḥīḥ; ṣāḥib; ṣawāb (ṣawābuhu); ṣallá Allāh ʿalayhi (ṣalwalah); Ṣafar
صح = ṣaḥīḥ
صل = aṣl
صم / صله / صلم / صلعم / صلع / صع = ṣallá Allāh ʿalayhi (ṣalwalah)
ض = bayāḍ; raḍiya Allāh

ʿanhu (tarḍiyah); ḍabbah (taḍbīb)
ط = ṭurrah; faqaṭ
طر / طه = ṭāba Allāh tharāhu
طره / طع / طع / طلع = aṭāla Allāh ʿumrahu
ظ = ẓann ; ẓāhir; unẓur
ع / ع = maʿṭūfah; taʿshīrah; samāʿ; ʿūriḍa; ʿan fulān; farʿ; rajʿ; laʿallahu; rukūʿ
ع لله = laʿanahu Allāh
ع / ع / عم / ع م /عسد / عه = ʿalayhi al-salām (taslīmah)
عج / ع ج = ʿazza wa-jalla
عج = ʿajjala Allāh farajahu
عط / عف = maʿṭūfah
ع ل / ع ١ = Rabīʿ al-Awwal
ع ٢ = Rabīʿ al-Thānī
عه = laʿallahu
غ = ghalaṭ
ف / فيه = fāʾidah
فتد = fa-taʾammal(hu); fa-tadabbar(hu)
فصد / فصل = fāʾidat al-aṣl
فق = fa-qāla
فيق = fa-yuqāl
ق = qāla; qabla; taqdīm (muqaddam); waraqah
ق / قد / قده / قس / ق س = qaddasa Allāh sirrahu or rūḥahu (taqdīs)
قع = Dhū al-Qaʿdah
قه = qawluhu
ك / ک = kurrās(ah); kadhā; kataba(hu)
كه = katabahu
ل = badal (baddilhu); aṣl; Shawwāl
لع = laʿanahu Allāh
م = matn; tamma; malzamah; Muḥarram; lāzim (see under waqf)
المح = al-muḥashshī
مخ = muʾakhkhar muqaddam
المصد = al-muṣannif
مض = Ramaḍān
معط = maʿṭūfah
مم = muqaddam muʾakhkhar
ن = bayān; nuskhah (ukhrá); Ramaḍān
نخ / نخ = nuskhah (ukhrá)
ه = hāmish
ه / ه = taʿlīqah
هی / ه = intahá
و = waraqah
يق = yuqāl

PART TWO

BIBLIOGRAPHY

The present bibliography, apart from a number of entries in Turkish and Persian, includes the research published in Arabic and European languages on various aspects of the Arabic manuscript tradition. It does not, however, reproduce all the entries found in the bibliographies listed below in Section I.1. The bibliography has been arranged by subject with the result that some entries are repeated in the various sections due to their broader coverage.

Arabic manuscripts cannot be studied in isolation. Indeed, many practices and phenomena connected with Arabic manuscripts are also to be found in the Hebrew, Greek and Latin manuscript traditions. It is therefore appropriate to mention here a number of important references dealing with the codicologies and palaeographies of the latter. Their usefulness for the study of Arabic manuscripts will be evident for anyone who consults them.

Ancient and medieval book materials and techniques, ed. M. Maniaci and P. Munafò. Vatican City, 1993. 2 vols.

Archéologie du livre médiéval: exposition organisée par le Centre national de la recherche scientifique et la Bibliothèque nationale. Paris, 1988.

Beit-Arié, Malachi. *Hebrew codicology: tentative typology of technical practices employed in Hebrew dated medieval manuscripts.* Paris, 1976.

——— *The makings of the medieval Hebrew book: studies in palaeography and codicology.* Jerusalem, 1993.

Bischoff, Bernhard. *Latin palaeography: Antiquity and the Middle Ages.* Transl. by Dáibhí Ó Cróinín and David Ganz. Cambridge, 1990.

Boyle, Leonard. *Medieval Latin palaeography: a bibliographical introduction.* Toronto, 1984.

Bozzolo, Carla. *Pour une histoire du livre manuscrit au Moyen Age: trois essais de codicologie quantitative.* Paris, 1983.

Cockerell, Sydney M. *Bookbinding, and the care of books: a text-book for book-binders and librarians.* 5th ed. London/New York, 1953 (repr. 1979).

Codicologica: towards a science of handwritten books, ed. A. Gruys and J.P. Gumbert. Leiden, 1976-1980. 5 vols.

Dain, Alphonse. *Les manuscrits.* Paris, 1997.

Les débuts du codex, ed. A. Blanchard. Turnhout, 1989.

Delamare, François and Guineau, Bernard. *Les matériaux de la couleur*. Paris, 1999.

Diringer, David. *The hand-produced book*. New York, 1953.

Dukan, M. *La réglure des manuscrits hébreux au Moyen-Age*. Paris, 1988.

Gallo, Italo. *Greek and Latin papyrology*. London, 1986.

Glaister, Geoffrey Ashall. *Encyclopedia of the book*. 2nd ed. New Castle, Del., 1996.

Glenisson, Jean. *Le livre au Moyen Age*. Paris, 1988.

Gruijs, M. Albert. "Paléographie, codicologie et archéologie du livre. Questions de méthodologie et de terminologie". *La paléographie hébraïque médiévale, Paris, 11-13 septembre 1972*. Paris, 1974 : 19-25.

Johnston, Edward. *Writing & illuminating, & lettering*. London/New York, 1977.

Kristeller, Paul O. "Tasks and problems of manuscripts research". *Codicologica*, 1 (1976): 84-90.

Lemaire, Jacques. *Introduction à la codicologie*. Louvain-la-Neuve, 1989.

Maniaci, M. *Terminologia del libro manuscritto*. Rome, 1996.

Les manuscrits datés: premiers bilans et perspectives (= *Die datierten Handschriften: erste Bilanz und Perspektiven*). *Neuchâtel/Neuenburg, 1983*. Paris, 1985.

Murdoch, John E. *Album of science: Antiquity and the Middle Ages*. New York, 1984.

Muzerelle, Denis. *Vocabulaire codicologique: répertoire méthodique des termes français relatifs aux manuscrits*. Paris, 1985.

Pigments et colorants de l'Antiquité et du Moyen-Age: teinture, peinture, enluminure, études historiques et physico-chimiques. Paris, 1990.

Recherches de codicologie comparée: la composition du codex au Moyen-Age en Orient et en Occident, ed. P. Hoffmann. Paris, 1998.

Reynolds, L.D. and Wilson, N.G. *Scribes and scholars: a guide to the transmission of Greek and Latin literature*. 2nd ed. Oxford, 1974.

Roberts, C. H. "The codex". *Proceedings of the British Academy*, 40 (1954): 169-204.

Roberts, C.H. and Skeat, T.C. *The birth of the codex*. London, 1983.

Shailor, Barbara A. *The medieval book: illustrated from the Beinecke Rare Book and Manuscript Library, Yale University*. Toronto, 1991.
Sirat, Colette. *Du scribe au livre: les manuscrits hébreux au Moyen Age*. Paris, 1994.
Les techniques de laboratoire dans l'étude des manuscrits. Paris, 13-15 septembre 1972. Paris, CNRS, 1974.
Thompson, E. Maunde. *An introduction to Greek and Latin palaeography*. Oxford, 1912.
Les tranchefiles brodées: études historique et technique. Paris, 1989.
Turner, Eric G. *The typology of the early codex*. [Philadelphia], 1977.
West, Martin L. *Textual criticism and editorial technique applicable to Greek and Latin texts*. Stuttgart, 1972.
Wouters, A. "From papyrus roll to papyrus codex: some technical aspects of the ancient book fabrication". *Manuscripts of the Middle East*, 5 (1990-91): 9-19.

I. GENERAL AND INTRODUCTORY STUDIES

I. 1. Bibliographies

ʿAbd al-Hādī, Maḥammad Fatḥī. *Al-Turāth al-ʿArabī al-Islāmī: biblyūj-rāfīyah bi-al-intāj al-fikrī al-ʿArabī min 1882 ilá 1998*. London, Muʾassasat al-Furqān lil-Turāth al-Islāmī. 1419/1999.
ʿAbd al-Raḥmān, ʿAbd al-Jabbār. *Kashshāf al-dawrīyāt al-ʿArabīyah*. Baghdad, 1989. 4 vols.
Dhayyāb, Miftāḥ Muḥammad. "Ḥarakat al-taʾlīf wa-al-kutub wa-al-maktabāt". *Majallat Kullīyat al-Daʿwah al-Islāmīyah* (Tripoli, Libya), 6 (1989): 367-398.
Endress, Gerhard. "Handschriftenkunde". *Grundriss der arabischen Philologie*. Band I: *Sprachwissenschaft*, herausgegeben von W. Fischer. Wiesbaden, 1982: 306-315.
Gacek, Adam. "A select bibliography of Arabic language publications concerning Arabic manuscripts". *Manuscripts of the Middle East*, 1 (1986): 106-108.
——— "Arabic language publications on manuscripts (Part I)". *Nouvelles des manuscrits du Moyen-Orient*, VII/1 (1998): 3-8.
——— "Arabic language publications on manuscripts (Part II)". *Nouvelles des manuscrits du Moyen-Orient*, VII/2 (1998): 2-7.
Index Islamicus on CD-ROM. London/New York, 1998.

I. 2. Periodicals

ʿĀlam al-makhṭūṭāṭ wa-al-nawādir. Riyad, 1 (1996) – .

Fichier des manuscrits moyen-orientaux datés (FiMMOD). (Published in loose-leaf format within *Nouvelles des manuscrits du Moyen-Orient*), ed. François Déroche. Paris, 1991- .

Majallat Maʿhad al-Makhṭūṭāt al-ʿArabīyah. Cairo, 1 (1955) – .

Manuscripta Orientalia. International journal for Oriental manuscript research. St.Petersburg/Helsinki, 1, no.1 (1995) – .

Manuscripts of the Middle East: a journal devoted to the study of hand written materials of the Middle East, ed. J.J. Witkam. Leiden, 1 (1986) – .

Nouvelles des manuscrits du Moyen-Orient, ed. François Déroche et al. Paris, 1991– .

I. 3. Conference proceedings and composite works

Ahammīyat al-makhṭūṭāt al-Islāmīyah. Aʿmāl al-Muʾtamar al-Iftitāḥī li-Muʾassasat al-Furqān lil-Turāth al-Islāmī. London, 1992.

The book in the Islamic world: the written word and communication in the Middle East, ed. George N. Atiyeh. Albany, NY, 1995.

The codicology of Islamic manuscripts. Proceedings of the Second Conference of al-Furqān Islamic Heritage Foundation, 1993, ed. Y. Dutton. London, 1995.

The conservation and preservation of Islamic manuscripts. Proceedings of the Third Conference of al-Furqān Islamic Heritage Foundation 18th-19th November 1995, ed. Yusuf Ibish and George Atiyeh. London, 1996.

Dirāsāt al-makhṭūṭāt al-Islāmīyah bayna iʿtibārāt al-māddah wa-al-bashar. Aʿmāl al-Muʾtamar al-Thānī li-Muʾassasat al-Furqān lil-Turāth al-Islāmī, ed. Rashīd al-ʿInānī. London, 1997.

Editing Islamic manuscripts on science. Proceedings of the Fourth Conference of al-Furqān Islamic Heritage Foundation, 29th-30th November 1997, ed. Yusuf Ibish. London, 1420/1999.

Fann fahrasat al-makhṭūṭāt: madkhal wa-qaḍāyā, ed. Fayṣal al-Ḥafyān. Cairo, Maʿhad al-Makhṭūṭāt al-ʿArabīyah, 1999.

"Livres et lecture dans le monde ottoman", thème sous la responsabilité de Frédéric Hitzel. *Revue des mondes musulmans et de la Méditerranée*, 87/88 (1999).

Al-Makhṭūṭ al-ʿArabī wa-ʿilm al-makhṭūṭāt (= Le manuscrit arabe et la codicologie). Rabat, 1994.

Al-Makhṭūṭāt al-ʿArabīyah fī al-Gharb al-Islāmī: waḍʿīyat al-majmūʿāt wa-āfāq al-baḥth (= Manuscrits arabes en occident musulman). Casablanca, Muʾassasat al-Malik ʿAbd al-ʿAzīz, 1990.

Les manuscrits du Moyen-Orient: essais de codicologie et de paléographie. Actes du colloque d'Istanbul (Istanbul, 26-29 mai 1986), ed. F. Déroche. Istanbul/Paris, 1989.

Le papier au moyen âge: histoire et techniques, ed. M. Zerdoun Bat-Yehouda. Turnhout, 1999.

"Patrimoine manuscrit et vie intellectuelle de l'Asie centrale islamique", sous la direction de Ashirbek Muminov, Francis Richard et Maria Szuppe. *Cahiers d'Asie centrale*, 7 (1999).

Recherches de codicologie comparée: la composition du codex au Moyen Age en Orient et en Occident. Paris, 1998.

Scribes et manuscrits du Moyen-Orient, ed. F. Déroche and F. Richard. Paris, 1997.

The significance of Islamic manuscripts. Proceedings of the Inaugural Conference of al-Furqān Islamic Heritage Foundation (30th November – 1st December 1991), ed. John Cooper. London, 1992.

Ṣināʿat al-makhṭūṭ al-ʿArabī al-Islāmī min al-tarmīm ilá al-tajlīd: al-dawrah al-tadrībīyah al-dawlīyah al-ūlá, Dubayy, al-Imārāt al-ʿArabīyah al-Muttaḥidah, min 26 Dhū al-Ḥijjah 1417 h. ilá 9 Muḥarram 1418 h. al-muwāfiq 3 Māyū 1997 m. ilá 15 Māyū 1997 m. Dubai, Markaz al-Jumʿah al-Majīd lil-Thaqāfah wa-al-Turāth, [1997].

Ṣiyānah wa-ḥifẓ al-makhṭūṭāt al-Islāmīyah. Aʿmāl al-Muʾtamar al-Thālith li-Muʾassasat al-Furqān lil-Turāth al-Islāmī, 18-19 Nov. 1995, ed. Ibrāhīm Shabbūḥ. London, 1998.

Taḥqīq makhṭūṭāt al-ʿulūm fī al-turāth al-Islāmī: abḥāth al-Muʾtamar al-Rābiʿ li-Muʾassasat al-Furqān lil-Turāth al-Islāmī, 29-30 Nov. 1997, ed. Ibrāhīm Shabbūḥ. London, 1999.

Al-Tajārib al-ʿArabīyah fī fahrasat al-makhṭūṭāt, ed. Fayṣal al-Ḥafyān. Cairo, Maʿhad al-Makhṭūṭāt al-ʿArabīyah, 1998.

"La tradition manuscrite en écriture arabe", thème sous la responsabilité de Geneviève Humbert. *Revue des mondes musulmans et de la Méditerranée*, (forthcoming).

Al-Turāth al-ʿilmī al-ʿArabī: manāhij taḥqīqih wa-ishkālat nashrih, ed. Fayṣal al-Ḥafyān. Cairo, Maʿhad al-Makhṭūṭāt al-ʿArabīyah, 2000.

I. 4. General studies and surveys

ʿAbd al-Hādī, ʿAdnān. "Tadwīn al-makhṭūṭ al-ʿArabī fī al-ʿaṣr al-ʿUthmānī, 922-1225". *ʿĀlam al-kutub*, 11, no.2 (1990): 189-197.

Akimushkin, Oleg F., Khalidov, Anas B. and Rezvan, Efim A. "The triumph of the qalam". *Pages of perfection. Islamic paintings and calligraphy from the Russian Academy of Sciences, St. Petersburg*. Lugano/Milan, 1995: 35-75.

al-ʿAlī, Ṣāliḥ Aḥmad. "Al-Tadwīn wa-ẓuhūr al-kutub al-muṣannafah fī al-ʿuhūd al-Islāmīyah al-ūlá". *Majallat al-Majmaʿ al-ʿIlmī al-ʿIrāqī*, 31, no.2 (1980): 3-46.

Amān, Muḥammad Muḥammad. *Al-Kutub al-Islāmīyah*. Tarjamah wa-taʿlīq Saʿd ibn ʿAbd Allāh al-Ḥubayʿān. Riyad, Maktabat al-Malik Fahd al-Waṭanīyah, 1411/ 1990. [Based on his "Islamic books", *Encyclopaedia of Library and Information Science*. New York, 1968-83: 13, 90-111.]

Arnold, T.W. and Grohmann, Adolf. *The Islamic book: a contribution to its art and history from the VIIth to the XIIIth century*. [Florence], 1929.

ʿAṭāʾ Allāh, Samīr. *Taʾrīkh wa-fann ṣināʿat al-kitāb*. Beirut, Dār ʿAṭāʾ Allāh, 1993.

ʿAṭīyah, Muḥyī al-Dīn. *Al-Kitāb al-Islāmī*. Kuwait, Dār al-Buḥūth al-ʿIlmīyah, 1982.

Bencherifa (Binsharīfah), Mohamed. "Problems of attribution in historical and geographical works". *The codicology of Islamic manuscripts. Proceedings of the Second Conference of al-Furqān Islamic Heritage Foundation, 1993*, ed. Y. Dutton. London, 1995: 103-121.

——— "Ẓāhirat al-makhṭūṭāt majhūlat al-muʾallif: al-makhṭūṭāt al-taʾrīkhīyah wa-al-jughrāfīyah mithālan". *Dirāsāt al-makhṭūṭāt al-Islāmīyah bayna iʿtibārāt al-māddah wa-al-bashar. Aʿmāl al-Muʾtamar al-Thānī li-Muʾassasat al-Furqān lil-Turāth al-Islāmī*, ed. Rashīd al-ʿInānī. London, 1997: 207-227.

Bielawski, Józef. *Książka w świecie Islamu*. Warsaw, 1961.

Binbīn, Aḥmad Shawqī. *Dirāsāt fī ʿilm al-makhṭūṭāt wa-al-baḥth al-bibliyūghrāfī*. Rabat, Jāmiʿat Muḥammad al-Khāmis, Kullīyat al-Ādāb wa-al-ʿUlūm al-Insānīyah, 1993.

Bin Zuwaytīn, al-Shādhilī. *Ta'rīkh al-kitāb bi-Tūnis qadīman wa-ḥadīthan, khaṭṭan wa-nasākhatan, ṭibā'an wa-nashran, ishāratan wa-tawzī'an* .... Tunis, 1997.

Déroche, François et al. *Manuel de codicologie des manuscrits en écriture arabe*. Paris, Bibliothèque nationale de France, 2000.

Endress, Gerhard. "Handschriftenkunde". *Grundriss der arabischen Philologie*, Band I: *Sprachwissenschaft*, herausgegeben von W. Fischer. Wiesbaden, 1982: 271-291.

al-Ḥalwajī, ʿAbd al-Sattār. *Al-Makhṭūṭ al-ʿArabī*. Cairo, Dār al-Thaqāfah, 1986. [2nd revised ed.: Jeddah, Maktabat Miṣbāḥ, 1989.]

——— "Al-Makhṭūṭāt al-ʿArabīyah bayna al-ta'līf wa-al-imlā'". *Majallat Kullīyat al-Lughah al-ʿArabīyah* (Riyad), 4 (1974): 303-311.

Ḥammūdah, Maḥmūd ʿAbbās. *Ta'rīkh al-kitāb al-Islāmī al-makhṭūṭ*. Cairo, Dār Gharīb, 1994.

al-Jubūrī, Yaḥyá Wahīb. *Al-Kitāb fī al-ḥaḍārah al-Islāmīyah (=The book in Islamic civilization)*. Beirut, Dār al-Gharb al-Islāmī, 1998.

al-Ka"āk, ʿUthmān. "Al-Khiṭāṭah al-Tūnisīyah". *Majallat al-Maktabah al-ʿArabīyah* (Cairo), 1, no.1 (1963): 26-48; 1, no.3 (1964): 19-33.

al-Kattānī, Muḥammad Ibrāhīm. "Al-Kitāb al-Maghribī wa-qīmatuh". *Al-Baḥth al-ʿilmī*, 4-6 (1965): 9-57.

Khalidov, A. B. *Arabskie rukopisi i arabskaia rukopisnaia traditsiia*. Moscow, 1985.

Koningsveld, P.S. van. "Andalusian-Arabic manuscripts from Christian Spain: a comparative intercultural approach". *Israel Oriental studies*, 12 (1992): 75-110.

——— "Andalusian-Arabic manuscripts in Christian Spain: some supplementary notes". *Festgabe für Hans-Rudolf Singer zum 65. Geburtstag*. Frankfurt am Main, 1991: 811-823.

Krachkovskii, I.Y. *Among Arabic manuscripts*. Transl. by Tatiana Minorsky. Leiden, 1953.

al-Kūtī, Aḥmad. "Al-Kitābah ʿinda al-ʿArab fī al-jāhilīyah wa-ṣadr al-Islām". *Majallat Majmaʿ al-Lughah al-ʿArabīyah bi-Dimashq*, 61, no.2 (1986): 348-361.

al-Maḥāsinī, Samā' Zakī. *Dirāsāt fī al-makhṭūṭāt al-ʿArabīyah*. Riyad, Maktabat al-Malik al-Fahd al-Waṭanīyah, 1999.

al-Manūnī, Muḥammad. *Ta'rīkh al-wirāqah al-Maghribīyah: ṣināʿat al-makhṭūṭ al-ʿArabī min al-ʿaṣr al-wasīṭ ilá al-fatrah al-*

muʿāṣirah. Rabat, Jāmiʿat Muḥammad al-Khāmis, Kullīyat al-Ādāb wa-al-ʿUlūm al-Insānīyah, 1991.

——— *Qabas min ʿaṭāʾ al-makhṭūṭ al-Maghribī (= Quintessence des manuscrits marocains)*. Beirut, Dār al-Gharb al-Islāmī, 1999. 4 vols. in 3.

Maqdisī, Jūrj. "Al-Ḥifāẓ ʿalá al-turāth wa-al-daʿwah ilá dirāsatih". *Ahammīyat al-makhṭūṭāt al-Islāmīyah. Aʿmāl al-Muʾtamar al-Iftitāḥī li-Muʾassasat al-Furqān lil-Turāth al-Islāmī*. London, 1992: 17-22.

Murūwah, Ibrāhīm Ibrāhīm. *Fī al-makhṭūṭāt al-ʿArabīyah: qirāʾāt taṭbīqīyah*. Beirut/ Damascus, Dār al-Fikr, 1997.

al-Musfir, ʿAbd al-ʿAzīz ibn Muḥammad. *Al-Makhṭūṭ al-ʿArabī wa-shayʾ min qaḍāyāh*. Riyad, Dār al-Mirrīkh, 1999.

Nasr, Sayyid Husayn. "Ahammīyat al-makhṭūṭāt al-Islāmīyah". *Ahammīyat al-makhṭūṭāt al-Islāmīyah. Aʿmāl al-Muʾtamar al-Iftitāḥī li-Muʾassasat al-Furqān lil-Turāth al-Islāmī*. London, 1992: 29-42.

——— "The significance of Islamic manuscripts". *The significance of Islamic manuscripts. Proceedings of the Inaugural Conference of al-Furqān Islamic Heritage Foundation (30th November – 1st December 1991)*, ed. John Cooper. London, 1992: 7-17.

Orsatti, Paola. "Il manoscritto come specchio di una cultura: il caso dell'Islam". *Gazette du livre médiéval*, 24 (1994): 1-7.

——— "Le manuscrit islamique: caractéristiques matérielles et typologie". *Ancient and medieval book materials and techniques*, ed. M. Maniaci and P. Munafò. Vatican City, 1993: 2, 269-331.

Pedersen, Johannes. *The Arabic book*. Transl. [from the Danish *Den Arabiske Bog*] by G. French, ed. R. Hillenbrand. Princeton, 1984. [Also translated from the English into Arabic: *al-Kitāb al-ʿArabī mundhu nashʾatih ḥattá ʿaṣr al-ṭibāʿah*, tarjamat Ḥaydar Ghaybah. Damascus, al-Ahālī , 1409/1989.]

Piemontese, Angelo Michele. "Islamic manuscripts in the West". *The significance of Islamic manuscripts. Proceedings of the Inaugural Conference of al-Furqān Islamic Heritage Foundation (30th November – 1st December 1991)*, ed. John Cooper. London, 1992: 45-54.

Rosenthal, Franz. "'Of making many books there is no end': the classical Muslim view". *The book in the Islamic world: the written word and communication in the Middle East*, ed. George N. Atiyeh. Albany, N.Y., 1995: 33-55.

Sadan, J. "Genizah and Genizah-like practices in Islamic and Jewish traditions". *Bibliotheca Orientalis*, 43, 1-2 (1986), 36-58.

Sayyid, Aymān Fu'ād. *Al-Kitāb al-ʿArabī al-makhṭūṭ wa-ʿilm al-makhṭūṭāt (=Le manuscrit arabe et la codicologie)*. Cairo: al-Dār al-Miṣrīyah al-Lubnānīyah, 1997. 2 vols.

——— "Ṣināʿat al-kitāb al-ʿArabī al-makhṭūṭ". *Annales islamologiques (= Ḥawlīyāt Islāmīyah)*, 31, (1997): 1-39.

Sellheim, Rudolf. "Kitāb". *EI*, new ed., 5: 207-208.

Shākir, Maḥmūd Abū Fahr. "Dhikrīyāt maʿa muḥibbī al-makhṭūṭāt". *Ahammīyat al-makhṭūṭāt al-Islāmīyah. Aʿmāl al-Mu'tamar al-Iftitāḥī li-Mu'assasat al-Furqān lil-Turāth al-Islāmī*. London, 1992: 23-28.

Sharpe, J.L. "Books and book-making". *Encyclopedia of Arabic literature*, ed. J.S. Meisami and P. Starkey. London/New York, 1988: 1, 154-160.

al-Shaybānī, Muḥammad ibn Ibrāhīm. *Al-Makhṭūṭ al-ʿArabī wa-al-Islāmī: fawā'id, qīmah, ṣiyānah*. Kuwait, Markaz al-Makhṭūṭāt wa-al-Turāth wa-al-Wathā'iq, 1999.

Witkam, J.J. and Sukanda-Tessier, Viviane. "Nuskha". *EI*, new ed., 8: 149-154.

Zaydān, Yūsuf. *Al-Turāth al-majhūl: iṭlālah ʿalá ʿālam al-makhṭūṭāt*. Cairo, Dār al-Amīn, 1996.

Ždralović, Muhamed. *Bosansko-Hercegovački prepisivači djela u arabičkim rukopisima*. Sarajevo, Svjetlost, 1988. 2 vols.

I. 5. Selected studies of one or more manuscripts

Abbott, Nabia. "A ninth-century fragment of the 'Thousand Nights': new light on the early history of the Arabian Nights". *Journal of Near Eastern studies*, 8 (1949): 129-164, pl. XV-XVIII.

Arberry, A.J. "Two rare manuscripts". *Journal of Arabic literature*, 1 (1970): 112-113.

Birnbaum, Eleazar. "Kātib Chelebi (1609-1657) and alphabetization: a methodological investigation of the autographs of his 'Kashf al-ẓunūn' and 'Sullam al-wuṣūl'". *Scribes et manuscrits du Moyen-Orient*, ed. F. Déroche and F. Richard. Paris, 1997: 235-263.

Bivar, A.D.H. "A possible Fulani autograph in the Library of SOAS". *Threefold wisdom: Islam, the Arab world and Africa. Papers in honour of Ivan Hrbek*. Prague, 1993: 39-46.

Bonebakker, S.A. "Notes on some old manuscripts of the *Adab al-*

kātib of Ibn Qutayba, the *Kitāb aṣ-ṣinā'atayn* of Abū Hilāl al-ʿAskarī and the *Maṯal as-sā'ir* of Ḍiyā' ad-Dīn ibn al-Aṯīr". *Oriens*, 13-14 (1960-61): 159-194.

Daiber, Hans. "An Arabic manuscript library: some important discoveries". *Manuscripts of the Middle East*, 2 (1987): 18-36.

De Blois, François. "The oldest known Fāṭimid manuscript from Yemen". *Proceedings of the Seminar for Arabian studies*, 14 (1984): 1-7.

Déroche, François. "A propos du manuscrit 'arabe 6726', Bibliothèque nationale, Paris (al-Aṣmaʿī, Ta'rīkh mulūk al-ʿArab al-awwalīn)". *Revue des études islamiques*, 58 (1990): 209-212.

Géhin, Paul. "Un manuscrit bilingue grec-arabe, BnF, Supplément grec 911 (année 1043)". *Scribes et manuscrits du Moyen-Orient*, ed. F. Déroche and F. Richard. Paris, 1997: 161-175.

Hartmann, Angelika. "Codicologie comme source biographique: à propos d'un autographe inédit d'Ibn al-Ğauzī". *Les manuscrits du Moyen-Orient*, ed. F. Déroche. Istanbul/Paris, 1989: 23-30.

——— "Bemerkungen zu Handschriften ʿUmar as-Suhrawardīs, echten und vermeintlichen Autographen". *Der Islam*, 60, no.1 (1983): 112-142, 6 pl.

Humbert, Geneviève. "Copie 'à la pecia' à Baghdad au IXe siècle?". *Gazette du livre médiéval*, no.12 (1988): 12-15.

——— "Le Kitāb de Sībawayhi d'après l'autographe d'un grammairien andalou du XIIe siècle". *Al-Makhṭūṭ al-ʿArabī wa-ʿilm al-makhṭūṭāt (= Le manuscrit arabe et la codicologie)*. Rabat, 1994: 9-20.

Koningsveld, P.S. van. *The Latin-Arabic glossary of the Leiden University Library. A contribution to the study of Mozarabic manuscripts and literature*. Leiden, 1977.

Lévi-Provençal, E. "Un manuscrit de la bibliothèque du calife al-Ḥakam II". *Hespéris*, 18 (1934): 198-200.

——— "Note sur l'exemplaire du 'Kitāb al-ʿibar' offert par Ibn Ḥaldūn à la bibliothèque d'al-Ḳarawīyīn à Fèz". *Journal asiatique*, 203 (1923): 161-168.

Mingana, A. *An important manuscript of the traditions of Bukhāri: with nine facsimile reproductions*. Cambridge, 1936.

Muranyi, Miklos. "Über ein Muwaṭṭa'-Fragment in der Zāwiya al-Nāṣiriyya in Tamagrūt (Marokko)". *Die Welt des Orients*, 29 (1998): 149-157.

Palmer, H. R. "Two Sudanese manuscripts of the 17th century". *Bulletin of the School of Oriental Studies. London Institution*, 5 (1928-30): 541-560.

Ritter, Hellmut. "Autographs in Turkish libraries". *Oriens*, 6 (1953): 63-90.

Sayyid, Aymān Fu'ād. "Early methods of book composition: al-Maqrīzī's draft of 'Kitāb al-khiṭaṭ'". *The Codicology of Islamic manuscripts. Proceedings of the Second Conference of Al-Furqān Islamic Heritage Foundation, 4-5 Dec.1993*. London, 1995: 93-101.

——— "Ṭarīqat al-ta'līf ʿinda al-qudamā' min khilāl musawwadat al-Maqrīzī li-Kitāb al-khiṭaṭ". *Dirāsāt al-makhṭūṭāt al-Islāmīyah bayna iʿtibārāt al-māddah wa-al-bashar. Aʿmāl al-Mu'tamar al-Thānī li-Mu'assasat al-Furqān lil-Turāth al-Islāmī*, ed. Rashīd al-ʿInānī. London, 1997: 153-162.

Schacht, J. "On some manuscripts in the libraries of Kairouan and Tunis". *Arabica*, 14 (1967): 225-258.

——— "Sur quelques manuscrits de la bibliothèque de la mosquée d'al-Qarawiyyīn". *Etudes d'orientalisme dédiées à la mémoire de Lévi-Provençal*. Paris, 1962: 1, 271-284.

Sellheim, R. "Neue Materialien zur Biographie des Yāqūt". *Schriften und Bilder: drei orientalistische Untersuchungen*. Wiesbaden, 1967: 41(87)-72(118), Taf. VII(XI)-XXX(XXXIV).

Sidarus, Adel. "Un recueil original de philologie gréco-copto-arabe: la Scala Copte 43 de la Bibliothèque nationale de France". *Scribes et manuscrits du Moyen-Orient*, ed. F. Déroche and F. Richard. Paris, 1997: 293-326.

Stern, S.M. "A manuscript from the Library of the Ghaznawid Amīr ʿAbd al-Rashīd". *Paintings from Islamic lands*, ed. R. Pinder-Wilson. Oxford, 1969: 7-31.

——— "Some noteworthy manuscripts of the poems of Abu'l-ʿAlā' al-Maʿarrī". *Oriens*, 7 (1954): 322-347.[Reprinted in his *History and culture in the medieval Islamic world*. London, 1984.]

Vajda, G. "Trois manuscrits de la bibliothèque du savant damascain Yūsuf ibn ʿAbd al-Hādī". *Journal asiatique*, 270 (1982): 229-256.

Witkam, J.J. "Les autographs d'al-Maqrīzī". *Al-Makhṭūṭ al-ʿArabī wa-ʿilm al-makhṭūṭāt (= Le manuscrit arabe et la codicologie)*. Rabat, 1994: 89-98.

——— "Ḥasan Kāfī al-Aqḥiṣārī and his 'Niẓām al-ʿulamāʾ ilā ḵātam al-anbiyā': a facsimile edition of MS Bratislava TF 136". *Manuscripts of the Middle East*, 4 (1989): 85-114.
——— "The 'Kitāb Qamʿ al-wāšīn fī ḏamm al-barrāšīn' by Nūr al-Dīn ʿAlī b. al-Ǧazzār: a facsimile edition of the unique manuscript". *Manuscripts of the Middle East*, 1 (1986): 86-99.
——— "Manuscripts & manuscripts". *Manuscripts of the Middle East*, 1 (1986): 111-117; 2 (1987): 111-125; 4 (1988): 155-180.

I. 6. Manuscript production and culture (wirāqah)

ʿAbd al-Wahhāb, Ḥasan Ḥusnī. "Al-ʿInāyah bi-al-kutub wa-jamʿuhā fī Ifrīqīyah al-Tūnisīyah (min al-qarn al-thālith ilá al-khāmis lil-hijrah)". *Majallat Maʿhad al-Makhṭūṭāt al-ʿArabīyah*, 1 (1955): 72-90.
Akhtar, Ahmadmian. "The art of waraqat during the Abbasid period". *Islamic culture*, 9 (1935): 131-143.
——— "More about the art of waraqat". *All-India Oriental Conference*, 9 (1937): 294-310.
Déroche, François. "Copier des manuscrits: remarques sur le travail du copiste". *Revue des mondes musulmans et de la Méditerranée* (forthcoming).
Jamil, Muhammad Faris. "Islamic wiraqah 'stationery' during the early Middle Ages (bookmaking, Muslim bookproducing)". Ph.D. diss., University of Michigan, 1985.
Karbāj, Jūrj. "Al-Wirāqah wa-al-warrāqūn ʿinda al-ʿArab". *Āfāq ʿArabīyah*, 9 (1984): 66-71.
al-Manūnī, Muḥammad. "Shawāhid min izdihār al-wirāqah fī Sabtah al-Islāmīyah". *Majallat Kullīyat al-Ādāb bi-Tiṭwān*, 3 (1989): 117-119.
——— *Taʾrīkh al-wirāqah al-Maghribīyah. Ṣināʿat al-makhṭūṭ al-ʿArabī min al-ʿaṣr al-wasīṭ ilá al-fatrah al-muʿāṣirah*. Rabat, Jāmiʿat Muḥammad al-Khāmis, Kullīyat al-Ādāb wa-al-ʿUlūm al-Insānīyah, 1991.
——— "Al-Wirāqah al-ʿAlawīyah ʿabra sabʿat ʿuqūd min al-miʾah al-hijrīyah al-thālithah ʿashrata". *Daʿwat al-ḥaqq*, 23, no.4 (1982): 10-24; 24, no.246 (1985): 133-151.
——— "Al-Wirāqah al-Maghribīyah fī ʿahd al-Sulṭān al-ʿAlawī Muḥammad al-Thālith". *Daʿwat al-ḥaqq*, 18, no.2 (1977): 45-56.

——— "Al-Wirāqah al-Maghribīyah fī al-ʿaṣr al-ʿAlawī al-awwal". *Daʿwat al-ḥaqq*, 16, no.10 (1975): 80-92.
——— "Al-Wirāqah al-Maghribīyah min al-fatḥ al-Islāmī ḥattá nihāyat al-Dawlah al-Waṭṭāsīyah". *Al-Baḥth al-ʿilmī*, 16 (1970): 37-65.
——— "Al-Wirāqah al-Maghribīyah: al-Dawlah al-Saʿdīyah". *Al-Baḥth al-ʿilmī*, 18 (1971): 17-47.
——— "Al-Wirāqah al-Maghribīyah fī al-ʿaṣr al-ʿAlawī al-rābiʿ". *Al-Manāhil*, 26 (1987): 37-90.
al-Namlah, ʿAlī ibn Ibrāhīm. *Al-Wirāqah wa-ashhar aʿlām al-warrāqīn: dirāsah fī al-nashr al-qadīm wa-naql al-maʿlūmat*. Riyad, Maktabat al-Malik Fahd al-Waṭanīyah, 1415/1995.
al-Nāṣirī, Aḥmad ʿAlī. "Al-Warrāqūn wa-al-nassākhūn wa-dawruhum fī al-ḥaḍārah al-ʿArabīyah al-Islāmīyah". *Al-Dārah*, 14, no.4 (1989): 178-195.
Ṭayyib, Asʿad. "Min aḥwāl al-nussākh fī turāthinā al-ʿArabī al-Islāmī". *Turāthunā*, 29 (1412 A.H.):90-104.
Zayyāt, Ḥabīb. "Al-Wirāqah wa-al-warrāqūn fī al-Islām". *Al-Mashriq*, 41 (1947): 305- 350.
Ždralović, Muhamed. *Bosansko-Hercegovački prepisivači djela u arabičkim rukopisima*. Sarajevo, Svjetlost, 1988. 2 vols.

I. 7. Libraries (selected bibliographies and studies)

Auchterlonie, J.P.C. "Libraries". *Arab Islamic bibliography: the Middle East Library Committee guide*, ed. D. Grimwood-Jones et al. Hassocks, England, 1977: 235-265.
Binebine, Ahmed Chouqui. *Histoire des bibliothèques au Maroc*. Rabat, 1992.
Binbīn, Aḥmad Shawqī. "Ẓāhirat waqf al-kutub fī taʾrīkh al-khizānah al-Maghribīyah". *Majallat Majmaʿ al-Lughah al-ʿArabīyah bi-Dimashq*, 63, no.3 (1988): 409-436.
De Jong, Frederick and Witkam, Jan Just. "The library of šayḵ Ḵālid al-Šahrazūrī al-Naqšabandī (d.1242/1827): a facsimile of the inventory of his library (MS Damascus, Maktabat al-Asad, no.259)". *Manuscripts of the Middle East*, 2 (1987): 68-87.
Deverdun, G. "Un registre d'inventaire et de prêt de la bibliothèque de la mosquée ʿAli ben Youssef à Marrakech daté de 1111 H.-1700 J.C.". *Hespéris*, 31 (1944): 55-59.

Eche, Yussef. *Les bibliothèques arabes publiques et semi-publiques en Mesopotamie, en Syrie et en Egypte au moyen âge*. Damascus, 1967.

Endress, Gerhard. "Handschriftenkunde". *Grundriss der arabischen Philologie*. Band I: *Sprachwissenschaft*, herausgegeben von W. Fischer. Wiesbaden, 1982: 306-308.

Gacek, Adam. "The ancient 'sijill' of Qayrawan". *MELA notes*, no.46 (1989): 26-29.

Ḥammādah, Muḥammad Māhir. *Al-Maktabāt fī al-Islām: nashʾatuhā wa-taṭawwuruhā wa-maṣāʾiruhā*. Beirut, Muʾassasat al-Risālah, 1978.

Heffening, W. and Pearson, J.D. "Maktaba". *EI*, new ed., 6: 197-200.

Ibrāhīm, ʿAbd al-Laṭīf. *Dirāsāt fī al-kutub wa-al-maktabāt al-Islāmīyah*. Cairo, Maṭbaʿat Jāmiʿat al-Qāhirah, 1962.

al-Manūnī, Muḥammad. "Al-Khizānah al-Maghribīyah fī ʿaṣr al-Sulṭān al-Ḥasan al-Awwal". *Al-Manāhil*, 38 (1989): 7-103.

Muminov, Ashirbek and Ziyadov, Shavasil. "L'horizon intellectuel d'un érudit du XVe siècle: nouvelles découvertes sur la bibliothèque de Muḥammad Pârsâ". *Cahiers de l'Asie centrale*, 7 (1999): 77-98.

Richter-Bernburg, L. "Libraries, medieval". *Encyclopaedia of Arabic literature*, ed. J.S. Meisami and P. Starkey. New York, 1998: 2, 470-471.

Sāʿātī, Yaḥyá Maḥmūd. *Al-Waqf wa-binyat al-maktabah al-ʿArabīyah: istibṭān lil-mawrūth al-thaqāfī*. Riyad, Markaz al-Malik Fayṣal lil-Buḥūth wa-al-Dirāsāt al-Islāmīyah, 1996.

Sayyid, Ayman Fuʾād. "Khizānat kutub al-Fāṭimīyīn: hal baqiya minhā shayʾ?" *Majallat Maʿhad al-Makhṭūṭāt al-ʿArabīyah*, 42, no.1 (1998): 7-32.

Sayyid, Fuʾād. "Naṣṣān qadīmān fī iʿārat al-kutub". *Majallat Maʿhad al-Makhṭūṭāt al-ʿArabīyah*, 4, no. 1 (1958): 125-136. [Contains Jalāl al-Dīn al-Suyūṭī's *Badhl al-majhūd fī khizānat Maḥmūd*.]

Shabbūḥ, Ibrāhīm. "Sijill qadīm li-maktabat Jāmiʿ al-Qayrawān". *Majallat Maʿhad al-Makhṭūṭāt al-ʿArabīyah*, 2 (1956): 339-372.

Sibai, Mohamed Makki. *Mosque libraries: an historical study*. London/ New York, 1987.

Wasserstein, David. "The library of al-Ḥakam II al-Mustanṣir and the culture of Islamic Spain". *Manuscripts of the Middle East*, 5 (1990-91): 99-105.

I. 8. History of manuscripts (ownership statements, seal impressions, waqf-statements, etc.)

Afshar, Iraj. "ʿArż (عرض) dans la tradition bibliothéconomique irano-indienne". *Scribes et manuscrits du Moyen-Orient*, ed. F. Déroche and F. Richard. Paris, 1997: 331-343.

Allan, J. and Sourdel, D. "Khātam, khātim". *EI*, new ed., 4: 1102-1105.

Binbīn, Aḥmad Shawqī. "Ẓāhirat waqf al-kutub fī taʾrīkh al-khizānah al-Maghribīyah". *Majallat Majmaʿ al-Lughah al-ʿArabīyah bi-Dimashq*, 63, no.3 (1988): 409-436.

Deny, J. and Nizami, K.A. "Muhr". *EI*, new ed. 7: 472-473.

Deverdun, Gaston and Ghiati, Mhammed ben Abdeslem. "Deux taḥbīs almohades (milieu du XIIIe s. J.-C.)". *Hespéris*, 41 (1954): 411-423.

Gacek, Adam. "Ownership statements and seals in Arabic manuscripts". *Manuscripts of the Middle East*, 2 (1987): 88-95. [Persian translation by Nūsh Āfrīn Anṣārī (Muḥaqqiq), *Āyinah-i pizhūhish*, 13-14 (1371), 711-718 (33-40).]

Hammer-Purgstall, J. *Abhandlung über die Siegel der Araber, Perser und Türken*. Vienna, 1849.

Kalus, Ludvik. *Catalogue des cachets, bulles et talismans islamiques*. Paris, 1981.

——— *Catalogue of Islamic seals and talismans*. Oxford, 1986.

——— "Islamic art, VIII, 14. Seals". *The dictionary of art*, ed. J. Turner. New York, 1996: 16, 542-543.

Rosenthal, Franz. "'Blurbs' (*taqrīẓ*) from fourteenth-century Egypt". *Oriens*, 27-28 (1981): 177-196.

al-Qaḥṭānī, Rāshid ibn Saʿd. "Ṣafaḥāt al-ʿanāwīn fī al-makhṭūṭāt al-ʿArabīyah". *ʿĀlam al-makhṭūṭāt wa-al-nawādir*, 2, no.2 (1997-8): 365-383.

Sāʿātī, Yaḥyá Maḥmūd. *Al-Waqf wa-binyat al-maktabah al-ʿArabīyah: istibṭān lil-mawrūth al-thaqāfī*. Riyad, Markaz al-Malik Fayṣal lil-Buḥūth wa-al-Dirāsāt al-Islāmīyah, 1996: 130-171 and 31 illus. (in particular).

Shishin (Şeşen), Ramaḍān. "Ahammīyat ṣafḥat al-ʿunwān (al-ẓahrīyah) fī tawṣīf al-makhūṭāt". *Dirāsāt al-makhṭūṭāt al-Islāmīyah bayna iʿtibārāt al-māddah wa-al-bashar. Aʿmāl al-Muʾtamar al-Thānī li-Muʾassasat al-Furqān lil-Turāth al-Islāmī*, ed. Rashīd al-ʿInānī. London, 1997: 179-196.

Wenzel, Marian. *Ornament and amulet: rings of the Islamic lands*. London/Oxford, 1993 (*The Nasser D. Khalili Collection of Islamic Art, XVI*).

I. 9. Popular culture in manuscripts

Canaan, Tawfik. "The decipherment of Arabic talismans". *Berytus. Archaeological studies*, 4, fasc.1 (1937):69-110; 5, fasc.2 (1938):141-151.

Casanova, M. "Alphabets magiques arabes". *Journal asiatique*, série II, 18 (1921): 37-55; 19 (1922): 250-262.

Dawkins, J. McG. "The seal of Solomon". *Journal of the Royal Asiatic Society*, (1944): 145-150.

Fahd, T. "Tamīma". *EI*, new ed., 10: 177-178.

Gacek, Adam. "The use of 'kabīkaj' in Arabic manuscripts". *Manuscripts of the Middle East*, 2 (1987): 49-53. [Persian translation by Nūsh Āfrīn Anṣārī (Muḥaqiq), *Kitābdārī*, 14 (1989): 5-12; Turkish translation by A. Yaycioğlu, *Kebikeç*, 5 (1997): 5-8.]

MacDonald, D.B. "Budūḥ". *EI*, new ed., suppl.3-4: 153-154.

Matton, Sylvain. *La magie arabe traditionelle*. Paris, 1977. [Contains Ibn Waḥhīyah's *Shawq al-mustahām fī maʿrifat rumūz al-aqlām*.]

Piemontese, Angelo M. "Aspetti magici e valori funzionali della scrittura araba". *La Ricerca folklorica*, 5 (1984): 27-55.

Pollock, James. "Kabi:kaj to book pouches. Library preservation, magic and technique in Syria of the 1880's and the 1980's West". *MELA notes*, 44 (1988): 8-10.

Saidan, A.S. "Magic squares in an Arabic manuscript". *Journal for the history of Arabic science*, 4, no.1 (1980): 87-88.

"Tilsam". *EI*, new ed., 10: 500-502.

Winkel, H.A. *Siegel und Charactere in der mohammedanischen Zauberei*. Tübingen, 1930.

I. 10. Forgeries

ʿAbd al-Majīd, Rashīd et al. *Al-Tazwīr wa-taṭbīq al-makhṭūṭāt*. Baghdad, 1941.

Denny, Walter B. "Islamic art, IX. Forgeries". *The dictionary of art*, ed. J. Turner. New York, 1996: 16, 545-546.

Duda, Dorothea. "Alte Restaurierungen und Falschungen bei orientalischen Handschriften". *Les manuscrits du Moyen-Orient*, ed. F. Déroche. Istanbul/Paris, 1989: 39-43.
"Forgeries of art objects and manuscripts". *Encyclopaedia Iranica*, ed. E. Yarshater, 10: 90-100.
Frye, Richard N. "Islamic book forgeries from Iran". *Islamwissenschaftliche Abhandlungen Fritz Meier zum sechzigsten Geburtstag*, herausgegeben von R. Gramlich. Wiesbaden, 1974: 106-109.
Gacek, Adam. "Tazwīr". *EI*, new ed., 10: 408-409 or 10: 437-438 (French).

I. 11. Terminology

al-Bahnassī, ʿAfīf. *Muʿjam al-muṣṭalaḥāt al-khaṭṭ al-ʿArabī wa-al-khaṭṭāṭīn*. Beirut, Maktabat Lubnān, 1995.
Gacek, Adam. "The language of catalogues of Arabic manuscripts". *MELA notes*, no.48 (1989): 21-29.
——— "Some technical terms relative to the execution of Arabic manuscripts". *MELA notes*, nos.50-51 (1990): 13-18.
Maḥfūẓ, Ḥusayn ʿAlī. "ʿIlm al-makhṭūṭāt". *Al-Mawrid*, 5 (1976): 144-145.
Mihdād, al-Zabīr. "Al-Muṣṭalaḥ al-tarbawī fī al-turāth al-ʿArabī". *Al-Lisān al-ʿArabī*, 44 (1997): 233-274.
Shabbūḥ, Ibrāhīm. "Naḥwa muʿjam taʾrīkhī li-muṣṭalaḥ wa-nuṣūṣ funūn ṣināʿat al-makhṭūṭ al-ʿArabī". *Ṣiyānah wa-ḥifẓ al-makhṭūṭāt al-Islāmīyah. Aʿmāl al-Muʾtamar al-Thālith li-Muʾassasat al-Furqān lil-Turāth al-Islāmī, Lundun 18-19 Nūfimbir 1995*, ed. Ibrāhīm Shabbūḥ. London, 1998: 341-393.

II. WRITING SURFACES, MATERIALS AND IMPLEMENTS

II. 1. General studies

Acar, M. Şinasi. *Türk hat sanati: araç, gereç ve formlar (= Turkish calligraphy: materials, tools and forms*. Istanbul, Antik A.Ş., 1999. [Text in Turkish and English.]
Amīn, Niḍāl ʿAbd al-ʿĀlī. "Adawāt al-kitābah wa-mawādduhā fī al-ʿuṣūr al-Islāmīyah". *Al-Mawrid*, 15, no.4 (1986): 131-140.

Būbū, Mas'ūd. "Min ta'rīkh al-lughah al-'Arabīyah: adawāt al-kitābah wa-al-wirāqah". *Dirāsāt ta'rīkhīyah* (Damascus), 17, nos.55-56 (1996): 53-62.

al-Dimashqī, Muḥammad ibn Abī al-Khayr. *Al-Nujūm al-shāriqāt fī dhikr ba'ḍ al-ṣanā'i' al-muḥtāj ilayhā fī 'ilm al-mīqāt (!).* Aleppo, Maṭba'at Muḥammad Rāghib al-'Ilmīyah, 1928.

Ghédirah, A. "Ṣaḥīfa". *EI*, new ed., 8: 834-835.

Grohmann, A. *Arabische Paläographie.* Teil 1. Wien, 1961: 66-131.

Ibn Bādīs, al-Mu'izz. "'Umdat al-kuttāb wa-'uddat dhawī al-albāb", ed. 'Abd al-Sattār al-Ḥalwajī and 'Alī 'Abd al-Muḥsin Zakī. *Majallat Ma'had al-Makhṭūṭāt al-'Arabīyah*, 17 (1971).

——— *'Umdat al-kuttāb wa-'uddat dhawī al-albāb: fīhi ṣifat al-khaṭṭ wa-al-aqlām wa-al-midād wa-al-liyaq wa-al-ḥibr wa-al-aṣbāgh wa-ālāt al-tajlīd*, ed. Najīb Māyil Haravī and 'Iṣām Makkīyah. Mashhad, Majma' al-Buḥūth al-Islāmīyah, 1989.

Ibn Qutaybah, 'Abd Allāh ibn Muslim. *Risālat al-khaṭṭ wa-al-qalam al-mansūbah ilá Ibn Qutaybah*, ed. Ḥātim Ṣāliḥ al-Ḍāmin. Beirut, Mu'assasat al-Risālah, 1989.

——— "Risālat Ibn Qutaybah fī al-khaṭṭ wa-al-qalam", ed. Hilāl Nājī. *Al-Mawrid*, 19, no.1 (1990):156-170.

Janert, Klaus Ludwig. *Bibliographie mit Berichten über die mündliche und schriftliche Textweitergabe sowie die Schreibmaterialen in Indien.* Bonn, 1995 – .

al-Kurdī, Muḥammad Ṭāhir. *Ḥusn al-du'ābah fīmā warada fī al-khaṭṭ wa-adawāt al-kitābah.* Cairo, Muṣṭafá al-Bābī al-Ḥalabī, 1938.

al-Malik al-Muẓaffar, Yūsuf ibn 'Umar. *Al-Mukhtara' fī funūn min al-ṣuna'.* Kuwait, Mu'assasat al-Shirā' al-'Arabī, 1989.

al-Manūnī, Muḥammad. "Taqnīyāt i'dād al-makhṭūṭ al-Maghribī". *Al-Makhṭūṭ al-Arabī wa-'ilm al-makhṭūṭāt (= Le manuscrit arabe et la codicologie).* Rabat, 1994: 11-32.

Naṣṣār, Ḍiyā' Muḥammad Ḥasan. "Ma'a ālāt al-khaṭṭ al-'Arabī". *Al-Turāth al-sha'bī*, no.4 (1976): 99-106.

Porter, Yves. "Une traduction persane du traité d'Ibn Bādīs: 'Umdat al-kuttāb (ca.1025)". *Les manuscrits du Moyen-Orient*, ed. F. Déroche. Istanbul/Paris, 1989: 61-67.

Rahman, P.I.S.M. "Calligrapher's tools and materials". *Journal of the Asiatic Society of Bangladesh*, 20, no.1 (1975): 83-90.

"Risālah fī ṣinā'at al-kitābah", ed. 'Abd al-Laṭīf al-Rāwī and 'Abd al-Ilāh Nabhān. *Majallat Majma' al-Lughah al-'Arabīyah bi-Dimashq*, 62, no.4 (1987): 760-795; 63, no.1 (1988): 50-65.

Sadan, J. "Nouveaux documents sur scribes et copistes". *Revue des études islamiques*, 45 (1977): 41-87. [Contains *al-bāb al-thānī fī dhikr al-khaṭṭ wa-al-qalam* by Ibn Qutaybah, both original text and translation.]

Sauvan, Yvette. "Un traité à l'usage des scribes à l'époque nasride". *Les manuscrits du Moyen-Orient*, ed. F. Déroche. Istanbul/Paris, 1989: 49-50.

Thackston, Wheeler M. "Treatise on calligraphic arts: a disquisition on paper, colors, inks, and pens by Sami of Nishapur". *Intellectual studies on Islam. Essays written in honor of Martin B. Dickson*, ed. Michel M. Mazzaoui. Salt Lake City, Utah, 1990: 219-228.

II. 2. Papyrus

Grohmann, Adolf. "Aperçu de papyrologie arabe". *Etudes de papyrologie*, 1 (1932): 23-95.

——— "Arabische Papyruskunde". *Arabische Chronologie. Arabische Papyruskunde*, by Adolf Grohmann. Leiden/Köln, 1966: 49-118, 10 pl. (*Handbuch der Orientalistik*. Abt.1, Erg.2).

Hüttermann, A. et al. "Making of papyrus: an ancient biotechnology or Pliny was right indeed". *Naturwissenschaften*, 82, Heft 9 (1995): 414-416.

Khan, Geoffrey. "Arabic papyri". *The codicology of Islamic manuscripts. Proceedings of the Second Conference of al-Furqān Islamic Heritage Foundation, 1993*. London, 1995: 1-16.

——— "Al-Bardīyāt al-ʿArabīyah". *Dirāsāt al-makhṭūṭāt al-Islāmīyah bayna iʿtibārāt al-māddah wa-al-bashar. Aʿmāl al-Muʾtamar al-Thānī li-Muʾassasat al-Furqān lil-Turāth al-Islāmī*, ed. Rashīd al-ʿInānī. London, 1997: 57-76.

——— *Bills, letters and deeds: Arabic papyri of the 7th to 11th centuries*. London/ Oxford, 1993: 11-22 [in particular].

Khoury, R.G. "Papyrus". *EI*, new ed., 8: 261-265.

——— "Papyruskunde". *Grundriss der arabischen Philologie*. Band I: *Sprachwissenschaft*, herausgegeben von W. Fischer. Wiesbaden, 1982: 251-270.

Rāġib, Yūsuf. "Les plus anciens papyrus arabes". *Annales islamologiques (= Ḥawlīyāt Islāmīyah)*, 30 (1996): 1-19.

Sellheim, R. "Ḳirṭās". *EI*, new ed., 5:173-174.

II. 3. Parchment

Déroche, François. "L'emploi du parchemin dans les manuscrits islamiques: quelques remarques liminaires". *The codicology of Islamic manuscripts. Proceedings of the Second Conference of Al-Furqān Islamic Heritage Foundation, 1993*. London, 1995: 17-57.

——— "Istikhdām al-raqq fī al-makhṭūṭāt al-Islāmīyah: mulāḥaẓāt tamhīdīyah". *Dirāsāt al-makhṭūṭāt al-Islāmīyah bayna iʿtibārāt al-māddah wa-al-bashar. Aʿmāl al-Muʾtamar al-Thānī li-Muʾassasat al-Furqān lil-Turāth al-Islāmī*, ed. Rashīd al-ʿInānī. London, 1997: 93-134.

Endress, G. "Pergament in der Codicologie des islamisch-arabischen Mittelalters". *Pergament: Geschichte, Structur, Restaurierung, Herstellung*, ed. P. Rück. Sigmaringen, 1991: 45-46.

Grohmann, A. "Djild". *EI*, new ed., 2: 540-541.

Khoury, R.G. and Witkam, J.J. "Rakk". *EI*, new ed., 8: 407-410.

Reed, Ronald. *The nature and making of parchment*. Leeds, 1975.

al-Zayyāt, Ḥabīb. "Al-Julūd wa-al-ruqūq wa-al-ṭurūs fī al-Islām". *Al-Kitāb*, 4 (1947): 1358-1366.

II. 4. Paper (for decorated paper see VII. 7.)

a) Non-watermarked paper and paper in the Islamic world

- Bibliography

Le Léannec-Bavavéas, Marie-Thérèse. *Les papiers non-filigranés médiévaux de la Perse à l'Espagne: bibliographie 1950-1995*. Paris, 1998.

- Papermaking recipes and ethics

Gacek, Adam. "On the making of local paper: a thirteenth century Yemeni recipe". *Revue des mondes musulmans et de la Méditerranée* (forthcoming).

Ibn al-Ḥājj al-Fāsī, Muḥammad ibn Muḥammad. *Al-Madkhal*. Cairo, 1929 : 4, 79-83.

Ibn Bādīs, al-Muʿizz. "ʿUmdat al-kuttāb wa-ʿuddat dhawī al-albāb", ed. ʿAbd al-Sattār al-Ḥalwajī and ʿAlī ʿAbd al-Muḥsin Zakī. *Majallat*

Maʿhad al-Makhṭūṭāt al-ʿArabīyah, 17 (1971): 147-152. [For translations of the chapter on papermaking see: Karabacek, "Neue Quellen"; Briquet, "Le papier arabe"; Levey, "Mediaeval Arabic bookmaking"; Irigoin, "Les papiers non filigranés".]

Richard, Francis. "Une recette en persan pour colorer le papier". *Revue des mondes musulmans et de la Méditerranée* (forthcoming).

Tawfīq, Barwīn Badrī. "Risālatān fī ṣināʿat al-makhṭūṭ al-ʿArabī". *Al-Mawrid*, 14, no.4 (1985): 275-286 ['fī ʿamal al-khāghad al-baladī'].

al-Wansharīsī, Aḥmad ibn Yaḥyá. *al-Miʿyār al-muʿrib wa-al-jāmiʿ al-mughrib*. Beirut, Dār al-Gharb al-Islāmī, 1981: 1, 75-104. [Includes a fragment of Ibn Marzūq's *Taqrīr al-dalīl al-wāḍiḥ al-maʿlūm ʿalá jawāz al-naskh fī kāghad al-Rūm*.]

Zayyāt, Ḥabīb. *Al-Wirāqah wa-ṣināʿat al-kitābah wa-muʿjam al-sufun*. Beirut, Dār al-Ḥamrāʾ, 1992. [Contains an edition of the chapter on papermaking by Ibn Bādīs, pp.79-81.]

- Studies

Afshār, Īraj. "The use of paper in Islamic manuscripts as documented in classical Persian texts". *The codicology of Islamic manuscripts. Proceedings of the Second Conference of Al-Furqān Islamic Heritage Foundation, 1993*. London, 1995: 77-91.

——— "Istikhdām al-waraq fī al makhṭūṭāt al-Islāmīyah: kamā sajjalathu al-nuṣūṣ al-Fārisīyah al-qadīmah". *Dirāsāt al-makhṭūṭāt al-Islāmīyah bayna iʿtibārāt al-māddah wa-al-bashar. Aʿmāl al-Muʾtamar al-Thānī li-Muʾassasat al-Furqān lil-Turāth al-Islāmī*, ed. Rashīd al-ʿInānī. London, 1997: 35-55.

Babinger, Franz. *Zur Geschichte der Papiererzeugung im osmanischen Reiche*. Berlin, 1931.

Baker, Don. "Arab papermaking". *The paper conservator*, 15 (1991): 28-35.

——— "A note on the expression '... a manuscript on Oriental paper'". *Manuscripts of the Middle East*, 4 (1989): 67-68.

Bavavéas, M. Th. and Humbert, G. "Une méthode de description du papier non filigrané (dit 'oriental')". *Gazette du livre médiéval*, 17 (1990): 24-30.

Beit-Arié, M. "Quantitative typology of Oriental paper patterns". *Le papier au moyen âge: histoire et techniques*, ed. M. Zerdoun Bat-Yehouda. Turnhout, 1999: 41-53.

——— "The Oriental Arabic paper". *Gazette du livre médiéval*, 28 (1996), 9-12.

Björkman, W. "Ḳaṭʿ". *EI*, new ed., 4: 741-743.

Bloom, Jonathan M. "Paper in Fatimid Egypt". *L'Egypte fatimide: son art et son histoire. Actes du colloque organisé à Paris les 28, 29 et 30 mai 1998*, ed. Marianne Barrucand. Paris, 1999: 395-401.

——— "Revolution by the ream: a history of paper". *Aramco world*, 50, no.3 (May/June) 1999: 26-39.

Bockwitz, Hans Heinrich. "Ein Papierfund aus dem Anfang des 8. Jahrhunderts am Berge Mugh bei Samarkand". *Papiergeschichte*, 5 (1995): 42-44.

——— "Zu Karabacek's Forschungen über das Papier im islamischen Kulturkreis". *Buch und Schrift*, N.F., 1 (1938): 83-86.

——— "Zur Gechichte des Papiers: die Erfindung und Ausbreitung im Fernen Osten". *Einfürung in die Papierkunde*, by Fritz Hoyer. Leipzig, 1941: 1-42.

Briquet, C.-M. "Le papier arabe au moyen âge et sa fabrication". *Briquet's Opuscula*, ed. E.J. Labarre. Hilversum, 1955: 162-169.

——— "Recherches sur les premiers papiers employés en Occident et en Orient du Xe au XIVe siècle". *Briquet's Opuscula*, ed. E.J. Labarre. Hilversum, 1955: 129-161.

Canat, Paul et al. "Une enquête sur le papier de type 'arabe occidental' ou 'espagnol non filigrané'". *Ancient and medieval book materials and techniques*, ed. M. Maniaci and P. Munafò. Vatican City, 1993: 1, 313-393.

Déroche, F. "Islamic art, III, 5. Paper". *The dictionary of art*, ed. J. Turner. New York, 1996: 16, 351-354.

Huart, Cl. and Grohmann, A. "Kāg͟had, kāg͟hid". *EI*, new ed., 4: 419-420.

Humbert, Geneviève. "Un papier fabriqué vers 1350 en Egypte". *Le papier au moyen âge: histoire et techniques*, ed. M. Zerdoun Bat-Yehouda. Turnhout, 1999: 61-73.

——— "Les papiers 'arabes': un état de la recherche". *Revue des mondes musulmans et de la Méditerranée* (forthcoming).

——— "Papiers non filigranés utilisés au Proche-Orient jusqu'en 1450: essai de typologie". *Journal asiatique*, 286, no.1 (1998): 1-54.

Hunter, Dart. *Papermaking: the history and technique of an ancient craft*. New York, 1978.

Irigoin, Jean. "Papiers orientaux et papiers occidentaux". *La paléographie grecque et byzantine*. Paris, 1997: 45-54.

——— "Les premiers manuscrits grecs écrits sur papier et le problème de bombycin". *Scriptorium*, IV/1 (1950): 194-204.

——— "Les papiers non filigranés: état présent des recherches et perspectives d'avenir". *Ancient and medieval book materials and techniques*, ed. M. Maniaci and P. Munafò. Vatican City, 1993: 1, 265-312.

——— "Papiers orientaux et papiers occidentaux: les techniques de confection de la feuille". *Bollettino dell'Istituto Centrale per la Patologia del Libro*, 42 (1988): 57-79.

——— "Les types des formes utilisés dans l'Orient méditerranéen (Syrie, Egypte) du XIe au XIVe siècle". *Papiergeschichte*, 13/1-2 (1963): 18-21.

Jones, Russell. "European and Asian papers in Malay manuscripts: a provisional assessment". *Bijdragen tot de taal-, land- en volkenkunde*, 149 (1993): 475-502.

——— "From papermill to scribe: the lapse of time". *Papers from the III European Colloquium on Malay and Indonesian Studies, Naples, 2-4 June 1981*, ed. Luigi Santa Maria et al. Naples, 1988: 153-169.

Kâgitçi, Mehmed Ali. "Beitrag zur türkischen Papiergeschichte". *Papiergeschichte*, 13/4 (1963): 37-44.

——— "A brief history of papermaking in Turkey". *The paper maker* 34 (1965): 41-51.

——— *Historical study of paper industry in Turkey (= Historique de l'industrie papetière en Turquie).* [Istanbul], 1976. [Text in English and French.]

Karabacek, J. von. "Das arabische Papier". *Mittheilungen aus der Sammlung der Papyrus Erzherzog Rainer*, 2-3 (1887): 87-178.

——— *Arab paper,1887*. Additional notes by D. Baker. Transl. by D. Baker and S. Dittmar. London, Islington Books, 1991.

——— "Neue Quellen zur Papiergeschichte". *Mittheilungen aus der Sammlung der Papyrus Erzherzog Rainer*, 4 (1888): 75-122.

Le Léannec-Bavavéas, Marie-Thérèse. "Zigzag et filigrane sont-ils incompatibles? Enquête dans les manuscrits de la Bibliothèque nationale de France". *Le papier au moyen âge: histoire et techniques*, ed. M. Zerdoun Bat-Yehouda. Turnhout, 1999: 119-134.

Macfarlane, N. *Handmade papers of India*. Winchester, Alembic Press, 1987. [In particular: pp. [9-15]: 'Islamic paper in India' and pp. [17-23]: 'The making of Islamic paper'.]

Porter, Yves. "Notes sur la fabrication du papier dans le monde iranien médiéval (VIIIe-XVIe siècle)". *Le papier au moyen âge: histoire et techniques*, ed. M. Zerdoun Bat-Yehouda. Turnhout, 1999: 19-30.

Premchand, Neeta. *Off the deckle edge: a paper making journey through India*. Bombay, 1995.

Quraishi, Salim. "A survey of the development of papermaking in Islamic countries". *Bookbinder*, 3 (1989): 29-36.

Qureshi, Salimuddin. "Paper making in Islamic countries". *Pakistan library bulletin*, 21, no.2 (1990): 1-11.

Rantoandro, Gabriel. "Contribution à la connaissance du 'papier antemoro' (sud-est de Madagaskar)". *Archipel*, 26 (1983): 86-116.

Richard, Francis. "Le papier utilisé dans les manuscrits persans du XVe siècle de la Bibliothèque nationale de France". *Le papier au moyen âge: histoire et techniques*, ed. M. Zerdoun Bat-Yehouda. Turnhout, 1999: 31-40.

Ṣābāt, Khalīl. "Taṭawwur ṣināʿat al-waraq fī Miṣr". *Majallat Kullīyat al-Ādāb* (Cairo), 19, no.1 (1957): 245-261.

Sistach, M. Carme. "Les papiers non filigranés dans les archives de la Couronne d'Aragon du XIIe au XIVe siècle". *Le papier au moyen âge: histoire et techniques*, ed. M. Zerdoun Bat-Yehouda. Turnhout, 1999: 105-118.

Soteriou, Alexandra. *Gift of conquerors: hand papermaking in India*. New Delhi, Mappin, 1999.

Tschudin, Peter F. "Zu Geschichte und Technik des Papiers in der arabischen Welt". *International paper history (IPH)*, 8, no.2 (1998): 20-24.

Valls i Subirà, Oriol. "Arabian paper in Catalonia: notes on Arabian documents in the Royal Archives of the kings of Aragon in Barcelona". *The paper maker*, 32, no.1 (1963): 21-30.

——— *The history of paper in Spain*. Transl. by Sarah Nicholson. Madrid, 1978-82. 3 vols.

Vidal, L. and Bouvier, R. "Le papier de Khanbaligh et quelques autres anciens papiers asiatiques". *Journal asiatique*, 206 (1925):159-170.

Walz, Terence. "A note on the Trans-Saharan paper trade in the 18th and 19th centuries". *Research bulletin. Centre of Arabic Documentation. Institute of African Studies* (Ibadan), 13, nos. 1-2 (1980-82): 42-47.

——— "The paper trade of Egypt and the Sudan in the 18th and 19th centuries". *Modernization in the Sudan*, ed. M.W. Daly. New York, 1985: 29-49.

Zayyāt, Ḥabīb. *Al-Wirāqah wa-ṣināʿat al-kitābah wa-muʿjam al-sufun*. Beirut, Dār al-Ḥamrā', 1992.

b) Watermarked paper and filigranology

Bogdán, István. "La datation du papier à partir des ses propriétés matérielles". *Avant-texte, texte, après-texte*, by L. Hay and P. Nagy. Paris/Budapest, 1982: 27-40.

Briquet, C.M. *Les filigranes. Dictionnaire historique des marques du papier dès leur apparition vers 1282 jusqu'en 1600*. Amsterdam, 1968. 4 vols.

Churchill, W.A. *Watermarks in paper in Holland, England and France, etc. in the XVII & XVIII centuries and their interconnection*. Amsterdam, 1935. [Repr. 1967.]

Eineder, Georg. *The ancient paper-mills of the former Austro-Hungarian Empire and their watermarks*. Hilversum, 1960 (*Monumenta Chartae Papyraceae Historiam Illustrantia, VIII*).

Heawood, Edward. *Watermarks, mainly of the 17th and the 18th centuries*. Hilversum, 1960 (*Monumenta Chartae, I*).

Hills, Richard L. "The importance of laid and chain line spacing". *Le papier au moyen âge: histoire et techniques*, ed. M. Zerdoun Bat-Yehouda. Turnhout, 1999: 149-163.

Horst, K. van der. "The reliability of watermarks". *Gazette du livre médiéval*, 15 (1989): 15-19.

Irigoin, Jean. "La datation par les filigranes du papier". *Codicologica*, 5 (1980): 9-36.

Labarre, E.J. "English index to Briquet's watermarks". *The Briquet album*. Hilversum, 1952: 138-145 (*Monumenta Chartae, II*).

——— (ed.). *The Nostitz papers: notes on watermarks found in the German imperial archives of the 17th & 18th centuries, and essays showing the evolution of a number of watermarks*. Hilversum, 1956 (*Monumenta Chartae, V*).

Mošin, Vladimir. *Anchor watermarks*. Amsterdam, 1973 (*Monumenta Chartae, XIII*).

Mošin, Vladimir and Traljič, Seid. *Filigranes des XIIIe et XIVe siècles*. Zaghreb, 1957. 2 vols.

Nikolaev, V. *Watermarks of the Ottoman Empire*. Sofia, 1954.

Piccard, Gerhard. *Wasserzeichenkartei Piccard im Hauptstaatsarchiv Stuttgart: Findbuch.* Stuttgart, 1961 – .

Shorter, A.H. *Paper mills and paper makers in England, 1495-1800.* Hilversum, 1957 (*Monumenta Chartae, VI*).

Stevenson, Allan H. "Watermarks are twins". *Studies in bibliography*, 4 (1952): 57-91.

Uchastkina, Zoia Vasilevna and Simmons, J.S.G. *A history of Russian hand paper-mills and their water-marks.* Hilversum, 1962 (*Monumenta Chartae, IX*).

Valls i Subirà, Oriol. *Paper and watermarks in Catalonia.* Amsterdam, 1970 (*Monumenta Chartae, XII*). 2 vols.

Velkov, Asparukh and Andreev, Stefan. *Vodni znatsi v osmano-turskite dokumenti, I: tri luni (= Filigranes dans les documents ottomans, I: trois croissants).* Sofia, SS. Cyril and Methodius National Library, 1983.

Weiss, Karl Th. *Handbuch der Wasserzeichenkunde.* Leipzig, 1962.

Zonghi, Aurelo et al. *Zonghi's watermarks.* Hilversum, 1953 (*Monumenta Chartae, III*).

II. 5. Inks, inkwells, pens and other writing accessories

Abouricha, Noureddin. "L'encre au Maghreb". *Nouvelles des manuscrits du Moyen Orient*, III/1 (1993): 3-4.

Baer, E. "Dawāt". *EI*, new ed., suppl. 3-4: 203-204.

Derman, M. Uğur. "The mıstar, the ruler and scissors for paper". *İlgi*, 27 (1979): 32-35.

——— "The tools of Turkish calligraphy". *İlgi*, 19 (1974): 40-43; 22 (1976): 36-39; 23 (1976): 33-35; 24 (1976): 33-35.

Dukan, Michèle. "De la difficulté à reconnaître des instruments de réglure: planche à régler (mastara) et cadre-patron". *Scriptorium*, 40, no.2 (1986): 257-261.

Greenfield, Jane. "Notable bindings XVII". *The Yale University Library gazette*, 72, nos. 3-4 (1998): 168-170. [On misṭarah.]

Huart, Cl. and Grohmann, A. "Ḳalam". *EI*, new ed., 4: 471.

Kalus, Ludvik et Naffah, Christine. "Deux écritoires mameloukes des collections nationales françaises". *Revue des études islamiques*, 51 (1983): 89-145.

Komaroff, Linda. "Dawāt". *Encyclopaedia Iranica*, ed. E. Yarshater, 7: 137-139.

Levey, Martin. *Medieval Arabic bookmaking and its relation to early chemistry and pharmacology*. Philadelphia, 1962. [Contains translations of *ʿUmdat al-kuttāb* of Ibn Bādīs and *Ṣināʿat tasfīr al-kutub wa-ḥall al-dhahab* of Aḥmad al-Sufyānī.]

Lucas, A. "The inks of ancient and modern Egypt". *Analyst*, 47 (1922): 9-14.

Qāshā, Suhayl. "Al-Ḥibr wa-adawāt al-kitābah fī al-turāth al-ʿArabī". *Al-Turāth al-shaʿbī*, no.5 (1978): 5-36.

Shabbūḥ (Chabbouh), Ibrāhīm. "Maṣdarān jadīdān ʿan ṣināʿat al-makhṭūṭ: ḥawla funūn tarkīb al-midād". *Dirāsāt al-makhṭūṭāt al-Islāmīah bayna iʿtibārāt al-māddah wa-al-bashar. Aʿmāl al-Muʾtamar al-Thānī li-Muʾassasat al-Furqān lil-Turāth al-Islāmī*, ed. Rashīd al-ʿInānī. London, 1997: 15-34.

——— "Two new sources on the art of mixing ink". *The codicology of Islamic manuscripts. Proceedings of the Second Conference of Al-Furqān Islamic Heritage Foundation, 1993*. London, 1995: 59-76.

Talbot, Roseline. "La restauration des encres métallo-galliques". *Avant-texte, texte, après-texte*, by L. Hay and P. Nagy. Paris/ Budapest, 1982: 69-73.

Tawfīq, Barwīn Badrī. "Midād al-dhahab, ṣināʿatuh fī al-ʿuṣūr al-Islāmīyah". *Al-Mawrid*, 18, no.1 (1989): 137-141.

——— (ed.). "Risālah fī ṣināʿat al-aḥbār wa-al-liyaq". *Majallat al-maktabah al-ʿArabīyah* (Baghdad), 2 (1982): 149-163.

——— "Risālatān fī ṣināʿat al-makhṭūṭ al-ʿArabī". *Al-Mawrid*, 14, no.4 (1985): 269-274 ['anwāʿ al-liyaq wa-kayfīyat aʿmālihā'].

——— "Ṣīnāʿat al-aḥbār wa-al-liyaq wa-al-aṣbāgh: fuṣūl min makhṭūṭat 'Qaṭf al-azhār' lil-Maghribī". *Al-Mawrid*, 12, no.3 (1983): 251-278.

ʿUbaydī, Ṣāliḥ Ḥasan. "Al-Dawāh wa-al-qalam fī al-āthār al-ʿArabīyah al-Islāmīyah fī al-ʿaṣr al-ʿAbbāsī". *Majallat Kullīyat al-Ādāb* (Baghdad), 28 (1980): 637-658.

al-ʿUsaylī, Nūr al-Dīn. "Urjūzah fī ālāt dawāt al-kātib". *Al-Durar al-farāʾid al-munaẓẓamah fī akhbār al-ḥajj wa-ṭarīq Makkah al-muʿaẓẓamah*, by ʿAbd al-Qādir al-Anṣārī al-Jazīlī. Riyad, 1983: 1, 392-393.

Witkam, J.J. "Midād". *EI*, new ed., 6: 1031.

Zerdoun Bat-Yehouda, Monique. *Les encres noires au Moyen Age (jusqu'à 1600)*. Paris, 1983: 123-141 [in particular].

——— "La fabrication des encres noires d'après les textes". *Codicologica*, 5 (1980): 52-58.

III. TEXTBLOCK (QUIRES, SIGNATURES AND FOLIATION)

Binbīn, Aḥmad Shawqī. "Niẓām al-taʿqībah". *Fann fahrasat al-makhṭūṭāt: madkhal wa-qaḍāyā*, ed. Fayṣal al-Ḥafyān. Cairo, Maʿhad al-Makhṭūṭāt al-ʿArabīyah, 1999: 65-72.

——— "Al-Taʿqībah fī al-makhṭūṭ al-ʿArabī". *ʿĀlam al-kutub*, 14, no.5 (1993): 519-523.

Déroche, François. "L'emploi du parchemin dans les manuscrits islamiques, quelques remarques liminaires". *The codicology of Islamic manuscripts. Proceedings of the Second Conference of Al-Furqān Islamic Heritage Foundation, 1993*. London, 1995: 17-57.

Déroche, François and Richard, Francis. "Du parchemin au papier: remarques sur quelques manuscrits du Proche-Orient". *Recherches de codicologie comparée: la composition du codex au Moyen Age en Orient et en Occident*, ed. Ph. Hoffmann. Paris, 1998: 183-197.

Guesdon, Marie-Geneviève. "L'assemblage des cahiers: remarques à propos d'un échantillon de manuscrits arabes récemment catalogués". *Al-Makhṭūṭ al-ʿArabī wa-ʿilm al-makhṭūṭāt (= Le manuscrit arabe et la codicologie)*. Rabat, 1994: 57-67.

——— "La numérotation des cahiers et la foliotation dans les manuscrits arabes datés jusqu'en 1450". *Revue des mondes musulmans et de la Méditerranée* (forthcoming).

——— "Les réclames dans les manuscrits arabes datés à 1450". *Scribes et manuscrits du Moyen-Orient*, ed. F. Déroche and F. Richard. Paris, 1997: 65-75.

Humbert, Geneviève. "Le ǧuzʾ dans les manuscrits arabes médiévaux". *Scribes et manuscrits du Moyen-Orient*, ed. F. Déroche and F. Richard. Paris, 1997: 77-86.

Keller, Adriaan. "Codicologia comparativa de los manuscritos medievales españoles, latinos, árabes y hebreos". *Estudios sobre Alfonso VI y la reconquista de Toledo. Actas del II Congreso Internacional de Estudios Mozárabes, Toledo, 20-26 Mayo 1985*. Toledo, 1987-89: 3, 207-218.

Orsatti, Paola. "Le manuscrit islamique: caractéristiques matérielles et typologie". *Ancient and medieval book materials and tech-*

niques, ed. M. Maniaci and P. Munafò. Vatican City, 1993: 2, 269-331.
Ritter, H. "Griechisch-koptische Ziffern in arabischen Manuskripten". *Rivista degli studi orientali*, 16 (1936): 212-214.
Troupeau, G. "A propos des chiffres utilisés pour le foliotage des manuscrits arabes". *Arabica*, 21 (1974): 84.

IV. THE TEXT, ITS COMPOSITION AND ARRANGEMENT

IV. 1. Types of compositions, their parts, etc.

al-ʿAmad, Hānī. *Muqawwimāt manāhij al-taʾlīf al-ʿArabī fī muqaddimāt al-muʾallifīn*. Amman, al-Jāmiʿah al-Urdunīyah, 1987.
Ambros, Arne A. "Beobachtungen zu Aufbau und Funktionen der gereimten klassisch-arabischen Buchtitel". *Wiener Zeitschrift für die Kunde des Morgenlandes*, 80 (1990): 13-57.
——— "ʿUnwān: literary aspects of book titles". *EI*, new ed., 10: 871-872.
Arazi, A. and Ben Shammai, H. "Mukhtaṣar". *EI*, new ed., 7: 536-540.
Arazi, A. et al. "Risāla". *EI*, new ed., 8: 532-544.
Barabanov, A.M. "Poyasnitel'nie znachki v arabskikh rukopisyakh i dokumentakh Severnogo Kavkaza". *Sovetzkoie Vostokovedenie*, 3 (1945): 183-214.
Bonebakker, S.A. "Ibtidāʾ". *EI*, new ed., 3: 1006.
——— "Intihāʾ". *EI*, new ed., 3: 1246.
Carmona González, Alfonso. "La estructura del titulo en los libros árabes medievales". *Estudios románicos*, 4 (1987-9): 181-187.
——— "Sobre la estructura convencional del titulo en los libros árabes". *Al-Qanṭara, revista de estudios árabes*, 21, fasc.1 (2000): 85-96.
Carra de Vaux, B. and Gardet, L. "Basmala". *EI*, new ed., 1: 1084-1085.
Fekete, Lajos. "Tamma und seine synonyme". *Trudy Dvadtsat' pjatogo Mezhdunarodnogo Kongressa Vostokovedov, Moskva 9-16 avgusta 1960 g*. Moscow, 1963: 2, 374-377.
Freimark, P. "Mukaddima". *EI*, new ed., 7: 495-496.
——— "Das Vorwort als literarische Form in der arabischen Literatur". Ph.D. diss., Münster (Westfalen), 1967.
Gilliot, Cl. "Sharḥ". *EI*, new ed., 9: 317-320.

Gimaret, D. "S̲h̲ahāda". *EI*, new ed., 9: 201.
Macdonald, D.B. "Ḥamdala". *EI*, new ed., 3: 122-123.
Rippin, A. "Taṣliya". *EI*, new ed., 10: 358-359.
Rosenthal, F. "Ḥās̲h̲iya". *EI*, new ed., 3: 268-269.
——— " Taʿlīḳ ". *EI*, new ed. 10: 165.
Wensinck, A.J. and Rippin, A. "Tas̲h̲ahhud". *EI*, new ed., 10: 340-341.

IV. 2. Page lay-out (mise en page)

Bakhti, M. "Réglure et mise en page des manuscrits maghrébins datés: essai de définition des pratiques observables sur quelques exemples datés du XIVe s.". Doctoral thesis, EPHE (Paris), 1985.
Polosin, Val. V. "Arabic manuscripts: text density and its convertibility in copies of the same work". *Manuscripta Orientalia*, 3, no.2 (1997): 3-17.
——— "Ṣaḥīfat al-makhṭūṭ al-ʿArabī ka-mawḍūʿ lil-baḥth wa-al-waṣf". *Al-Makhṭūṭ al-ʿArabī wa-ʿilm al-makhṭūṭāt (= Le manuscrit arabe et la codicologie)*. Rabat, 1994: 57-60.

IV. 3. Colophon and scribal verses

al-Abbās, Aḥmad al-Muʿtaṣim et al. "A colophon from eighteenth-century Sinnār". *Bulletin d'information. Fontes Historiae Africanae*, 6 (1981): 13-165.
Hunwick, J.O. "West African Arabic manuscript colophons". *Bulletin d'information. Fontes Historiae Africanae*, 7/8 (1982/3): 51-58; 9/10 (1984/5): 49-69.
——— "West African Arabic manuscript colophons II: a sixteenth-century Timbuktu copy of the Muḥkam of Ibn Sīda". *Bulletin d'information. Fontes Historiae Africanae*, 9/10 (1984/85): 49-69.
Koningsveld, P.S. van and al-Samarrai, Q. *Localities and dates in Arabic manuscripts. Descriptive catalogue of a collection of Arabic manuscripts in the possession of E.J. Brill*. Leiden, 1978 (Catalogue no.500).
Şeşen, Ramazan. "Esquisse d'une histoire du développement des colophons dans les manuscrits musulmans". *Scribes et manuscrits du Moyen-Orient*, ed. F. Déroche and F. Richard. Paris, 1997: 189-221.

Troupeau, Gérard. "Les colophons des manuscrits arabes chrétiens". *Scribes et manuscrits du Moyen-Orient*, ed. F. Déroche and F. Richard. Paris, 1997: 224-231.

Weisweiler, Max. "Arabische Schreiberverse". *Orientalische Studien Enno Littmann zu seinem 60. Geburtstag am 16. September 1935 überreicht...*, herausgegeben von R. Paret. Leiden, 1935: 101-120.

IV. 4. Dates, dating and numerals

a) Bibliography, chronology

Grohmann, Adolf. "Arabische Chronologie". *Arabische Chronologie. Arabische Papyruskunde*, by Adolf Grohmann. Leiden/Köln, 1966: 1-48 (*Handbuch der Orientalistik*. Abt.1, Erg.2).

al-Ḥājirī, ʿAbd Allāh. "Al-Arqām al-ʿArabīyah: qāʾimah bībliyūghrāfīyah mukhtārah". *ʿĀlam al-kutub*, 19, no.5-6 (1998): 531-534.

Horovitz, J. "Zu den Ehrennamen der islamischen Monate". *Der Islam*, 13 (1923): 281.

Littmann, Enno. "Über die Ehrennamen und Neubenennungen der islamische Monate". *Der Islam*, 8 (1918): 228-236.

"Taʾrīkh". *EI*, new ed., 10: 257-302.

b) Alpha-numerical and numerical systems

al-Bakrī, Muḥammad Ḥamdī. "Rumūz al-aʿdād fī al-kitābāt al-ʿArabīyah". *Majallat Kullīyat al-Ādāb* (Cairo), 16, no.2 (1954): 73-84.

Farrāj, ʿAbd al-Raḥmān. "Al-Arqām fī intāj al-fikr al-ʿArabī: qāʾimah wirāqīyah". *ʿĀlam al-kutub*, 19, no.5-6 (1998): 535-541.

Ifrah, Georges. *Histoire universelle des chiffres*. Paris, 1981: 298-305, 317-320, 453-503 [in particular].

Irani, Rida A.K. "Arabic numeral forms". *Centaurus*, 4 (1955-56): 1-12.

Labarta, Ana and Barceló, Carmen. *Números y cifras en los documentos arábigohispanos*. Cordoba, 1988.

Lemay, R. "Arabic numerals". *Dictionary of the Middle Ages*, ed. J.R. Strayer. New York, 1982-89: 1, 382-398.

al-Munīf, ʿAbd Allāh ibn Muḥammad. "Al-Arqām al-ʿArabīyah: namādhij min al-makhṭūṭāt al-Maghribīyah". *ʿĀlam al-kutub*, 19, no.5-6 (1998): 474-485.

Souissi, M. "Ḥisāb al-ghubār". *EI*, new ed., 3: 468-469.
Welborn, M.C. "Ghubār numerals". *Isis*, 17 (1932): 260-263.

c) Abjad, ḥisāb al-jummal, chronograms

Ahmad, Qeyamuddin. "A note on the art of composing chronograms". *Islamic culture*, 46 (1972): 163-169.
Bruijn, J.T.P. de. "Chronograms". *Encyclopaedia Iranica*, ed. E. Yarshater, 5: 550-551.
Colin, G. "Ḥisāb al-djummal". *EI*, new ed., 3: 468.
Gwarzo, Hassan Ibrahim. "The theory of chronograms as expanded by the 8th century Katsina astronomer-mathematician Muhammad b. Muhammad". *Research bulletin. Centre for Arabic Documentation. Institute of African Studies* (Ibadan), 3, no.2 (1967): 116-123.
Schanzlin, G.L. "The abjad notation". *Muslim world*, 24 (1934): 257-261.
al-Tāzī, ʿAbd al-Hādī. "Tartīb al-ḥurūf al-abjadīyah bayna al-mashāriqah wa-al-maghāribah". *Majallat Majmaʿ al-Lughah al-ʿArabiyah* (Cairo), 56 (1985): 197-198.
Weil, Gotthold and Colin, Georges S. "Abdjad". *EI*, new ed., 1: 97-98.

d) Greek (Coptic) numerals

Ritter, H. "Griechisch-koptische Ziffern in arabischen Manuskripten". *Rivista degli studi orientali*, 16 (1936): 212-214.
Troupeau, G. "A propos des chiffres utilisés pour le foliotage des manuscrits arabes". *Arabica*, 21 (1974): 84.

e) Rūmī (Fāsī) numerals

Colin, Georges S. "De l'origine grecque des 'chiffres de Fès' et de nos 'chiffres arabes'". *Journal asiatique*, 222 (1933): 193-215.
Fāsī, Muḥammad. "Ḥisāb al-qalam al-Fāsī". *Daʿwat al-ḥaqq*, no.269 (1988): 180-182.
Rey, Abel. "A propos de l'origine grecque des 'chiffres de Fès' et de nos 'chiffres arabes'". *Revue des études grecques*, 48 (1935): 525-539.
Sánchez Pérez, José A. "Sobre las cifras rummies". *Al-Andalus:*

revista de las escuelas de estudios árabes de Madrid y Granada, 3 (1935): 97-125.

Sukayrij, Aḥmad ibn al-Ḥājj al-ʿAyyāshī. *Irshād al-mutaʿallim wa-al-nāsī fī ṣifat ashkāl al-qalam al-Fāsī*. Fez, 1317 A.H. (lithographed). [Printed with *al-Rawḍah al-yāniʿah*.]

Viala, M. E. *Le mécanisme du partage des successions en droit musulman, suivie de l'exposé des 'signes de Fèz'*. Algiers, 1917. [Contains a translation of *Irshād al-mutaʿallim wa-al-nāsī* of Sukayrij, see above.]

f) Dating by fractions

Dietrich, A. "Zur Datierung durch Brüche in arabischen Handschriften". *Nachrichten der Akademie der Wissenschaften in Göttingen,* Band I, Phil. Hist. Klasse, nr.2 (1961): 27-33.

Ḥasan, Jaʿfar Hādī. "Ṭarīqat taʾrīkh Ibn Kamāl Bāshā fī al-makhṭūṭ al-Islāmī". *ʿĀlam al-kutub*, 7, no.2 (1986): 164-170.

——— "Namūdhaj min al-taʾrīkh bi-al-kusūr fī al-makhṭūṭ al-ʿArabī". *Majallat Maʿhad al-Makhṭūṭāt al-ʿArabīyah*, 32, no.2 (1988): 393-402.

Mawālidī, Muṣṭafá. "Ḥall taʿmiyat al-taʾrīkh bi-al-kusūr". *Majallat Maʿhad al-Makhṭūṭāt al-ʿArabīyah*, 39, no.2 (1996): 213-255.

Ritter, Hellmut. "Philologika XII: Datierung durch Brüche". *Oriens*, 1 (1948): 237-247.

Ṣadrī Afandī. "Sharḥ taʾrīkh Ibn Kamāl Pāshā". *Catalogue of Arabic manuscripts in the Library of the Institute of Ismaili Studies*, by A. Gacek. London, 1984-1985: 2, 178 (facsimile).

g) Calendars, conversion tables, dynasties

Bacharach, J.A. *A Near East studies handbook*. 3rd ed. Seattle, 1984.

Bosworth, Clifford Edmund. *The new Islamic dynaties: a chronological and genealogical manual*. Edinburgh, 1996.

"Calendars". *Encyclopaedia Iranica*, ed. E. Yarshater, 4: 668-675 (in particular).

Freeman-Grenville, G.S.P. *The Muslim and Christian calendars, being tables for the conversion of Muslim and Christian dates from the Hijra to the year A.D. 2000*. London, 1977.

Mayr, J. and Spuler, B. (eds). *Wüstenfeld-Mahler'sche Vergleichungs-*

Tabellen zur muslimischen und iranischen Zeitrechnung mit Tafeln zur Umrechnung orient-christlicher Ären. Wiesbaden, 1961.
"Taʾrīkh". *EI*, new ed., 10: 257-302.

IV. 5. Abbreviations

"Abbreviations". *EI*, new ed., suppl., fasc.1-2, p.2.
ʿAlawān, Muḥammad Bāqir. "Thalāth arājīz fī rumūz 'al-Jāmiʿ al-ṣaghīr'". *Majallat Maʿhad al-Makhṭūṭāt al-ʿArabīyah*, 18 (1972): 151-158.
Alič, Salih H. "Problem kratica u arapskim rukopisima (sa spiskom arapskih kratica iz 16. vjeka)". *Prilozi za orientalnu filologiju*, 26 (1976):199-212.
Ben Cheneb, M. "Liste des abréviations employées par les auteurs arabes". *Revue africaine*, nos.302-303 (1920): 134-138.
Fekete, Lajos. "Tamma und seine synonyme". *Trudy Dvadtsat' pjatogo Mezhdunarodnogo Kongressa Vostokovedov, Moskva 9-16 avgusta 1960 g*. Moscow, 1963: 2, 374-377.
Gacek, Adam. *Catalogue of Arabic manuscripts in the library of the Institute of Ismaili Studies*. London, 1984-1985: 2, xiv.
Maḥfūẓ, Ḥusayn ʿAlī. "Al-ʿAlāmāt wa-al-rumūz ʿinda al-muʾallifīn al-ʿArab qadīman wa-ḥadīthan". *Al-Turāth al-shaʿbī*, no.1 (1963/64): 23-27 [436-451]. Also: Baghdad, Maṭbaʿat al-Maʿārif, 1964.
al-Māmaqānī, Muḥmmad Riḍá. "Muʿjam al-rumūz wa-al-ishārāt". *Turāthunā*, 2, no.1 (1407 H): 159-171; 2, nos 2-3 (1407 H): 164-219.
——— *Muʿjam al-rumūz wa-al-ishārāt*. Beirut, Dār al-Muʾarrikh al-ʿArabī, 1992.
Quiring-Zoche, Rosemarie. "How al-Buḫārī's 'Ṣaḥīḥ' was edited in the Middle Ages: ʿAlī al-Yūnīnī and his 'Rumūz'". *Bulletin d'études orientales*, 50 (1998): 191-222.
al-Samarrāʾī, Ibrāhīm. "Al-Mukhtaṣarāt wa-al-rumūz fī al-turāth al-ʿArabī". *Majallat Majmaʿ al-Lughah al-ʿArabīyah al-Urdunī*, 32 (1987): 105-114.

IV. 6. Arabic nomenclature

Ašraf, A. "Alqāb va ʿAnāwīn". *Encyclopaedia Iranica*, ed. E. Yarshater, 1: 898-906.
Beeston, A.F.L. *Arabic nomenclature: a summary guide for beginners*. Oxford, 1971.
Bosworth, C.E. "Laḳab". *EI*, new ed., 5: 618-631.
Bruijn, J.T.P. de. "Ta<u>kh</u>alluṣ". *EI*, new ed., 10: 123.
"Ibn". *EI*, new ed., 3: 669-670.
"Ism". *EI*, new ed., 4: 179-181.
"Nisba". *EI*, new ed., 8: 53-56.
Rosenthal, F. "Nasab". *EI*, new ed., 7: 967-968.
Schimmel, Annemarie. *Islamic names*. Edinburgh, 1989.
Sublet, Jacqueline. *Le voile du nom: essai sur le nom propre arabe*. Paris, 1991.
Wensinck, A.J. "Kunya". *EI*, new ed., 5: 395-396.

IV. 7. Transcription, corrections and etiquette

al-ʿAmad, Hānī. *Adab al-kitābah wa-al-taʾlīf ʿinda al-ʿArab: naẓrah ʿāmmah*. Amman, al-Jāmiʿah al-Urdunīyah, 1986.
Arḥīlah, ʿAbbās. "Al-Qaḍī ʿIyāḍ wa-naẓratuh fī manhaj taḥqīq al-makhṭūṭāt". *ʿĀlam al-kutub*, 26, no.1 (1995): 19-26.
al-Balghīthī, Aḥmad ibn al-Maʾmūn. *Al-Ibtihāj bi-nūr al-Sirāj*. Cairo, 1319 A.H.: 1, 211-257 [in particular].
Gacek, Adam. "Technical practices and recommendations recorded by classical and post-classical Arabic scholars concerning the copying and correction of manuscripts". *Les manuscrits du Moyen Orient*, ed. F. Déroche. Paris/Istanbul, 1989: 51-60. [Contains a facsimile reproduction of Chapter Six of *al-Durr al-naḍīd fī ādāb al-mufīd wa-al-mustafīd* by Badr al-Dīn al-Ghazzī, pl. XX-XXXII.]
Ibn al-Ḥājj al-Fāsī, Muḥammad ibn Muḥammad. *Al-Madkhal*. Cairo, al-Maṭbaʿah al-Miṣrīyah, 1348/1929, 4: 79-93.
Juynboll, G.H.A. "Mustamlī". *EI*, new ed., 7: 725-726.
al-Khūlī, Muḥammad Mursī. "Naṣṣ fī ḍabṭ al-kutub wa-taṣḥīḥihā wa-dhikr al-rumūz wa-al-iṣṭilāḥāt al-wāridah fīhā lil-ʿAllāmah Badr al-Dīn al-Ghazzī". *Majallat Maʿhad al-Makhṭūṭāt al-ʿArabīyah*, 10 (1964): 167-184.
al-Manūnī, Muḥammad. "ʿAlāmat al-kitābah al-ʿArabīyah fī al-

makhṭūṭāt: al-nuqaṭ, al-shakl wa-ishārāt ukhrá". *Al-Maṣādir al-ʿArabīyah li-taʾrīkh al-Maghrib, al-fatrah al-muʿāṣirah, 1790-1930*, by Muḥammad al-Manūnī. Rabat, 1989: 2, 349-360.

al-Mashūkhī, ʿĀbid Sulaymān. *Anmāṭ al-tawthīq fī al-makhṭūṭ al-ʿArabī fī al-qarn al-tāsiʿ al-hijrī*. Riyad, Maktabat al-Malik Fahd al-Waṭanīyah, 1414/1994.

——— "Naskh al-makhṭūṭāt". *ʿĀlam al-kutub*, 15, no.3 (1994): 322-326.

Rosenthal. F. "Muḳābala". *EI*, new ed., 7: 490-491.

——— " Taʿlīḳ". *EI*, new ed., 10: 165.

——— "Taṣḥīf". *EI*, new ed., 10: 347-348.

——— *The technique and approach of Muslim scholarship*. Rome, 1947. [Contains a translation of Chapter Six of *al-Muʿīd fī adab al-mufīd wa-al-mustafīd* by ʿAbd al-Bāsiṭ al-ʿAlmawī.]

al-Samʿānī, ʿAbd al-Karīm ibn Muḥammad. *Adab al-imlāʾ wa-al-istimlāʾ*. Beirut, Dār al-Kitāb al-ʿArabī, 1981.

——— *Die Methodik des Diktatkollegs* (*Adab al-imlāʾ waʾl-istimlāʾ*), herausgegeben von Max Weisweiler. Leiden, 1952.

al-Sarāqabī, Walīd Muḥammad. "Mafhūm al-taṣḥīf: dirāsah fī taʾṣīl al-muṣṭalaḥ". *ʿĀlam al-kutub*, 17, no.1 (1996): 29-33.

al-Sawāḥilī, Aḥmad Rizq Muṣṭafá. "Min qaḍāyā al-ḥarf al-ʿArabī, al-taṣḥīf wa-al-taḥrīf". *ʿĀlam al-kutub*, 14, no.6 (1993): 641-649.

Sayf, Aḥmad Muḥammad Nūr. *ʿInāyat al-muḥaddithīn bi-tawthīq al-marwīyāt wa-athar dhālika fī taḥqīq al-makhṭūṭāt*. Damascus, Dār al-Maʾmūn lil-Turāth, 1987.

Sayyid, Ayman Fuʾād. "Manāhij al-ʿulamāʾ al-Muslimīn fī al-baḥth min khilāl al-makhṭūṭāt". *Majallat Maʿhad al-Makhṭūṭāt al-ʿArabīyah*, 43, no.2 (1999): 99-131.

Shākir, Aḥmad. *Taṣḥīḥ al-kutub wa-ṣunʿ al-fahāris al-muʿjamah wa-kayfīyat ḍabṭ al-kitāb wa-sabq al-Muslimīn wa-al-Ifranj fī dhālik*. Beirut: Dār al-Jīl, 1995.

Weisweiler, Max. "Das Amt des Mustamlī in der arabischen Wissenschaft". *Oriens*, 4 (1951): 27-57.

al-Yūsī, al-Ḥasan ibn Masʿūd. *Qānūn yashtamil ʿalá aḥkām al-ʿilm wa-aḥkām al-ʿālim wa-al-mutaʿallim*. Fez, 1310 A.H. (lithographed), malzamah 24: 1-7.

V. TRANSMISSION OF KNOWLEDGE

V. 1. General studies

Berkey, Jonathan Porter. *The transmission of knowledge in medieval Cairo: a social history of Islamic education*. Princeton, N.J., 1992.

Leder, Stefan. "Authorship and transmission in unauthored literature". *Oriens*, 31 (1988): 67-81.

——— "Riwāya". *EI*, new ed., 8: 545-547.

Makdisi, George. *The rise of colleges: institutions of learning in Islam and the West*. Edinburgh, 1981.

——— *The rise of humanism in classical Islam and the Christian West with special reference to scholasticism*. Edinburgh, 1990.

——— "Madrasa and university in the Middle Ages". *Studia Islamica*, 32 (1970): 255-264.

Messick, Brinkley. *The calligraphic state. Textual domination and history in a Muslim society*. Berkeley/Oxford, 1993.

Nasr, Seyyed Hossein. "Oral transmission and the book in Islamic education: the spoken and the written word". *Journal of Islamic studies*, 3, no.1 (1992): 1-14.

Reichmuth, Stefan. "Murtaḍā az-Zabīdī (d.1791) in biographical and autobiographical accounts: glimpses of Islamic scholarship in the 18th century". *Die Welt des Islams*, 39, no.1 (1999): 64-102.

Schoeler, Gregor. "Die Frage der schriftlichen oder mündlichen Überlieferung der Wissenschaften im frühen Islam". *Der Islam*, 62 (1985): 210-230.

——— "Weiteres zur Frage der schriftlichen oder mündlichen Überlieferung der Wissenschaften im Islam". *Der Islam*, 66 (1989): 38-67.

Sellheim, R. *Al-ʿIlm wa-al-ʿulamāʾ fī ʿuṣūr al-khulafāʾ*. Beirut, 1972.

Sizkīn (Sezgin), Fuʾād. "Ahammīyat al-isnād fī al-ʿulūm al-ʿArabīyah wa-al-Islāmīyah". *Muḥāḍarāt fī taʾrīkh al-ʿulūm al-ʿArabīyah wa-al-Islāmīyah (= Vorträge zur Geschichte der arabisch-islamischen Wissenschaften)*, by Fuʾād Sizkīn. Frankfurt am Main, 1984.

Vajda, Georges. "De la transmission orale du savoir dans l'Islam traditionnel". *L'Arabisant*, 4 (1975): 2-8.

——— *La transmission du savoir en Islam (VII-XVIIIe siècles)*, ed. N. Cottart. London, 1983.

V. 2. Transmission of individual works

Fück, Johann. "Beiträge zur Überlieferungsgeschichte von Buḫārī's Traditionssammlung". *Zeitschrift der Deutschen Morgenländischen Gesellschaft*, 92 (1938): 60-87.

Humbert, Geneviève. *Les voies de la transmission du Kitāb de Sībawayh*. Leiden, 1995.

al-Kattānī, Yūsuf. "Khatamāt Ṣaḥīḥ al-Bukhārī". *Daʿwat al-ḥaqq*, 240 (1984): 61-68.

Lévi-Provençal, E. "La recension maghribine du *Ṣaḥīḥ* d'al-Boḫārī". *Journal asiaique*, 202 (1923): 209-233.

Quiring-Zoche, Rosemarie. "How al-Buḫārī's 'Ṣaḥīḥ' was edited in the Middle Ages: ʿAlī al-Yūnīnī and his 'Rumūz'". *Bulletin d'études orientales*, 50 (1998): 191-222.

Robson, J. "The transmission of Abū Dāwūd's 'Sunan'". *Bulletin of the School of Oriental and African Studies, University of London*, 14 (1952): 579-588.

——— "The transmission of Muslim's 'Ṣaḥīḥ'". *Journal of the Royal Asiatic Society of Great Britain and Ireland*, (1949): 46-60.

——— "The transmission if Tirmīdhī's 'Jāmiʿ'". *Bulletin of the School of Oriental and African Studies, University of London*, 16 (1954): 258-270.

Schacht, Joseph. "Deux éditions inconnues du 'Muwaṭṭa''". *Studi orientalistici in onore di Giorgio Levi della Vida*. Rome, 1956: 2, 477-492.

Vajda, Georges. "La transmission de la 'Kifāya fī maʿrifat uṣūl ʿilm al-riwāyah' d'al-Ḫaṭīb al-Baġdādī". *Arabica*, 4 (1957): 304-307.

——— "La transmission de l'éloge de Zayn al-ʿĀbidīn". *Journal asiatique*, 244 (1956): 433-437.

——— "La transmission de la mašyaḫa (Ansal al-maqāṣid wa-aʿdab al-mawārid) d'Ibn al-Buḫārī d'après le manuscrit Reisülküttab 262 de la Bibliothèque Süleymaniye d'Istanbul". *Rivista degli studi orientali*, 48 (1973-74): 55-74.

V. 3. Ijāzāt and samāʿāt (for *ijāzāt* in calligraphy see the section on calligraphy below)

Aḥmad, Aḥmad Ramaḍān. *Al-Ijāzāt wa-al-tawthīqāt al-maktūbah fī al-ʿulūm al-naqlīyah wa-al-ʿaqlīyah min al-qarn 4 h../10 m. ilá*

10 h./16 m. Cairo, Wizārat al-Thaqāfah, Hay'at al-Āthār al-Miṣrīyah, 1986.

Bāshā, ʿUmar Mūsá "Dawr al-ʿilm: al-ijāzāt al-ʿilmīyah". *Al-Turāth al-ʿArabī*, 4 (1981): 82-103.

Ben Shemesh, A. *Taxation in Islam.* Leiden, 1967. [Vol.1 contains 25 pages of specimens of *samāʿāt.*]

Ebied, R.Y. and Young, M.J.L. "An early eighteenth-century ijāzah issued in Damietta". *Le Muséon*, 87 (1974): 445-465.

——— "New light on the origin of the term 'baccalaureate'". *Islamic quarterly*, 18, nos.1-2 (1974): 3-7.

Gleave, Robert. "The ijāza from Yūsuf al-Baḥrānī (d.1186/1772) to Sayyid Muḥamad Mahdī Baḥr al-ʿUlūm (d.1212/1797-8)". *Iran. Journal of the British Institute of Persian Studies*, 32 (1994): 115-123.

al-Ḥusaynī, Aḥmad. *Ijāzat al-ḥadīth allatī katabahā Shaykh al-muḥaddithīn ... Muḥammad Bāqir al-Majlisī al-Iṣfahānī, 1037-1110 h.* Qum, Maktabat Ayat Allāh Marʿashī al-ʿĀmmah, 1410 A.H.

Ibn Ṭūlūn al-Dimashqī, Muḥammad ibn ʿAlī et al. *Nawādir al-ijāzāt wa-al-samāʿāt: ʿalayhā khuṭūṭ kibār al-ḥuffāẓ wa-al-muḥaddithīn al-Makkīyīn wa-al-Miṣrīyīn wa-al-Shāmīyīn (= Rare licenses and hearings)*, ed. Muṭīʿ al-Ḥāfiẓ. Damascus, Dār al-Fikr/Beirut, Dār al-Fikr al-Muʿāṣir, 1998.

al-Jalālī al-Ḥusaynī, Muḥammad Riḍā. "Dīwān al-ijāzāt al-manẓūmah". *Turāthunā*, 35-36 (1414 A.H.): 270-372.

Jallāb, Ḥasan. "Al-Ijāzāt al-ʿilmīyah ʿalá ʿahd al-Dawlah al-ʿAlawīyah: ijāzat al-Shaykh al-Murābiṭ al-Dalāʾī li-Abī ʿAlī al-Yūsī". *Daʿwat al-ḥaqq*, 326 (1997): 97-102.

al-Jawharjī, Muḥammad ʿAdnān. "Al-Ijāzah wa-ahammīyatuhā fī al-makhṭūṭ al-ʿArabī". *Al-Baṣāʾir* (Cyprus), 26 (1994): 75-96.

Khān, Aḥmad. "Samāʿāt muʾallafāt al-Ṣaghānī al-lughawīyah". *Majallat al-Maʿhad al-Makhṭūṭāt al-ʿArabīyah*, 41, no.1 (1997): 55-90.

Koningsveld, P.S. van. "Ten Arabic manuscript-volumes of historical contents acquired by the Leyden University Library after 1957". *Studies on Islam. A symposium on Islamic studies organized in cooperation with the Accademia dei Lincei in Rome, Amsterdam, 18-19 October 1973.* Amsterdam, 1974:92-110. [Contains a number of specimens of *samāʿāt.*]

Lecomte, Gérard. "A propos de la résurgence des ouvrages d'Ibn Qutayba sur le ḥadiṯ aux VIe/XIIe et VIIe/XIIIe siècles. Les

certificats de lecture du 'K. Ġarīb al-ḥadīṯ' et de 'K. Iṣlāḥ al-ġalaṭ fī ġarīb al-ḥadīṯ' li-Abī ʿUbayd al-Qāsim b. Sallām". *Bulletin d'études orientales*, 21 (1968): 347-409.
——— "Bedeutung der 'Randzeugnisse' (samāʿāt) in den alten arabischen Handschriften". *Zeitschrift der Deutschen Morgenländischen Gesellschaft*, Suppl.1, Teil 2 (1969): 562-566.
Leder, Stefan. " Dokumente zum Ḥadīṯ in Schrifttum und Unterricht aus Damascus im 6./12. Jhdt.". *Oriens*, 34 (1994): 57-75.
Leder, Stefan, Sawwās, Yāsīn Muḥammad and Sāgharjī, Maʾmūn. *Muʿjam al-samāʿāt al-Dimashqīyah: les certificats d'audition à Damas, 550-750/1155-1349.* Damas: Institut français, 1996 – .
MacKay, Pierre A. "Certificates of transmission on a manuscript of the 'Maqāmāt' of al-Ḥarīrī (MS. Cairo, Adab 105)". *Transactions of the American Philosophical Society*, n.s., 61, no.4 (1971.
al-Maslūtī, Muṣṭafá. "Al-Ijāzah al-ʿilmīyah wa-ishāmuhā fī al-ḥarakah al-fikrīyah bi-al-Maghrib". *Majallat Dār al-Ḥadīth al-Ḥasanīyah*, 7 (1989): 238-252.
Michaux-Bellaire, E. "Essai sur les samāʿs ou la transmission orale". *Hespéris*, 4 (1924): 345-355.
al-Munajjid, Ṣalāḥ al-Dīn. "Ijāzāt al-samāʿ fī al-makhṭūṭāt al-qadīmah". *Majallat Maʿhad al-Makhṭūṭāt al-ʿArabīyah*, 1, no.1 (1955): 232-251.
Nashabi, Hisham. "The 'ijāza': academic certificate in Muslim education". *Hamdard Islamicus*, 8, no.1 (1985): 7-20.
al-Sammānī al-Ḥāʾirī, Muḥammad. "Al-Ijāzāt ʿinda ʿulamāʾ al-Imāmīyah". *Turāthunā*, 2, no.1 (1407 A.H): 172-182; 3, no.1 (1408 A.H): 107-114.
——— "Al-Ijāzah al-kabīrah lil-Sayyid ʿAbd Allāh al-Jazāʾirī". *Turāthunā*, 1, no.2 (1406 A.H): 115-117.
Sayyid, Ayman Fuʾād. "Al-Samāʿ wa-al-qirāʾah wa-al-munāwalah wa-quyūd al-al-muqābalah wa-al-muʿāraḍah". *Fann fahrasat al-makhṭūṭāt: madkhal wa-qaḍāyā*, ed. Fayṣal al-Ḥafyān. Cairo, Maʿhad al-Makhṭūṭāt al-ʿArabīyah, 1999: 73-101.
Sellheim, R. "Samāʿ". *EI*, new ed., 8: 1019-1020.
Shishin (Şeşen), Ramaḍān. "Ahammīyat ṣafḥat al-ʿunwān (al-ẓahrīyah) fī tawṣīf al-makhṭūṭāt". *Dirāsāt al-makhṭūṭāt al-Islāmīyah bayna iʿtibārāt al-māddah wa-al-bashar. Aʿmāl al-Muʾtamar al-Thānī li-Muʾassasat al-Furqān lil-Turāth al-Islāmī*, ed. Rashīd al-ʿInānī. London, 1997: 179-196.

Stewart, Devin J. "Ejāza". *Encyclopaedia Iranica*, ed. E. Yarshater, 8: 273-275.

Vajda, Georges. *Les certificats de lecture et de transmission dans les manuscrits arabes de la Bibliothèque nationale de Paris*. Paris, 1957.

——— "Idjāza". *EI*, new ed., 3: 1020-1021.

——— "Un opuscule inédit d'as-Silafī". *La transmission du savoir en Islam (VIIe-XVIIIe siècles)*. London, 1983: 85-92.

——— "Quelques certificats de lecture dans les manuscrits arabes de la Bibliothèque nationale de Paris". *Arabica*, 1, no.3 (1954): 337-342.

Witkam, Jan Just. "The human element between text and reader. The ijāza in Arabic manuscripts". *The codicology of Islamic manuscripts. Proceedings of the Second Conference of Al-Furqān Islamic Heritage Foundation, 1993*. London, 1995: 123-136.

——— "Al-ʿUnṣūr al-basharī bayna al-naṣṣ wa-al-qāriʾ: al-ijāzah fī al-makhṭūṭāt al-ʿArabīyah". *Dirāsāt al-makhṭūṭāt al-Islāmīyah bayna iʿtibārāt al-māddah wa-al-bashar. Aʿmāl al-Muʾtamar al-Thānī li-Muʾassasat al-Furqān lil-Turāth al-Islāmī*, ed. Rashīd al-ʿInānī. London, 1997: 163-177.

VI. ARABIC ALPHABET, SCRIPTS AND PALAEOGRAPHY

VI. 1. Albums and exhibition catalogues

Ahlwardt, Wilhelm. *Zwölf arabische Schrifttaffeln*. Berlin, 1899. [Also in: idem, *Verzeichnis der arabischen Handschriften*. Hildesheim/New York, 1981, vol.10.]

Amīnī, Fakhr al-Dīn Naṣīrī. *Ganjīnah-ʾi khuṭūṭ-i ʿulamāʾ-i aʿlām va dānishmandān-i kirām va shuʿarā-yi ʿiẓām va khūshnavīsān-i chīrahdast va muʿāṣirān*. Tajrīsh (Iran), 1409 [1988 or 9]. 3 vols.

Arberry, A.J. *Specimens of Arabic and Persian palaeography*. London, 1939.

[Cheikho (Shaykhū), Louis]. *Kitāb maʿriḍ al-khuṭūṭ al-ʿArabīyah. (= Spécimens d'écritures arabes pour la lecture des manuscrits anciens et modernes)*. 2nd ed. Beirut, 1888.

Fichier des manuscrits moyen-orientaux datés (FiMMOD), ed. François Déroche. Paris, 1991- .

King Faisal Center for Research and Islamic Studies. *Al-Khaṭṭ al-ʿArabī min khilāl al-makhṭūṭāt*. Riyad, 1986.

——— *Arabic calligraphy in manuscripts*. Riyad, 1986.

Moritz, Bernhard. *Arabic palaeography: a collecton of Arabic texts from the first century of the Hidjra till the year 1000*. Cairo, 1905.

al-Munajjid, Ṣalāḥ al-Dīn. *Al-Kitāb al-ʿArabī al-makhṭūṭ ilá al-qarn al-ʿāshir al-hirjī (= Le Manuscrit arabe jusqu'au Xe s. de l'H.)*. al-Juzʾ al-awwal: al-namādhij. Cairo, 1960.

Shabbūḥ (Chabbouh), Ibrāhīm. *Al-Makhṭūṭ (= Le manuscrit)*. Tunis, al-Wikālah al-Qawmīyah li-Iḥyāʾ wa-Istighlāl al-Turāth al-Atharī wa-al-Taʾrīkhī, Alīf, 1989.

Tisserant, Eugenius. *Specimena codicum orientalium*. Bonn, 1914.

Vajda, Georges. *Album de paléographie arabe*. Paris, 1958.

Witkam, J.J. *Seven specimens of Arabic manuscripts*. Leiden, 1978.

Wright, William. *Facsimiles of manuscripts and inscriptions. Oriental series*. London, 1875-83.

al-Ziriklī, Khayr al-Dīn. *al-Aʿlām: qāmūs tarājim ashhar al-rijāl wa-al-nisāʾ min al-ʿArab wa-al-mustaʿribīn*. Vol.11, mustadrak 2: *al-Khuṭūṭ wa-al-ṣuwar*. Beirut, 1970.

VI. 2. Library catalogues with reproductions of specimens

Arberry, A.J. *Chester Beatty Library. A handlist of the Arabic manuscripts*. Dublin, 1955-66.

Gacek, Adam. *Arabic manuscripts in the libraries of McGill University: union catalogue*. Montreal, 1991.

——— *Catalogue of Arabic manuscripts in the library of the Institute of Ismaili Studies*. London, 1984-85. 2 vols.

Ḥusaynī, Aḥmad. *Fihrist-i nuskhah'hā-yi khaṭṭī-i Kitābkhānah-i ʿUmūmī-i Ḥaẓrat Āyat Allāh al-ʿUẓmá Najafī Marʿashī*...Qum, 1395 [1975] – . [28 vols. to date.]

Quiring-Zoche, Rosemarie. *Arabische Handschriften*. Teil III. Stuttgart, 1994.

Iskandar, Albert Zaki. *A catalogue of Arabic manuscripts on medicine and science in the Wellcome Historical Medical Library*. London, 1967.

Löfgren, Oscar and Traini, Renato. *Catalogue of the Arabic manuscripts in the Biblioteca Ambrosiana*. Vicenza, 1975 – .

Rasmussen, Stig T. (ed.). *Catalogue of Oriental manuscripts, xylographs etc. in Danish collections*. Vol. 5, pt. 1: *Catalogue of Arabic manuscripts. Codices Arabici additamenta & codices*

Simonseniani Arabici (= *al-Dhakhā'ir al-'Arabīyah fī al-Maktabah al-Malakīyah*), by Ali Abd Alhussein Alhaidary and Stig T. Rasmussen. Copenhagen, 1995.

Safadi, Yasin Hamid. *Select Arabic manuscripts. Descriptive and illustrated catalogue of a collection of Arabic manuscripts.* London, 1979.

Schoeler, Gregor. *Arabische Handschriften.* Teil II. Stuttgart, 1990.

Sellheim, Rudolf. *Materialien zur arabischen Literaturgeschichte.* Wiesbaden/ Stuttgart, 1976-87. 2 vols.

Witkam, J.J. *Catalogue of Arabic manuscripts in the library of the University of Leiden and other collections in the Netherlands.* Leiden, 1983 – .

VI. 3. Studies (for other works see the sections on calligraphy, VII.2 and Qur'anic manuscripts, VIII.)

a) General

Abbott, Nabia. "Arabic palaeography: the development of early Islamic scripts". *Ars Islamica*, 8 (1941): 65-104.

Briquel-Chatonnet, Françoise. "De l'araméen à l'arabe: quelques réflections sur la genèse de l'écriture arabe". *Scribes et manuscrits du Moyen-Orient*, ed. F. Déroche and F. Richard. Paris, 1997: 135-149.

Déroche, François. "Les études de paléographie des écritures livresques arabes: quelques observations". *Al-Qanṭara, revista de estudios árabes*, 19, fasc.2 (1998), 365-381.

——— "Les manuscrits arabes datés du IIIe/IXe siècle". *Revue des études islamiques*, 55/57 (1987/89): 343-379.

——— "La paléographie des écritures livresques dans le domaine arabe". *Gazette du livre médiéval*, 28 (1996), 1-8.

Endress, Gerhard. "Die arabische Schrift". *Grundriss der arabischen Philologie.* Band I: *Sprachwissenschaft*, herausgegeben von W. Fischer. Wiesbaden, 1982: 165-197.

Fleisch, H. "Ḥurūf al-hidjā". *EI*, new ed., 3: 596-600.

Frye, Richard N. "An early Arabic script in eastern Iran". *Orientalia Suecana*, 3 (1954): 67-74.

Gruendler, Beatrice. *The development of the Arabic scripts from the Nabatean era to the first Islamic century according to dated texts.* Atlanta, Ga., 1993.

Ḥamad, Ghānim Qaddūrī. "Muwāzanah bayna rasm al-muṣḥaf wa-al-nuqūsh al-ʿArabīyah al-qadīmah". *Al-Mawrid*, 15, no.4 (1986): 27-44.

Hanaway, William L. and Spooner, Brian. *Reading nastaʿliq: Persian and Urdu hands from 1500 to the present*. Costa Mesa, Ca., 1995.

Healey, John F. "Nabataean to Arabic. Calligraphy and script development among the pre-Islamic Arabs". *Manuscripts of the Middle East*, 5 (1990-91): 41-52.

Karabacek, Josef von. "Arabic palaeography". *Wiener Zeitschrift für die Kunde des Morgenlandes*, 20 (1906):131-148.

Mādun, Muḥammad ʿAlī. *Khaṭṭ al-jazm ibn khaṭṭ al-musnad*. Damascus, Ṭalās, 1989.

Minovi, M. "The so-called Badīʿ script". *Bulletin of the American Institute of Iranian Art and Archeology*, 5 (1937): 143-146.

Muḥaffal, Muḥammad. "Fī uṣūl al-kitābah al-ʿArabīyah". *Dirāsāt taʾrīkhīyah* (Damascus), 6 (1981): 59-111.

al-Naqshabandī, Usāmah Nāṣir. "Mabdaʾ ẓuhūr al-ḥurūf al-ʿArabīyah wa-taṭawwuruhā fī ghāyat al-qarn al-awwal al-hijrī". *Al-Mawrid*, 15, no.4 (1986): 83-102.

Orsatti, Paola. "Gli studi di paleografia araba oggi: problemi e metodi". *Scrittura e civiltà*, 14 (1990): 281-331.

Rāġib, Yūsuf. "L'écriture des papyrus arabes aux premiers siècles de l'Islam". *Revue du monde musulman et de la Méditerranée*, 58 (1991): 14-29.

Rezvan, E. and Kondybaev, N.S. "New tool for analysis of handwritten script". *Manuscripta Orientalia*, 2, no. 3 (1996): 43-53.

Robin, Christian. "Les écritures de l'Arabie avant l'Islam". *Revue du monde musulman et de la Méditerranée*, 61 (1991):127-137.

Rosenthal, Franz. "Significant uses of Arabic writing". *Ars Orientalis*, 4 (1961): 15-23. [Reprinted in his *Four essays on art and literature in Islam*. Leiden, 1971: 50-62.]

Schroeder, Eric. "What was the Badīʿscript?". *Ars Islamica*, 4 (1937):232-248.

——— "The so-called Badīʿ script, a mistaken identification". *Bulletin of the American Insitute of Iranian Art and Archaeology*, 5 (1937): 146-147.

Şeşen, Ramazan. "Les caractéristiques de l'écriture de quatre manuscrits du IVe s. H/Xe s. AD". *Les manuscrits du Moyen-Orient*, ed. F. Déroche. Istanbul/Paris, 1989: 45-48.

Shabbūḥ, Ibrāhīm. *Ba'ḍ mulāḥaẓāt 'alá khaṭṭ al-bardīyāt al-'Arabīyah al-Miṣrīyah al-mubakkarah wa-madá ta'aththurihā bi-ḥarakāt iṣlāḥ al-kitābah.* Cairo, Maṭba'at Dār al-Kutub, 1970.

Silvestre de Sacy, A.I. "Nouveaux aperçus sur l'histoire de l'écriture chez les arabes du Hedjaz". *Journal asiatique*, 10 (1827): 209-231.

——— "Mémoire sur l'origine et les anciens monuments de la littérature parmi les arabes". *Mémoires de littérature tirés des registres de l'Académie royale des Inscriptions et Belles-Lettres*, 1 (1808): 247-440. [1ère partie: 'Histoire de l'écriture parmi les arabes', reprinted in F. Déroche, *Sources de la transmission manuscrite du texte coranique* I, vol.1. Lesa, 1998: XXIX-XCII.]

Sourdel-Thomine, J. "Les origines de l'écriture arabe: à propos d'une hypothèse récente". *Revue des études islamiques*, 34 (1966): 151-157.

al-Zarkān, Muḥammad 'Alī. "Al-Kitābah bayna al-Suryānīyah wa-al-'Arabīyah". *Al-Lisān al-'Arabī*, 40 (1995): 53-76.

b) Maghribi and African scripts

Binsharīfah, Muḥammad. "Naẓrah ḥawla al-khaṭṭ al-Andalusī". *Al-Makhṭūṭ al-'Arabī wa-'ilm al-makhṭūṭāt (= Le manuscrit arabe et la codicologie).* Rabat, 1994: 73-85.

Bivar, A.D.H. "The Arabic calligraphy of West Africa". *African languages review*, 7 (1968): 3-15.

Boogert, N. van den. "Some notes on Maghribi script". *Manuscripts of the Middle East*, 4 (1989): 30-43.

Déroche, François. "O. Houdas et les écritures maghrébines". *Al-Makhṭūṭ al-'Arabī wa-'ilm al-makhṭūṭāt (= Le manuscrit arabe et la codicologie).* Rabat, 1994: 75-81.

——— "Tradition et innovation dans la pratique de l'écriture au Maghreb pendant les IVe/Xe et Ve/Xie siècles". *Numismatique, langues, écritures et arts du livre, spécificité des arts figurés: actes du VIIe Colloque international sur l'histoire et archéologie de l'Afrique du nord, réunis dans le cadre du 121e Congrès des sociétés historiques et scientifiques, Nice, 21 au 31 octobre 1996*, ed. Serge Lancel. Paris, 1999 : 233-247.

Houdas, O. "Essai sur l'écriture maghrébine". *Nouveaux mélanges orientaux*, (1886): 85-112.

al-Manūnī, Muḥammad . "Lamḥah 'an ta'rīkh al-khaṭṭ al-'Arabī wa-al-zakhrafah fī al-Gharb al-Islāmī". *Al-Majallah al-ta'rīkhīyah al-Maghribīyah*, 16, nos.53-54 (1989): 205-230.

al-Nājī, al-Amjad. "Al-Khaṭṭ al-Maghribī wa-al-huwīyah al-mafqūdah". *Al-Makhṭūṭ al-'Arabī wa-'ilm al-makhṭūṭāt (= Le manuscrit arabe et la codicologie)*. Rabat, 1994: 87-97.

Sukayrij, 'Abd al-Karīm. "Al-Khaṭṭ al-Maghribī". *Majallat al-thaqāfah al-Maghribīyah*, no.2 (1941): 67-72.

——— "Al-Khaṭṭ al-'Arabī al-Maghribī". *Ta'rīkh al-wirāqah al-Maghribīyah. Ṣinā'at al-makhṭūṭ al-Maghribī min al-'aṣr al-wasīṭ ilá al-fatrah al-mu'āṣirah*, by Muḥammad al-Manūnī. Rabat, 1991: 320-325.

VII. THE ARTS OF THE BOOK

VII. 1. General

a) Bibliographies

Creswell, K.A.C. *A bibliography of the architecture, arts and crafts of Islam to 1st Jan. 1960*. Cairo,1978: 608-624 (bookbinding), 627-674 (calligraphy and palaeography), 979-1087 (painting). *Supplement Jan.1960 to Jan 1972*. Cairo, 1973: 199-214, 293-316. *Second supplement* Jan.1972 to Dec. 1980 (with omissions from previous years), by J.D. Pearson, Cairo, 1984: 309-412, 455-498.

Jachimowicz, E.M.F. "Illuminated Arabic manuscripts". *Arab Islamic bibliography: the Middle East Library Committee guide*, ed. D. Grimwood-Jones, D. Hopwood, and J.D. Pearson. Hassocks, England, 1977: 164-186.

b) General studies and exhibition catalogues

Arnold, T.W. and Grohmann, Adolf. *The Islamic book: a contribution to its art and history from the VIIth to the XIIIth century*. [Florence], 1929.

The arts of Islam: catalogue of an exhibition at the Hayward Gallery. London, 1976.

Berthier, A. "L'art du livre ottoman". *Arts et métiers du livre*, 163 (1990): 41-47.

Blair, Sheila and Bloom, Jonathan M. "Islamic art: arts of the book, III. introduction". *The dictionary of art*, ed. J. Turner. New York, 1996: 16, 271-273.

Bothmer, Hans-Caspar Graf von. "Islamische Buchkunst". *Das Buch im Orient: Handschriften und kostbare Drucke aus zwei Jahrtausenden. Ausstellung 16. Nov. 1982 – 5. Feb. 1983*. Wiesbaden, 1982: 109-220.

Brend, Barbara. "The arts of the book". *The arts of Persia*, ed. R.W. Ferrier. New Haven/London, 1989: 232-242.

Carboni, Stefano. "The Arabic manuscripts". *Pages of perfection. Islamic paintings and calligraphy from the Russian Academy of Sciences, St. Petersburg*. Lugano/Milan, 1995: 77-91.

Denny, Walter B. "Dating Ottoman Turkish works in the saz style". *Muqarnas*, 1 (1983): 103-121.

——— *The image and the word: Islamic painting and calligraphy*. Springfield, Mass, Museum of Fine Arts, 1976.

Dreaming of paradise. Islamic art from the collection of the Museum of Ethnology, Rotterdam. [Rotterdam], 1993.

Duda, D. *Islamische Handschriften*. Wien, 1992-1993. 2 vols.

Fisher, Carol G. "Naḳḳāsh-khāna". *EI*, new ed., 7: 931-932.

Gray, Basil (ed.). *The arts of the book in Central Asia, 14th-16th centuries*. Paris/ London, 1979.

James, David. *The Arabic book (= Das arabische Buch). An exhibition of Arabic manuscripts from the Chester Beatty Library, Dublin at the Museum für Kunst und Gewerbe, Hamburg on the occasion of the Euro-Arab Dialogue, Cultural Symposium, April 1983*. Dublin, 1983.

——— *Islamic masterpieces of the Chester Beatty Library*. London, World of Islam Festival Trust, 1981.

Losty, J. *The art of the book in India*. London, 1982.

Lowry, Glen and Nemazee, Susan. *A jeweler's eye: Islamic arts of the book from the Vever Collection*. Washington, D.C. 1988.

Orientalische Buchkunst in Gotha: Ausstellung zum 350 jährigen Jubiläum der Forschungs- und Landesbibliothek Gotha. Gotha, 1997. [In particular: 'Die Buchkunst des Islams', 49-175.]

Pages of perfection. Islamic paintings and calligraphy from the Russian Academy of Sciences, St. Petersburg. Lugano/Milan, 1995.

Piemontese, Angelo M. "Arte persiana del libro e scrittura araba". *Scrittura e civiltà*, 4 (1980): 103-156.

Richard, Francis. *Splendeurs persanes: manuscrits du XIIe au XVIIe siècle*. Paris, Bibliothèque nationale de France, 1997.
Roxburgh, David J. "The study of painting and the arts of the book". *Muqarnas*, 17 (2000): 1-16.
Rührdanz, K. "The arts of the book in Central Asia". *Uzbekistan: heirs to the silk road*, ed. J. Kalter and M. Pavaloi. London/New York, 1997: 101-115.
Tanindi, Zeren. "Additions to illustrated manuscripts in Ottoman workshops". *Muqarnas*, 17 (2000): 147-161.
——— "Manuscript production in the Ottoman Palace workshop". *Manuscripts of the Middle East*, 5 (1990-91): 67-98.
Taylor, Alice. *Book arts of Isfahan: diversity and identity in seventeenth-century Persia*. Malibu, Ca., J. Paul Getty Museum, 1995.
Vernoit, Stephen. *Occidentalism: Islamic art in the 19th century*. London/Oxford, 1997 (*The Nasser D. Khalili Collection of Islamic Art, XXIII*).
Welch, A. and Welch, S.C. *Arts of the Islamic book. The collection of Prince Sadruddin Agha Khan*. Ithaca/London, 1982.

c) Albums (muraqqaʿāt)

Derman, M. Uğur. "The murakka, an album of calligraphic collage". *İlgi*, 32 (1981): 40-43.
——— "The Turkish calligraphic art: the kıtʿa". *İlgi*, 30 (1980): 32-35.
Mahdī'zādah, Muṣṭafá and Razzāqī, Ḥusayn. *Muntakhabī az muraqqaʿāt-i Kitābkhānah-i Markazī-yi Astān-i Quds-i Raẕavī* (= *Selected calligraphy from the Central Library of Astane Qods Razavi*). [Mashhad], 1368 [1990].
Mustafa İzzet. *Kazasker Mustafa İzzet Efendi'nin sülüs ve nesih meşk murakkai*. Istanbul, Kubbealtı Neşriyâtı, 1996.
Robinson, B.W. "Muraḳḳaʿ". *EI*, new ed., 7: 602-603.
Roxburgh, David J. "Catalogue of scripts by seven masters (H.2310): a Timurid calligraphy album at the Ottoman court". *Art turc (= Turkish art): 10e Congrès international d'art turc*, ed. F. Déroche et al. Geneva, 1999: 587-597.
——— "'Our works point to us': album making, collecting, and art (1427-1565) under the Timurids and Safavids". Ph.D. diss., Univ. of Pennsylvania, 1996.

Şevki Efendi, Mehmed. *Şevki Efendi'nin sülüs ve nesih meşk murakkai.* Istanbul, Kubbealtı Neşriyâtı, 1996.

The St. Petersburg muraqqaʿ: album of Indian and Persian miniatures from the 16th through the 18th century and specimens of Persian calligraphy by ʿImâd al-Hasanî. Lugano/Milan, 1996.

Thackston, Wheeler M. "Album, 3. Islamic world". *The dictionary of art*, ed. J. Turner. New York, 1996: 1, 583-584.

VII. 2. Calligraphy (see also VIII. Qurʾanic manuscripts)

a) Bibliographies and dictionaries

Akgül, Medine and Yiğitbaş, Ayeşe Kızıltepe. *Uğur Derman bibliyografyası.* Istanbul, Türk Kütübhaneciler Derneği, 1996.

ʿAwwād, Kūrkīs. "Al-Khaṭṭ al-ʿArabī fī āthār al-dārisīn qadīman wa-ḥadīthan". *Al-Mawrid*, 15 (1986): 377-412.

al-Bahnassī, ʿAfīf . *Muʿjam muṣṭalaḥāt al-khaṭṭ al-ʿArabī wa-al-khaṭṭāṭīn.* Beirut, Maktabat Lubnān, 1995.

Gacek, Adam. "Al-Nuwayrī's classification of Arabic scripts". *Manuscripts of the Middle East*, 2 (1987): 126-130. [Includes an appendix: 'A select bibliography of classical and post-classical texts on penmanship'.]

Shaykh Mūsá, Muḥammad Khayr. "Ḥarakat al-taʾlīf fī al-kitābah wa-al-kuttāb wa-maṣādir naqd al-tarassul wa-al-kitābah (ḥattá al-qarn al-rābiʿ al-hijrī)". *Majallat Majmaʿ al-Lughah al-ʿArabīyah bi-Dimashq*, 72, no.3 (1997): 481-526.

al-Yūsuf, Khālid Aḥmad and Sayyid, Amīn Sulaymān. "Marājiʿ al-khaṭṭ al-ʿArabī". *Al-Khaṭṭ al-ʿArabī min khilāl al-makhṭūṭāt.* Riyad, 1406 [1986] : 241-254. [See also the English version : *Arabic calligraphy in manuscripts*, 259-267.]

b) Exhibition catalogues

Derman, M. Uğur. *Letters in gold: Ottoman calligraphy from the Sakip Sabanci collection, Istanbul.* New York, Metropolitan Museum of Art, 1998.

Grube, Ernst J. *Calligraphy and the decorative arts of Islam.* London, Bluett, 1976.

Hoare, Oliver. *The calligrapher's craft. Summer exhibition, 1-27 June 1987, Ahuan Gallery of Islamic Art.* London,1987.

Islamic calligraphy: sacred and secular writings (= Calligraphie islamique). Geneva, Musée d'art et d'histoire, 1988.

Musée de la calligraphie arabe. *Calligraphie arabe: oeuvres du Musée de Damas, [exposition], 25 mai –19 juin 1977*. Paris, 1977.

Safwat, Nabil F., Fehérvári, Géza and Zakariya, Mohamed U. *The harmony of letters: Islamic calligraphy from the Tareq Rajab Museum*. Singapore, 1997.

c) Pre-20th century texts on calligraphy and penmanship

Abouricha, Noureddine. "Recherches autour l'opuscule la 'Ḥikmat al-ishrāq ilā kuttāb al-āfāq' de Murtaḍā al-Zabīdī". Doctoral thesis, EPHE (Paris), 2000.

Gacek, Adam. "Arabic scripts and their characteristics as seen through the eyes of Mamluk authors". *Manuscripts of the Middle East*, 4 (1989): 144-149.

——— "Al-Nuwayrī's classification of Arabic scripts". *Manuscripts of the Middle East*, 2 (1987): 126-130.

Hilmi Efendi, Mustafa Hakkâk-zâde. *Mizânü'l-hatt (=Mīzān al-khaṭṭ)*. Istanbul, Osmanlı Yayınevi, 1986. [Facsimile edition of an album calligraphed by Ḥakkāk zādah in 1266/1850 and containing a number of texts in Arabic and Turkish, including *Tuḥfat ūlī al-albāb* by Ibn al-Ṣā'igh, 3 ijāzāt and *Handasat al-khaṭṭ* by Shaykh Ḥamd Allāh.]

Ibn Muqlah, Muḥammd ibn ʿAlī. "Risālah fī al-khaṭṭ wa-al-qalam". *Ibn Muqlah, khaṭṭāṭan wa-adīban wa-insānan*, by Hilāl Nājī. Baghdad, Dār al-Shu'ūn al-Thaqāfīyah al-ʿĀmmah, 1991: 113-126.

James, David. "The commentaries of Ibn al-Baṣīṣ and Ibn al-Waḥīd on Ibn al-Bawwāb's 'Ode on the art of calligraphy' (Rā'iyyah fī l-khaṭṭ)". *Back to the sources. Biblical and Near Eastern studies in honour of Dermot Ryan*, ed. K.J. Cathcart and J.F. Healey. Sandycove,1989: 164-191.

al-Kātib, Ḥusayn ibn Yāsīn ibn Muḥammad. *Lamḥat al-mukhtaṭif fī ṣināʿat al-khaṭṭ al-ṣalif*, ed. Hayā Muḥammad Dawsarī. Kuwait, Mu'assasat al-Kuwayt lil-Taqaddum al-ʿIlmī, Idārat al-Ta'līf wa-al-Tarjamah wa-al-Nashr, 1992.

Nājī, Hilāl. "Nuṣūṣ fī al-khaṭṭ al-ʿArabī". *Al-Mawrid*, 15, no.4 (1986): 157-270. [Contains five texts: *Waḍḍāḥat al-uṣūl fī al-khaṭṭ* by ʿAbd al-Qādir al-Ṣaydāwī, *Naẓm la'ālī al-simṭ* by Aḥmad al-

Rifāʿī al-Qasṭālī, *Minhāj al-iṣābah* by Muḥammad al-Ziftāwī, *Biḍāʿat al-mujawwid* by Muḥammad al-Sinjārī and *Sharḥ al-manẓūmah al-mustaṭābah fī ʿilm al-kitābah* by Ibn Baṣīṣ and Ibn al-Waḥīd.]

"Risālah fī ṣināʿat al-kitābah", ed. ʿAbd al-Laṭīf al-Rāwī and ʿAbd al-Ilāh Nabhān. *Majallat Majmaʿ al-Lughah al-ʿArabīyah bi-Dimashq*, 62, no.4 (1987): 760-795; 63, no.1 (1988): 50-65.

Rudolph, Ekkehard. "Der Wettsreit der Schriftarten – eine arabische Handschrift aus der Forschungsbibliothek Gotha". *Der Islam*, 65, Heft 2 (1988): 301-316. [Contains a facsimile of *Ghāyat al-marām fī takhāṭub al-aqlām* by ʿAbd Allāh ibn Aḥmad al-Maqdisī.]

Saʿd, Fārūq. *Risālah fī al-khaṭṭ wa-bary al-qalam li-Ibn al-Ṣāʾigh.* Beirut, Sharikat al-Maṭbūʿāt, 1997.

al-Saʿdī al-Mawṣilī, Sāliḥ. "Urjūzah fī ʿilm rasm al-khaṭṭ", ed. Zuhayr Zāhid and Hilāl Nājī. *Al-Mawrid*, 15, no.4 (1986): 345-376.

al-Sāwirī, ʿAbd al-ʿAzīz. "Kitāb al-qalam li-Abī Muḥammad al-Sarrāj al-Baghdādī". *ʿĀlam al-kutub*, 15, no.1 (1994): 70-73.

al-Zabīdī, Muḥammad Murtaḍá. *Ḥikmat al-ishrāq ilá kuttāb al-āfāq*, ed. Muḥammad Ṭalḥah Bilāl. Jedda, Dār al-Madanī, 1990. [Contains (pp.113-138) a compilation by the editor entitled: *Tatimmah fī naqd al-athār al-maʿrūfah ʿan al-khaṭṭ wa-al-kitābah.*]

d) Calligraphers and calligraphers' diplomas

ʿAbbās, Ẓamyāʾ Muḥammad. "Nisāʾ khaṭṭāṭāt". *Al-Mawrid*, 15, no.4 (1986): 141-148.

Abbott, Nabia. "The contribution of Ibn Muḳlah to the North-Arabic script". *American journal of Semitic languages and literatures*, 56 (1939): 71-83.

Albin, M.W. "Index of penmen in Nājī Zayn al-Dīn's 'Muṣawwar al-khaṭṭ al-ʿArabī'". *MELA notes*, 13 (1978): 27-35.

al-Atharī, Muḥammad Bahjah. *Taḥqīqāt wa-taʿlīqāt ʿalá kitāb 'al-Khaṭṭāṭ al-Baghdādī ʿAlī ibn Hilāl al-mashhūr bi-Ibn al-Bawwāb'*. Baghdād, al-Majmaʿ al-ʿIlmī al-ʿIrāqī, 1958.

al-Aʿẓamī, Walīd. *Jamharat al-khaṭṭāṭīn al- Baghdādīyīn mundhu taʾsīs Baghdād ḥattá nihāyat al-qarn al-rābiʿ ʿashar al-hijrī.* Baghdad, Wizārat al-Thaqāfah wa-al-Iʿlām, Dār al-Shuʾūn al-Thaqāfīyah al-ʿĀmmah, 1989. 2 vols.

ʿAzzāwī, ʿAbbās. "Khaṭṭ al-muṣḥaf al-sharīf wa-al-khaṭṭāṭ al-Shāh Maḥmūd al-Nīsābūrī". *Sumer*, 23 (1967): 151-156, 5 illus.

——— "Al-Khaṭṭ wa-mashāhīr al-khaṭṭāṭīn fī al-waṭan al-ʿArabī", ed. Fāḍil ʿAbbās al-ʿAzzāwī. *Sumer*, 38, nos.1-2 (1982): 284-302.

——— "Mashāhīr al-khaṭṭāṭīn fī al-ʿIrāq fī ʿahd al-Mamālīk". *Sumer*, 5 (1949): 85-91.

——— "Mashāhīr al-khaṭṭ al-ʿArabī fī Turkiyā". *Sumer*, 36, no.1-2 (1980): 334-352.

——— "Nuṣūṣ ijāzāt al-khaṭṭāṭīn". *Al-Mawrid*, 1, no.3-4 (1972): 180-186.

al-Bahnassī, ʿAfīf. *Muʿjam muṣṭalaḥāt al-khaṭṭ al-ʿArabī wa-al-khaṭṭāṭīn*. Beirut, Maktabat Lubnān, 1995.

Déroche, François. "The Ottoman roots of a Tunisian calligrapher's 'tour de force'". *Sanatta etkilesim* (= *Interactions in art*), ed. Z. Yasa Yaman. Ankara (forthcoming).

Gacek, Adam. "The diploma of the Egyptian calligrapher Ḥasan al-Rushdī". *Manuscripts of the Middle East*, 4 (1989): 44-55.

Hassan, Ahmed Moustafa M. "The scientific foundation of Arabic lettershapes according to the theory of 'the proportioned script' by Ibn Muqla (272-328 AH / 886-940 AD)". Ph.D, London Institute – Central Saint Martin's College of Art and Design, 1989.

Huart, Cl. *Les calligraphes et les miniaturistes de l'Orient musulman*. Paris, 1908.

Ibrāhīm, ʿAbd al-Laṭīf. "Ibn al-Ṣāʾigh al-khaṭṭāṭ wa-madrasatuh". *Majallat al-maktabah al-ʿArabīyah* (Cairo), 1, no.3 (1964): 80-93, 7 illus.

al-Jubūrī, Maḥmūd Shukr. "Al-Khaṭṭāṭ Yāqūt al-Mustaʿṣimī". *Al-Mawrid*, 15, no.4 (1896): 149-156.

al-Kurdī, Muḥammad Ṭāhir. *Taʾrīkh al-khaṭṭ al-ʿArabī wa-ādābuh*. Cairo, 1939. [Also published: Riyad, al-Jamʿīyah al-ʿArabīyah al-Saʿūdīyah lil-Thaqāfah wa-al-Funūn, 1982.]

al-Munajjid, Ṣalāḥ al-Dīn. *Yāqūt al-Mustaʿṣimī*. Beirut, Dār al-Kitāb al-Jadīd, 1985.

——— "Women's roles in the art of Arabic calligraphy". *The book in the Islamic world: the written word and communication in the Middle East*, ed. George N. Atiyeh. Albany, NY, 1995: 141-148.

Nājī, Hilāl. *Ibn al-Bawwāb – ʿabqarī al-khaṭṭ al-ʿArabī ʿabra al-ʿuṣūr: majmūʿah nafīsah min khuṭūṭ Ibn al-Bawwāb*. Beirut, Dār al-Gharb al-Islāmī, 1998.

——— *Ibn Muqlah, khaṭṭāṭan wa-adīban wa-insānan*. Baghdad, Dār al-Shu'ūn al-Thaqāfīyah al-ʿĀmmah, 1991.

Porter, Yves. "Notes sur le 'Golestān-e honar' de Qāżi Aḥmad Qomi". *Studia Iranica*, 17 (1988): 207-223.

Qāḍī Aḥmad. *Calligraphers and painters: a treatise by Qāḍī Aḥmad, son of Mīr-Munshī (circa A.H. 1015/A.D. 1606)*. Transl. by V. and T. Minorsky. Washington, D.C., 1959.

al-Qaysī, Nūrī Ḥammūdī. "Madrasat al-khaṭṭ al-ʿIrāqīyah min Ibn Muqlah ilá Hāshim al-Baghdādī". *Al-Mawrid*, 15, no.4 (1986): 69-82.

Rado, Şevket. *Türk hattatları XV. yüzyıldan günümüze kadar gelmiş ünlü hattatların hayatları ve yazılarından örnekler*. Istanbul, 1982.

Rayef, Ahmad Maher. "Die ästhetischen Grundlagen der arabischen Schrift bei Ibn Muqlah". Diss. Köln, 1975.

Richard, Francis. "Dīvānī ou Taʿlīq: un calligraphe au service de Mehmet II Sayyidī Mohammad Monšī". *Les manuscrits du Moyen Orient*, ed. F. Déroche. Istanbul/ Paris, 1989: 89-93.

Ribera y Tarragó, J. "Escuela valenciana de calígrafos árabes". *Disertaciones y opúsculos*, by J. Ribera y Tarragó. Madrid, 1928: 2, 304-306.

Saʿīd, Khayr Allāh. *Khaṭṭāṭū Baghdād fī al-ʿaṣr al-ʿAbbāsī*. Damascus, Dār al-Numayr, 1996.

Salmān, ʿĪsá. "Al-Shāh Maḥmūd al-Nīsābūrī: khaṭṭāṭ wa-madhhab". *Sumer*, 33, no.1 (1977): 104-111.

Serin, Muhittin. *Hat sanatı ve meşhur hattatlar*. Istanbul, Kubbealtı Neşriyâtı, 1999.

——— *Hattat Aziz Efendi*. Istanbul, Kubbealtı Akademisi Kültür ve San'at Vakfı, 1999.

——— *Hattat Şeyh Hamdullah: hayâtı, talebeleri, eserleri*. Istanbul, Kubbealtı Akademisi Kültür ve San'at Vakfı, 1992.

Soucek, P.P. "ʿAbdallah Ṣayrafī". *Encyclopaedia Iranica*, ed. E. Yarshater, 1: 203-205.

Sourdel, D. "Ibn Muḳla". *EI*, new ed., 3: 886-887.

Sourdel-Thomine, J. "Ibn al-Bawwāb". *EI*, new ed., 3: 736-737.

Tabrizi, Mohammad Ali Karimzadeh. *Ijazat nameh (= Icâzet name): the most unique and precious document in Ottoman calligraphy*. London, 1999.

Ünver, A. Süheyl. *Al-Khaṭṭāṭ al-Baghdādī ʿAlī ibn Hilāl al-mashhūr bi-Ibn al-Bawwāb*. Transl. by Muḥammad Bahjah al-Atharī and ʿAzīz Shāmī. Baghdad, Maṭbaʿat al-Majmaʿ al-ʿIlmī al-ʿIrāqī, 1958.

Welch, A. "Patrons and calligraphers in Safavi Iran". *MELA notes*, 12 (1977): 10-15.

Zāyid, Aḥmad Ṣabrī. *Ta'rīkh al-khaṭṭ al-'Arabī wa-a'lām al-khaṭṭāṭīn: muzawwad bi-al-ṣuwar wa-al-lawḥāt li-ashhar al-khaṭṭāṭīn*. Cairo, Dār al-Faḍīlah, [1999].

e) Studies and albums (by modern calligraphers) (see also VII.1.c)

al-ʿAbbāsī, Yaḥyá Sallūm. *Al-Khaṭṭ al-ʿArabī: ta'rīkhuh wa-anwāʿuh muzayyan bi-al-lawḥāt al-khaṭṭīyah wa-al-ṣuwar*. Baghdad, Maktabat al-Nahḍah, 1984.

Acar, M. Şinasi. *Türk hat sanati: araç, gereç ve formlar (= Turkish calligraphy: materials, tools and forms*. Istanbul, Antik A.Ş., 1999.[Text in Turkish and English.]

ʿAfīfī, Fawzī Sālim. *Jāmiʿ al-khaṭṭ al-ʿArabī*. Damascus/Cairo, Dār al-Kitāb al-ʿArabī, 1996.

Akimushkin, Oleg. "The calligraphy of the St. Petersburg Album". *The St. Petersburg muraqqaʿ. Album of Indian and Persian miniatures from the 16th through the 18th century and specimens of Persian calligraphy by ʿImâd al-Hasanî*. Lugano/Milan, 1996: 39-46.

Āl Saʿīd, Shākir Ḥasan. "Al-Khaṭṭ al-ʿArabī jamālīyan wa-ḥaḍārīyan". *Al-Mawrid*, 15, no.4 (1986): 51-68.

Alani, Ghani. "Calligraphy: the writing of script". *Dreaming of paradise. Islamic art from the collection of the Museum of Ethnology, Rotterdam*. [Rotterdam], 1993: 41-61.

al-Ali, Salih. "Remarks on style". *Islamic calligraphy, sacred and secular writings*. Geneva, 1988: 30-39.

Alparslan, Ali. "L'art de la calligraphie en Turquie aux XVe et XVIe siècles". *Revue des études islamiques*, 35 (1967): 219-224.

——— "Ecoles calligraphiques turques". *Islam Tetkikleri Enstitüsü Dergisi*, 5, nos. 1-4 (1973): 265-278.

——— "The influence of the court and the courtly milieu on the development of Islamic calligraphy". *Actes du XXIXe Congrès international des orientalistes. Etudes arabes et islamiques. 1. Histoire et civilisation*. Paris, 1975 : 23-28.

Atanasiu, V. *De la fréquence des lettres et de son influence en calligraphie arabe*. Paris, 1999.

Aziza, Mohamed. *La calligraphie arabe*. Tunis, 1973.

al-Bahnassī, ʿAfīf. *Al-Khaṭṭ al-ʿArabī: uṣūluh, nahḍatuh, intishāruh*. Damascus, Dār al-Fikr, 1984.

al-Baghdādī, Hāshim Muḥammad. *Qawāʿid al-khaṭṭ al-ʿArabī: majmūʿah khaṭṭīyah li-anwāʿ al-khuṭūṭ al-ʿArabīyah*. Al-Ṭabʿah al-muzayyadah. Baghdad, Maktabat al-Nahḍah, Beirut, Dār al-Qalam, 1980.

Bhutta, Muhammad Iqbal. "Muslim calligraphy in the Subcontinent". *Journal of the Research Society of Pakistan*, 36, no.2 (1999): 43-67, 2 p. of illus.

Bidīwī, Yūsuf ʿAlī. *Al-Dirāsāt al-akādīmīyah fī taʾrīkh al-khaṭṭ al-ʿArabī wa-jamālīyātih wa-tiqnīyātih*. Damascus, Dār al-Waʿy, 1996.

"Calligraphy". *A survey of Persian art from prehistoric times to the present*, ed. A.U. Pope and P. Ackerman. Ashiya/New York, 1977: 2, 1707-1742.

Derman, M. Uğur. "A remarkable collection of mashq". *Art turc (= Turkish art): 10e Congrès international d'art turc*, ed. F. Déroche et al. Geneva, 1999: 253-259.

——— "The Turks and the art of calligraphy". *Islam sanatında Türkler (= The Turkish contribution to Islamic arts)*. Istanbul, 1976: 58-83, 235-236.

Derman, M. Uğur and Çetin, Nihad M. *The art of calligraphy in the Islamic heritage*. Istanbul, IRCICA, 1998.

Déroche, François. "Maîtres et disciples: la transmission de la culture calligraphique dans le monde ottoman". *Revue du monde musulman et de la Méditerranée*, 75-76 (1995): 81-90.

Dhannūn, Yūsuf. "Qadīm wa-jadīd fī aṣl al-khaṭṭ al-ʿArabī wa-taṭawwuruh fī ʿuṣūrih al-mukhtalifah". *Al-Mawrid,* 15, no.4 (1986): 7-26.

Faẕāʾilī, Ḥabīb Allāh. *Aṭlas-i khaṭṭ: taḥqīq dar khuṭūṭ-i Islāmī*. Isfahan, [1971].

——— *Taʿlīm-i khaṭṭ*. Tehran, Surūsh, 1363 [1984 or 1985].

Gacek, Adam. "Arabic calligraphy and the 'Herbal' of al-Ghāfiqī: a survey of Arabic manuscripts at McGill University". *Fontanus: from the collections of McGill University*, 2 (1989): 37-53.

Ḥanash, Idhān Muḥammad. *Al-Khaṭṭ al-ʿArabī fī al-wathāʾiq al-ʿUthmānīyah*. Amman, Dār al-Manāhij, 1998.

——— *Al-Khaṭṭ al-ʿArabī wa-ishkālīyāt al-naqd al-fannī*. Amman, Dār al-Manāhij, 1998.

Harātī, Muḥammad Mahdī. *Tajallī-i hunar dar kitābat-i Bism Allāh (= Wuḍūḥ al-fann fī kitābat al-basmalah)*. Mashhad, 1367/ [1988].

James, David. "Calligraphy, epigraphy and the art of the book".

Louisiana revy, 27, no.3 (March 1987): 20-23.

——— "Islamic calligraphy, an outline". *Islamic calligraphy: sacred and secular writings*. Geneva, 1988: 12-19.

al-Jubūrī, Kāmil Salmān. *Mawsūʿat al-khaṭṭ al-ʿArabī*. Beirut, Dār wa-Maktabat al-Hilāl, 1999. 8 vols.

——— *Uṣūl al-khaṭṭ al-ʿArabī: nashʾatuh, anwāʿuh, taṭawwuruh, namādhijuh*. Beirut, Dār wa-Maktabat al-Hilāl, 2000.

al-Jubūrī, Yaḥyá Wahīb. *Al-Khaṭṭ wa-al-kitābah fī al-ḥaḍārah al-ʿArabīyah*. Beirut, Dār al-Gharb al-Islāmī, 1994.

Khatibi, Abdelkabir and Sijelmassi, Mohammed. *The splendor of Islamic calligraphy*. London, 1976.

Kühnel, Ernst. *Islamische Schriftkunst*. 3. Auflage. Graz, 1986.

al-Kurdī, Muḥammad Ṭāhir. *Taʾrīkh al-khaṭṭ al-ʿArabī wa-ādābuh*. Cairo, 1939. [New ed.: Riyad, al-Jamʿīyah al-ʿArabīyah al-Saʿūdīyah lil-Thaqāfah wa-al-Funūn, 1982.]

Lowry, Glenn D. "Introduction to Islamic calligraphy". *From concept to context. Approaches to Asian and Islamic calligraphy*, by Shen Fu, G. D. Lowry and A. Yonemura. Washington, 1986: 102-149.

Lowry, Heath. "Calligraphy – Hüsn-i hat". *Tulips, arabesques & turbans: decorative arts from the Ottoman empire*, ed. Y. Petsopoulos. London, 1982: 169-191.

al-Manūnī, Muḥammad. "Lamḥah ʿan taʾrīkh al-khaṭṭ al-ʿArabī: awwalan bi-al-Mashriq al-Islāmī". *Al-Manāhil*, 24 (1982): 238-266.

Mitchell, T.F. *Writing Arabic: a practical introduction to ruqʿah script*. London, 1953.

Naef, Silvia. *L'art de l'écriture arabe: passé et présent*. Geneva, 1992.

Raby, Julian. "The Nayrizi tradition: Naskh in Safavid and Qajar Iran". *The art of the pen: calligraphy of the 14th to 20th centuries*, by Nabil F. Safwat. Oxford, 1996: 212-227.

Rahman, Parez Islam Syed Mustafizur. *Islamic calligraphy in medieval India*. Dacca, 1979.

——— "An introduction to Islamic calligraphy, techniques and terminology". *Dacca University Studies*, 22a (1974): 203-210.

al-Rifāʿī, Bilāl ʿAbd al-Wahhāb. *Al-Khaṭṭ al-ʿArabī: taʾrīkhuh wa-ḥāḍiruh*. Damascus/ Beirut, Dār Ibn Kathīr, 1990.

Rodari, Florian. "The imponderable, improbable writing". *Islamic calligraphy: sacred and secular writings*. Geneva, 1988: 40-47.

Safadi, Yasin Hamid. *Islamic calligraphy*. London, 1978. [French translation, *Calligraphie islamique,* by Michel Garell, Paris, 1978.]

Safwat, Nabil F. *The art of the pen: calligraphy of the 14th to 20th centuries.* London/ Oxford, 1996 (*The Nasser D. Khalili Collection of Islamic Art, V*).

al-Samarrāʾī, Qāsim Aḥmad. "Taʾrīkh al-khaṭṭ al-ʿArabī wa-arqāmih: muqaddimah mūjazah". *ʿĀlam al-kutub*, 16, no.6 (1995): 523-537.

Schimmel, Annemarie. "The art of calligraphy". *The arts of Persia*, ed. R.W. Ferrier. New Haven/London, 1989: 306-314.

——— *Calligraphy and Islamic culture.* New York, 1984.

——— "Calligraphy and sufism in Ottoman Turkey". *The dervish lodge: architecture, art and sufism in Ottoman Turkey*, ed. R. Lifchez. Los Angeles/ Oxford, 1992: 242-252.

——— *Islamic calligraphy.* Leiden, 1970.

——— "Die Schriftarten und ihr kalligraphischer Gebrauch". *Grundriss der arabischen Philologie.* Band I: *Sprachwissenschaft*, herausgegeben von W. Fischer. Wiesbaden, 1982: 198-209.

Schimmel, Annemarie , Déroche, François and Thackston, Wheeler M. "Islamic art, III, 2. Calligraphy". *The dictionary of art*, ed. J. Turner. New York, 1996: 16, 273-288.

Schimmel, Annemarie and Rivolta, Barbara. "Islamic calligraphy". *The Metropolitan Museum of Art bulletin,* (Summer, 1992).

Selim, George Dimitri. "Arabic calligraphy in the Library of Congress". *Quarterly journal of the Library of Congress*, 36 (1979): 140-177.

Sharīfī, Muḥammad. "Al-Khaṭṭ al-ʿArabī fī al-ḥaḍārah al-Islamīyah". *Al-Āthār al-Islāmīyah fī al-waṭan al-ʿArabī.* Tunis, al-Munaẓẓamah al-ʿArabīyah lil-Tarbiyah wa-al-Thaqāfah wa-al-ʿUlūm, Idārat al-Thaqāfah, 1985: 172-193.

Siddiqui, Atiq R. *The story of Islamic calligraphy.* Delhi, 1990.

Soucek, Priscilla P. "The arts of calligraphy". *The arts of the book in Central Asia, 14th-16th centuries*, ed. Basil Gray. Paris/London, 1979: 7-33.

Sourdel-Thomine, J., Alparslan, Ali and Chaghatai, M. Abdullah. "Khaṭṭ". *EI*, new ed., 4: 1113-1128.

Ülker, Muammer. *Başlangıçtan günümüze Türk hat sanatı (= The art of Turkish calligraphy from the beginning up to present).* Ankara, 1987. [Text in Turkish, English and Arabic.]

Welch, Anthony. *Calligraphy in the arts of the Muslim world*. Austin, 1979.

Yaqub Ali, A.K.M. "Muslim calligraphy, its beginning and major styles". *Islamic studies*, 23, no.4 (1984): 373-379.

Yūsofī, Ġolām-Ḥosayn. "Calligraphy". *Encyclopaedia Iranica*, ed. E. Yarshater, 4: 680-718.

Yusuf, K. M. "Muslim calligraphy under the Mughals". *Indo-Iranica*, 10, no.1 (1957): 9-13.

Zakariya, Mohamed U. *The calligraphy of Islam. Reflections on the state of the art*. Washington, D.C., 1979.

——— "A compendium of Arabic scripts". *The art of the pen: calligraphy of the 14th to 20th centuries*, by Nabil F. Safwat. Oxford, 1996: 228-234.

——— *Observations on Islamic calligraphy*. Washington, D.C., 1978.

——— "Islamic calligraphy: a technical overview". *Brocade of the pen. The art of Islamic writing*, ed. Carol Garrett Fisher. Michigan, Kresge Art Museum, Michigan State University, 1991: 1-17.

Zayn al-Dīn, Nājī. *Badāʾiʿ al-khaṭṭ al-ʿArabī*, ed. ʿAbd al-Razzāq ʿAbd al-Wāḥid. Baghdad, Wizārat al-Iʿlām, 1972.

——— *Muṣawwar al-khaṭṭ al-ʿArabī*. Baghdad, Maktabat al-Nahḍah, Beirut, Dār al-Qalam, 1980/1400.

Ziauddin, M. *Moslem calligraphy*. Calcutta, 1936.

VII. 3. Ornament and painted decoration

Baer, E. *Islamic ornament*. Edinburgh, 1998.

Akimushkin, Oleg F. "The art of illumination". *The arts of the book in Central Asia, 14th-16th centuries*, ed. Basil Gray. Paris/ London, 1979: 35-67.

Arberry, A. J. *The Koran illuminated: a handlist of the Korans in the Chester Beatty Library*. Dublin, 1967.

Barrucand, Marianne. "Remarques sur le décor des manuscrits religieux hispano-maghrébins du moyen-âge". *Histoire et archéologie de l'Afrique du Nord: actes du Ve colloque international réuni dans le cadre du 115e Congrès national des societés savantes (Avignon, 9-13 avril 1990)*. Paris, 1992: 235-248.

Ettinghausen, R. "Manuscript illumination". *A survey of Persian art from prehistoric times to the present,* ed. A.U. Pope and P. Ackerman. Ashiya/New York, 1977: 5, 1937-1974.

Déroche, F. and Simpson, Marianna S. "Islamic art, III, 3. Painted decoration". *The dictionary of art*, ed. J. Turner. New York, 1996: 16, 288-293.

Gacek, Adam. "ʿUnwān: in manuscript production". *EI*, new ed., 10: 870-871.

Kühnel, E. "Arabesque". *EI*, new ed., 1: 558-561.

——— *The arabesque: meaning and transformation of an ornament*. Graz, n.d.

Monneret de Villard, U. "Codici magrebini decorati della Biblioteca Vaticana". *Annali. Istituto Universitario Orientale di Napoli*, n.s., 3 (1949): 83-91.

Polosin, Val. V. "'All is numbers'? An unknown numerical component in the design of medieval Arabic manuscripts". *Manuscripta Orientalia*, 5, no.1 (1999): 7-11.

——— "Frontispieces on scale canvas in Arabic manuscripts". *Manuscripta Orientalia*, 2, no.1 (1996): 5-19.

——— "To the method of describing illuminated Arabic manuscripts". *Manuscripta Orientalia*, 1, no.2 (1995): 16-21.

Richard, Francis. "La signature discrète d'un doreur persan à la fin du XVe s. Mīr ʿAzod al-Mo̱zahheb". *Revue des études islamiques*, 61/62 (1993/94): 88-108.

Sijelmassi, Mohamed. *Enluminures des manuscrits royaux au Maroc (Bibliothèque al-Hassania)*. Paris, 1987.

Simpson, Marianna S. "Manuscript illumination, Islamic". *Dictionary of the Middle Ages*, ed. J. R. Strayer. New York, 1982-89: 8, 112-118.

Tanindi, Zeren. "An illuminated manuscript of the wandering scholar Ibn al-Jazari and the wandering illuminators between Tabriz, Shiraz, Herat, Bursa, Edirne, Istanbul in the 15th century". *Art turc (= Turkish art): 10e Congrès international d'art turc*, ed. F. Déroche et al. Geneva, 1999: 647-655.

Waley, Muhammad Isa. "Illumination and its functions in Islamic manuscripts". *Scribes et manuscrits du Moyen-Orient*, ed. F. Déroche and F. Richard. Paris, 1997: 87-112.

VII. 4. Painted illustration

a) Drawing

Brend, Barbara. "Rasm". *EI*, new ed., 8:451-453.
Swietochowski, M.L. "Drawing". *Encyclopaedia Iranica*, ed. E. Yarshater, 7: 537-547.

b) Other studies

Barrucand, Marianne. "Héritage et emprunts culturels dans la miniature islamique du XIIIe au XVe siècle". *Revue des études islamiques*, 55/57, fasc.1 (1987-89): 239-253.
al-Bāshā, Ḥasan. *Funūn al-taṣwīr al-Islāmī fī Miṣr*. Cairo, al-Hay'ah al-Miṣrīyah al-ʿĀmmah lil-Kitāb, 1994.
Berthier, A. "Qalamus, pinceau, ciseaux. Ombres chinoises sur la miniature persane et turque". *Etudes orientales* (= *Dirāsāt Sharqīyah*), 11/12 (1991):116-125.
Blair, Sheila S. "The development of the illuminated book in Iran". *Muqarnas*, 10 (1993): 266-274.
Blair, Sheila S. et al. "Islamic art, III, 4. Painted book illustration". *The dictionary of art*, ed. J. Turner. New York, 1996: 16, 293-351.
Bloom, Jonathan M. "The introduction of paper to the Islamic world and the development of the illustrated manuscript". *Muqarnas*, 17 (2000): 17-23.
"Book painting". *A survey of Persian art from prehistoric times to the present,* ed. A.U. Pope and P. Ackerman. Ashiya/New York, 1977: 5: 1809-1927.
Brandenburg, Dietrich. *Islamic miniature painting in medical manuscripts*. 2nd ed. Basle, 1984.
Canby, Sheila R. *Princes, poets & paladins: Islamic and Indian paintings from the collection of Prince and Princess Sadruddin Aga Khan*. London, 1998.
Farghalī, Abū al-Ḥamd Maḥmūd. "Al-Khaṣā'iṣ al-fannīyah li-madrasat al-taṣwīr al-maḥallīyah fī Miṣr fī al-ʿaṣr al-ʿUthmānī 923-1220/1517-1805". *Al-Majallah al-ta'rīkhīyah al-Miṣrīyah,* 38 (1991-95): 185-231.
Grabar, Oleg. *La peinture persane, une introduction*. Paris, 1999.
Hoffman, Eva R. "The beginnings of the illustrated Arabic book: an

intersection between art and scholarship". *Muqarnas*, 17 (2000): 37-52.

——— "The emergence of illustration in Arabic manuscripts: classical legacy and Islamic transformation". Ph.D. diss., Harvard University, 1982.

King, David. "Some illustrations in Islamic scientific manuscripts and their secrets". *The book in the Islamic world: the written word and communication in the Middle East*, ed. George N. Atiyeh. Albany, NY, 1995: 149-177.

Milstein, Rachel. *Miniature painting in Ottoman Baghdad*. Costa Mesa, Ca., 1990.

Papadopoulo, Alexandre. "Al-Taṣwīr fī al-makhṭūṭāt al-ʿArabīyah". Transl. by Nahād Takrālī. *Funūn ʿArabīyah*, 2, no.1 (1982): 12-20.

Porter, Yves. "Arts du livre et illustrations". *Entre l'Iran et l'Occident: adaptation et assimilation des idées et techniques occidentales en Iran*, ed. Yann Richard. Paris, 1989: 157-169.

——— *Painters, paintings, and books: an essay on Indo-Persian technical littérature, 12-19th centuries*. New Delhi, 1994.

——— *Peinture et arts du livre: essai sur la litérature technique indo-persane*. Paris, 1992.

Robinson, B.W. et al. *Islamic painting and the arts of the book*. London, 1976.

Schmitz, Barbara. "Arabic illustrated manuscripts". *Islamic manuscripts in the New York Public Library*. New York, 1992: 1-50.

——— *Islamic and Indian manuscripts and paintings in the Pierpont Morgan Library*. New York, 1997.

Shams al-Dīn, ʿAlī Maḥmūd. "Fann tazwīq al-makhṭūṭāt fī al-ʿuṣūr al-Islāmīyah mā bayna al-qarn al-thānī ʿashar wa-al-thāmin ʿashar". *Al-Waḥdah*, 3, nos.33-34 (1987): 169-184.

Soucek, Priscilla P. "Persian artists in Mughal India: influences and transformations". *Muqarnas*, 4 (1987):166-181.

——— "Taṣwīr". *EI*, new ed., 10: 361-363.

Wensinck, A.J. and Fahd, T. "Ṣūra". *EI*, new ed., 9: 889-892.

c) Descriptions of individual works

Alikberov, A. and Rezvan, E. "ʿAjāʾib al-makhlūqāt by Zakariyā al-Qazwīnī (d.682/1283): 16th-century illuminated manuscript from the St. Petersburg Academic Collection". *Manuscripta Orientalia*, 1, no.1 (1995): 56-67.

Alikberov, A. and Rezvan, E. "Ibn Abī Khazzām and his Kitāb al-makhzūn: the Mamlūk military manual". *Manuscripta Orientalia,* 1, no.1 (1995): 21-28.

al-ʿArrīqī, Samīr Muqbil. "Al-Madrasah al-Yamanīyah fī fann tazwīq al-makhṭūṭāt al-Islāmīyah". *ʿĀlam al-makhṭūṭāt wa-al-nawādir*, 2, no.2 (1997-8): 343-364.

Barrucand, Marianne. "Le Kalīla wa Dimna de la Bibliothèque royale de Rabat: un manuscrit illustré Il-khānide". *Revue des études islamiques*, 54 (1986): 17-48.

——— "Un manuscrit arabe illustré de Kalila wa Dimna du XIIIe siècle et sa copie ottomane". *Archéologie islamique*, 2 (1991): 81-95.

Blair, Sheila S. *A compendium of chronicles. Rashid al-Din's illustrated history of the world.* London/Oxford, 1995 (*The Nasser D. Khalili Collection of Islamic Art, XXVII*).

Carboni, Stefano. "Constellations, giants and angels from al-Qazwini manuscripts". *Islamic art in the Ashmolean Museum*, ed. James Allen. Oxford, 1995: 83-97 (*Oxford Studies in Islamic Art, X, pt.1*).

——— "An illustrated copy of al-Qazwīnī's 'The Wonders of creation'". *Sotheby's art at auction*, 1990: 229-234.

——— "The London Qazwīnī: an early 14th-century copy of the ʿAjāʾib al-makhlūqāt". *Islamic art*, 3 (1989): 15-31.

Contadini, Anna. "The Kitāb manāfiʿ al-ḥayawān in the Escorial Library". *Islamic art*, 3 (1989): 33-57.

Cowen, Jill Sanchia. *Kalila wa-Dimna: an animal allegory of the Mongol court*. New York, 1989.

Grabar, Oleg. *The illustrations of the Maqamat*. Chicago, 1984.

Grube, Ernst J. "Prolegomena for a corpus publication of illustrated Kalīlah wa Dimnah manuscripts". *Islamic art*, 4 (1991): 301-481.

VII. 5. Lacquer

Diba, L. "Lacquer work". *The arts of Persia*, ed. R.W. Ferrier. New Haven/London, 1989: 243-253.

Grube, Ernst J. "A lacquered panel painting from the collection of Lester Wolfe in the Museum of the University of Notre-Dame".

Orientalia Hispanica sive studia F.M. Pareja octogenario dicata. Leiden, 1974: 1, 376-397.

Khalili, Nasser D., Robinson, B.W. and Stanley, Tim. *Lacquer of the Islamic lands*. London/Oxford, 1996 (*The Nasser D. Khalili Collection of Islamic Art, XXII, pt.1-2*).

Lacquer: an international history and illustrated survey. New York, 1984.

Motamed, Said. "Lackerwork from Iran". *Dreaming of paradise. Islamic art from the collection of the Museum of Ethnology, Rotterdam*. [Rotterdam], 1993: 173-186.

[Robinson, B.W.]. *An exhibition of 50 pieces of Persian, Indian and Turkish lacquer at Bernheimer Fine Arts Ltd. from 10 June to 27 June 1986*. London, 1986.

——— "Islamic art, VIII, 10. Lacquer". *The dictionary of art*, ed. J. Turner. New York, 1996: 16, 533-535.

——— "Lacquer in the University of Oxford". *Islamic art in the Ashmolean Museum*, ed. James Allen. Oxford, 1995: 45-61 (*Oxford Studies in Islamic Art, X, pt.2*).

——— "Persian lacquer in the Bern Historical Museum". *Iran*, 8 (1970): 47-50.

——— "Qajar lacquer". *Muqarnas*, 6 (1989): 131-146.

VII. 6. Papercuts

Schmitz, Barbara. "Cut-paper". *Encyclopaedia Iranica*, ed. E.Yarshater, 6: 475-478.

Thackston, Wheeler M. "Islamic art, III, 6. Papercuts". *The dictionary of art*, ed. J. Turner. New York, 1996: 16, 354-355.

VII. 7. Decorated paper (marbled paper, etc.)

Arndt, R. "Ebru, the cloud art". *Aramco world*, 24, no.3 (1973): 26-32.

Blair, Sheila S. "Color and gold: the decorated papers used in manuscripts in later Islamic times". *Muqarnas*, 17 (2000): 24-36.

Derman, M. Uğur. "Colouring and sizing of paper". *İlgi*, 25 (1977): 32-35.

Doizy, Marie-Ange. *De la dominoterie à la marbrure: histoire des techniques traditionnelles de la décoration du papier*. Paris, 1996.

Kâgitçi, M.A. "Ebrû : Turkish marbled papers". *Palette*, 30 (1968): 14-20, pl.

Porter, Yves. "Kāqaẕe-e abri: notes sur la technique de la marbrure". *Studia Iranica*, 17 (1988): 47-55.

Soucek, P.P. "Afšān". *Encyclopaedia Iranica*, ed. E. Yarshater, 1: 581-582.

Wolfe, Richard J. *Marbled paper: its history, techniques and patterns, with special reference to the relationship of marbling to bookbinding in Europe and the Western World*. Philadelphia, 1990.

VII. 8. Bookbinding (for lacquer bindings see also VII. 5.)

a) Bibliography

Gratzl, Emil, Creswell, K.A.C. and Ettinghausen, R. "Bibliographie der islamischen Einbandkunst, 1871 bis 1956". *Ars Orientalis*, 2 (1957): 519-540.

b) Pre-18th century texts

Bosch, Gulnar K. "The staff of the scribes and the implements of the discerning, an excerpt". *Ars Orientalis*, 4 (1961): 1-13. [Translation of the chapter on bookbinding from *'Umdat al-kuttāb* of Ibn Bādīs.]

Bosch, G., Carswell, J. and Petherbridge, G. *Islamic bindings and bookmaking. A catalogue of an exhibition*. Chicago, 1982. [Contains essays on Islamic bookmaking, its materials, techniques and structures based principally on the works of Ibn Bādīs and Aḥmad al-Sufyānī.]

Gacek, Adam. "Arabic bookmaking and terminology as portrayed by Bakr al-Ishbīlī in his 'Kitāb al-taysīr fī ṣinā'at al-tasfīr'". *Manuscripts of the Middle East*, 5 (1990-91): 106-113.

——— "Ibn Abī Ḥamīdah's didactic poem for bookbinders". *Manuscripts of the Middle East*, 6 (1991): 41-58. [Persian translation by Mahdī Arjumand, *Mīrāṣ-i Islāmī-i Īrān*, 3 (1375/1996): 857-867.]

——— "Instructions on the art of bookbinding attributed to the Rasulid ruler of Yemen al-Malik al-Muẓaffar". *Scribes et manuscrits du Moyen-Orient*, ed. F. Déroche and F. Richard. Paris, 1997: 57-63.

Ibn Bādīs, al-Muʿizz. "ʿUmdat al-kuttāb wa-ʿuddat dhawī al-albāb", ed. ʿAbd al-Sattār al-Ḥalwajī and ʿAlī ʿAbd al-Muḥsin Zakī. *Majallat Maʿhad al-Makhṭūṭāt al-ʿArabīyah*, 17 (1971): 153-166. [Another edition by Najīb Māyil Haravī and ʿIṣām Makkīyah, Mashhad, Majmaʿ al-Buḥūth al-Islāmīyah, 1989.]

al-Ishbīlī, Bakr ibn Ibrāhīm. "Kitāb al-taysīr fī ṣināʿat al-tasfīr", ed. ʿAbd Allāh Kannūn. *Revista del Instituto de Estudios Islámicos en Madrid (= Ṣaḥīfat Maʿhad al-Dirāsāt al-Islāmīyah fī Madrīd)*, 7-8 (1959-60): 1-42 [Spanish resumé: 197-199.]

Levey, Martin. *Mediaeval Arabic bookmaking and its relation to early chemistry and pharmacology*. Philadelphia, 1962. [Contains translations of *ʿUmdat al-kuttāb* of Ibn Bādīs and *Ṣināʿat tasfīr al-kutub wa-ḥall al-dhahab* of Aḥmad al-Sufyānī.]

al-Malik al-Muẓaffar, Yūsuf ibn ʿUmar. *Al-Mukhtaraʿ fī funūn min al-ṣunaʿ*. Kuwait, Muʾassasat al-Shirāʿ al-ʿArabī, 1989: 103-119.

al-Sufyānī, Aḥmad ibn Muḥammad. *Art de la reliure et de la dorure (= Ṣināʿat tasfīr al-kutub wa-ḥall al-dhahab). Texte arabe accompagné d'un index de termes techniques par P. Ricard.* 2nd ed. Paris, 1925. [Reprinted: Cairo, Maktabat al-Thaqāfah al-Dīnīyah, 1999.]

c) Other studies

Ağa-Oğlu, Mehmet. *Persian bookbindings of the fifteenth century*. Ann Arbor, 1935.

Aslanapa, Oktay. "The art of bookbinding". *The arts of the book in Central Asia, 14th-16th centuries*, ed. Basil Gray. Paris/London, 1979: 59-91.

Binmūsá, al-Saʿīd. *Taʾrīkh tasfīr al-maṣāḥif al-sharīfah wa-al-kutub al-makhṭūṭah bi-al-Maghrib min ʿahd al-Muwaḥḥidīn ilá ʿahd al-shurafāʾ al-ʿAlawīyīn*. Rabat, Sharikat Bābil, 1996.

——— *Tasfīr wa-tadhhīb al-kutub wa-tarmīm al-makhṭūṭāt*. Rabat, Sharikat Bābil, 1994.

Bosch, Gulnar K. "Islamic book-bindings: twelfth to seventeenth centuries". Ph.D. diss., Univ. of Chicago, 1952.

——— "Medieval Islamic bookbinding, doublures as a dating factor". *Proceedings of the Twenty-sixth International Congress of Orientalists*. Poona,1970: 4, 217-221.

Bosch, Gulnar K. and Petherbridge, Guy. "Islamic art, III, 7. Binding". *The dictionary of art*, ed. J. Turner. New York, 1966: 16, 355-359.

Bosch, Gulnar K., Carswell, J. and Petherbridge, G. *Islamic bindings and bookmaking. A catalogue of an exhibition.* Chicago, 1982. [Contains essays on Islamic bookmaking, its materials, techniques and structures based principally on the works of Ibn Bādīs and Aḥmad al-Sufyānī.]

Chabrov, G.N.K. "K izucheniyu sredneaziatskogo knizhnogo perepleta". *Narody Azii i Afriki*, no.2 (1964): 136-141.

Déroche, François. "Quelques reliures médiévales de provenance damscaine". *Revue des études islamiques*, 54 (1986): 85-99.

——— "Un manuscrit coranique du IIIe/IXe siècle: contribution à l'histoire du livre islamique au Moyen-Age". *Revue des études islamiques*, 60 (1992): 585- 595.

——— "Une reliure du Ve/XIe siècle". *Nouvelles des manuscrits du Moyen-Orient*, IV/1 (1195): 2-8.

Dolinskaya, V.G. "Kashmirskie knizhnyie pereplety iz sobraniya Instituta Vostokovedenia AN UzSSR". *Narody Azii i Afriki*, no.6 (1964): 120-121.

Dreibholtz, Ursula. "Some aspects of early Islamic bookbindings from the Great Mosque of Sanaʿa, Yemen". *Scribes et manuscrits du Moyen-Orient*, ed. F. Déroche and F. Richard. Paris, 1997: 15-63.

Ettinghausen, R. "The covers of the Morgan Manāfiʿ manuscript and other early Persian bookbindings". *Studies in art and literature for Belle da Costa Greene*, ed. D. Miner. Princeton, 1954: 459-473.

——— "Near Eastern book covers and their influence on European bindings: a report on the exhibition 'History of bookbinding' at the Baltimore Museum of Art, 1957-58". *Ars Orientalis*, 3 (1959): 113-131.

Fischer, Barbara. "Sewing and endband in the Islamic technique of binding". *Restaurator*, 7, iv (1986): 181-201.

Gardner, K.B. "Three early Islamic bookbindings". *British Museum quarterly*, 26 (1962): 28-30.

——— "A Persian bookbinding of the sixteenth century". *British Museum quarterly*, 29 (1964-65): 10-11.

Gast, Monika. "A history of endbands based on a study by Karl Jäckel". *The new bookbinder*, 3 (1983): 42-58.

Gratzl, Emil. "Book covers". *A survey of Persian art from prehistoric times to the present,* ed. A.U. Pope and P. Ackerman. Ashiya/ New York, 1977: 5, 1975-1994.

——— *Islamische Bucheinbände des 14. bis 19. Jahrhunderts aus den Handschriften der Bayerischen Staatsbibliothek ausgewählt und beschrieben.* Leipzig, 1924.

Haldane, Duncan. "Aghlifat al-makhṭūṭāt al-ʿArabīyah fī Mathaf Fiktūriyā wa-Albirt". *Funūn ʿArabīyah,* 2, no.5 (1982): 60-65.

——— "Bookbinding". *Encyclopaedia Iranica,* ed. E. Yarshater, 4: 363-365.

——— *Islamic bookindings in the Victoria and Albert Museum.* London, 1983.

Ibrāhīm, ʿAbd al-Laṭīf. "Jildat muṣḥaf bi-Dār al-Kutub al-Miṣrīyah". *Majallat Kullīyat al-Ādāb* (Cairo), 20, no.1 (1958): 91-106.

——— "Al-Tajlīd fī Miṣr al-Islāmīyah: jildat muṣḥaf bi-Dār al-Kutub al-Miṣrīyah". *Dirāsāt fī al-kutub wa-al-maktabāt al-Islāmīyah,* by ʿAbd al-Laṭīf Ibrāhīm. Cairo, Maṭbaʿ Jāmiʿat al-Qāhirah, 1962: al-baḥth al-rābiʿ, 1-32.

Levey, M., Krek, M. and Haddad, H. "Some notes on the chemical technology in an eleventh century work on bookbinding". *Isis,* 47 (1956): 239-243.

al-Mahdī, Sihām Muḥammad. "Khaṣāʾiṣ tajlīd al-makhṭūṭāt fī al-ʿaṣr al-Mamlūkī". *Dirāsāt al-makhṭūṭāt al-Islāmīyah bayna iʿtibārāt al-māddah wa-al-bashar. Aʿmāl al-Muʾtamar al-Thānī li-Muʾassasat al-Furqān lil-Turāth al-Islāmī,* ed. Rashīd al-ʿInānī. London, 1997: 77-91.

Marçais, Georges and Poinssot, Louis. *Objets kairouanais, IXe au XIIIe siècles.* Tunis, 1948: 1, 11-61 [la reliure à Kairouan].

Muḥammad, Maḥmūd. "Al-Tajlīd". *Risālat al-maṭbaʿah,* 3, no.2 (1958): 37-39.

Petersen, Theodore C. "Early Islamic bookbindings and their Coptic relations". *Ars Orientalis,* 1 (1954): 41-64.

Pinder-Wilson, Ralph. "Stone-press moulds and leatherworking in Khurasan". *Science, tools & magic.* Part Two: *Mundane worlds.* London/Oxford, 1997: 338-355 (*The Nasser D. Khalili Collection of Islamic Art, XII*).

Plomp, M. "Traditional bookbindings from Indonesia: materials and decoration". *Bijdragen tot de taal-, land- en volkenkunde,* 149 (1993): 571-592.

Polosin, Val. V. "Muslim bindings with al-Khālidiānī double borders". *Manuscripta Orientalia,* 2, no. 2 (1996): 9-12.

Raby, Julian and Tanindi, Zeren. *Turkish bookbinding in the 15th century. The foundation of an Ottoman court style*. London, 1993.

Rammāḥ, Murād. "Tasāfīr Maktabat al-Qayrawān al-ʿatīqah". *Dirāsāt al-makhṭūṭāt al-Islāmīyah bayna iʿtibārāt al-māddah wa-al-bashar. Aʿmāl al-Muʾtamar al-Thānī li-Muʾassasat al-Furqān lil-Turāth al-Islāmī*, ed. Rashīd al-ʿInānī. London,1997: 135-150.

Regemorter, Berthe van. *Some Oriental bindings in the Chester Beatty Library*. Dublin, 1961.

Ricard, Prosper. "Reliures marocaines du XIIIe siècle: notes sur des spécimens d'époque et de tradition almohades". *Hespéris*, 17 (1933): 109-127.

——— "Sur un type de reliure des temps almohades". *Ars Islamica*, 1 (1934): 74-79.

Richard, Francis. "Trois reliures persanes laquées à décor animalier de la Bibliothèque nationale". *Revue française d'histoire du livre*, 36 (1982): 445-454.

Sakisian, A. "La reliure turque du XVe au XIXe siècle". *La revue de l'art ancien et moderne*, 51 (1927): 277-284; 52 (1927): 141-154, 286-298.

——— "La reliure persane au XVe siècle sous les Timourides". *La revue de l'art ancien et moderne*, 66 (1934): 145-168.

Sarre, F. *Islamic bookbindings*. Transl. by F.D. O'Byrne. London, Kegan Paul, [1923]. [Translation of the German *Islamische Bucheinbände*.]

Shore, A.F. "Fragment of a decorated leather binding from Egypt". *British Museum quarterly*, 36 (1971): 19-23.

Tanindi, Zeren. "15th-century Ottoman manuscripts and bindings in Bursa libraries". *Islamic art*, 4 (1991):143-174.

Vicat, Michèle. "Arts du livre: la reliure. Evolution de la reliure d'art depuis l'époque qājār jusqu'à nos jours". *Entre l'Iran et l'Occident. Adaptation et assimilation des idées et techniques occidentals en Iran*, ed. Yann Richard. Paris, 1989: 171-183.

Weisweiler, Max. *Der islamische Bucheinband des Mittelalters*. Wiesbaden, 1962.

VIII. QUR'ANIC MANUSCRIPTS

VIII. 1. Exhibition catalogues

The Holy Quran in manuscript. A selection of fine and rare Holy Quran leaves and manuscripts exhibited by the National Bank of the Kingdom of Saudi Arabia (= Maʿriḍ al-Muṣḥaf al-Sharīf). Jeddah, 1991/1412.

James, David. *Masterpieces of the Holy Qur'anic manuscripts: selections from the Islamic world (= Badāʾiʿ al-makhṭūṭāt al-Qurʾānīyah. Mukhtārāt min al-ʿālam al-Islāmī)*. Kuwait, National Council for Culture, Arts and Letters, [1987].

——— *Qurʾans and bindings from the Chester Beatty Library: a facsimile exhibition*. London, 1980.

Kuwait National Museum. *Maṣāḥif Ṣanʿāʾ (19th March – 19th May 1985)*. Kuwait, 1985.

Lings, Martin and Safadi, Yasin Hamid. *The Qurʾān: catalogue of an exhibition of Qurʾan manuscripts at the British Library 3 April – 15 August 1976*. London, 1976.

[Rebhan, Helga and Riesterer, Winfried]. *Prachtkorane aus tausend Jahren: Handschriften aus dem Bestand der Bayerischen Staatsbibliothek München*. Munich, 1998.

Splendeur et majesté: Corans de la Bibliothèque nationale. Paris, IMA and BN, 1987.

Stoilova, A. and Ivanova, Z. *The Holy Qurʾān through the ages: a catalogue of the exhibition of manuscripts and printed editions preserved in the SS. Cyril and Methodius National Library*. Sofia, 1995.

Tādrus, Fawzī. *Dalīl maʿriḍ makhṭūṭāt al-Qurʾān al-karīm*. Doha, Jāmiʿat Qaṭar, 1991.

VIII. 2. Early Qurʾans and fragments

Abbott, Nabia. *The rise of the North Arabic script and its Ḳurʾānic development. With a full description of the Ḳurʾān manuscripts in the Oriental Institute*. Chicago, 1939.

Aḥmad, ʿAbd al-Rāziq Aḥmad. "Nashʾat al-khaṭṭ al-ʿArabī wa-taṭawwuruh ʿalá al-maṣāḥif". *Maṣāḥif Ṣanʿāʾ*. Kuwait, 1985: 31-40.

Arberry, A.J. "A Koran in 'Persian' kufic". *Oriental College magazine*, 40/3-4 (1964): 9-16.

Berque, Jacques. "The Koranic text: from revelation to compilation". *The book in the Islamic world: the written word and communication in the Middle East*, ed. George N. Atiyeh. Albany, NY, 1995: 17-32.

Bloom, Jonathan M. "The blue Koran: an early Fatimid Kufic manuscript from the Maghrib". *Les manuscrits du Moyen-Orient*, ed. F. Déroche. Istanbul/Paris, 1989: 95-99.

——— "Al-Maʾmun's blue Koran?". *Revue des études islamiques*, 54 (1986): 59-65.

——— "The early Fatimid blue Koran manuscript". *Graeco-Arabica*, 4 (1991):171-178.

Bothmer, H.-C. von. "Architekturbilder im Koran: eine Prachthandschrift der Umayyadenzeit aus dem Yemen". *Pantheon*, 45 (1987): 4-20.

——— "Frühislamische Koran-Illuminationen: Meisterwerke aus dem Handschriftenfund der Grossen Moschee in Sanaa/Yemen". *Kunst und Antiquitäten*, 1 (1986): 22-33.

——— "Masterworks of Islamic book art: Koranic calligraphy and illumination in the manuscripts found in the Great Mosque in Sanaa". *Yemen: 3000 years of art and civilization in Arabia Felix*, ed. Werner Daum. Innsbruck, 1988: 178-181, 185-187.

——— "Meisterwerke islamischer Buchkunst: koranische Kalligraphie und Illuminationen im Handschriftenfund aus der Grossen Moschee in Sanaa". *Jemen: 3000 Jahre Kunst und Kultur des glücklichen Arabien*, ed. W. Davies. Innsbruck, 1987: 177-187.

——— "Ein seltenes Beispiel für die ornamentale Vorwendung der Schrift in frühen Koranhandschriften: die Fragmentgruppe Inv. Nr.17-15.3 im 'Haus der Handschriften' in Sanaa". *Ars et ecclesia. Festschrift F.J. Ronig*, ed. H.W. Stork, Ch. Gerhard and A. Thomas. Trier, 1989: 45-67.

Burton, J. "Muṣḥaf". *EI*, new ed., 7: 668-669.

Colombo, Valentina. "Une hypothèse sur le retour de l'alif dans l'écriture ḥiǧāzī". *Scribes et manuscrits du Moyen-Orient*, ed. F. Déroche and F. Richard. Paris, 1997: 151-159.

Coomaraswamy, A.K. "Leaf of a Koran". *Bulletin of the Museum of Fine Arts, Boston*, 18 (1920): 52-53.

Croisier, Faïka. "Un manuscrit coranique attribué au calife 'Uṯmān". *L'art de l'écriture arabe: passé et présent*, by Silvia Naef. Geneva, 1992: 68-73.

Déroche, François. "A propos d'une série de manuscrits coraniques anciens". *Les manuscrits du Moyen-Orient*, ed. F. Déroche. Istanbul/Paris, 1989: 101-111.

——— *The Abbasid tradition: Qur'ans of the 8th to 10th centuries AD*. London/ Oxford, 1992. (*The Nasser D.Khalili Collection of Islamic Art, I*).

——— *Catalogue des manuscrits arabes. Les manuscrits du Coran*. Paris, Bibliothèque nationale, 1983-85: vol.1.

——— "Collections de manuscrits anciens du Coran à Istanbul, rapport préliminaire". *Etudes médiévales et patrimoine turc*, ed. J. Sourdel-Thomine. Paris, 1983: 145-165.

——— "Un critère de datation des écritures coraniques anciennes: le kâf final ou isolé". *Damaszener Mitteilungen*, 11 (1999): 87-94, pl. 15-16.

——— "Deux fragments coraniques maghrébins anciens au Musée des arts turc et islamique d'Istanbul". *Revue des études islamiques*, 59 (1991): 229-235.

——— "Les écritures coraniques anciennes, bilan et perspectives". *Revue des études islamiques*, 48 (1980): 207-224.

——— *Les manuscrits du Coran en caractères higâzî: position du problème et éléments préliminaires pour une enquête*. Lesa, Fondazione Ferni Noja Noseda, 1996 (*Quinterni,1*).

——— "Note sur les fragments coraniques anciens de Katta Langar (Ouzbékistan)". *Cahiers d'Asie centrale*, 7 (1999): 65-73, pl. 7 and 8.

——— "The origins of Islamic calligraphy". *Islamic calligraphy: sacred and secular writings*. Geneva, 1988: 20-29.

——— "A Qur'an from Umayyad times". *Manuscripts of the Middle East* (forthcoming).

——— "The Qur'ān of Amājūr". *Manuscripts of the Middle East*, 5 (1990): 59-66.

Déroche, François and Noseda, S. Noja. *Le manuscrit arabe 328 (a) de la Bibliothèque nationale de France*. Lesa, 1998 (*Sources de la transmission manuscrite du texte coranique. I: Les manuscrits de style ḥiǧāzī*).

Dreibholz, Ursula. "Der Fund von Sanaa: frühislamische Handschriften auf Pergament". *Pergament: Geschichte, Struktur, Restaurierung, Herstellung*, herausgegeben von Peter Rück. Sigmaringen, 1991: 299-313.

Dutton, Yasin. "Red dots, green dots, yellow dots and blue: some reflections on the vocalization of early Qur'anic manuscripts – Part 1". *Journal of Qur'anic studies*, 1, issue 1 (1999): 115-140.

Gacek, Adam. "Early Qur'anic fragments". *Fontanus: from the collections of McGill University*, 3 (1990): 45-64.

Grohmann, Adolf. "The problem of dating early Qur'āns". *Der Islam*, 33 (1958): 213-231.

Jenkins, Marilyn. "A vocabulary of Umayyad ornament: new foundations for the study of early Qur'an manuscripts". *Maṣāḥif Ṣan'ā'*. Kuwait, 1985: 19-23.

al-Jubūrī, Kāmil Salmān. *Wathā'iq nādirah min al-khaṭṭ al-'Arabī*. Beirut, Dār wa-Maktabat al-Hilāl, 1998. [Contains reproductions from Qur'āns attributed to the early caliphs and imams.]

Kanū, 'Abd al-Laṭīf Jāsim. "Ma'a al-Qur'ān: dirāsah fī kitābat al-muṣḥaf al-sharīf, hal al-maṣaḥif al-atharīyah allatī 'uthira 'alayhā hiya maṣaḥif al-Khalīfah 'Uthmān? Maṣaḥif bi-al-Baḥrayn ta'ūd ilà al-qarn al-awwal al-hijrī". *Al-Wathīqah*, 4 (1983):102-149.

Karabacek, J. von. *Ein Koranfragment des IX. Jahrhunderts*. Vienna, 1913 (*Zur orientalischen Altertumskunde, 6*).

Lamare, A. "Le muṣḥaf de la mosquée de Cordoue". *Journal asiatique*, 230 (1938): 551-575.

Levi della Vida, G. *Frammenti coranici in carattere cufico nella Biblioteca Vaticana*. Vatican City, 1947.

Loebenstein, Helene. *Koranfragmente auf Pergament aus der Papyrussammlung der Österreichischen Nationalbibliothek*. Wien, 1982. 2 vols.

McAllister, H.E. "Acquisitions of leaves from early Korans". *Bulletin of the Metropolitan Museum of Art*, 36 (1941): 165-168.

——— "Leaves from three early Korans". *Bulletin of the Metropolitan Museum of Art*, 32 (1937): 264-265.

Milo, Thomas. "The Koran fragments from the Lodewijk Houthakker collection". *MELA notes*, no.62 (1995): 15-34.

Mingana, A. and Lewis, A. *Leaves from three ancient Qur'āns possibly pre-'Othmanic, with a list of their variants*. Cambridge, 1914.

Munīf, 'Abd Allāh ibn Muḥammad ibn 'Abd Allāh. *Dirāsah fannīyah li-muṣḥaf mubakkir ya'ūd lil-qarn al-thālith al-hijrī / al-tāsi' al-*

milādī maktūb bi-khaṭṭ al-Jalīl aw al-Jalīl al-Shāmī, maḥfūẓ fī Maktabat al-Malik Fahd al-Waṭanīyah. Riyad, 1998.
al-Naqshabandī, Nāṣir. "Al-Maṣāḥif al-karīma fī ṣadr al-Islām". *Sumer*, 12 (1956): 33-37.
Ory, Solange. "Un nouveau type de muṣḥaf, inventaire de Corans en rouleau de provenance damascaine conservés à Istanbul". *Revue des études islamique*, 33 (1965): 87-149.
Puin, Gerd-R. "Methods of research on Qur'anic manuscripts, a few ideas". *Maṣāḥif Ṣan'ā'*. Kuwait, 1985: 9-17.
——— "Observations on early Qur'an manuscripts in San'ā'". *The Qur'an as text*, ed. Stefan Wild. Leiden, 1996: 107-111.
Rezvan, Efim A. "The first Qur'ans". *Pages of perfection. Islamic paintings and calligraphy from the Russian Academy of Sciences, St. Petersburg*. Lugano/Milan, 1995: 108-117.
——— "Yet another "Uthmānic Qur'ān' (On the history of Manuscript E20 from the St. Petersburg Branch of the Institute of Oriental Studies)". *Manuscripta Orientalia*, 6, no.1 (2000): 49-68.
Rezvan, Efim A. and Kondybaev, N.S. "The ENTRAP software: tests results". *Manuscripta Orientalia*, 5, no.2 (1999): 58-64. [Computer analysis of an early fragment of the Qur'an.]
Saint Laurent, Beatrice. "The identification of a magnificent Koran manuscript". *Les manuscrits du Moyen-Orient*, ed. F. Déroche. Istanbul/Paris, 1989: 115-124.
Shānehchī Kāẓim Mudīr. "Some old manuscripts of the Holy Qur'ān". Transl. by Mujāhid Ḥusayn. *Al-Tawḥīd*, 8, no.4 (May-July 1991): 15-34.
Tabbaa, Yasser. "The transformation of Arabic writing: Part 1, Qur'anic calligraphy". *Ars Orientalis*, 21 (1991): 119-148.
——— "The transformation of Arabic writing. Part 2: the public text". *Ars Orientalis*, 24 (1994): 119-147.
Whelan, Estelle. "Forgotten witness: evidence for the early codification of the Qur'ān". *Journal of the American Oriental Society*, 118, no.1 (1998): 1-14.
——— "Writing the word of God: some early Qur'an manuscripts and their milieu, pt.1". *Ars Orientalis*, 20 (1990): 113-147.

VIII. 3. Later Qur'ans

Abbott, Nabia. "Arabic-Persian Koran of the late 15th or early 16th century". *Ars Islamica*, 6 (1939): 91-94.

——— "An Arabic-Persian wooden Kur'anic manuscript from the Royal Library of Shah Husain Safawi I, 1105-35 H.". *Ars Islamica*, 5 (1938): 89-94.

——— "Maghribi Koran manuscripts of the seventeenth and the eighteenth centuries (in possession of Dr. and Mrs. Paul Hudson, Ohio State University)". *American Journal of Semitic languages and literatures*, 55 (1938): 61-65.

Arberry, A. J. *The Koran illuminated: a handlist of the Korans in the Chester Beatty Library*. Dublin, 1967.

ʿAṭīyah, Jūrj. "Al-Makhṭūṭāt al-ʿArabīyah wa-al-Islāmīyah fī Maktabat al-Kūnghris al-Amrīkīyah: Muṣḥaf al-Shaykh Ḥamd Allāh al-Amāsī". *Al-Makhṭūṭ al-ʿArabī wa-ʿilm al-makhṭūṭāt (= Le manuscrit arabe et la codicologie)*. Rabat, 1994: 45-56.

Bayani, Manijeh, Contadini, Anna and Stanley, Tim. *The decorated word: Qur'ans of the 17th to 19th centuries*. London/Oxford, 1999. (*The Nasser D. Khalili Collection of Islamic Art, IV, pt.1*).

Bivar, A.D.H. "A dated Kuran from Bornu". *Nigeria magazine*, (1960): 199-205.

Brockett, A.A. "Aspects of the physical transmission of the Qur'ān in the 19th-century Sudan: script, decoration, binding and paper". *Manuscripts of the Middle East*, 2 (1987): 45-67.

——— "St. Andrews University Oriental manuscript no.16: fragment of a Qur'ān on paper in Maghribi script, probably Spanish...". *Codices Manuscripti*, 10 (1984): 41-51.

Dandel, E. "A propos d'un Coran almohade copié en soixante volumes". *Numismatique, langues, écritures et arts du livre, spécificité des arts figurés: actes du VIIe Colloque international sur l'histoire et archéologie de l'Afrique du nord, réunis dans le cadre du 121e Congrès des sociétés historiques et scientifiques, Nice, 21 au 31 octobre 1996*, ed. Serge Lancel. Paris, 1999: 249-265.

Derman, Uğur. "Une sourate coranique calligraphiée au XVIe s. en caractères coufiques lacqués". *Les manuscrits du Moyen-Orient*, ed. F. Déroche. Istanbul/ Paris, 1989: 113.

Déroche, François. *Catalogue des manuscrits arabes. Les manuscrits du Coran*. Paris, Bibliothèque nationale, 1983-85: vol.2.

——— "Coran, couleur et calligraphie". *I primi sessanta anni di scuola: studi dedicati dagli amici a S. Noja Nosseda nello 65° compleanno, 7 luglio 1996*. Lesa (forthcoming).

——— "La fonction et l'histoire des Corans : quelques observations". *Revue de l'histoire des religions* (forthcoming).

——— "Les manuscrits du Coran". *Arts et métiers du livre*, no.217 (1999-2000): 52-54.

Déroche, François and Gladiss, Almut von. *Buchkunst zur Ehre Allāhs: der Prachtkoran im Museum für Islamische Kunst*. Berlin, 1999.

Digby, S. "A Qur'an from the East African coast". *Art and archeology research papers*, 7 (1975): 49-55.

Ettinghausen, R. "A signed and dated Seljuq Qur'an". *Bulletin of the American Institute of Persian Art and Archeology*, 4 (1935): 92-102. [Reprinted in his *Islamic art and archeology: collected papers*, ed. M. Rosen-Ayalon. Berlin, 1984: 510-20.]

Gacek, Adam. "A collection of Qur'anic codices". *Fontanus: from the collections of McGill University*, 4 (1991): 35-53.

Gottheil, Richard. "An illustrated copy of the Koran". *Revue des études islamiques*, 5 (1931): 21-24, 4 pl.

Gray, Basil. "The monumental Qur'ans of the Il-khanid and Mamluk ateliers of the first quarter of the fourteenth century (eighth century H.)". *Rivista degli studi orientali*, 59, fasc.1-4 (1985): 135-146.

Ḥabash al-Bayātī, Ḥasan Qāsim. *Riḥlat al-Muṣḥaf al-Sharīf min al-jarīd ilá al-tajlīd*. Beirut, Dār al-Qalam, 1993.

İhsanoğlu, Ekmeleddin. "A study on the manuscript translations of the Holy Qur'ān". *The significance of Islamic manuscripts. Proceedings of the Inaugural Conference of al-Furqān Islamic Heritage Foundation (30th November – 1st December 1991)*, ed. John Cooper. London, 1992: 79-105.

Iqbal, M. "Some specimens of the calligraphy of the Qur'an from the Library of Meshed". *Woolner commemorative volume*. Lahore, 1940: 109-112.

James, David. *After Timur: Qur'ans of the 15th and 16th centuries A.D.* London/ Oxford, 1992. (*The Nasser D. Khalili Collection of Islamic Art, III*).

——— *The master scribes: Qur'ans of the 11th to 14th centuries A.D.* London/ Oxford, 1992. (*The Nasser D. Khalili Collection of Islamic Art, II*).

——— *Qur'ans of the Mamluks*. London, 1988.

——— "Some observations on the calligrapher and illuminators of the Koran of Rukn al-Dīn Baybars al-Jāshnagīr". *Muqarnas*, 2 (1984): 147-157.

Janér, Florencio. "El-Koran: códice árabe llamado de Muley Cidan, rey de Marruecos, conservado en la Biblioteca del Escorial". *Museo Español de Antiguedades*, 3 (1874): 409-431.

Lévi-Provençal, E. "Note sur un Qor'ān royal du XIVe siècle". *Hespéris*, 1 (1921): 83-86.

Lings, Martin. "Andalusian Qorans". *British Museum quarterly*, 24 (1961): 94-96, pl. 29-32.

——— *The Qur'anic art of calligraphy and illumination*. London, 1976.

al-Manūnī, Muḥammad. "Markaz al-Muṣḥaf al-sharīf bi-al-Maghrib". *Da'wat al-ḥaqq*, 11, no.3 (1968): 71-77.

——— "Ta'rīkh al-Muṣḥaf al-sharīf bi-al-Maghrib". *Majallat Ma'had al-Makhṭūṭāt al-'Arabīyah*, 15, no.1 (1969): 3-47.

Marzūq, Muḥammad 'Abd al-'Azīz. "Al-Muṣḥaf al-sharīf: dirāsah fannīyah". *Majallat al-Majma' al-Ilmī al-'Irāqī*, 20 (1970): 88-137.

——— *Al-Muṣḥaf al-sharīf: dirāsah ta'rīkhīyah wa-fannīyah*. Cairo, al-Hay'ah al-'Āmmah lil-Kitāb, 1975.

Mingana, A. "Notes upon some of the Kuranic manuscripts in the John Rylands Library". *Bulletin of the John Rylands University Library of Manchester*, 2 (1914-15): 240-250.

Monneret de Villard, Ugo. "Codici magrebini decorati della Biblioteca Vaticana". *Annali. Istituto Universitario Orientale di Napoli*, n.s., 3 (1949): 83-91.

Muḥriz, Jamāl Muḥammad. "Muṣḥaf mudhahhab min al-'aṣr al-Gharnāṭī". *Revista del Instituto Egipcio de Estudios Islámicos en Madrid*, 3 (1955): 141-147.

Ory, Solange. "Du Coran récité au Coran calligraphié". *Arabica*, 47, fasc. 3-4 (2000): 366-380.

Rice, D.S. *The unique Ibn al-Bawwāb manuscript in the Chester Beatty Library, Dublin*. Dublin, 1955.

Rosen-Ayalon, Myriam. "Some comments on a Maghribī Qur'ān". *Jerusalem studies in Arabic and Islam*, 19 (1995): 73-80.

Shāfi'ī, Farīd. "Zakhārif muṣḥaf bi-Dār al-Kutub al-Miṣrīyah". *Majallat Kullīyat al-Ādāb* (Cairo), 17, no.1 (1955): 43-48.

Sharīfī, Muḥammad ibn Sa'īd. *Khuṭūṭ al-maṣāḥif 'inda al-mashāriqah wa-al-maghāribah min al-qarn al-rābi' ilá al-'āshir al-hijrī*. Algiers, al-Sharikah al-Waṭanīyah, 1982.

Sims, Eleanor. "An illuminated manuscript copied by Shaykh Hamdullah in the Library of Congress in Washington, DC". *9th*

International Congress of Turkish Art, Istanbul, 1991. Ankara, 1995: 3, 203-212.
[Stanley, Tim]. *The Qur'an and calligraphy. A selection of fine manuscript material*. London, [1995]. [Bernard Quaritch, catalogue 1213.]
Witkam, Jan Just. "Manuscripts & manuscripts: [6] Qur'ān fragments from Ḍawrān (Yemen)". *Manuscripts of the Middle East*, 4 (1989): 155-174.
Wright, E. "An Indian Qur'an and its 14th century model". *Oriental art*, (Winter 1996/97): 8-12.
Zahradeen, Muhammad Sani. "Islamic calligraphy in West Africa, the Qur'ans of Northern Nigeria". *Dirasat Islamiyyah* (Kano), (1979/80 – 1980/81): 1-18.

VIII. 4. Facsimile editions

Corán de Muley Zaydán: historia de un manuscrito árabe de la Real Biblioteca de El Escorial, estudio critico de José Manuel Ruiz Asencio. Madrid, 1996.
Déroche, François and Noseda, S. Noja. *Le manuscrit arabe 328 (a) de la Bibliothèque nationale de France*. Lesa, 1998. (*Sources de la transmission manuscrite du texte coranique. I: Les manuscrits de style ḥiǧāzī*).
The Holy Qur'an manuscripted in 927/16th century by Muhammed bin Na'im al-Tab'i 'Ruzbihan'. Dublin, Chester Beatty Library, 1991.
The Holy Qur'an manuscripted in 953/1546 by Ahmed Karahisari for Sultan Süleyman the Magnificent. Rome, Fideurart Edizioni d'arte, [198?].
[*Kur'an-i Karim*]. Ankara, Kültür Bakanlığı, 1991. [Attributed to Ḥamd Allāh al-Amāsī.]
[*Muṣḥaf sharīf*]. Tunis, 1983. [Calligraphed by al-Shaykh al-Ḥājj Zuhayr Bāsh Mamlūk, d.1305/1885.]
The unique Ibn al-Bawwab manuscript: complete facsimile edition of the earliest surviving naskhi Qur'an, Chester Beatty Library, Dublin, Manuscript K.16. Graz: Akademische Druck-u. Verlags-anstalt, 1983. 2 vols. [Text of commentary by D.S. Rice, in English and Arabic.]

IX. TEXTUAL CRITICISM AND EDITING

IX. 1. General studies

ʿAbd al-Tawwāb, Ramaḍān. *Manāhij taḥqīq al-turāth bayna al-qudamāʾ wa-al-muḥdathīn.* Cairo, Maktabat Khānjī, 1985.

——— "Min tajribatī fī taḥqīq nisbat al-kitāb wa-tawthīq ʿunwānih". *Majallat Maʿhad al-Makhṭūṭāt al-ʿArabīyah*, 34 (1990): 7-24.

Akimushkin, O.F. "Textological studies and the 'critical text' problem". *Manuscripta Orientalia*, 1, no.2 (1995): 22-28.

ʿAlī, ʿAbd al-Wahhāb Muḥammad. "Amālī Muṣṭafá Jawād fī fann taḥqīq al-nuṣūṣ". *Al-Mawrid*, 6, no.1 (1977): 117-138.

al-Anṣārī, Muḥammad Riḍá. *Fawāʾid wa-hafawāt taḥqīqīyah.* Qum, Maktabat Āyat Allāh al-ʿUẓmá al-Marʿashī al-Najafī al-ʿĀmmah, 1214 A.H.

al-ʿAwnī, Ḥātim ibn ʿĀrif. *Al-ʿUnwān al-ṣaḥīḥ lil-kitāb.* Mecca, Dār ʿĀlam al-Fawāʾid, 1414 A.H.

al-ʿAzzām, Muḥammad ibn ʿAbd Allāh. "Namaṭ min al-taḥqīq". *ʿĀlam al-kutub*, 26, no.1 (1995): 3-18.

Ben Murad, Ibrahim. "Le terme scientifique dans le patrimoine arabe manuscrit: problématiques du passé et perspectives de l'avenir". *Editing Islamic manuscripts on science. Proceedings of the Fourth Conference of al-Furqān Islamic Heritage Foundation, 29th-30th November 1997*, ed. Yusuf Ibish. London, 1420/ 1999: 193-222.

Binbīn, Aḥmad Shawqī. "ʿIlm al-makhṭūṭāt wa-al-taḥqīq al-ʿilmī". *Majallat Majmaʿ al-Lughah al-ʿArabīyah bi-Dimashq*, 68, no.2 (1993): 236-250. [See also the same article in *al-Makhṭūṭ al-ʿArabī wa-ʿilm al-makhṭūṭāt (= Le manuscrit arabe et la codicologie).* Rabat, 1994: 33-43.]

Blachère, Régis and Sauvaget, J. *Règles pour éditions et traductions de textes arabes.* Paris, 1953. [Translated into Arabic by Maḥmūd al-Muqdād under the title: *Qawāʿid taḥqīq al-makhṭūṭāt al-ʿArabīyah wa-tarjamatuhā: wajhat naẓar al-istiʿrāb al-Faransī.* Damascus, Dār al-Fikr, 1988.]

Carter, M.G. "Arabic literature". *Scholarly editing: a guide to research*, ed. D.C. Greetham. New York, 1995: 546-574.

Dallal, Ahmad. "Between reproduction and recovery: notes on editing classical Arabic manuscripts on astronomy". *Editing Islamic manuscripts on science. Proceedings of the Fourth Conference of al-Furqān Islamic Heritage Foundation, 29th-30th November 1997*, ed. Yusuf Ibish. London, 1420/1999: 59-73.

al-Dannā', Muḥammad Khalīfah. *Qirā'at al-nuṣūṣ al-turāthīyah, ishkālīyāt wa-ḍawābiṭ*.. Tripoli (Libya), Manshūrāt Kullīyat al-Da'wah al-Islāmīyah wa-Lajnat al-Ḥifāẓ 'alá al-Turāth al-Islāmī, 1994.

Dayyāb, 'Abd al-Majīd. *Taḥqīq al-turāth al-'Arabī*. Cairo, 1983.

al-Ḥafyān, Fayṣal (ed.). *Al-Turāth al-'ilmī al-'Arabī: manāhij taḥqīqih wa-ishkālat nashrih*. Cairo, Ma'had al-Makhṭūṭāt al-'Arabīyah, 2000.

al-Ḥalwajī, 'Abd al-Sattār. "Turāthunā al-makhṭūṭ: dirāsah fī ta'rīkh al-nash'ah wa-al-taṭawwur". *Al-Dārah*, 4 (1975): 169-173.

Ḥallāq, Ḥassān. *Muqaddimah fī manāhij al-baḥth al-ta'rīkhī wa-al-'ulūm al-musā'idah wa-taḥqīq al-makhṭūṭāt bayna al-naẓarīyah wa-al-taṭbīq*. Beirut, Dār al-Nahḍah al-'Arabīyah, 1986.

al-Jubūrī, Yaḥyá Wahīd. *Manhaj al-baḥth wa-taḥqīq al-nuṣūṣ (= Research methods and transcript analysis)*. Beirut, Dār al-Gharb al-Islāmī, 1993.

Karbāj, Jūrj Mīkhā'il. "Al-Turāth al-'Arabī: al-makhṭūṭ bayna māḍīh wa-ḥāḍirih". *Al-Turāth al-'Arabī*, 5 (1985): 124-131.

al-Kharrāṭ, Aḥmad Muḥammad. *Muḥāḍarāt fī taḥqīq al-nuṣūṣ*. Jedda, Dār al-Manārah, 1988.

Maas, Paul. "Naqd al-naṣṣ". *Al-Naqd al-ta'rīkhī*. Transl. by 'Abd al-Raḥmān Badawī. Cairo, Dār al-Nahḍah, 1963: 253-278. [Translation of his *Textkritik*, Leipzig, 1950.]

Madelung, Wilferd F. "Manuscripts in historical research and text edition". *The significance of Islamic manuscripts. Proceedings of the Inaugural Conference of al-Furqān Islamic Heritage Foundation (30th November – 1st December 1991)*, ed. John Cooper. London, 1992: 1-6.

——— "Al-Makhṭūṭāt fī al-abḥāth al-ta'rīkhīyah". *Ahammīyat al-makhṭūṭāt al-Islāmīyah. A'māl al-Mu'tamar al-Iftitāḥī li-Mu'assasat al-Furqān lil-Turāth al-Islāmī*. London, 1992: 43-49.

al-Manūnī, Muḥammad. "Qawā'id taḥqīq al-nuṣūṣ wa-ikhrājihā: naṣṣ mawḍū'ī". *Al-Maṣādir al-'Arabīyah li-ta'rīkh al-Maghrib: al-fatrah al-mu'āṣirah 1790-1930*, by Muḥammad al-Manūnī. Rabat, 1989: 2, 335-348.

al-Mawālidī, Muṣṭafá. "Ṭarīqah jadīdah fī ta'ṣīl al-nusakh al-khaṭṭīyah (asās qawā'id namūdhajan)". *Majallat Ma'had al-Makhṭūṭāt al-'Arabīyah*, 36 (1992): 169-201.

Molina, Luis. "Consideraciones sobre la édicion de manuscritos árabes". *Al-Qanṭara, revista de estudios árabes*, 19, fasc.2 (1998): 393-416.

Muʾassasat Āl al-Bayt li-Iḥyāʾ al-Turāth. *Manhaj taḥqīq al-makhṭūṭāt*. Qum, 1408 A.H.

Mahdi, Muhsin. "From the manuscript age to the age of printed books". *The book in the Islamic world: the written word and communication in the Middle East*, ed. George N. Atiyeh. Albany, N.Y., 1995: 1-15.

al-Munajjid, Ṣalāḥ al-Dīn. "Régles pour l'édition des textes arabes". *Mélanges. Institut dominicain d'études orientales du Caire (MIDEO)*, 3 (1956): 359-374.

Nājī, Hilāl. "Min qawāʿid al-taḥqīq al-ʿilmī: tawthīq ʿunwān al-makhṭūṭ wa-muʾallifih". *Al-Mawrid*, 21, no.1 (1993): 41-49.

——— "Muwaḍḍiḥat al-ṭarīq ilá ṣuwá manāhij al-taḥqīq". *Al-Mawrid*, 15, no.3 (1986): 169-182.

Rashed, Roshdi. "Conceptual tradition and textual tradition: Arabic manuscripts on science". *Editing Islamic manuscripts on science. Proceedings of the Fourth Conference of al-Furqān Islamic Heritage Foundation, 29th-30th November 1997*, ed. Yusuf Ibish. London, 1420/1999: 15-57.

al-Rifāʿī, Usāmah Ṭāhā. "Kayfa tuḥaqqiq naṣṣan makhṭūṭan?". *Ḥawlīyāt Kullīyat al-Ādāb wa-al-ʿUlūm al-Insānīyah* (al-Dār al-Bayḍāʾ), 5 (1988): 21-48.

Saʿd, Fahmī et al. *Taḥqīq al-makhṭūṭāt bayna al-naẓarīyah wa-al-taṭbīq*. Beirut, ʿĀlam al-Kutub, 1993.

Saʿīdān, Aḥmad Salīm. "Maʿa taḥqīq kutub al-turāth". *Majallat Majmaʿ al-Lughah al-ʿArabīyah al-Urdunī*, 13-14 (1981): 193-205.

——— "Al-Turāth al-ʿArabī li-madhā nuḥaqqiquh wa-kayfa?". *Majallat Majmaʿ al-Lughah al-ʿArabīyah al-Urdunī*, 23-24 (1984): 7-19.

al-Samarrāʾī, Ibrāhīm. "Maʿa taḥqīq kutub al-turāth". *Majallat Majmaʿ al-Lughah al-ʿArabīyah al-Urdunī*, 11-12 (1981): 92-115.

Samsó, Julio. "Andalusī and Maghribī astronomical sources: what has been done and what remains to be done". *Editing Islamic manuscripts on science. Proceedings of the Fourth Conference of al-Furqān Islamic Heritage Foundation, 29th-30th November 1997*, ed. Yusuf Ibish. London, 1420/1999: 75-104.

Sarḥān, Muḥyī Hilāl. *Taḥqīq makhṭūṭāt al-ʿulūm al-sharʿīyah.* Baghdad, Maṭbaʿat al-Irshād, 1984.

Shabbūḥ, Ibrāhīm (ed.). *Taḥqīq makhṭūṭāt al-ʿulūm fī al-turāth al-Islāmī: abḥāth al-Muʾtamar al-Rābiʿ li-Muʾassasat al-Furqān lil-Turāth al-Islāmī, 29-30 Nov. 1997.* London, 1999.

Shāfiʿī, Ḥasan. "Baʿḍ ṣuʿūbāt taḥqīq al-makhṭūṭāt al-ʿArabīyah". *Ḥawlīyāt Kullīyat Dār al-ʿUlūm* (Cairo), 10 (1980): 231-258.

Shākir, Aḥmad. *Taṣḥīḥ al-kutub wa-ṣunʿ al-fahāris al-muʿjamah wa-kayfīyat ḍabṭ al-kitāb wa-sabq al-Muslimīn wa-al-Ifranj fī dhālik.* Beirut, Dār al-Jīl, 1995.

al-Ṭanāḥī, Maḥmūd Muḥammad. *Madkhal ilá taʾrīkh nashr al-turāth al-ʿArabī maʿa muḥāḍarah ʿan taṣḥīḥ wa-taḥrīf.* Cairo, Maktabat Khānjī, 1984.

al-Tūnjī, Muḥammad. "Al-Makhṭūṭāt al-ʿArabīyah bayna yaday al-taḥqīq". *Al-Turāth al-ʿArabī*, 3 (1982): 197-208.

al-ʿUmarī, Akram Ḍiyāʾ. *Dirāsāt taʾrīkhīyah: maʿa taʿlīqah fī manhaj al-baḥth wa-taḥqīq al-makhṭūṭāt.* Medina, al-Jāmiʿah al-Islāmīyah, 1983.

——— *Manāhij al-baḥth wa-taḥqīq al-turāth.* Medina, Maktabat al-ʿUlūm wa-al-Ḥikam, 1995.

ʿUsaylān, ʿAbd Allāh ibn ʿAbd al-Raḥīm. *Taḥqīq al-makhṭūṭāt bayna al-wāqiʿ wa-al-nahj al-amthal.* Riyad, Maktabat al-Malik Fahd al-Waṭanīyah, 1415/1994.

Witkam, Jan Just. "Establishing the stemma, fact or fiction?". *Manuscripts of the Middle East*, 3 (1988): 88-101.

Yūsuf, Irshīd. *Al-Kitāb al-Islāmī al-makhṭūṭ: tadwīnan wa-taḥqīqan.* Amman, Maṭābiʿ al-Muʾassasah al-Ṣuḥufīyah al-Urdūnīyah, 1993 (?).

IX. 2. Some specific cases

Bellosta, Hélène. "The specific case of geometrical manuscripts using the example of manuscript B.N. 2457 (Paris)". *Editing Islamic manuscripts on science. Proceedings of the Fourth Conference of al-Furqān Islamic Heritage Foundation, 29th-30th November 1997*, ed. Yusuf Ibish. London, 1420/1999: 181-191.

Crozet, Pascal. "A propos des figures dans les manuscrits arabes de géométrie: l'example de Siǧzī". *Editing Islamic manuscripts on science. Proceedings of the Fourth Conference of al-Furqān*

Islamic Heritage Foundation, 29th-30th November 1997, ed. Yusuf Ibish. London, 1420/1999: 131-163.

Gutas, Dimitri. "Editing Arabic philosophical texts". *Orientalistische Literaturzeitung*, 75 (1980): 214-222.

Hartmann, Angelika. "Sur l'édition d'un texte arabe médiéval: le 'Rašf an-naṣā'iḥ al-īmānīya wa-kašf al-faḍā'iḥ al-yūnānīya' de ʿUmar as-Suhrawardī, composé à Baġdād en 621/1224". *Der Islam*, 62 (1985): 71-97.

Humbert, Geneviève. "Remarques sur les éditions du 'Kitāb' de Sībawayhi et leur base manuscrite". *Studies in the history of Arabic grammar II*, ed. K. Versteegh and M. G. Carter. Amsterdam/Philadelphia, 1990: 179-194.

Mahdi, Muhsin. "Al-Farabi's 'Imperfect state'". *Journal of the American Oriental Society*, 110, no.4 (1990): 691-726.

Masoumi Hamedani, Hossein. "Remarks on the manuscript tradition of some optical works of Ibn al-Haytham". *Editing Islamic manuscripts on science. Proceedings of the Fourth Conference of al-Furqān Islamic Heritage Foundation, 29th-30th November 1997*, ed. Yusuf Ibish. London, 1420/1999: 165-180.

Morelon, Régis. "Le corpus des manuscrits arabes des oeuvres d'astronomie de Thābit b. Qurra". *Editing Islamic manuscripts on science. Proceedings of the Fourth Conference of al-Furqān Islamic Heritage Foundation, 29th-30th November 1997*, ed. Yusuf Ibish. London, 1420/1999: 115-130.

Pingree, David. "A preliminary assessment of the problems of editing the Zīj al-Sanjarī of al-Khāzinī". *Editing Islamic manuscripts on science. Proceedings of the Fourth Conference of al-Furqān Islamic Heritage Foundation, 29th-30th November 1997*, ed. Yusuf Ibish. London, 1420/1999: 105-113.

Raven, Wim. "The manuscripts and editions of Ibn Dāwūd's 'Kitāb al-zahra'". *Manuscripts of the Middle East*, 4 (1989): 133-137.

Rezvan, Efim A. "The Qur'ān: between textus receptus and critical edition". *Les problèmes posés par l'édition critique des textes anciens et médiévaux*, ed. J. Hamesse. Louvain-La-Neuve, 1992: 291-310.

Scattolin, Giuseppe. "The oldest text of Ibn Fāriḍ's Dīwān? A manuscript of Yusufağa Kütüphanesi of Konya". *Quaderni di studi arabi*, 16 (1998): 143-163.

al-Wafā'ī, Muḥammad Ẓāfir. "The editing and publication of the

Islamic medicine series: ʿIlm al-kīḥālah". *Editing Islamic manuscripts on science. Proceedings of the Fourth Conference of al-Furqān Islamic Heritage Foundation, 29th-30th November 1997*, ed. Yusuf Ibish. London, 1420/1999: 223-241.

X. CATALOGUING

ʿAbd al-Hādī, Fatḥī. "Taṣnīf al-makhṭūṭāt al-ʿArabīyah". *Fann fahrasat al-makhṭūṭāt: madkhal wa-qaḍāyā*, ed. Fayṣal al-Ḥafyān. Cairo, Maʿhad al-Makhṭūṭāt al-ʿArabīyah, 1999: 155-173.

Abū Haybah, ʿIzzat Yāsīn. *Al-Makhṭūṭāt al-ʿArabīyah: fahārisuhā wa-fahrasatuhā fī Jumhurīyat Miṣr al-ʿArabīyah*. Cairo, al-Hayʾah al-Miṣrīyah al-ʿĀmmah lil-Kitāb, 1989.

Binbīn, Aḥmad Shawqī. "ʿAlāqat al-fahrasah bi-ʿilm al-makhṭūṭāt". *Fann fahrasat al-makhṭūṭāt: madkhal wa-qaḍāyā*, ed. Fayṣal al-Ḥafyān. Cairo, Maʿhad al-Makhṭūṭāt al-ʿArabīyah, 1999: 33-44.

——— "Fahrasat al-makhṭūṭāt al-ʿArabīyah fī al-Maghrib". *Al-Lisān al-ʿArabī*, 45 (1998): 165-192.

——— "Taqnīyāt fahrasat al-makhtūṭāṭ al-ʿArabīyah". *Al-Makhṭūṭāt al-ʿArabīyah fī al-Gharb al-Islāmī: waḍʿīyat al-majmūʿāt wa-āfāq al-baḥth (= Manuscrits arabes en occident musulman)*. Casablanca, Muʾassasat al-Malik ʿAbd al-ʿAzīz, 1990: 227-237.

Gacek, Adam. "Some remarks on the cataloguing of Arabic manuscripts". *British Society for Middle Eastern Studies bulletin*, 10 (1983): 173-179.

Guesdon, M.-G. "The Bibliothèque nationale de France and the UNESCO's MEDLIB project: a seminar on Arabic manuscripts computerised cataloguing". *Manuscripta Orientalia*, 5, no.3 (1999): 59-61.

al-Ḥafyān, Fayṣal (ed.). *Al-Tajārib al-ʿArabīyah fī fahrasat al-makhṭūṭāt*. Cairo, Maʿhad al-Makhṭūṭāt al-ʿArabīyah, 1998.

al-Ḥalwajī, ʿAbd al-Sattār. "Fann al-fahrasah: al-muṣṭalaḥ wa-al-ḥudūd". *Fann fahrasat al-makhṭūṭāt: madkhal wa-qaḍāyā*, ed. Fayṣal al-Ḥafyān. Cairo, Maʿhad al-Makhṭūṭāt al-ʿArabīyah, 1999: 19-31.

——— "Fahāris al-makhṭūṭāt". *Al-Ḥalqah al-dirāsīyah lil-khadamāt al-maktabīyah wa-al-wirāqah (...)*. Damascus, Maṭbaʿat Jāmiʿat Dimashq, 1392/1972: 284-300.

Jamāl, ʿĀdil Sulaymān. "Juhūd al-mustashriqīn wa-manāhijuhum fī fahrasat al-makhṭūṭāt". *Fann fahrasat al-makhṭūṭāt: madkhal wa-qaḍāyā*, ed. Fayṣal al-Ḥafyān. Cairo, Maʿhad al-Makhṭūṭāt al-ʿArabīyah, 1999: 235-302.

al-Mashūkhī, ʿĀbid Sulaymān. *Fahrasat al-makhṭūṭāt al-ʿArabīyah*. al-Zarqāʾ (Jordan), Maktabat al-Manār, 1989.

al-Samarrāʾī, Qāsim. "Mushkilāt fahrasat al-makhṭūṭāt al-ʿArabīyah". *Al-Makhṭūṭāt al-ʿArabīyah fī al-Gharb al-Islāmī: waḍʿīyat al-majmūʿāt wa-āfāq al-baḥth (= Manuscrits arabes en occident musulman)*. Casablanca, Muʾassasat al-Malik ʿAbd al-ʿAzīz, 1990: 215-226.

Sayyid, Ayman Fuʾād. "Al-Waṣf al-māddī lil-makhṭūṭāt". *Fann fahrasat al-makhṭūṭāt: madkhal wa-qaḍāyā*, ed. Fayṣal al-Ḥafyān. Cairo, Maʿhad al-Makhṭūṭāt al-ʿArabīyah, 1999: 55-64.

Sellheim, Rudolf. "The cataloguing of Arabic manuscripts as a literary problem". *Oriens*, 23-24 (1974): 306-311.

al-Shanṭī, ʿIṣām Muḥammad. "Awwal al-makhṭūṭah wa-ākhiruhā". *Fann fahrasat al-makhṭūṭāt: madkhal wa-qaḍāyā*, ed. Fayṣal al-Ḥafyān. Cairo, Maʿhad al-Makhṭūṭāt al-ʿArabīyah, 1999: 137-154.

——— "Al-Makhṭūṭāt al-ʿArabīyah, amākinuhā, al-istighlāl bihā, fahrasatuhā wa-taṣnīfuhā wa-mushkilātuhā". *Al-Makhṭūṭāt al-ʿArabīyah fī al-Gharb al-Islāmī: waḍʿīyat al-majmūʿāt wa-āfāq al-baḥth (= Manuscrits arabes en occident musulman)*. Casablanca, Muʾassasat al-Malik ʿAbd al-ʿAzīz, 1990: 201-213.

al-Ṭanāḥī, Maḥmūd Muḥammad. "Thaqāfat al-mufahris". *Fann fahrasat al-makhṭūṭāt: madkhal wa-qaḍāyā*, ed. Fayṣal al-Ḥafyān. Cairo, Maʿhad al-Makhṭūṭāt al-ʿArabīyah, 1999: 189-234.

Ṭashkandī, ʿAbbās. "Fahāris al-makhṭūṭāt, dirāsah taḥlīlīyah". *Al-Dārah*, 4, no.2 (1400/1979): 219-242.

Torres Santo Domingo, Nuria. "Reflexiones sobre catálogos y catalogación de manuscritos árabes". *Al-Qanṭara, revista de estudios árabes*, 19, fasc.2 (1998): 343-364.

Voorhoeve, P. "Het Beschrijven van oosterse Handschriften". *Bibliotheekleven*, 41 (1965):321-334.

Witkam, Jan Just. "Aims and methods of cataloguing manuscripts of the Middle East". *Les manuscrits du Moyen-Orient*, ed. F. Déroche. Istanbul/Paris, 1989: 1-5.

Zaydān, Yūsuf. "Mushkilāt tawthīq al-ʿunwān wa-al-muʾallif". *Fann fahrasat al-makhṭūṭāt: madkhal wa-qaḍāyā*, ed. Fayṣal al-Ḥafyān. Cairo, Maʿhad al-Makhṭūṭāt al-ʿArabīyah, 1999: 117-135.

XI. PRESERVATION AND CONSERVATION

ʿAtīqī, Mahdī. "Problems relating to the treatment of Islamic manuscripts: paper". *The conservation and preservation of Islamic manuscripts. Proceedings of the Third Conference of al-Furqān Islamic Heritage Foundation 18th-19th November 1995*, ed. Yusuf Ibish and George Atiyeh. London, 1996: 151-156.

Bedar, Abid Reza. "The preservation of Islamic manuscripts in India". *The conservation and preservation of Islamic manuscripts. Proceedings of the Third Conference of al-Furqān Islamic Heritage Foundation 18th –19th November 1995*, ed. Yusuf Ibish and George Atiyeh. London, 1996: 15-19.

Bencherifa, Mohamed. "The restoration of manuscripts in Morocco". *The conservation and preservation of Islamic manuscripts. Proceedings of the Third Conference of al-Furqān Islamic Heritage Foundation 18th –19th November 1995*, ed. Yusuf Ibish and George Atiyeh. London, 1996: 21-27.

Bish, Tony. "Conservation at the Khālidī Library in the old city of Jerusalem". *The conservation and preservation of Islamic manuscripts. Proceedings of the Third Conference of al-Furqān Islamic Heritage Foundation 18th-19th November 1995*, ed. Yusuf Ibish and George Atiyeh. London, 1996: 49-52.

Bull, W. "Rebinding Islamic manuscripts: a new direction". *Bookbinder*, 1 (1987): 21-38.

Bürgel, Johann Christoph. "Von Buchern und Termiten". *Festschrift Ewald Wagner zum 65. Geburtstag*, herausgegeben von W. Heinrichs and G. Schoeler. Beirut/ Stuttgart, 1994: 2, 337-349.

Clare, Julian and Marsh, Frederick. "A dry repair method for Islamic illuminated manuscript leaves". *The paper conservator*, 4 (1979): 3-9.

De Torres, Amparo R. "Preventive conservation: global trends". *The conservation and preservation of Islamic manuscripts. Proceedings of the Third Conference of al-Furqān Islamic Heritage Foundation 18th -19th November 1995*, ed. Yusuf Ibish and George Atiyeh. London, 1996: 185-194.

Dreibholtz, Ursula. "Conservation of the manuscripts". *Maṣāḥif Ṣanʿāʾ*. Kuwait, 1985: 24-30.

——— "Treatment of early Islamic manuscript fragments on parchment. A case history: the find of Sanaʿa, Yemen". *The conservation and preservation of Islamic manuscripts. Proceedings of the Third Conference of al-Furqān Islamic Heritage Foundation 18th-19th November 1995*, ed. Yusuf Ibish and George Atiyeh. London, 1996: 131-145.

Gacek, Adam. "The use of 'kabīkaj' in Arabic manuscripts". *Manuscripts of the Middle East*, 2 (1987): 49-53. [Persian translation by Nūsh Āfrīn Anṣārī (Muḥaqqiq), *Kitābdārī*, 14 (1989): 5-12; Turkish translation by A. Yaycioğlu, *Kebikeç*, 5 (1997): 5-8.]

Hegazi, Mahmoud F. "Conservation and preservation policy at the National Library of Egypt (Dār al-Kutub)". *The conservation and preservation of Islamic manuscripts. Proceedings of the Third Conference of al-Furqān Islamic Heritage Foundation 18th-19th November 1995*, ed. Yusuf Ibish and George Atiyeh. London, 1996: 7-14.

Iskander, Nasry. "The conservation and preservation of Islamic books, papers, manuscripts, papyri, and parchments". *The conservation and preservation of Islamic manuscripts. Proceedings of the Third Conference of al-Furqān Islamic Heritage Foundation 18th-19th November 1995*, ed. Yusuf Ibish and George Atiyeh. London, 1996: 119-130.

Jacobs, David. "A simple book support for Islamic manuscripts". *British Library conservation news*, 33 (1991): 3, 8.

Jacobs, David and Rodgers, Barbara. "Developments in the conservation of Oriental (Islamic) manuscripts at the India Office Library, London". *Restaurator*, 11, ii (1990): 110-138.

Jacobs, David and Rodgers, Barbara. "Developments in Islamic bindings and conservation in the Oriental and India Office Collections of the British Library". *The conservation and preservation of Islamic manuscripts. Proceedings of the Third Conference of al-Furqān Islamic Heritage Foundation 18th-19th November 1995*, ed. Yusuf Ibish and George Atiyeh. London, 1996: 81-92.

Jarjis, Raik. "Ion-beam codicology, its potential in developing scientific conservation of Islamic manuscripts". *The conservation and preservation of Islamic manuscripts. Proceedings of the Third Conference of al-Furqān Islamic Heritage Foundation 18th-19th*

November 1995, ed. Yusuf Ibish and George Atiyeh. London, 1996: 93-117.

Mintzer, Frederick C. et al. "Towards on-line worldwide access to Vatican Library materials". *The conservation and preservation of Islamic manuscripts. Proceedings of the Third Conference of al-Furqān Islamic Heritage Foundation 18th-19th November 1995*, ed. Yusuf Ibish and George Atiyeh. London, 1996: 53-79.

al-Naqshabandī, Usāmah Nāṣir. "Khazn wa-ṣiyānat al-makhṭūṭāt". *Sumer*, 31 (1975): 311-319.

Pollock, James. "Kabi:kaj to book pouches: library preservation, magic and technique in Syria of the 1880's and the 1980's West". *MELA notes*, 44 (1988): 8-10.

al-Rammāḥ, Murād. "The ancient library of Kairouan and its methods of conservation". *The conservation and preservation of Islamic manuscripts. Proceedings of the Third Conference of al-Furqān Islamic Heritage Foundation 18th-19th November 1995*, ed. Yusuf Ibish and George Atiyeh. London, 1996: 29-47.

Richard, F. and Aubry, T. "Un cas intéressant de restauration d'un Coran indien de la fin du XVIe siècle (BnF, manuscrit arabe 7260)". *La conservation: une science en évolution : bilan et perspectives. [Actes des troisièmes journées internationales d'études de l'ARSAC, Paris, 21 au 25 avril 1997]*. Paris, ARSAC, 1997:109-115.

Schwartz, Werner. "Preserving manuscript works in the original or by reformatting? The usefulness of an international database". *The conservation and preservation of Islamic manuscripts. Proceedings of the Third Conference of al-Furqān Islamic Heritage Foundation 18th-19th November 1995*, ed. Yusuf Ibish and George Atiyeh. London, 1996: 175-183.

Seibert, Ann. "New trends in preventive conservation: what can be done about climate, emergencies, and pests?". *The conservation and preservation of Islamic manuscripts. Proceedings of the Third Conference of al-Furqān Islamic Heritage Foundation 18th-19th November 1995*, ed. Yusuf Ibish and George Atiyeh. London, 1996: 157-174.

Shāhīn, ʿAbd al-Muʿizz. *Al-Usus al-ʿilmīyah li-ʿilāj wa-ṣiyānat al-raqq wa-al-bardī wa-taṭbīqatuhā ʿalá baʿḍ qiṭaʿ al-mustakhrajah min al-ḥafāʾir al-atharīyah*. Cairo, 1981.

——— *Al-Usus al-ʿilmīyah li-al-ʿilāj wa-tarmīm wa-ṣiyānat al-kutub wa-al-makhṭūṭāt wa-al-wathā'iq al-ta'rīkhiyah*. Cairo, al-Hay'ah al-Miṣrīyah al-ʿĀmmah lil-Kitāb, 1990.

Ṣināʿat al-makhṭūṭ al-ʿArabī al-Islāmī min al-tarmīm ilá al-tajlīd: al-dawrah al-tadrībīyah al-dawlīyah al-ūlá, Dubayy, al-Imārāt al-ʿArabīyah al-Muttaḥidah, min 26 Dhū al-Ḥijjah 1417 h. ilá 9 Muḥarram 1418 h. al-muwāfiq 3 Māyū 1997 m. ilá 15 Māyū 1997 m. Dubai, Markaz al-Jumʿah al-Majīd lil-Thaqāfah wa-al-Turāth, [1997].

Ṣiyānah wa-ḥifẓ al-makhṭūṭāt al-Islāmīyah. Aʿmāl al-Mu'tamar al-Thālith li-Mu'assasat al-Furqān lil-Turāth al-Islāmī, 18-19 Nov. 1995, ed. Ibrāhīm Shabbūḥ. London, 1998.

XII. CATALOGUES OF MANUSCRIPTS, COLLECTIONS, ETC.

XII. 1. Bibliographies and bio-bibliographies of the Arabic heritage

[Gacek, Adam]. "Manuscripts". *Introductory guide to Middle Eastern and Islamic studies*, ed. Paul Auchterlonie. Oxford, Middle East Libraries Committee, 1990: 25-29.

Monzawī, Aḥmad and Monzawī, ʿAlī-Naqī. "Bibliographies and catalogues". *Encyclopaedia Iranica*, ed. E. Yarshater, 4: 214-235.

Pearson, J.D. "Bibliography". *EI*, new ed., 1: 1197-1199.

Pellat, Ch. "Fahrasa". *EI*, new ed., 2: 743-744.

Sayyid, Ayman Fu'ād. "Maṣādir maʿrifat al-turāth al-ʿArabī". *Al-Mawrid*, 6, no.1 (1977): 7-12.

Witkam, Jan Just. "Lists of books in Arabic manuscripts". *Manuscripts of the Middle East*, 5 (1990-91): 123-136.

XII. 2. Lists of dated manuscripts

ʿAwwād, Kūrkīs. *Aqdam al-makhṭūṭāt al-ʿArabīyah fī maktabāt al-ʿālam al-maktūbah mundhu ṣadr al-Islām ḥattá sanah 500.* Baghdad, Wizārat al-Thaqāfah wa-al-Iʿlām, 1982.

Déroche, François. "Les manuscrits arabes datés du IIIe/IXe siècle". *Revue des études islamiques*, 55/57 (1987/89): 343-379.

Vajda, Georges. "Les manuscrits arabes datés de la Bibliothèque nationale de Paris". *Bulletin d'information de l'Institut de recherche et d'histore des textes*, 7 (1958): 47-69.

XII. 3. Catalogues of catalogues

ʿAwwād, Kūrkīs. *Fahāris al-makhṭūṭāt al-ʿArabīyah fī al-ʿālam*. Kuwait, Maʿhad al-Makhṭūṭāt al-ʿArabīyah, 1984. 2 vols.

Bakkār, Yūsuf Ḥusayn. "Fahāris al-makhṭūṭāt al-ʿArabīyah fī al-ʿālam lil-Ustādh Kūrkīs ʿAwwād: mulāḥaẓāt wa-iḍāfāt". *Majallat Maʿhad al-Makhṭūṭāt al-ʿArabīyah*, 29, no.1 (1985): 323-352.

——— "Fahāris al-makhṭūṭāt al-ʿArabīyah fī al-ʿālam: iḍāfāt ukhrá". *Majallat Maʿhad al-Makhṭūṭāt al-ʿArabīyah*, 30, no.1 (1986): 345-380.

Ḥujjātī, Muḥammad Bāqir. *Kashshāf al-fahāris wa-waṣṣāf al-makhṭūṭāt al-ʿArabīyah fī maktabāt Fāris (= Fihrist-i mawẓūʿī-i nuskhahʾhā-yi khaṭṭī-i ʿArabī-i kitābkhānahʾhā-yi Jumhūrī-i Islāmī-i Īrān va tarīkh-i ʿulūm va tarājim-i dānishmandān-i Islāmī)*. Tehran, 1991 – .

al-Majmaʿ al-Malakī li-Buḥūth al-Ḥaḍārah al-Islāmīyah (Royal Academy for Islamic Civilization Research). *Dalīl fahāris al-makhṭūṭāt fī al-Majmaʿ al-Malakī li-Buḥūth al-Ḥaḍārah al-Islāmīyah*. Amman, 1986.

——— *Dalīl fahāris al-makhṭūṭāt fī al-Majmaʿ al-Malakī li-Buḥūth al-Ḥaḍārah al-Islāmīyah: al-mulḥaq al-awwal*. Amman, 1987.

——— *Dalīl fahāris al-makhṭūṭāt fī al-Majmaʿ al-Malakī li-Buḥūth al-Ḥaḍārah al-Islāmīyah: al-mulḥaq al-thānī*. Amman, 1991.

Mikhailova, I.B. and Khalidov, A.B. *Bibliografiia arabskikh rukopisei*. Moscow, 1982.

Roper, Geoffrey (ed.). *World survey of Islamic manuscripts*. London, 1992-1994. 4 vols.

——— (ed.). *Al-Makhṭūṭāt al-Islāmīyah fī al-ʿālam*. Transl. by ʿAbd al-Sattār al-Ḥalwajī. London, al-Furqān Islamic Heritage Foundation, 1997- .

al-Shāhīn (Şahin), Shāmil. *Fihris al-fahāris al-maṭbūʿah lil-makhṭūṭāt al-ʿArabīyah fī Turkiyā, 1262/1845 – 1413/1992 (= Türkiye'de Arapça yazmalara dair basılmış fihristlerin fihristi)*. Istanbul, 1993.

XII. 4. Descriptions of collections and catalogues

Bayraktar, Nimet and Lugal, Mihin. *Bibliography on manuscript libraries in Turkey and the publications on the manuscripts located in these libraries*, ed. Ekmeleddin Ihsan İhsanoğlu.

Istanbul, Research Centre for Islamic History, Art and Culture, 1995.

Benjelloun-Laroui, Latifa. *Les bibliothèques au Maroc*. Paris, 1990.

Berthier, A. "Manuscrits orientaux et connaissance de l'Orient: éléments pour une enquête culturelle". *Moyen-Orient et Océan Indien, XVIe-XIXe s.*, 2, no.2 (1985): 79-108.

Dodkhudoeva, Larisa and Dodkhudoeva, Lola. "Manuscrits orientaux du Tadjikistan: la collection Semenov." *Cahiers de l'Asie centrale*, 7 (1999): 39-55.

Jones, Robert. "Piracy, war, and the acquisition of Arabic manuscripts in Renaissance Europe". *Manuscripts of the Middle East*, 2 (1987): 96-110.

Khan, Geoffrey A. "The Arabic fragments in the Cambridge Genizah collections". *Manuscripts of the Middle East*, 1 (1986): 54-60.

al-Manūnī, Muḥammad. "Adillat al-makhṭūṭāt wa-marākizuhā bi-al-Maghrib wa-al-bilād al-ʿArabīyah". *Majallat Dār al-Ḥadīth al-Ḥasanīyah*, 8 (1990): 11-46.

al-Makhṭūṭāt al-ʿArabīyah fī al-Gharb al-Islāmī: waḍʿīyat al-majmūʿāt wa-āfāq al-baḥth (= Manuscrits arabes en occident musulman). Casablanca, Muʾassasat al-Malik ʿAbd al-ʿAzīz, 1990.

Martel-Thoumian, Bernadette. "Achats et legs de manuscrits historiques à la bibliothèque Ẓāhiriyya de Damas (1943-1972)". *Scribes et manuscrits du Moyen-Orient*, ed. F. Déroche and F. Richard. Paris, 1997: 363-375.

Muminov, Ashirbek. "Fonds nationaux et collections privées de manuscrits en écriture arabe de l'Ouzbékistan". *Cahiers de l'Asie centrale*, 7 (1999): 17-38.

Sāʿātī, Yaḥyá Maḥmūd. *Waḍʿīyat al-makhṭūṭāt fī al-Mamlakah al-ʿArabīyah al-Saʿūdīyah ilá ʿām 1408 h.* Riyad, Maktabat al-Malik Fahd al-Waṭanīyah, 1993.

al-Shaybānī, Muḥammad ibn Ibrāhīm. *Awḍāʿ al-makhṭūṭāt al-ʿArabīyah fī al-Kuwayt mundhu al-nashʾah ḥattá ʿām 1418 h./1997 m.* Kuwait, Markaz al-Makhṭūṭāt wa-al-Turāth wa-al-Wathāʾiq, 1999.

XII. 5. Catalogues of edited manuscripts

ʿAbd al-Raḥmān, ʿAbd al-Jabbār. *Dhakhāʾir al-turāth al-ʿArabī al-Islāmī (= Printed Arabic manuscripts: a comprehensive bibliography of all printed works written by Arab authors from the advent of Islam to the end of the 12th century A.H./17th century A.D.*). Basra, 1981-83. 2 vols.

Āl Salmān, Mashhūr Ḥasan Maḥmūd. *Al-Ishārāt ilá asmā' al-rasā'il al-mūda'ah fī buṭūn al-mujalladāt wa-al-majallāt*. Riyad, Dār al-Ṣumayʿī, 1994.

al-Dakhlī, ʿAbd al-Wahhāb. *Al-Ishām al-Tūnisī fī taḥqīq al-turāth al-makhṭūṭ: fihris taḥlīlī bi-al-manshūrāt al-muḥaqqaqah fī Tūnis wa-al-ṣādirah khilāl al-fatrah 1860-1988*. Tunis, al-Mu'assasah al-Waṭanīyah lil-Tarjamah wa-al-Taḥqīq wa-al-Dirāsāt, 1990.

al-Munajjid, Ṣalāḥ al-Dīn. *Muʿjam al-makhṭūṭāt al-maṭbūʿah (1954-1980)*. Beirut, Dār al-Kitāb al-Jadīd, 1978-82. 5 vols.

Ṣāliḥīyah, Muḥammad ʿĪsá. *Al-Muʿjam al-shāmil lil-turāth al-ʿArabī al-maṭbūʿ*. Cairo, Maʿhad al-Makhṭūṭāt al-ʿArabīyah, 1992-1995. 5 vols.

HANDBUCH DER ORIENTALISTIK

Abt. I: DER NAHE UND MITTLERE OSTEN

ISSN 0169-9423

Band 12
JAYYUSI, S. K. (ed.). *The Legacy of Muslim Spain*. Chief consultant to the editor, M. Marín. 2nd ed. 1994. ISBN 90 04 09599 3

Band 13
HUNWICK, J. O. and O'FAHEY, R. S. (eds.). *Arabic Literature of Africa*. Editorial Consultant: Albrecht Hofheinz.
Volume I. *The Writings of Eastern Sudanic Africa to c. 1900*. Compiled by R. S. O'Fahey, with the assistance of M. I. Abu Salim, A. Hofheinz, Y. M. Ibrahim, B. Radtke and K. S. Vikør. 1994. ISBN 90 04 09450 4
Volume II. *The Writings of Central Sudanic Africa*. Compiled by John O. Hunwick, with the assistance of Razaq Abubakre, Hamidu Bobboyi, Roman Loimeier, Stefan Reichmuth and Muhammad Sani Umar. 1995. ISBN 90 04 10494 1

Band 14
Decker, W. und Herb, M. *Bildatlas zum Sport im alten Ägypten. Corpus der bildlichen Quellen zu Leibesübungen, Spiel, Jagd, Tanz und verwandten Themen*. Bd.1: Text. Bd. 2: Ab-bildungen. 1994. ISBN 90 04 09974 3 *(Set)*

Band 15
Haas, V. *Geschichte der hethitischen Religion*. 1994. ISBN 90 04 09799 6

Band 16
Neusner, J. (ed.). *Judaism in Late Antiquity*. Part One: The Literary and Archaeological Sources. 1994. ISBN 90 04 10129 2

Band 17
Neusner, J. (ed.). *Judaism in Late Antiquity*. Part Two: Historical Syntheses. 1994. ISBN 90 04 09799 6

Band 18
Orel, V. E. and Stolbova, O. V. (eds.). *Hamito-Semitic Etymological Dictionary*. Materials for a Reconstruction. 1994. ISBN 90 04 10051 2

Band 19
al-Zwaini, L. and Peters, R. *A Bibliography of Islamic Law, 1980-1993*. 1994. ISBN 90 04 10009 1

Band 20
Krings, V. (éd.). *La civilisation phénicienne et punique*. Manuel de recherche. 1995. ISBN 90 04 10068 7

Band 21
Hoftijzer, J. and Jongeling, K. *Dictionary of the North-West Semitic Inscriptions*. With appendices by R.C. Steiner, A. Mosak Moshavi and B. Porten. 1995. 2 Parts. ISBN *Set (2 Parts)* 90 04 09821 6 Part One: ʾ - L. ISBN 90 04 09817 8 Part Two: M - T. ISBN 90 04 9820 8.

Band 22
Lagarde, M. *Index du Grand Commentaire de Faḫr al-Dīn al-Rāzī*. 1996. ISBN 90 04 10362 7

Band 23
Kinberg, N. *A Lexicon of al-Farrāʾ's Terminology in his Qurʾān Commentary*. With Full Definitions, English Summaries and Extensive Citations. 1996. ISBN 90 04 10421 6

Band 24
Fähnrich, H. und Sardshweladse, S. *Etymologisches Wörterbuch der Kartwel-Sprachen*. 1995. ISBN 90 04 10444 5

Band 25
Rainey, A.F. *Canaanite in the Amarna Tablets*. A Linguistic Analysis of the Mixed Dialect used by Scribes from Canaan. 1996. ISBN *Set (4 Volumes)* 90 04 10503 4
Volume I. Orthography, Phonology. Morphosyntactic Analysis of the Pronouns, Nouns, Numerals. ISBN 90 04 10521 2 Volume II. Morphosyntactic Analysis of the Verbal System. ISBN 90 04 10522 0 Volume III. Morphosyntactic Analysis of the Particles and Adverbs. ISBN 90 04 10523 9 Volume IV. References and Index of Texts Cited. ISBN 90 04 10524 7

Band 26
Halm, H. *The Empire of the Mahdi.* The Rise of the Fatimids. Translated from the German by M. Bonner. 1996. ISBN 90 04 10056 3
Band 27
Strijp, R. *Cultural Anthropology of the Middle East.* A Bibliography. Vol. 2: 1988-1992. 1997. ISBN 90 04 010745 2
Band 28
Sivan, D. *A Grammar of the Ugaritic Language.* 1997. ISBN 90 04 10614 6
Band 29
Corriente, F. *A Dictionary of Andalusi Arabic.* 1997. ISBN 90 04 09846 1
Band 30
Sharon, M. *Corpus Inscriptionum Arabicarum Palaestinae (CIAP).* Vol. 1: A. 1997. ISBN 90 04 010745 2 Vol.1: B. 1999. ISBN 90 04 110836
Band 31
Török, L. *The Kingdom of Kush.* Handbook of the Napatan-Meroitic Civilization. 1997. ISBN 90 04 010448 8
Band 32
Muraoka, T. and Porten, B. *A Grammar of Egyptian Aramaic.* 1998. ISBN 90 04 10499 2
Band 33
Gessel, B.H.L. van. *Onomasticon of the Hittite Pantheon.* 1998. ISBN *Set (2 parts)* 90 04 10809 2
Band 34
Klengel, H. *Geschichte des hethitischen Reiches* 1998. ISBN 90 04 10201 9
Band 35
Hachlili, R. *Ancient Jewish Art and Archaeology in the Diaspora* 1998. ISBN 90 04 10878 5
Band 36
Westendorf, W. *Handbuch der altägyptischen Medizin.* 1999. ISBN *Set (2 Bände)* 90 04 10319 8
Band 37
Civil, M. *Mesopotamian Lexicography.* 1999. ISBN 90 04 11007 0
Band 38
Siegelová, J. and Souček, V. *Systematische Bibliographie der Hethitologie.* 1999. ISBN *Set (3 Bände)* 90 04 11205 7
Band 39
Watson, W.G.E. and Wyatt, N. *Handbook of Ugaritic Studies.* 1999. ISBN 90 04 10988 9
Band 40
Neusner, J. *Judaism in Late Antiquity, III,1.* 1999. ISBN 90 04 11186 7
Band 41
Neusner, J. *Judaism in Late Antiquity, III,2.* 1999. ISBN 90 04 11282 0
Band 42
Drijvers, H.J.W. and Healey, J.F. *The Old Syriac Inscriptions of Edessa and Osrhoene.* 1999. ISBN 90 04 11284 7
Band 43
Daiber, H. *Bibliography of Philosophical Thought in Islam.* 2 Volumes.
ISBN *Set (2 Volumes)* 90 04 11347 9
Volume I. Alphabetical List of Publications 1999. ISBN 90 04 09648 5
Volume II. Index of Names, Terms and Topics. 1999. ISBN 90 04 11348 7
Band 44
Hunger, H. and Pingree, D. *Astral Sciences in Mesopotamia.* 1999. ISBN 90 04 10127 6
Band 45
Neusner, J. *The Mishnah.* Religious Perspectives 1999. ISBN 90 04 11492 0
Band 46
Neusner, J. *The Mishnah.* Social Perspectives 1999. ISBN 90 04 11491 2
Band 47
Khan, G. *A Grammar of Neo-Aramaic.* 1999. ISBN 90 04 11510 2
Band 48
Takács, G. *Etymological Dictionary of Egyptian.* Vol. 1. 1999. ISBN 90 04 11538 2
Band 49
Avery-Peck, A.J. and Neusner, J. *Judaism in Late Antiquity IV.* 2000. ISBN 90 04 11262 6

Band 50
Tal, A. *A Dictionary of Samaritan Aramaic.* (2 Volumes) 2000. ISBN 90 04 11858 6 (dl. 1) ISBN 90 04 11859 4 (dl. 2) ISBN 90 04 11645 1 (set)
Band 51
Holes, C. *Dialect, Culture, and Society in Eastern Arabia.* Vol. 1 : Glossary 2001. ISBN 90 04 10763 0
Band 52
Jong, R.E. de. *A Grammar of the Bedouin Dialects of the Northern Sinai Littoral.* Bridging the Linguistic Gap between the Eastern and Western Arab World. 2000. ISBN 90 04 11868 3
Band 53
Avery-Peck, A.J. and Neusner, J. *Judaism in Late Antiquity III,3.* Where we stand: Issues and Debates in Ancient Judaism. 2000. ISBN 90 04 11892 6
Band 54
Krahmalkov, Ch. R. *A Phoenician-Punic Grammar.* 2001. ISBN 90 04 11771 7
Band 55
Avery-Peck, A.J. and Neusner, J. *Judaism in Late Antiquity III,4.* Where we stand: Issues and Debates in Ancient Judaism.. *The Special Problem of the Synagogue.* 2001. ISBN 90 04 12000 9.
Band 56
Avery-Peck, A.J., Neusner, J., and Chilton, B. *Judaism in Late Antiquity V,1.* The Judaism of Qumran: A Systemic Reading of the Dead Sea Scrolls. *Theory of Israel.* 2001. ISBN 90 04 12001 7
Band 57
Avery-Peck, A.J., Neusner, J., and Chilton, B. *Judaism in Late Antiquity V,2.* The Judaism of Qumran: A Systemic Reading of the Dead Sea Scrolls. *World View, Comparing Judaisms.* 2001. ISBN 90 04 12003 3
Band 58
Gacek, A. *The Arabic manuscript tradition.* A Glossary of Technical Terms and Bibliography. 2001. ISBN 90 04 12061 0
Band 60
Marzolph, U. *Narrative illustration in Persian lithographed books.* 2001. ISBN 90 04 12100 5

Printed in the United States
By Bookmasters